Photo: Clarence E. Premo

ABOUT THE AUTHOR

Educator, industrial marketing consultant, author, researcher, and professional speaker, George Risley has been on the faculty of Clarkson College of Technology since 1946 and has held visiting professorships at Syracuse University and The Graduate School, University of Pittsburgh. He helped pioneer the recognition of industrial marketing by the American Marketing Association, then served AMA for two terms as Vice President in charge of the Industrial Marketing Division. He was also on the Board of Directors and editor of industrial marketing monographs.

The author of numerous professional articles, Professor Risley is a frequent speaker before business groups in the United States and abroad. His research into industrial marketing measurements led to the creation in 1968 of The Marketing-Cost Institute, Inc. (now a division of The Conference Board).

In writing this book, he draws on 35 years of experience as consultant—including 25 years in research and teaching—a background that affords him an ideal combination of theory and practical application.

Modern
Industrial
Marketing

Modern Industrial Marketing

George Risley
Clarkson College of Technology

McGRAW-HILL BOOK COMPANY

New York   St. Louis   San Francisco   Düsseldorf   Johannesburg
Kuala Lumpur   London   Mexico   Montreal   New Delhi
Panama   Rio de Janeiro   Singapore   Sydney   Toronto

Library of Congress Cataloging in Publication Data

Risley, George
    Modern industrial marketing.

    1. Marketing.   2. Marketing management.   I. Title.
HF5415.R552   658.8   72-6106
ISBN 0-07-052941-8

1 2 3 4 5 6 7 8 9   DODO   7 6 5 4 3 2

*The editors for this book were William H. Mogan and Stanley E. Redka,
the designer was Naomi Auerbach, and its production was supervised
by George E. Oechsner.   It was set in Caledonia by The Maple Press Company.*

It was printed and bound by R. R. Donnelley and Sons Company.

For my severist critic—
and my most helpful colleague—
my wife, Dottie

Contents

Part 5   Costs, Pricing, and Financing

Part 6   Measurements of Marketing, Markets, and Men

Part 7   Industrial Marketing Management

Foreword

Industrial marketing has never received anywhere near as much attention as consumer marketing; has never received anywhere near as much attention as it deserves.

In my view, there are several reasons for this neglect:

1. The people who head industrial product companies, including those who are responsible for sales, are likely to have technical backgrounds.

2. The need for marketing—or to put it more positively, the potential value of marketing—is not so apparent as in consumer goods marketing.

Let me elaborate on that second point. There is a tendency to think that "we know our customers, especially our large customers, well; even the president of the company knows them on a first-name basis." Further, "they buy on a rational basis, matching specifications with needs, so what room is there for persuasion and other selling techniques?"

But industrial buyers are human beings too. They do not always reveal their feelings. They may not be activated by appeals to motivations of emulation, prestige, emotional satisfaction, and so on, but they do need to have a psychological feeling of confidence in their sources of supply.

Besides, marketing is more than persuasion. It is the strategy of how to organize all marketing resources (money, time, energy); how to integrate all marketing functions (product design and development, inventory and delivery policy, quality control and service follow-up, informational and promotional efforts, arrangement of sales territories and sales pesonnel, selection of customers by degree of salability and sales volume, frequency and length of sales calls, etc., etc.)—in order to optimize, not just sales, but profits and return on investment. And that means a *total* marketing approach.

Hence I welcome this book, with its breadth of vision and its penetration, which provides both a rich background of understanding and a deep insight into the decision-making process of industrial marketing.

Happy reading!   Successful marketing!

Edward C. Bursk

Preface

This book is written for the industrial manager—one relatively new to industrial marketing or one more experienced who seeks to broaden his perspective and thereby improve his skills as a decision maker. The emphasis is not on the development of a scholarly "theory" of industrial marketing. Rather, the essentials of theory are combined with the reality of current practice. Practical applicability to decision making in a realistic environment is stressed.

The decision-making approach means that the reader is placed in the position of a decision maker. There are no answers provided for him— there are no ready-made answers available within marketing. Rather, he is first provided with a perspective for all his marketing considerations as an approach, a guide to the problems. Then only that material which can contribute to improved decision making is included. The relevancy and value of any data are its ability to do that.

The reader is assumed to be knowledgeable and to have had some business experience. The student should have attained an upper-level status and have had basic courses in economics and marketing.

"Fundamental Concepts of Significance," Part One, is most important— a prerequisite to the realization of maximum benefit from the following sections. It is recognized that many readers do not read a book of this nature from cover to cover, as they would a novel. They tend to excerpt from it those portions most applicable to their current interests and needs. It is most strongly urged that such a reader may derive as much benefit from Part One as from the subsequent material, if not more. In fact, the fundamental concepts are the heart of modern industrial marketing—without which relatively little will be gained, but with which the rest of the material will take on immensely greater significance.

It is hoped that the reading of this book may stimulate thought. It contains many instances of treatments which differ somewhat from the traditional but are deemed to be applicable to the practical. At least one new concept, the "marketing profile" at the end of Chapter Two, may help point the way to further basic research, which will be followed by improved marketing practice. In several other areas, techniques are offered to aid in improved decision making. Some examples are marketing costs in Chapter Ten, the break-even analysis in Chapter Eleven, measurement of potentials in Chapter Fourteen, construction of quotas in Chapter Fifteen, planning in Chapter Seventeen, and the act of decision making in Chapter Eighteen.

The reader may or may not agree with the author on some of the points developed. This is good. Different people have different perspectives and value judgments which may lead to different conclusions. The important thing is that we seek to think, to broaden our considerations, and to continue to give attention to areas in need of improvement. By this means progress is achieved.

The author accepts full responsibility for any errors, omissions, and stupidity of thought contained herein—since there is no way to duck it, anyway. However, he will be particularly grateful to hear from anyone who might like to pursue anything further—or to offer constructive thinking.

Traditionally, it is now time to give thanks to all who have helped in any way—including the ever-loyal secretary who typed and retyped the manuscript. I wish to do so, too. But, because of the depth of this gratitude, it will not be buried in a preface. It is where it belongs—in a special section.

George Risley

Potsdam, New York

Acknowledgments

It is recognized that a list of names is not intrinsically interesting. It is also recognized that I (as author) and you (if you read this book) owe profound gratitude for the thinking of these men, who as contributing authors have added both the depth and the realism of practice to it.

We thank:

GORDON W. BENOIT, Manager—Marketing,

JOHN F. McNEILL, Manager—Sales,

WILLIAM W. POORMAN, Manager—Contracts, and

NORMAN J. CARDINAL, Specialist—Marketing Planning, Undersea Electronics Programs, Heavy Military Electronic Systems, General Electric Company, for their collective contribution to governmental/defense/space marketing.

EDWARD C. BURSK, Editor, *Harvard Business Review*, for his thinking on the total-marketing concept and the Foreword

DAN J. CANTILLON, Vice President, The Ferry Cap & Set Screw Company, for his sales planning and control system

BAY E. ESTES, JR., Vice President—Economist, American Iron and Steel Institute, for his preliminary review and many helpful suggestions

ALBERT W. FREY, retired Dean of The Graduate School of Business, University of Pittsburgh, for his penetrating thoughts on advertising and marketing management

MORLAN J. GRANDBOIS, Corporate Planning Coordinator, St. Regis Paper Company, for his help in providing a living example of corporate planning

LEE GUNLOGSON, Director of Marketing Services, Carrier Corporation, for his treatment of trade associations

WILLIAM W. CARPENTER, President, Smith, Bucklin & Associates, Inc., for his managerial perspective of trade-association operations

MERRITT D. HILL, Hill Associates, for his analysis of the top spot

A. P. MORAN, Manager, New Products, Electrical Components Division, The Bendix Corporation, for his contributions to both market research and new products

D. W. NEWCOMB, Executive Assistant to the Director of Marketing, Electrical Components Division, The Bendix Corporation, for his efforts in industrial distribution.

THOMAS F. PRAY, Instructor, Clarkson College, for his material on contract buying and inventory control

A. F. STORER, Assistant Vice President, St. Regis Paper Company, for his assistance in trade relations

J. C. YOUMANS, Director of Marketing, Electrical Components Division, The Bendix Corporation, for his research assistance and for motivating me to write this book

It is fitting here to express gratitude to two others: my wife, Dottie, for her questions—which invariably caused me to correct something—and my daughter, Pamela, who as proofreader found the mistakes my wife and I both missed.

George Risley

Modern
Industrial
Marketing

PART ONE

Fundamental Concepts of Significance

CHAPTER ONE

Perspectives of Modern Industrial Marketing

"A fish for a rabbit—a spear for a club" may well have been the beginning—the first acts of marketing. If we accept barter between cavemen as the beginning of marketing activities, then marketing is older than civilization itself! This makes it both the oldest and the youngest of our disciplines—oldest as to the act, youngest as to academic and professional attention. It has been characterized by an evolutionary growth, definitely not a directed development. Marketing, like Topsy, just "growed."

EVOLUTIONARY GROWTH OF MARKETING

Early man began about 20,000 B.C. as an uncivilized hunter and food gatherer, eking out a barely subsistence living. Human civilization probably began about 4000 B.C. Agriculture became sufficiently successful to create some surpluses, which permitted artisans to evolve. They traded their products for food and raw materials. Thus barter, the exchange of goods for goods, became the first marketing system of civilization, too—and lasted some 6,000 years.

The first set of laws to control commercial practices was probably the Code of Hammurabi, about 2000 B.C., followed much later by church canons.

The first philosophical writings were undoubtedly Chinese, and about 700 B.C., Buddha's, now Hinduism.   In Western civilization our earliest Greek literature started about 600 B.C. with Thales, then Socrates, Aristotle, and his pupil, Plato.   These early writings were both philosophical and religious in context.

Economics, born of philosophy, followed the mercantilism which characterized the colonial development of the fifteenth through the seventeenth centuries to the doctrines of free trade in the eighteenth century. By the end of the nineteenth century competition began to be regarded as wasteful.   In many countries cartels were born; in the United States, giant trusts.   State control was then invoked to promote economic welfare.

The earliest writers of economics were political philosophers by identification, but the subject matter was nevertheless heavily economic.   The first courses in economics began to appear in the curricula of leading universities around 1890, just before the turn of the century.

Marketing, born of economics, was first recognized just after the turn of the century, in the early 1900s.   This was followed by an increasingly rapid development, particularly since the 1920s, although, for the most part, marketing was viewed as being consumer marketing.   In the mid-thirties, the first books on industrial marketing,[1] as distinguished from consumer, appeared.   These fell upon somewhat barren soil as to recognition and interest.   It wasn't until the late 1940s, immediately after World War II, that special-interest sections of a few of the American Marketing Association's chapters began to meet separately to discuss their common problems, industrial marketing.   During the 1950s a few college courses in industrial marketing were started.   However, it was not until April 1962 that the American Marketing Association, the national professional association of marketing men, created two new divisions of marketing—the one consumer, and the other industrial—thereby giving official recognition to the existence of industrial marketing.

The Industrial Revolution

It is interesting to note that the industrial revolution, born in the vicinity of the North Sea in the early 1700s, is frequently referred to as a fait accompli—something over and done with.   However, if one were to take a map of the world and plot the spread of industrialization on it, say by twenty-five-year periods from 1730 until today, the result would clearly indicate that it is far from over—it has barely begun!   The areas remaining available for future industrialization are far greater than

[1] John H. Frederick, *Industrial Marketing*, Englewood Cliffs, N.J.: Prentice-Hall, Inc., 1934, and Robert F. Elder, *Fundamentals of Industrial Marketing*, New York: McGraw-Hill Book Company, 1935.

the total accomplished to date, both on a worldwide scale and within the United States. Incidentally, it might be interesting to start at about the same time and place, with the French Revolution, and plot the spread of democracy in a similar manner—then to superimpose and compare the two maps.

COMPETITION

Since the earliest economic developments began, the economies of the world have been characterized by scarcity. Economics, itself, has been predicated upon the assumption of scarce resources and their use to satisfy a relatively insatiable demand. Even today, it continues to be defined as "the study of the optimal use of scarce resources to satisfy human wants."[2]

Under conditions of true scarcity, that is, where demand is greater than either supply or the productive capacity to provide it, there is no real competition—no need for marketing, or even salesmanship. Competition is based on surplus, not scarcity.

All through history and up until the Great Depression of the 1930s, we have had an economy of scarcity. Starting in the late 1930s and through World War II, the 1940s, and into the early 1950s, our productive facilities were devoted to war materiel and then conversion from chiefly governmental to industrial and consumer needs. However, since about the mid-1950s, conditions of surplus, characterized in an increasing number of cases by surplus productive capacity, have created competition at an extremely high level—and for the first time in history. This competition is far from reaching its peak. It, like industrial development, has barely begun. With the rapid increases in technology, productive efficiencies, expansion abroad, and the long-term trend toward free trade, competition both at home and abroad will continue to grow. And the need for effective marketing will grow with it.

ORIENTATIONS

By far the most important characteristic of the modern industrial manager, other things being equal, is his orientation to business. This is of greatest significance and has far-reaching effects, since it underlies all his thinking concerning business problems—and guides his decision making. No other single factor even comes close in the influence it can exert toward improved decision making. Once the manager possesses the proper perspective toward his operations and his total situa-

[2] Marshall R. Colberg, Dascomb R. Forbush, and Gilbert R. Whitaker, Jr., *Business Economics*, Homewood, Ill.: Richard D. Irwin, Inc., 1970, chap. 1, p. 1.

tion, improvement in his decision making is bound to follow. He will recognize the strength of his position and can act with the confidence which comes from knowing that his premises are sound.

Failure to adopt the perspective of the orientation most suitable to the circumstances of the firm can produce most serious and sometimes fatal results. An excellent illustration of this is contained in Theodore Levitt's article, "Marketing Myopia,"[3] wherein he states:

> The railroads did not stop growing because the need for passenger and freight transportation declined. That grew. The railroads are in trouble today not because the need was filled by others (cars, trucks, airplanes, even telephones), but because it was *not* filled by the railroads themselves. They let others take customers away from them because they assumed themselves to be in the railroad business rather than in the transportation business. The reason they defined their industry wrong was because they were railroad-oriented instead of transportation-oriented; they were product-oriented instead of customer-oriented.

There are four recognizable orientations, which, like marketing itself, have come from an evolutionary process.

Product Orientation

In the earlier days of industrial development of this country, while our economy was characterized by scarcity, the job of business was to produce. Entrepreneurs entering business were quite properly product-oriented, their goal being to produce a product to satisfy an ever-increasing demand. Considerations of production and the quality of the product dominated decision making. The key to success in the marketplace was simply the product—anything else was secondary. Such is product orientation.

Sales Orientation

Later, as competition increased somewhat, managements began to shift their primary concern away from the product toward an awareness of the need for sales to provide for the continued growth of the firm. The Great Depression of the 1930s encouraged this change in emphasis with the need to stay alive, to keep in business in the minds of many. Managements became aware that other sources of supply existed and that their profit comes from their sales revenues, and the phrase "nothing happens around here until a sale is made" became popular. They hired good salesmen and gave them all possible assistance. The product became something to be converted into cash by the sale; sales considera-

---

[3] Theodore Levitt, "Marketing Myopia," *Harvard Business Review*, July-August 1960, p. 45.

tions began to dominate management's thinking. Such is sales orientation.

Marketing Orientation

Starting shortly after World War II, with our economy moving from one of scarcity toward one of plenty, with rapidly increasing competition, many more progressive managements tended to realize that successful sales results come from far more than good salesmanship. They recognized that good sales results were the reward of total corporate effort, that each element makes its own contribution to the corporate team— product development, the product itself, the advertising, promotion, packaging, pricing, delivery, customer service—and that the way to achieve this was to integrate all these aspects through marketing. Sales became a segment of marketing, with the sales manager reporting to a marketing manager. And this involved far more than renaming a sales department to a marketing one. Sales, like product orientation, places the interest of the firm first. Thus a change to marketing orientation, which places the interest of the customer first, was a significant one. This change in emphasis from sales to marketing started the recognition of the need for the complete integration of marketing considerations throughout all the functional areas of the corporation by both marketing and nonmarketing executives. Firms which treat marketing considerations as paramount in their decision making are truly marketing-oriented.

Market Orientation

The next step in this evolutionary development is still in process. It involves the replacement of *marketing* as the center of the business universe with the considerations of the *market,* that is, with customer satisfaction as the paramount consideration in decision making rather than the marketing department, per se. This may seem at first to be but a subtle difference, yet it is a very important one. Let us explore this further.

It should never be inferred that marketing considerations, stemming from customer satisfactions, are a property of the marketing department—nor that the promotion of such *considerations* promotes the marketing *department.* They are two entirely separate matters. In fact, a completely market-oriented firm need not even *have* a marketing department!

The marketing department is an organizational grouping of marketing specialists, experts in the *techniques* of marketing—advertising, sales management, market research, etc.—and guided by the same considerations, customer satisfaction, as anyone else. But, to say that this group, the marketing department, should command the corporate organization is silly. This group belongs on a par with the other major specialized functional groups—as is portrayed in Figure 1.1.

The market-oriented firm is not run by a marketing department. It is one wherein the creation of customer satisfaction has been adopted as the basic and most significant factor in all its decision making—and by all its decision makers, both marketing and nonmarketing executives. Thus, the implementation of marketing is not restricted to a marketing department. It is a function of the total firm.

It should be noted, too, that the orientation is of the individual, rather than the corporation. It is a perspective, a point of view, an attitude toward business possessed by a man. It varies from individual to individual on a personal basis, and it varies, in general, by job position within the corporate structure. Those individuals most closely in contact with the customers are apt to be far more market-oriented than those whose duties are largely internal and deal with technical aspects of engineering, production, and administrative detail. The latter, particularly at the lower levels, tend to be oriented first toward the importance of their own job function and then toward the product or, at the best, toward sales. It is the exceptional individual in such a capacity who has adopted either the marketing or the market concept.

Now then, I would expect you to expect me (as a marketing man, of sorts) to argue that market orientation is obviously the best one for the industrialist to adopt. I do not do so. The market concept just is not the best one for all circumstances. There are plenty of cases today where product orientation is and should be used. The best one to use is a function of the total circumstances faced by the firm.

Under circumstances of scarcity, and particularly where maximum quality is needed, the firm should be product-oriented. It best serves its customers thereby. There are many examples today where the firm

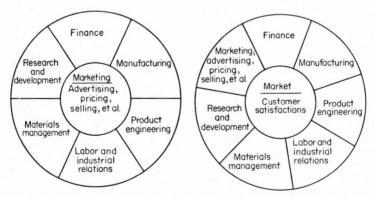

Fig. 1.1 Market versus marketing orientation.

need do very little beyond producing the best product to the specifications of the buyer that it can. Such examples are found in the foundry business, small tool and die makers who have a few accounts with whom they work intimately, and in many areas of governmental marketing where a relatively low volume is coupled with the need for the best possible product capable of being produced—such as nose cones for space capsules. Here the research capabilities of the firm together with productive capacity—all highly product-oriented—are the most important in the decision making of the firm.

Sales orientation seems proper for the sideshow owner and barker, and in many forms of entertainment, in raising funds for charitable causes, and even in persuading people to take a more active interest in both their local and national governments.

Marketing orientation becomes the most difficult of all to defend. Under conditions of relatively keen competition, the creation of customer satisfaction would seem to be paramount. There seems to be little to justify marketing's assuming the major role—except to provide a better place in the sun for the marketing personnel. The need for and the justification of the existence of any segment of the corporate entity comes from its ability to contribute to customer satisfaction. And this includes marketing. If customer satisfaction can be achieved as well, or more effectively, without the entity—away with it. It is the creation of customer satisfaction which should control.

In all fairness to the product-oriented industrialist, it must be admitted that consumer satisfaction in the industrial area is not based on the same set of criteria as it is in the consumer area. Typically, the industrial buyer is an expert whose buying decisions are far more rational than the ultimate consumer's. Therefore, product superiority in the form of cost saving, better technical performance, and perhaps superior product service become his major considerations as against the more emotional and self-rewarding personal reasons, the pride, social acceptability, sexual prowess, etc., of the typical consumer buyer.

Industrially, there is far less to no impulse buying, far less emotional satisfaction to be derived from the purchase decision on the part of the industrial buyer. Yet, there is still customer satisfaction to be realized from the function of the product purchased, even though the basis of judgment is far more impersonal and rational. This does not change in the slightest the position of customer satisfaction as the dominant characteristic for industrial decision making. It enhances it as the objective of industrial marketing. At the same time, it means that it must be real, rather than fancied or suggested by a highly emotional association. And too, it invites a further query, "How best to do the job?" as against how to better the competition.

MARKETING DEFINED

It is recognized that there are difficulties in writing a definition of "marketing" acceptable to everyone. A short, generalized statement appealing to some individuals would be criticized by others for its lack of specific identification of content. These difficulties stem from many things: the differing levels of generalization of different individuals (and businessmen hate to generalize, anyway); differing perspectives—the variation in the orientation of the individual to marketing, from product-oriented through sales-oriented, to marketing- or market-oriented; the variation in proximity to the customer of differing positions within the corporate structure from production workers through salesmen; and the interest in the definition from the standpoint of its purpose—practice (what we can use it for) versus theory (what it ought to be).

In addition to these differences in people, there are significant differences in the traditional practices of firms. Some are very broad in allocating responsibilities to marketing; others are more restrictive. Further, not all the marketing performance is done by the marketing department. Frequently, other corporate entities perform part of the marketing task. Examples are the packaging of finished goods by production workers, a shipping department located in and charged to production facilities, credit and collection, and in many cases, technical field engineering services, including application engineering. Then, too, marketing considerations permeate (or should permeate) many areas of decision making by nonmarketing as well as marketing executives.

Obviously, from the foregoing we would expect, and in fact, find that authorities offer various definitive statements and practitioners have somewhat differing concepts of what is or is not marketing. So, we offer for your critical examination a series of definitions rather than one. In reality, they are all one and the same—the difference being in the level of generalization—and moving as we go toward more and more refinement, from the general to the specific.

At a very high level of generalization: Marketing is the profitable creation of customer satisfactions. As such, it is no longer a set of laws, principles, or rules to dictate decisions. Rather, it is a perspective, a way of life, a point of view to aid business in creating satisfied customers. Marketing is the determination and profitable distribution of want satisfactions.

At a lower level: Marketing is the determination of, guidance to production in reference to, and distribution of goods and services to create optional satisfaction of customer wants, needs, and desires—and if successful, at a reasonable profit.

A somewhat more detailed version of our definition: Marketing starts with determining the present and future needs and wants of both present and prospective customers. It aids in interpreting these want-satisfying characteristics to product planning. Through forecasting, it aids in establishing the volume and timing of production. Then, once the goods have been produced, it assumes full responsibility for their advertising, promotion, sale, and distribution to create satisfied cutomers—and post-sale follow-up to keep the customers satisfied.

Last, and to be even more explicit: Marketing includes all business activities to determine the needs and wants of customers, develop new markets, aid in product development, estimate potentials, forecast, and aid in production planning; to operate a marketing organization, determine marketing strategy, select channels of distribution, inform and motivate customers, price, sell, and provide marketing services including order entry, customer financing, credit and collection, and both customer and product services; to provide for physical distribution, including packaging, transportation, field warehousing of finished goods, and delivery; to contribute to overall corporate planning and to plan and control this entire operation.

It should be noted that some firms may, because of organizational structure and traditional accounting practices, treat certain of these areas as being excluded from marketing. Credit, field warehousing, and transportation are the major borderline areas. In the case of credit, if it is used primarily as a sales aid to obtain business, it is typically treated as a part of marketing. If it is a necessary evil, with sales for cash but credit granted primarily because the competitors traditionally do so, it is frequently regarded as a financial operation. If sales are primarily for cash and credit is made available to help finance them, particularly on high-ticket items as in installment financing, credit is then regarded as an independent, profit-generating center.

In-plant and between-plant storage and transportation are typically included as part of production. Field storage and transportation of finished goods are generally included in marketing.

Thus, marketing includes all business activities that make possible the determination of what should be produced and control that which is produced from its creation to ultimate consumption. In doing this, marketing's role is a dual one—to represent the interests of the customer to the producer and to represent the interest of the producer to the customer. Successful marketing, then, maximizes the want satisfaction of the customer with optimal efficiency, and in so doing, helps provide the prerequisite profit to the corporation for the attainment of its goals.

INDUSTRIAL MARKETING

Obviously, industrial marketing is simply the performance of these marketing tasks and the furnishing of the marketing perspective within the

area of business and industry for business purposes—as against the marketing to families and individuals for personal use and consumption.

MARKETING: ART OR SCIENCE?

This is an age-old question, still being raised. Art is skill, an ability
to perform. Science is knowledge. Scientific procedures, then, simply
are based on knowledge to seek further truths, by providing a set of
rules to eliminate both chance and subjectivity.

Marketing is both—an art in performance, from planning through
selling to final decision making; a science in its body of truths, and
an avid user of scientific procedures in data processing, logistics, research, and innumerable areas of quantification.

MARKETING SEGMENTATION

Marketing, however defined, would indeed be simple if only the people,
the customers, were uniform in nature and behaved in a completely
predictable and rational manner. It is the people who are at the root
of all the problems and complications of marketing. Bless them!

And yet, there are recognizable patterns of similarity of problems,
which gives rise to the start of marketing segmentation. The basis for
consumer versus industrial marketing is the division of the people (the
customers) into two major groups, because of the marketing problems
created by these groups—problems that are different between groups
and uniform within each. This is becoming well recognized and accepted. Consumer and industrial marketing are two major segments
of marketing, based upon the differences in problems between and uniformity of problems within each segment. Applying this concept still
further, it is then both appropriate and logical to recognize a third
major area of marketing—governmental/defense/space.

Fundamentally, there are at least four ways in which these three
marketing segments differ:

1. The markets differ.
2. The buying considerations, reasons for purchase, differ.
3. The buying practices differ.
4. The marketing strategy and practices differ.

On the basis of this three-way segmentation, we now have three markets, three groups of customers, and three sets of problems.

From the foregoing it might appear that we would also have product
differences. However, we do and we don't. It is relatively easy to

identify some goods which are governmental only—a missile, a jet fighter, and a spaceship. There is no real difficulty in identifying goods which are industrial only—a Bessemer converter, a rolling mill, and perhaps a multiple-turret drill press. But, it is a far more difficult matter to identify goods which are consumer only. Almost all consumer goods, or all, have industrial and/or governmental counterparts in the same form. In fact, most products serve at least two areas and many serve all three. Automobiles, building supplies, carpeting, chalk, food, furniture, standardized hardware items and hand tools, packaged drugs, sheets, sundries, and many other items are sold in the same form to all three markets. Perhaps the best examples of strictly consumer goods would be an expensive wedding ring and dress.

For practical purposes, then, we may identify consumer marketing simply as the marketing of goods and services to ultimate consumers, individuals and families, for personal consumption. Obviously, this is a retail market. Industrial marketing is the marketing of goods and services to industrial customers for use in the production of goods, for use in the operations of businesses themselves, and for use by nonpolitical institutions. Governmental/defense/space marketing is the marketing of goods and services to any and all segments of government, including political subdivisions, for use in its general operations, defense, and space.

This three-way conceptual division of marketing is not merely theoretical. Based on the groupings of problem similarities stemming from these three groups, it becomes very real, very practical, indeed. As usual, leadership in this recognition of governmental/defense/space marketing comes from the marketing practitioners themselves. They have authored articles and held conferences which have been devoted to the problems within this area. And, as with the earlier development of industrial marketing within the American Marketing Association (AMA), special governmental/defense/space interest groups have been formed within many AMA chapters to discuss and study their particular problems. College courses in governmental/defense/space marketing are just starting.

Recognition of governmental/defense/space as a separate entity within total marketing is well advanced within many corporations. A few even go so far as to separate production and finance as well, in addition to the marketing separation. Some major examples of the strictly governmental entities of this three-way division are Avco's Government Products Group, Bendix's Aerospace Electronics Group, Burroughs Corporation's Defense, Space and Special Systems Group, Chrysler's Defense-Space Group, General Electric's Aerospace Business Group, Goodyear Aerospace Corporation, ITT's Defense/Space Group, and Westinghouse's Defense and Space Center. This separation is far more than merely on the organizational chart. The groups are frequently separated both geographically and mentally. The people engaged in one area have little to no contact in their business operations with their counterparts in another.

These three major areas are but a start in marketing segmentation, of course. The subdivision of marketing into finer and finer customer groups can be based on all sorts of statistical data—employment, geographical location, industry and product groupings, plants, etc. Just how far one should go is the responsibility of the marketing analyst. Much statistical data is already available to serve this need (and if it is not, a market study could produce it). The limit should be set not on what one can do (or what traditionally has been done), but rather on the actual contribution to improved decision making to be derived from such segmentation.

APPROACHES TO MARKETING

Traditional

During its relatively rapid development over the past half-century, the study of marketing has been approached from several points of view. The traditional writers dominated this period up until shortly after World War II. They presented their treatments of marketing from the historical, institutional, and functional approaches.

Historical   The historical approach, while interesting, contributes far more to culture than to improved marketing, to a major extent due to the rapidity of change in technology, in the marketing environment, and in marketing, itself.

Institutional   The institutional approach studies the marketing of sellers and resellers, manufacturer sellers and middlemen, from the point of view of each one's own problems, operations, and practices. This approach provides an in-depth study of major marketing institutions, but in providing this analysis of segments, it fails completely to consider the whole.

Functional   The functional approach was a definite step in the right direction. It started with a concept of total marketing, and then segmented this into various lists of functions. Depending upon the author, the length of such lists ranged from ten or twelve to nearly fifty. These lists were not contradictory—rather, they came about as a result of differing levels of generalization between individuals and the differing degrees of segmentation and subsegmentation provided to the subject matter, marketing. Into how many pieces should the cake be cut?

Such functional lists typically included buying, selling, pricing, standardizing and grading, storage, transportation, marketing finance, risk bearing, market information, advertising and promotion, packaging, and so on.

The basic assumption here is simply that the whole is divisible into its parts and that the study and improvement of each part will automatically result in the improvement of the whole. However, it was not long before many leading marketing thinkers began to challenge this. They swung over to the Gestalt doctrine, which, by extension, postulates that the whole is greater than the sum of its parts. While it lasted, the functional approach appealed to the analytical mind, became popular in colleges since it was easy to teach, and formed the basis for viewing marketing somewhat mathematically, as a functional relationship between sales and marketing efforts, opportunities, and resistances thereto.

No real attempt was made to substitute actual values in the equations so developed. They were used primarily to illustrate interrelationships and as a springboard for discussion of the factors involved.

The practical necessity of providing the data to make any such formula workable becomes a Gargantuan task. More fundamental than that, this perspective attributes sales results to the marketing effort of the firm and its impact upon the customer. Psychologically, it came at a time when marketing men were avidly seeking a better place in the sun, and this approach tended to substantiate such increased recognition. Overlooked conveniently was the simple fact that sales results are not just marketing's results but, if anything, attributable to the entire corporate effort. And, not all demand is a result of any one firm's marketing effort. It is, at best, an oversimplification which ignores the many intangibles in the marketplace (including competitive action) which combine in various ways to make for sales results.

More Recent

Ecological More recently, marketing has been treated as an ecological concept. Simply stated, this interprets marketing as a manifestation of organized group behavior. It represents still another step forward by recognizing the customer, a family or a business enterprise, as he or it relates to the business environment. The ecological approach provides a series of goals for attainment by the customer. The lowest level is survival, followed by security, stability, success, and finally satisfaction as one moves up the ladder of attainment. The recognition of these goals helps to guide the marketing planner in presenting his product in such a way as to aid the customer to buy in order to attain the goal he seeks. This is the first recognition of the interest of the customer in the acquisition of goods and services. It is indeed a most significant step forward in marketing thinking, although it achieved but little notice in the marketing literature.

Systems The systems concept of marketing is another of the more recent approaches. It treats the marketing organization as a system in itself. The system is visualized as a set of components and interrelationships. For example, a railroad system is composed of tracks, cars, engines, stations, etc., arranged in a schema. All interrelated components are deemed to be in the system. All other elements are deemed to be in the environment—outside the system. And, there are hierarchies of systems.

The systems approach brings to attention one other significant attribute of modern marketing. When marketing is treated as a system, attention is directed to just what is "interrelated" within it. This tends to broaden the concept of marketing quite significantly from the functional approach. It leads rapidly to the recognition of the need for the integration of marketing considerations throughout the firm by both marketing and nonmarketing executives—since it can be realized that they are interrelated.

Managerial Most recently, much of the marketing literature is presented from a managerial approach. This is an appealing label and seems to imply that marketing is done by managers and hence is a high-level activity. Such is obviously true, since marketing planning, decision making, controlling, and remedial action are the responsibility of management. However, examination of the writings reveals that most are, in fact, simply descriptive of the institutions, their operations, and the circumstances of the marketplace. Some description is essential to understanding, of course. The error is to stop there. A few include both theory and illustrative application of quantitative techniques to marketing problems, but most frequently fall far short of a truly managerial—that is, decision-making—approach.

Most Recent—and Ours

Presumably, the objective of the marketing student—and especially the practitioner and the manager—is to learn to solve marketing problems better, to arrive at the best solution in line with the corporate goals, which automatically include the creation of customer satisfactions with maximum efficiency.

Each of these approaches has made its own contribution to modern marketing thinking. The historical approach starts us with culture; the institutional provides a start toward segmentation; the functional furthers this analysis; the ecological contributes the start of customer recognition—the "why" of needs, wants, and desires; systems adds integration;

the managerial adds perspective—all evolutionary steps blended in to-day's decision-making concept.

Decision Making If we forget the weaknesses but borrow the above strengths from each of these approaches and combine them into our current, decision-making approach, it makes for a sophisticated, multi-faceted one, indeed. This is but a reflection of the nature of modern marketing, a sophisticated and multifaceted area. And yet, it is at the same time simple, easy to understand. It is merely the problems, stemming fundamentally from people, which are complex.

The decision-making approach, and the one we have attempted to use in this book, places the reader in the position of being a decision maker. Viewed in this light, traditional theory and description must meet the test of contributing to the understanding of current problems faced by the decision maker. The decision-making approach first recognizes the problems, then develops the factors bearing on them to broaden the scope of the considerations of the decision maker, but leaves the act of reaching the decision to the manager. From this point of view there is no limit to the scope of such considerations except the test of relevancy. Marketing, today, is no longer viewed as a set of functions, principles, or "laws" to dictate solutions; rather, it is a point of view, a perspective, a philosophy to aid in the identification of problems, the assembly of relevant information, both quantitative and qualitative, and an aid in the attainment of the objective, improved decision making.

THE MARKETING CONCEPT

The marketing concept has become popular. But, its implications are not always understood. It is not to be misinterpreted to mean the technical interests of a marketing department, or the techniques of marketing performed by such a department. It is far broader than that. In a very real way it brings together into an integrated whole several aspects of marketing. It involves:

1. Market orientation, with the satisfaction of the consumer paramount in decision making. Without wholehearted acceptance of this orientation to the customer, anything else will be purely mechanical.

2. Perspective in planning, with recognition of what we are selling, who our competitors really are, and our potentials.

3. Recognition of profitability (not just sales volume) as an honorable goal—a prerequisite to the attainment of corporate goals and of continued service to the customer.

4. Recognition of the scope of marketing, together with the need for

the complete integration of the marketing concept throughout the corporate structure.

The integration of marketing really involves several aspects. Edward C. Bursk, editor of the *Harvard Business Review,* once put it this way:[4]

> (1) Marketing must be integrated in the sense that it involves the welding of art and science. In turn, art must be made up both of conceptual imagination and of operational skill; while science must comprise all possible disciplines, particularly the statistical and the behavioral.
> (2) Marketing must be integrated in the sense that it makes use of a combination of all the possible elements of action for reaching and influencing consumers and customers—product design, price, physical location of the goods, and communication (including both selling and advertising).
> (3) Marketing must be integrated in the sense that all functions in the company, all top managers, regardless of their assigned responsibilities, must understand the importance of the consumer and must have marketing awareness, understanding, and sensitivity (if not actual dedication). And lip-service is not enough.
> (4) Marketing must be integrated in the sense that all the steps of action must be knit together in a purposeful plan.

Today, market orientation is accepted as sound, and the marketing concept, together with its implications, is readily lauded. All too many businessmen, including a great many so-called marketing executives, will readily agree with its merits—and then go right on with the business of selling *products,* emphasizing their product superiorities, competing most keenly for more sales, and never pausing to reflect, to give more than lip service, to that in which they profess to believe. It takes far more than that to become market-oriented—to adopt the marketing concept. Renaming a sales to a marketing department may look good on a chart for the directors or an annual report, but it accomplishes little except to kid both the viewer and the manager.

A rearrangement of people on the organizational chart will accomplish little. It is the individual who is oriented, not the company. Even though these individuals may now report to different entities in the organizational structure, this realignment of responsibilities will not have changed their perspective, their attitude, or their thinking.

The attainment of market orientation (part one of the marketing concept) in a company which does not now possess it is not easy. The simple reason is that it involves changing the attitudes, the perspectives, the thinking of people—a most difficult task! Ideally, this might start

---

[4] Used with permission of Edward C. Bursk.

with the corporate president, or with the top marketing executive. Both of these men are in a position to convince the rest of top management and product-division management of the merit of their thinking. From there, it is far easier to persuade the lower levels of management to the point of view of top management, and to develop the cooperation in both thinking and performance so necessary to the effective implementation of the marketing concept.

Approached from the other direction, that is, with the attainment of market orientation first in the lower levels of management, and in the face of product or sales orientation in the minds of top management, the task is even more difficult—but all the more necessary. It calls for persuasiveness, tact, perseverance, courage, and a logical presentation of the nature of market orientation (as against the product or sales orientation already present) directed toward the gradual reorientation of such individuals. This may or may not be successful. Unfortunately, many senior executives have spent most of their lives and attained a reasonable degree of success under the orientation they possess (most of which was prior to the present conditions of keen competition). They may use their lifetime of experience to overrule the drastic changes in their thinking proposed by younger men, and from their point of view, feel confident that they are right.

Never overlook the possibility that such individuals *may* be correct in their product or sales orientation, if the circumstances support it. On the other hand, never apologize for youth. Just be sure you're right, then go ahead. There are three choices. Keep trying in the hope of eventual success; sit it out and wait for death or retirement to provide changes in top management; or move to another company more receptive to a realistic recognition of today's circumstances.

Still another difficulty in securing complete integration of the marketing concept is found in cases where everyone agrees with it and each insists he is acting accordingly. Let's see. Try talking to the product engineer—but don't take his word for it, probe his thinking.

In one company, the chief product engineer, when asked for the source of his ideas for product improvements, replied, "We have our own sources. We know what the customers want—in fact, better than the customer does—or what marketing thinks he does."

This man *thinks* he is market-oriented. He thinks he is serving the customer best through his superior knowledge (admittedly of engineering, questionably of customer satisfaction). His thinking will build a better railroad train—but it is no assurance of patronage. It is product orientation at its finest.

All that is really needed is to change the perspective, not the application of the engineering skill. This should start with a real awareness, not of the product, but of the satisfaction the product is to serve, and from the customer's point of view. To continue product orientation *may* be correct—and it *can* be fatal. True market orientation minimizes the risk of the latter.

And yet, this engineer continues to decide what his customers want—completely blind to the simple (but, oh, so significant) change in perspective which, coupled with his engineering skill, could make him a real leader, perhaps an innovator.

Organization for the Marketing Concept

Probably there is no such thing as a typical or ideal organizational structure to illustrate the best interrelationships within a firm adopting the marketing concept. There are too many variables, too many differing sets of circumstances—from multidivisional conglomerates operating internationally down to the many small corporations with relatively restricted product line(s).

It is clear that marketing performance is not restricted to the marketing department and that market *considerations* permeate the entire structure. Who reports to whom on a chart is less important than the welding of the whole into a corporate team. In fact, many corporations get along pretty well in spite of their organizational chart—which is frequently at least six months behind operational changes, anyway.

The simplest corporate structure and the simplest way possible to create more and better customer satisfactions would seem to be the best. Anything beyond that becomes an economic waste and tends to detract from corporate efficiency.

Clearly, irrespective of detail, the top marketing executive belongs on a par with the other major functional areas. The marketing manager should control, or at least be a major party to, such things as product planning (often under product engineering), pricing, budgeting, advertising, sales forecasting, production planning, and both customer and product services. Clearly, marketing data should be provided by staff—and to all who can use it. Clearly, line authority and responsibility should be placed at the lowest level which can handle it. And, in no case must communication be restricted by lines on a chart. Cooperative working relationships are the important things, not to be impeded by structural insularity.

Perhaps the best approach is to develop the working relationships first. How best can the job be done? Who needs to relate to whom? Then, develop the organizational structure informally along such lines. Any attempt to put this on paper as a diagram should never be interpreted as a restriction of communication or performance.

RELEVANT READING

Bell, Martin L., *Marketing*, Boston: Houghton Mifflin Company, 1966.

Fisk, George, *Marketing Systems*, New York: Harper & Row, Publishers, Incorporated, 1967.

Frey, Albert W. (ed.), *Marketing Handbook*, 2d ed., New York: The Ronald Press Company, 1965, sec. 27, pp. 1–5.

Greenwood, Frank, *Casebook for Management and Business Policy*, Scranton, Pa.: International Textbook Company, 1968.

Jones, Manley Howe, *The Marketing Process*, New York: Harper & Row, Publishers, Incorporated, 1965, chap. 1.

Kotler, Philip, *Marketing Management*, Englewood Cliffs, N.J.: Prentice-Hall, Inc., 1967, chap. 1.

McCarthy, E. Jerome, *Basic Marketing*, 3d ed., Homewood, Ill.: Richard D. Irwin, Inc., 1968, chap. 1.

Westing, J. Howard, and Gerald Albaum, *Modern Marketing Thought*, 2d ed., New York: The Macmillan Company, 1969, chaps. 2 and 3.

CHAPTER TWO

The Industrial Market.

The orientations to and perspectives of modern industrial marketing, discussed in the previous chapter, are deemed to be basic—a prerequisite to modern marketing thinking. We now turn our attention from the act of marketing to the goods marketed, to the market, to the special characteristics of industrial demand, and to an entirely new concept, an approach to marketing problems based for the first time upon marketing rather than product characteristics.

INDUSTRIAL GOODS CLASSIFIED

Don't bother. That's right—don't bother to develop or learn a classification system of industrial goods. Any such system is far more apt to perpetuate a misdirection of marketing thinking than it is to contribute to a real understanding of marketing problems. It tends to perpetuate a product orientation in the minds of marketing men, even of those who profess to be market-oriented. Such men insist that they are selling products. Their whole pattern of thought originates from the intrinsic properties and superiorities of their product lines. A classification system of industrial goods is but an answer to the question, "What are we selling?" Industrial buyers don't want to buy products. They are but a means to an end.   Industrial buyers seek to buy benefits, industrial want satisfactions.

As Levitt[1] has succinctly observed:

> "Last year 1 million quarter-inch drills were sold," Leo McGivena once said, "not because people wanted quarter-inch drills but because they wanted quarter-inch holes."
>
> People don't buy products; they buy the expectation of benefits.   Yet narrow production-minded executives and most economic theorists are resolutely attached to the idea that goods have intrinsic properties.   A loaf of bread is presumed to be quite obviously something different from a diamond.   Each is somehow viewed as having inherent characteristics rather than as conveying benefits to buyers.   This accounts in the business world for pricing policies based one-sidedly on costs, and in the world of the economist for microeconomic demand curves that define consumer utility as, at best, indifference functions.
>
> Physics long ago abandoned the notion that things have intrinsic or inherent characteristics.   It is time that we do the same in business.   People spend their money not for goods and services, but to get the value satisfactions they believe are bestowed by what they are buying.   They buy quarter-inch holes, not quarter-inch drills.   That is the marketing view of the business process.

It is very easy to form the conviction that *what* we market *is* our product.   It may be somewhat difficult to broaden one's perspective to the realization that the product is but a means to an end.   You may sell a product—but your customer buys want satisfaction.   One might ask if you *want* to buy a new TV antenna.   Of course not!   But, you *may* want to buy improved reception, a clearer picture, improved entertainment.

The error is not in attending to our product and its advantages, plus our superior service, naturally.   The error is to place our product at the center of our attention, of our universe.   Customer benefit, customer want satisfaction belongs there!   Our product exists solely to create such benefit and satisfaction—and competes with anything else which might create the same satisfaction, no matter how.   We are really being paid for the satisfaction, and we will survive only so long as we continue to deliver customer satisfaction.   Our present product competitors may or may not be our real competition.   Is AC a competitor of Champion—or is it a steam engine or a gas turbine?

There are other reasons to question the practical value of attempting to classify industrial goods in the first place.   Such a classification might serve as a basis for generalization to aid in marketing planning and decision making—provided all the goods in one category possess com-

[1] From *The Marketing Mode* by Theodore Levitt, p. 1.   Copyright 1969, McGraw-Hill Book Company.   Used with permission of McGraw-Hill Book Company.

mon marketing problems. Obviously, such is not the case. The many considerations bearing upon the solution of industrial problems go so far beyond the preliminary identification of the goods as belonging to this or that classification that the awareness of the correct classification contributes little or nothing to the ultimate decisions reached.

Yet another purpose for a classification of industrial goods might be to indicate the scope of the industrial market. This has some merit, as a start. The traditional concept was based on the view of the industrial market as being composed primarily, if not exclusively, of manufacturing establishments. Overlooked completely were all other businesses and institutions. Industrial goods were deemed to consist of raw materials, partially fabricated goods and parts, operating supplies, installations, and accessory equipment—things sold to a manufacturing plant.

If we are to have a classification structure for industrial goods and services, at least let's have a complete one. From this point of view, and for whatever benefit it may provide, industrial goods and services might be visualized as being composed of the following:

1. Capital investment items:
   a. Equipment. Removable items with a depreciable life. Examples: cash registers, construction equipment, counters, desk calculators, electric typewriters, farm machinery, furniture and fixtures, and trucks.
   b. Installations. These items are not readily removable and typically form some part of the office building, plant, or store. Examples: air conditioning, automated machines, computers, cranes, elevators, escalators, blast furnaces, and safes.
   c. Real estate, plant, and buildings. This is all the real property of the enterprise, including offices, plants, warehouses, parking lots, facilities for employee relaxation, housing, etc., wherever located.
2. Manufacturing materials:
   a. Raw materials, primarily from agriculture and the various extractive industries. Examples: cacao beans, corn, livestock, logs, minerals, ores, petroleum, scrap, as well as dairy products, fruits, and vegetables sold to a processor.
   b. Semifinished goods. Some work has been applied. They are finished only in part, or they may have been formed into shapes and specifications to make them readily usable by the buyer. Examples: castings, chemicals, metals in many forms such as bars, sheets, tubing, wire, etc., shoe leather, salvage, sugar to a candy maker, and paper to a printer.
   c. Parts. These are the completely finished products of one firm which can be used as a part of a more complex product by another firm. Included here are the OEMs, original equipment

manufacturers. Examples: bearings, buttons, controls, dials, gauges, lenses, pulleys, spark plugs, transistors and tubes to radio and TV manufacturers, and windshields for automobiles.

3. Operational:
   a. Labor—any employment of people in business.
   b. Operating supplies. Consumable items used in the operations of the business enterprise. Examples: adding-machine tape, cutting oil, fasteners, insecticides, fuels, office supplies, small tools, sacks, and wrapping materials.
   c. Repair, maintenance, and replacement items. Here we find items which are needed repeatedly or recurrently in order to maintain the operational efficiency of the business. They are typically of relatively low unit cost and would not include major machine installations or other such items more properly classified under capital investment. Examples: electrical outlets and supplies, janitorial supplies, lubricants, paint, plumbing materials, and a wide variety of repair parts to both plant and equipment.

4. Services:
   a. Manufacturing services. This refers to the growing number of highly skilled and specialized services performed by one firm for another as a part of the latter's total manufacturing process. Examples: brazing and welding, casting, dyeing, finishing, glazing, and many applications of special forming and shaping services.
   b. Business services. These are somewhat parallel to the manufacturing services, except that here we are referring to business services to offices rather than manufacturing-process services to the plant. Examples: copying and reproducing services, EDP, maintenance and repair services on business machines and equipment, protection services, research—goods from R&D, trade shows, travel agents, and window cleaning.
   c. Professional services. It has not been generally recognized, but there is a wide range of professional services marketed to industry. They well deserve inclusion as part of the complex of industrial goods and services. Examples: accounting, advertising, consulting—both business management and engineering—educational, financial, insurance, legal—general corporate counsel and both patent and process-right protection—psychological testing, and tax.

THE INDUSTRIAL MARKET: AN OVERVIEW

Every business entity (and nonpolitical institution) from the smallest, one-man operation to the conglomerate is included in the industrial market. This means all sole proprietorships, partnerships, associations, and corporations, whenever they buy goods or services for further production or to operate their businesses (as against buying merchandise for resale in the same form to ultimate consumers—families and individuals).

The owner of a retail store would be considered as an industrial customer if he were to buy a counter or a cash register to operate his business. The merchandise he buys for resale to customers is consumer goods. A farmer would be considered to be an industrial purchaser when he buys fertilizer and farm equipment for use in the operation of his farm, but not when he buys a new rug for his living room. Construction materials and building supplies sold to contractors would generally be industrial. However, when they are resold to the homeowner, the do-it-yourself buyer, they should be classified as consumer goods.

For practical purposes, industrial goods are industrial because they are bought and sold that way. Yet, a manufacturer needing an ordinary broom might buy it at a nearby supermarket or hardware store. Or an accountant might buy a letter opener for use in his office at a retail store. By our definition, such sales are clearly industrial, since the goods are to be used in the operation of a business. From the point of view of the seller, they are clearly consumer sales at retail, sold and recorded as such. Similar borderline cases exist in other marketing situations—for example, a regular wholesaler who occasionally sells to an ultimate consumer. These are exceptions. The volume involved is so low as not to impair the working practicality of our basic definitive concepts. To argue whether they are or should be "industrial" is far more theoretical than practical, obviously.

Difficulty of Measurement

This market is big and almost impossible to measure accurately—and that's about all that can be said about it. There are just no statistical data available on a strictly industrial basis, and probably never will be. Whereas many firms are purely industrial in their operations, many more sell to the consumer and/or governmental/defense/space markets as well, while many others verge on being almost entirely consumer. Corporations are most reluctant to reveal sales by major product lines or even by operating division. They rarely refine sales data by industrial buyers versus consumer resellers even though many items fit both markets. The degree of involvement in each of these markets is not available for publication; but, even if it were, it is only a part of the problem.

Consumer sales at retail represent but the final step in the selling and reselling involved from raw material to end product. All marketing, all successive sales prior to the creation of the consumer good in its final form, is industrial. And to this may be added the industrial components of sales ending up as governmental, as well as the strictly industrial sales to businesses, of course.

These data just are not available—nor need they be. For, if they were, they would serve little purpose except to demonstrate what we already know, that the size of the industrial market is gigantic.

There are ways by which the total volume of industrial sales may be approximated. One is to start with total manufacturer sales, perhaps adjust them for net imports and exports, add all other industrial sales such as construction (except governmental), industrial services, etc., and accumulate a total. From this must be subtracted both governmental and consumer (retail) sales at the manufacturer level (i.e., adjusted for the cost of passing through the channel of distribution—the compensation paid to agents and wholesalers and the retailers' own markups). The net result would approximate an industrial sales estimate.

Size and Distribution of Firms

If we restrict our perspective to *primarily* consumer, governmental/defense/space, or industrial marketing, it is interesting to note the rapidly diminishing size of market as reflected by the number of customers. There are, literally, millions of families and individuals in the consumer area, thousands to hundreds of customers in the primarily industrial, and but one—or at the most a few hundred—in the governmental.

Obviously, it is impractical to present detailed statistical data on the industrial market in a book of this nature. Such information, to be useful, needs to be refined right down to the point where it is truly descriptive of both present and potential customers of the user, often including specifics of individual names and addresses within prospective firms, which is far beyond our spatial limitations for even one market. Also, and equally preclusive, these data are constantly changing and need to be updated frequently. It is hoped that the life of this book will exceed somewhat the life of presently current statistical data.

There are many sources of such information, presumably so well known as not to warrant repetition here. Included are governmental data, state directories, and services from many publishers, each specializing somewhat in coverage. Two examples are *Scott's Industrial Directories*, covering manufacturers in Canada, segmented to Quebec, Ontario, and the *Western Directory*, which combines the four Western provinces, Manitoba, Saskatchewan, Alberta, and British Columbia. Companies are listed alphabetically, geographically, and by SIC (Standard Industrial Classification) number together with names and addresses of executives, products, employment, plant locations, etc. Mailing address: P.O. Box 365, Oakville, Ontario, Canada.

McGraw-Hill, in its *Plant Census,* has data on approximately 75,000 establishments classified by four-digit SIC numbers in the manufacturing industries of SIC 19-39. Both primary and additional product groups are identified. In most industries all plants with 20 or more employees are included; in some 100 employees is the cutoff point. These data are available on 3 by 5 cards or magnetic tape. Included are the company name and division if applicable, physical address and mailing address, principal and additional SICs, and a plant-size code breaking the list in increments as the United States Census does.

Statistics can be developed by geographical subdivision and mailing lists on heat-transfer labels by job title. These lists can be selected and sorted by SIC, plant size, state, city, county, and Zip Code. See Figure 2.1 for an illustration of the card format.

For those whose market is created by construction, *Dodge Reports* are a vital information service. With complete data on the best selling opportunities—including the owner, architect, engineer, and contractor's name and address, project description and current status—marketing efforts can be directed to the right people at the right time. New construction projects are reported at each key step until contracts are awarded and ground is broken. Figure 2.2 illustrates one such report. Coverage of the Dodge service is limited to projects where the total

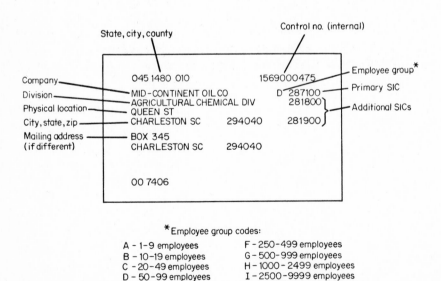

Fig. 2.1 McGraw-Hill census-card format.

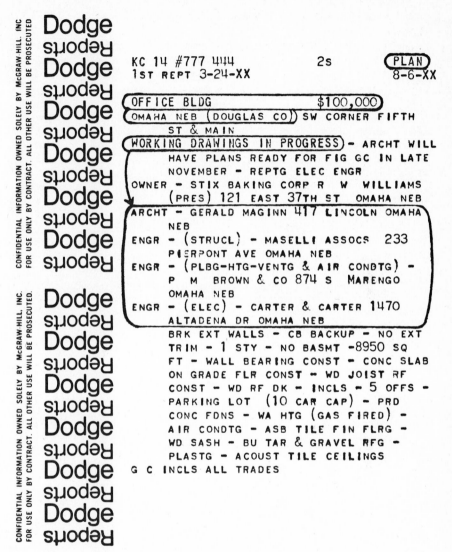

Dodge Reports
Dodge Reports
Dodge Reports
Dodge Reports
Dodge Reports
Dodge Reports
Dodge Reports

Dodge Reports
Dodge Reports
Dodge Reports
Dodge Reports
Dodge Reports
Dodge Reports
Dodge Reports

KC 14 #777 444   2s   (PLAN)
1ST REPT 3-24-XX   8-6-XX

(OFFICE BLDG $100,000)
(OMAHA NEB (DOUGLAS CO)) SW CORNER FIFTH
      ST & MAIN
(WORKING DRAWINGS IN PROGRESS)- ARCHT WILL
      HAVE PLANS READY FOR FIG GC IN LATE
      NOVEMBER - REPTG ELEC ENGR
OWNER - STIX BAKING CORP R W WILLIAMS
      (PRES) 121 EAST 37TH ST OMAHA NEB
ARCHT - GERALD MAGINN 417 LINCOLN OMAHA
      NEB
ENGR - (STRUCL) - MASELLI ASSOCS 233
      PIERPONT AVE OMAHA NEB
ENGR - (PLBG-HTG-VENTG & AIR CONDTG) -
      P M BROWN & CO 874 S MARENGO
      OMAHA NEB
ENGR - (ELEC) - CARTER & CARTER 1470
      ALTADENA DR OMAHA NEB
      BRK EXT WALLS - CB BACKUP - NO EXT
      TRIM - 1 STY - NO BASMT -8950 SQ
      FT - WALL BEARING CONST - CONC SLAB
      ON GRADE FLR CONST - WD JOIST RF
      CONST - WD RF DK - INCLS - 5 OFFS -
      PARKING LOT (10 CAR CAP) - PRD
      CONC FDNS - WA HTG (GAS FIRED) -
      AIR CONDTG - ASB TILE FIN FLRG -
      WD SASH - BU TAR & GRAVEL RFG -
      PLASTG - ACOUST TILE CEILINGS
G C INCLS ALL TRADES

Fig. 2.2 Sample *Dodge Report* of a project in planning stage.

cost exceeds $15,000 and to those projects located within forty-one states of the United States.   The Pacific Northwest is not covered.

Ancillary Dodge services are available for management's use in estimating potential and measuring sales penetration. National headquarters is located at 1221 Avenue of the Americas, New York, New York 10020.

TABLE 2.1   Distribution of United States Business Enterprises
(Figures in thousands)

Industry	Proprietorships	Partnerships	Corporations
Agriculture, forestry, fisheries	3,196	125	32
Mining	46	13	14
Construction	680	53	123
Manufacturing	170	35	197
Trans., commun., elec., gas	278	15	66
Wholesale trade	260	31	143
Retail trade	1,544	187	316
Finance, insurance, real estate	549	275	399
Services	2,328	165	221
Total	9,126	906	1,534

DERIVED FROM: *Statistical Abstract of U.S., 1970*, 91st ann. ed., U.S. Bureau of the Census, 1970, p. 468.

TABLE 2.2   Distribution of Business Enterprises by Size

Sales size brackets	Proprietorships	Partnerships	Corporations
Under $50,000	139,000		
50,000–99,999	17,000		
100,000+	14,000		
Under $100,000		25,000	
100,000–499,999		8,000	
500,000+		2,000	
Under $500,000			158,000
500,000–999,999			17,000
1,000,000+			22,000
Total	170,000	35,000	197,000

SOURCE: *Statistical Abstract of U.S., 1970*, 91st ann. ed., U.S. Bureau of the Census, 1970, p. 470.

In 1967, United States industry included:[2]

Proprietorships	9,126,000
Partnerships	906,000
Corporations	1,534,000

Table 2.1 shows the distribution of these business enterprises, broken down by industry.

Table 2.2 goes a step further and refines the 402,000 manufacturing enterprises by size categories.

[2] SOURCE: *Statistical Abstract of U.S., 1970*, 91st ann. ed., U.S. Bureau of the Census, 1970, p. 468.

The pattern is starting to emerge: 400,000 manufacturer-sellers—with a few, very large enterprises and a great number of small ones.

Then, from the standpoint of receipts, the picture in Table 2.3 is developed.

It might be noted that, in manufacturing, the 197,000 corporations sell $576.6 billion, whereas 170,000 proprietorships sell $6.5 billion.

A further refinement of these data provides a most significant picture of the distribution of manufacturing firms and the sales accounted for by those in each size bracket. It is tabulated in Table 2.4 and depicted graphically on Figure 2.3.

It is readily noted that the industrial market is extremely heavily concentrated in the relatively few, largest corporations—the giants, the conglomerates. They are the ones doing the most selling—and buying.

A more detailed examination of the foregoing can reveal many interesting points. For example, it can be noted that 70 percent of the business is done by less than 1 percent of the firms. Over 80 percent of the business is done by less than 5 percent of the firms. Firms with annual sales of $1 million or more amount to 23 percent of the total, but do 93 percent of the business. Other observations are left to you.

Irrespective of the mathematical precision of these statistics and with an awareness that the facts are constantly changing, the major pattern is both clear and well established. Figure 2.3 is not an "average," but it is indicative of the pattern found elsewhere. In fact, industrial segments of the overall picture, whereas they vary somewhat from one industry to another, conform quite closely in motif to this pattern.

TABLE 2.3 Distribution of Business Enterprises by Receipts
(Figures in millions of dollars)

Industry	Proprietorships	Partnerships	Corporations
Agriculture, forestry, fisheries	$35,271	$5,450	$8,855
Mining	1,323	1,045	12,754
Construction	18,334	7,129	66,828
Manufacturing	6,473	5,640	576,570
Trans., commun., elec., gas	5,539	1,310	99,191
Wholesale trade	19,712	10,796	182,687
Retail trade	81,116	16,925	216,341
Finance, insurance, real estate	6,738	9,131	131,983
Services	34,784	14,744	45,211
Total	$211,372	$79,020	$1,345,185

SOURCE: *Statistical Abstract of U.S., 1970*, 91st ann. ed., U.S. Bureau of the Census, 1970, p. 468.

TABLE 2.4   Distribution and Sales of 182,732 Primarily Industrial Firms by Sales Brackets

Sales brackets	Number of firms	Sales, in billions of dollars	Percent firms in each bracket	Percent sales in each bracket
Under $100M	48,892	2.05	26.76	0.37
$100–200M	26,989	3.95	14.77	0.71
$200–500M	39,110	12.74	21.40	2.29
$500–1MM	25,769	18.37	14.10	3.30
$1MM–2MM	15,955	19.14	8.73	3.43
$2MM–5MM	17,517	45.54	9.59	8.17
$5MM–10MM	3,958	28.45	2.17	5.10
$10MM–25MM	2,814	36.58	1.54	6.56
$25MM–50MM	691	20.73	0.38	3.72
$50MM–100MM	445	26.70	0.24	4.79
Over $100MM	592	343.07	0.32	61.56
Total	182,732	557.32	100.00	100.00

DERIVED AND COMPUTED FROM: *Statistics of Income 1966, Business Income Tax Returns*, U.S. Department of the Treasury, Internal Revenue Service, 1969, p. 218.

This distribution of industrial manufacturing has most serious implications to the market analyst, the researcher, and the sales manager. It is clear that the concept of the "average" customer becomes even more invalid than usual here. The use of any random sampling techniques becomes highly questionable. These points are more fully presented in Chapter Fourteen, "Measuring Markets: Past, Present, and Future."

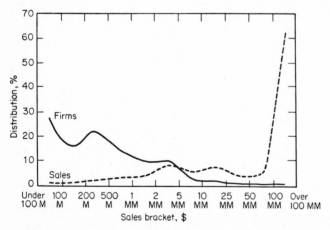

Fig. 2.3 Distribution and sales of 182,732 primarily industrial firms by sales brackets.

Power in the Marketplace

Another perspective of this industrial concentration is presented in Table 2.5. Here is depicted the share of market enjoyed by the top four and the top twenty firms in each of several markets. This concentration of sales, and therefore, also purchasing power in the hands of a few firms is, indeed, power in the marketplace.

This is a very significant situation to be faced by those responsible for the direction of marketing effort. In contrast with the consumer market, it means fewer customers, larger orders, far more concentration of marketing effort on a smaller target, and it is hoped, far more effective communication. Even more specifically, it typically means a few very important customers, then many more, perhaps hundreds of potential buyers which collectively represent only a small part of the potential of the first few.

It is appropriate to note that the trend is for this concentration of power to grow, rather than to diminish. The major corporate entities, the conglomerates, show a strong tendency to grow, in part by acquisition accomplished in any of several ways. They frequently seek allied but noncompetitive items for such addition, thereby tending to avoid difficulties of governmental interference on the grounds of monopolistic growth.

However, some firms are going beyond mere noncompetitive additions. They plan this growth to permit them to produce and market

TABLE 2.5   Concentration of Market in Top Four and Top Twenty Companies, by Percent of Value of Shipments, 1963

Industry SIC code no.	Product class	Top 4 companies	Top 20 companies
2621	Paper Mill Products	26	61
2818	Industrial Organic Chemicals	42	74
2819	Industrial Inorganic Chemicals	27	61
3011	Tires and Inner Tubes	72	97
33124	Steel, Hot Rolled Bars, Plates, etc.	63	89
3352	Aluminum Rolling and Drawing	67	85
34110	Metal Cans	73	94
3522	Farm Machinery and Equipment	42	65
3531	Construction Machinery	42	69
3571	Computers and Related Machines	63	89
3621	Electrical Motors and Generators	47	69
3721	Aircraft	58	98

SOURCE: *Concentration Ratios in Manufacturing Industry, 1963*, a report for the Subcommittee on Antitrust and Monopoly of the Committee of the Judiciary, United States Senate, U.S. Bureau of the Census, 1966, table 4.

TABLE 2.6   Manufacturing by Regions, Selected Years
(Percent of United States total)

Region	Employment			Value added		
	1958	1963	1967	1958	1963	1967
East North Central	26.6	26.4	26.7	28.9	29.3	28.6
Middle Atlantic	25.7	24.0	22.6	24.6	22.7	22.0
South Atlantic	11.8	12.5	12.9	10.1	11.0	11.2
Pacific	10.0	10.6	10.8	11.1	11.5	11.3
New England	8.7	8.4	8.1	7.4	7.1	7.3
West North Central	6.0	6.0	6.2	6.3	6.1	6.4
West South Central	5.0	5.1	5.6	5.5	5.7	6.3
East South Central	4.9	5.2	5.6	4.5	4.8	5.2
Mountain	1.4	1.7	1.6	1.6	1.8	1.7
United States total	100.0	100.0	100.0	100.0	100.0	100.0

SOURCE: *Statistical Abstract of U.S., 1970*, 91st ann. ed., U.S. Bureau of the Census, 1970, p. 697.

entirely integrated systems to their customers, not merely equipment for one step or random steps within such a system. Not only would this seem to strengthen them vastly as manufacturer-sellers by enhancing their competitive position in the right way, by delivering an integrated system to maximize the customer satisfaction—which is the true objective of marketing in the first place—but it also goes a long way toward justification of the existence of such conglomerates as total business entities.

Characteristics of the Industrial Market

Geographical: An Overview   Table 2.6 ranks the geographical regions of the United States by two major facets of industrial activity—percent of total of the United States employment and value added by manufacturing.

In general, the industrial market has not merely grown, but has been moving and continues to move south and west. Examination of Table 2.7 shows that the two historically leading areas, East North Central and Middle Atlantic, the largest to begin with, gained the most from 1958 to 1967. However, ranked by rate of growth, with the absolute growth expressed as a percent of the 1958 base data, they are in seventh and ninth places—at the other end of the scale. The following is the rank of these regions based on percentage of gain from 1958 to 1967 (see the last column in Table 2.7).

1. East South Central
2. West South Central

3. Mountain
4. South Atlantic
5. Pacific
6. West North Central
7. East North Central
8. New England
9. Middle Atlantic

The major industrial markets are quite heavily concentrated. Major metropolitan areas, including their immediate vicinities, are growing into huge industrial complexes. Chicago–Detroit and Washington–New York–Boston are living examples of this trend.

By states, the geographical concentration of industrial activities as reflected by employment is shown in Table 2.8. Here it can be readily seen that the top eight states account for more than 50 percent of the total. Statistics by industrialized areas across state lines, such as the Washington–New York–Boston complex, are not readily available. From that point of view, the concentration would appear to be even more intense in the leading areas, with but scattered development for the rest of the country.

TABLE 2.7 Regional Changes in Employment (Emp) and Value Added (V.A.), 1958–1967

Region	Factor*	1958	1967	Gain, 1958–1967 Amount	Percent
East North Central	Emp	4,261	5,169	908	21.3
	V.A.	40,962	75,046	34,084	83.2
Middle Atlantic	Emp	4,113	4,386	273	6.6
	V.A.	34,814	57,613	22,799	65.5
South Atlantic	Emp	1,885	2,502	617	32.7
	V.A.	14,355	29,300	14,945	104.1
Pacific	Emp	1,595	2,052	457	28.7
	V.A.	15,666	29,704	14,038	89.6
West South Central	Emp	795	1,088	293	36.9
	V.A.	7,791	16,639	8,848	113.6
New England	Emp	1,400	1,566	166	11.9
	V.A.	10,440	19,030	8,590	82.3
West North Central	Emp	964	1,207	243	25.2
	V.A.	8,870	16,764	7,894	89.0
East South Central	Emp	783	1,093	310	39.6
	V.A.	6,389	13,739	7,350	115.0
Mountain	Emp	229	316	87	38.0
	V.A.	2,244	4,524	2,280	101.6

* Employment in thousands; value added in millions of dollars.
COMPUTED FROM: *Statistical Abstract of U.S., 1970*, 91st ann. ed., U.S. Bureau of the Census, 1970, pp. 698–699.

TABLE 2.8   Production Workers by Leading States, 1967

State	Number of workers, in thousands	Percent
New York	1,291	9.2
Pennsylvania	1,142	8.2
California	1,049	7.5
Ohio	1,007	7.2
Illinois	997	7.1
Michigan	819	5.9
New Jersey	607	4.3
Indiana	544	3.9
Total, top 8 states	7,456	53.3
Rest of U.S.	6,543	46.7
Total, United States	13,999	100.0

SOURCE: *Statistical Abstract of U.S., 1970*, 91st ann. ed., U.S. Bureau of the Census, 1970, p. 699.

TABLE 2.9   Extent of Variation in Industrial versus Consumer Activities

Year	GNP — Amount, in billions of dollars	Percent change	Manufacturing — Amount, in billions of dollars	Percent change	Retailing — Amount, in billions of dollars	Percent change
1950	284.8		76.2		27.6	
		39.7		41.6		24.6
1955	398.0		107.9		34.4	
		26.6		16.6		20.1
1960	503.7		125.8		41.3	
		36.0		37.2		30.8
1965	684.9		172.6		54.0	
		26.4		24.8		24.4
1968	865.7		215.4		67.2	
Percent range of variation		13.3		25.0		10.7

COMPUTED FROM: *Statistical Abstract of U.S., 1970*, 91st ann. ed., U.S. Bureau of the Census, 1970, pp. 312 and 317.

One further observation of the characteristics of the industrial market, as against the consumer market, is that the consumer market tends to follow quite closely, but to a lesser degree, the pattern of changes in our gross national product.   The industrial market varies more.   A look at Table 2.9 should help illustrate this point.

Contrast in Characteristics: Industrial versus Consumer Market. The industrial marketing situation is just about the reverse of the consumer. In retailing to the ultimate consumer, one finds long channels of distribution; a great number and variety of resellers and customers; extensive use of self-service; the one-price plan; mass merchandising; a large number of relatively small transactions; and extensive advertising and promotional techniques, frequently stressing very minor differences and appealing to highly emotional buying motives of uninformed buyers.

In the industrial market, one sees short channels of distribution to relatively concentrated markets; heavy emphasis on direct relationships; far fewer sellers and buyers; much use of negotiation; far larger units of sale; infrequent purchases with fewer total transactions; well-informed buyers; highly organized and sophisticated procurement function; diverse and multiple purchasing influentials contributing to the buying decision from several points of view; predominately rational buying motives; heavy reliance on well-structured value and vendor analysis; the use of computers wherever applicable; and technical testing procedures by many of the larger firms.

In addition, there are considerations uniquely industrial: reciprocity, trade relations, order splitting, buying for a supplier, a relatively small number of buyers in a vertical market within any one industry, but a vast horizontal one across industry lines. Industrial marketers are keenly aware of the influence of government on industrial relationships. Even the objectives and roles of advertising and personal salesmanship differ significantly from consumer.

Thus, the industrial environment creates its own set of circumstances for decision making. The industrial marketer stands on his own and can borrow little from his consumer counterparts.

Yet, even these differences in characteristics are not the whole story. One of the most significant differences, one with far-reaching implications, has not been mentioned—the unique characteristics of industrial demand, particularly as contrasted with the typical treatment of demand predicated upon consumer behavior.

INDUSTRIAL DEMAND

Industrial demand is unique in that it does not exist by itself. It is completely derived from the demand for the goods of the other two major segments of marketing, consumer and governmental/defense/space. To this, of course, must be added the demand derived from the operations of all other businesses and institutions, including retail enterprises.

All this means that industrial demand is a function of the variation in consumer demand, but only in part. It also means that the industrialist is faced with the need for providing increased plant, equipment, and tooling for anticipated increases in consumer demand or curtailed expenditures in anticipation of decreased levels of consumer expenditures. In addition, he is faced with the impact of sales changes at the consumer level as these are reflected back to him through the channel of distribution. These changes are magnified by changes in inventory levels and also affected by inventory-policy changes. They can even be distorted by the time lag—with sales moving one way while manufacturers' orders are moving in the opposite direction.

Variation—and Why

This derived industrial demand follows generally, and frequently anticipates, the pattern of seasonal and cyclical variation present in consumer demand. However, the variation is substantially greater at the industrial level, both overall as was shown in Table 2.9 and even more so when viewed by specific product lines and for shorter periods of time. There are several phenomena which combine in various ways to produce this result.

Industrial goods are bought to fill an anticipated need. In the case of capital goods, they are purchased not only to fill current requirements, but also in the anticipation of a net profit from an expected future usage. This means that the variation in levels of business, the stage of the business cycle, can produce an exaggerated impact on the industrial sales of capital goods. In periods of recovery, real or anticipated, and in prosperity, the sale of such items is vastly stimulated. One tempering factor to this increased purchase rate lies in the financial structure of the industrial buyers. Because the amounts of money involved are substantial, the cash requirements, the cash flow, and the resultant cash position of the buyer are seriously involved. Under such circumstances, whereas the demand for capital goods may be rapidly increasing, the cash resources of the buyer may be inadequate to his total demand. Therefore, the sellers should be prepared not only to demonstrate effectively the financial advantages involved in the use of such new equipment, but also, in many cases, to provide assistance in the financing of them. Failure to recognize the probable financial position of any prospective buyers, particularly in periods of tight credit and high interest rates, may seriously detract from the total potential market.

In addition to the already high demand for industrial goods and services during periods of prosperity to satisfy current needs, the businessman in anticipation of increases in both future sales and prices may accumulate inventories, thereby stimulating the demand for industrial goods even further.

In periods of recession and in depression, the reduced consumer demand can readily be met by a reduction in inventories, by a reduced level of production, or both. Even a relatively slight threat of such a decrease in consumer buying can slow up not only the purchase of the industrial goods from which to make the consumer products, but also capital expenditures to replace present productive facilities.

One other significant aspect of the purchase of industrial goods in anticipation of a future need or profit lies in the reaction to a change in the economic climate as viewed by businessmen generally. It is this reaction which is most important—far more so than a slight change in economic welfare which may trigger it. If businessmen *feel* that the near future is apt to mean a slight recession, they act accordingly, and industrial sales are apt to be drastically curtailed. On the other hand, if the attitude of businessmen is favorable, that is, if they anticipate that business is on the upgrade, their investment in both capital goods and other industrial materials is apt to increase. This means that the attitude of businessmen may be far more significant than the actual level of our economy.

During periods of prosperity, the increased production of consumer goods, with the attendant increased demand for both industrial goods and capital equipment to increase productive capacity for the future, along with the increase in operational items for all businesses, at first tends to create conditions of relatively high demand and short supply. This places the seller in an advantageous position. Under such conditions price increases are most readily acceptable. Frequently, availability and shorter delivery times become very important. New firms will seek to enter the industrial market, wherever they can. The major delimiting factors to this increase in the number of firms are the cost of entry into the industry and the attitude of the businessman toward the permanency of the demand he currently sees.

On the other hand, whenever consumer demand falls off, with the attendant repercussions on the demand for the industrial counterparts, the reduction in capital expenditures, the generally unfavorable attitude of businessmen, the tightening of the belt via expense-reduction programs, we then find rapidly increasing conditions of both surplus goods and surplus productive capacity. This vastly increases competition and places the economic advantage in the hands of the buyer. Under these conditions, very few firms will seek to enter. In fact, this retrenchment may cause many of them to fail.

Industrial sales frequently accumulate to a far greater total than the consumer or governmental sources from which they are derived. No studies appear to have been made to document this point. It may not be true in every instance. Table 2.10 should help you visualize and

TABLE 2.10   Industrial Sales from $1 of Consumer Goods

Entity	Item	Amount	Industrial sale
Primary Producer	Raw Materials	$0.10	
	Labor et al.	.03	$0.13
	Profit	.02	
Primary Producer's		$0.15	
Selling Price Mill	Material	$0.15	
	Labor et al.	.06	0.21
	Profit	.04	
Mill's Selling Price		$0.25	
Parts Supplier	Material	$0.25	
	Labor et al.	.25	0.50
	Profit	.09	
Parts Supplier's			
Selling Price		$0.59	
Manufacturer	Material	$0.59	
	Labor et al.	.26	0.85
	Profit	.15	
Manufacturer's			
Selling Price of			
Consumer Good		$1.00	
Accumulated Industrial Sales			$1.69

evaluate this point. This is a purely hypothetical example. It illustrates the accumulation of the industrial sales involved as raw materials become finished consumer goods by the application of labor and other costs as they pass through the trade channel from primary producer, to mill, to parts supplier, and to the final manufacturer, possibly an assembler, who creates and sells the consumer good. Here it can be seen that the successive reselling (which includes as material cost of one stage, the selling price of the previous one) accumulates total industrial sales of 69 percent more than the consumer sale from which it is derived.

Obviously, this illustration is far from "typical." A thorough study of this process of accumulation would involve many more suppliers and subsuppliers, and frequently more than four levels. Although accurate information of this process would be most interesting, it is most likely that it would not change the basic point of the industrial accumulation being in excess of its source; rather, it would simply tend to define it more precisely.

Many manufacturers sell through middlemen, rather than directly. In all cases where goods are purchased for inventory as against current usage, a new set of complications arises. In the first place, the manufacturer loses control of, and in most cases even knowledge of, the inventories of his numerous customers. He may record on his books "sales" what are actually merely shipments. Because of the time lag in reflecting sales through the channel and the decisions of his customers to increase or decrease inventories, the sales may be moving at a far different rate or even in the opposite direction from his orders and shipments.

The existence of inventories in the hands of customers, and particularly if middlemen are also involved, is most apt to magnify even slight changes in the ultimate sales. Further, changes in inventories may come from simply a change in inventory policy by the customer, with or without any change in his sales. Or, a sales change in either direction may very well cause a reassessment of inventory policy. The result can be that a change in desired inventory levels is added to and still further exaggerates the change in ultimate sales, as it is reflected back to the manufacturer. The following mathematical example may help explain what happens under such circumstances.

First, inventory policy is the desired amount of inventory to be kept on hand. It may be expressed in any one of three ways: in dollars, in units, or in time supply, i.e., ninety-day supply. Now, let us suppose that a using manufacturer maintains a sixty-day inventory policy, uses 500 units per month, and reorders them twice a month, 250 at a time. Under normal circumstances he will maintain an inventory of 1,000 units. Let us now suppose that ultimate sales decrease 20 percent. Assuming no change in inventory policy, the manufacturer will now require only 800 units for inventory, which gives him an immediate surplus of 200 units. His normal reorders of 500 per month, 250 at a time, are reduced by the 20 percent sales drop to 400 per month, 200 at a time. If he now cancels his next reorder (and uses up his surplus inventory in place of it) while at the same time amending his future reorders to the 200 level, in the first month following this 20 percent sales decrease, his ordering will have dropped 60 percent—from the 500 to the 200. Thereafter, once this adjustment has been completed, his orders will be at the 400-per-month level. Thus, this magnification is not permanent, but it is drastic immediately following the sales change.

The manufacturer might have decided to change his inventory policy, perhaps to continue with a one-month supply, in which case he could have canceled his orders completely for the next month and a half, taking only 200 over the next two months instead of his customary 1,000. To make matters even worse, if we now visualize this manufacturer as buying through a distributor, then this impact of the manufacturer's order change will be magnified even further by the distributor as he adjusts to it, thus producing a most serious impact on the distributor's supplier. And yet, even this is not the end of the story. This reaction is not apt to be confined to one distributor, but may exist across the board. And, each such manufacturer serves many distributors. The simultaneous collective reaction of many such customers can produce a most serious cutback in the shipments of a manufacturer.

Changes which occur as a result of a sales decrease are apt to be both drastic and immediate. Obviously, the multiplier effect applies equally well in the reverse situation—that of a sales increase. However, since inventory policy provides a reserve from· which initial increased orders can be filled, adjustments upward are apt to be spread over a considerably longer period of time, thereby significantly reducing this impact all along the line.

Demand Schedule

Demand schedules are frequently found in textbooks on economics and in some student notebooks. They are very useful to the economist and the student—but rarely are they found on the desk of a businessman, particularly an industrial businessman. They come in a wide variety of shapes and levels of sophistication—complexity might be a better word—typically attained by the addition of more lines to represent additional factors involved in the situation being depicted.

Such schedules are simply an attempt to diagram on paper that which is noted to happen in the marketplace. Then, by study of the relationships within the diagram, by restructuring it to represent changes in some of the factors, conclusions can be reached to explain or predict market behavior. This is wonderful, in theory. In practice, the trouble is that such diagrams are a gross oversimplification of a most complex phenomenon. Even the most complex, and thereby realistic, diagrams include a recognition of supply, demand, various items of cost and revenue, and little else. Repeated use of such a limited set of basic factors quickly leads to the implication, all too frequently resulting in belief, that these are all the important factors which need be taken into account. This may not be a serious criticism in the analysis of many aspects of the market behavior for consumer goods. It is a most serious shortcoming in industrial.

One of the major reasons for the lack of use of demand schedules by the industrialist is, very simply, the difficulty of obtaining them. It is easy to draw such a diagram on paper using assumed data. It is an entirely different matter to construct such a diagram from reality—and particularly if it is to be refined to the specific brand of the seller as against the total market for the good.

The difficulty in the anticipation of demand is a variable within industrial marketing. Many standardized items with a low unit price are relatively easy to predict. Others, and particularly nonstandardized items with a high unit price, present great difficulty in determining the anticipated demand, even for relatively short future time periods. A

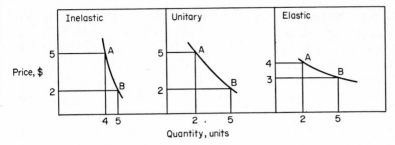

Fig. 2.4 Elasticity of demand.

good example of this is in the construction machinery industry, where high-ticket items tend to be built to order even in the face of an immediate need.

The usual demand schedule is downward sloping to the right. That is, as price is lowered, demand increases. Or, conversely, as price is raised, demand will decrease. It is actually a smoothed series of points, each one representing a quantity demanded at the price indicated. Figure 2.4 illustrates this.

The equation to measure demand elasticity actually is

$$E = \frac{\dfrac{Q_1 - Q_2}{Q_1 + Q_2}}{\dfrac{P_1 - P_2}{P_1 + P_2}}$$

E is the elasticity. Q_1 is the quantity before the price change, Q_2 after it. P_1 is the price before and P_2 the price after the change. The demand schedule is inelastic when E equals less than -1.0. It is unitary at E equals -1.0 exactly. Values greater than -1.0 are elastic. The negative sign comes from the negative slope of the demand curve.

Such demand schedules are highly typical of most consumer market situations. They are far less so of industrial. Industrial demand is derived with little bearing on the industrial price. The demand, coming from the needs of the consumer and governmental markets, exists any-way—irrespective of the industrial price or of a change in it. A price change may seriously affect the total taken as to consumer goods, and over relatively long periods of time. It will have far less impact on the total quantity taken of industrial goods. The impact is far more apt to be on the revenue, rather than the quantity.

Elasticity

Elasticity is simply the change in demand from a change in price. Per-centages are used to measure the changes relatively. Demand is deemed to be inelastic if the percentage change in quantity demanded is less than the percentage change in price. See Figure 2.4. It is said to possess unitary elasticity if the percentage change in price is matched by an equal percentage change in quantity. Demand is elastic if the percentage change in price is less than the percentage change in quantity demanded.

A common misconception is to interpret the *slope* of the demand-schedule line to mean elasticity. It is not the slope alone which indicates relative elasticity—rather, it is its position taken together with the slope which indicates this. The reason is that the ratio of elasticity is a reflection of the *percent* of change in the base—not merely the absolute amount of it. This is illustrated in Figure 2.5, where at A a 20 percent price decrease is accompanied by a 66⅔ percent increase in quantity, indicating that at this point, elasticity exists. However, at B this same 20 percent price decrease is accompanied by only a 12½ percent increase in quantity—quite inelastic.

The market for most industrial goods can be quite inelastic for the industry, but at the same time, highly elastic between firms. The total industry demand comes from the collective customer needs rather than the price. As such, it is relatively inelastic. Yet, as between sellers, even a slight change in price may create a major change in quantity and thereby be highly elastic for any one firm.

Many industrial products are essentially homogeneous, with many sellers. The market for such products tends to approach that of pure competition. Thus, if the wire available from many suppliers were uniform in quality, and one supplier were to increase his price, buyers would immediately purchase from the competition. Or, if one supplier were to lower his price, his orders would increase substantially for as long as he remained in this competitively advantageous position. Assuming this supplier is big enough to attract attention in the marketplace, chances are good that other suppliers may also cut their prices. The

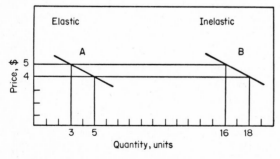

Fig. 2.5 Effect of position on elasticity.

net result can well be that they would collectively be selling the same volume as they did before, but for less money. This price cut by an individual seller may increase his share temporarily at the expense of his competitors, but a general price decline is most apt to decrease the revenue of all sellers, without seriously affecting the relative shares of the market or the total taken.

Reverse Elasticity

A unique and most interesting characteristic of industrial demand is that of a reverse elasticity as an immediate reaction to a price change. A price increase can cause an increase in demand, and a price decrease be followed by a decreased demand—just the opposite from what we would normally expect from observing consumer behavior. There, a reduction in the price of sirloin will sell more steak, not less. This reverse elasticity is not only possible in the industrial market, it is most likely to obtain as an immediate reaction, that is, in the short run.

In the long run industrial demand is simply the reflection of consumer and governmental demand—but in the short run, it is far more variable and may even be reversed.

The reason for this seemingly illogical reaction by industrial buyers is that they regard the initial price change as merely the first step in that direction with more to come. Then, in seeking to minimize their costs, they act very logically indeed to increase purchases immediately after a price increase in the anticipation of even higher prices later—and to decrease purchases, to start buying hand-to-mouth, to follow a price decline downward, and then to enter the market after the price decline has stopped.

These reactions are not uniform for all buyers. The cost advantage to be gained is tempered by several other factors involved in each of their purchase decisions. To increase purchases involves the probable duration of the need, the nature of the product from staple to speciality, the amount of money involved, the financial resources of the firm available for this use, and the corporate attitude toward speculation. The postponement of purchases involves the buyer's usage rate, his inventory policy and position within it, i.e., the effect on production of a short time lag in procurement, and the amount of money involved—the significance of the cost saving over any other considerations, such as the interruption of regularly scheduled deliveries.

These reactions do have the effect of further augmenting the price-level change in either direction. A decline in price which causes demand to diminish can thereby trigger a further price decline. Conversely, an increase in price which stimulates demand, in turn, can trigger further price increases. Thus, this reverse elasticity becomes yet another reason for the greater fluctuation in industrial over consumer demand and prices.

Cross Elasticity

Cross elasticity of demand is the responsiveness of the sales of one product to a price change for another. This concept is present in both consumer and industrial marketing—but is far more important in industrial. It helps to identify the competition between industrial materials, and in some cases interindustry competition itself.

An illustration of this might be in the case of the impact on the sale of steel of a price change for aluminum. Not all steel products would be affected, and those that are would most likely be affected in varying degrees. The cross elasticity is actually a ratio between the percentage of change in the quantity of the steel products to the percentage of change in the aluminum price. The higher this ratio, that is, the greater the percentage of change in quantity, the higher the cross elasticity and the more definitely the products compete in the same market. Incidentally, the concept works both ways. The same results should be produced when reflected by a change in the quantity of aluminum to a change in the price of steel.

It should be noted that cross elasticity of demand operates only when the price change in one product is *not* met by the other Common sense dictates that if, indeed, cross elasticity exists to a noticeable degree, the price change is very apt to be met. It could not be overlooked. This changes the impact on demand from the price change back to a question of general elasticity for the products involved.

Stimulation of Industrial Demand

Since industrial demand is derived to a major extent from consumer, obviously one good way to increase industrial demand is to increase the demand for the consumer counterparts. This has been the philosophy behind much thinking and planning by industrial marketing men in reaching decisions concerning the direction of their marketing efforts. See "Push-Pull" in Chapter Six, "Advertising," for an application of this to the direction of marketing effort.

THE SIC

The Standard Industrial Classification (SIC) system (together with its international counterpart, the ISIC) has made a major contribution to the analysis and measurement of industrial markets. This system was set up by the federal government to provide a numerical classification of our economy. The results are contained in the *Standard Industrial*

Classification Manual for sale by the Superintendent of Documents, U.S. Government Printing Office, Washington, D.C. 20402, for $4.50. The first edition was published in 1945. Since then it has been periodically revised and updated to reflect technological advancement, expansion, and contraction of industry.

The SIC is implemented through two committees whose major activities are the technical assignment and revision of the code numbers. Then, these code numbers are used as a basis for the compilation of all sorts of statistical data for both governmental and other publications.

The system first divides the economy into ten major divisions, identified alphabetically from A to J as follows:

Division A   Agriculture, Forestry, and Fisheries
Division B   Mining
Division C   Contract Construction
Division D   Manufacturing
Division E   Transportation, Communication, Electric, Gas, and Sanitary Services
Division F   Wholesale and Retail Trade
Division G   Finance, Insurance, and Real Estate
Division H   Services
Division I   Government
Division J   Nonclassifiable Establishments

These broad industrial divisions are then subdivided numerically into major groups. Each is given a two-digit identifier, with further subdivision within each group achieved by adding additional digits. For example, major group 35 is Machinery Except Electrical, 351 is Engines and Turbines, and 3519 is Internal Combustion Engines. The basis for the divisions and subsequent subdivisions is the product produced or the type of activity performed.

This grouping of establishments, based on comparable production procedures and products produced, is both the greatest strength and the greatest weakness of this system, from the standpoint of the industrial-marketing man. It would at first seem to provide an excellent basis for the compilation of data on product markets. In actuality, the groupings under many of the four-digit levels contain such vastly differentiated products as to destroy the meaningfulness of the data accumulated under that SIC number. For example, SIC 3548, Metal Working Machinery, Except Machine Tools, and Power Driven Hand Tools contains such extremes as attachments for portable drills and wire drawing and fabricating machinery; blooming and slabbing mills and caulking hammers; steel rolling machinery and valve grinding machines. In order to overcome this lack of meaningfulness, further refinement in the form of additional subdivisions, identified by additional digits to the five- or even seven-digit level, becomes necessary. This, in itself, would not be too bad except for the inability of many respondents to refine their own data to such a level—resulting in a breakdown in results. The simple fact is that we just do not have statistics refined to this point.

A second major weakness of the SIC system, and from an entirely different point of view, lies in the fact that this system is completely production-oriented, being based on processes and products. Marketing considerations are notable for their absence. If one attempts to use a four-digit SIC category to assemble marketing data, the lack of comparability contained within this category renders the data almost meaningless. To go beyond a four-digit level, say to a five or seven, compounds the difficulties of reporting but, even worse, directories and other sources of identification of such firms just do not provide refinement beyond four digits. From this point of view, what is needed is a marketing classification system—that is, a system based upon similarities in the act of marketing as against similarities in that which is marketed. This brings us to the considerations of a unique, new concept, the "marketing profile."

THE MARKETING PROFILE: A NEW CONCEPT

Many practitioners object to the use of SIC as a base for the assembly of data relating to their situations. They view their marketing problems as unique and are somewhat skeptical of the applicability of generalizations. They object to other products being included with theirs in any compilation of data since, they insist, their product situations differ significantly from that of other products which are combined in such statistics. If this position were sound, then little or no generalization would be possible. Marketing would indeed be segmented—a different segment for each seller.

This thinking is both traditional and very realistic. But, this does not make it correct! Such businessmen clearly are still thinking along product lines. When they say their situation is unique to their product, they are merely using their *product* to identify the uniqueness of their *marketing* situation. This is just the reverse of what it should be.

It is not the differences between products that become important in marketing—it is the differences between the markets and the marketing problems involved. If these problem circumstances differ, then truly, they may create a unique marketing situation. And, it is these marketing differences that become significant, not the technical or other differences between products.

Aspirin, toothpaste, and razor blades are highly differentiated products. Yet, when they are sold to the same market and share the same channel of distribution, they become highly similar from the standpoint of marketing considerations. The same thing can be said about almost any two completely differentiated items sold to end-user manufacturers through the same channel, say, via industrial distributors. Again, it is the similarity of the market and the means used to reach it which bring the products together, not the product characteristics, per se.

"Let Us Suppose. . . ." With an Open Mind

Now, let us suppose that we ask two manufacturers to describe completely and accurately the markets to which they sell and the marketing decisions made to reach those markets. Let us suppose, further, that their two answers are the same. Then quite clearly, these two firms reach identical markets, employ the same means to reach them, and share the same marketing problems—irrespective of product, that is, irrespective of that which is marketed.

Let us designate this complete set of circumstances, that is, the market criteria and the marketing decisions involved, as a "marketing profile." Any one firm selling a product in one way to one market would have one marketing profile. If the firm sells the same product to two different markets, or uses a second channel of distribution, etc., then for each major change it would have an additional profile. For any one product, it may well be that there are several profiles.

Let us pursue this approach a bit further and visualize an assembly of all marketing profiles—a master list of each significantly different set of circumstances. We might arrange them logically and give each one some sort of identifier. This brings us to the consideration of an MCS, a marketing-classification system.

A Marketing-Classification System

This system would be based on the circumstances of the market and the marketing considerations, rather than the product. It would provide a master list of all the different markets together with the various means by which they are reached. Nor would such a list be absurdly long. Research on marketing profiles has made it clear that there are far fewer significantly differing marketing profiles than one might at first suppose.

This would be a completely unique approach to the identification, analysis, and study of marketing problems. At the same time, it would provide a framework for the assembly of data relevant to marketing problems and based on marketing considerations, as against the historical product ones. For example, it could readily identify all products using any one profile and all the different profiles for any one product.

It might be most illuminating to see the differing products which comprise one marketing profile. However, of even greater significance would be the identification of the different profiles in use by any one firm and by the others—its competition. The assembly of market and marketing data, including marketing costs, based on each such profile could open the door to an entirely new approach to the analysis of marketing problems, to the comparison of efficiency and effectiveness of differing marketing-profile decisions, and to the evaluation of marketing strategy and techniques, at a level of accuracy and comparability infinitely beyond current capabilities.

For example, let us suppose that a manufacturer-seller were to learn that for one of his major product lines there were several different marketing profiles in current use and that he is using two of them. He could then compare his own results with the others using the same profiles he is using, and with those who market differently. He would have available to him the data with which to compare the effectiveness and efficiency of each different profile, together with the attainment of each. This, coupled with an awareness of the potentials, could provide him with not only a most meaningful share-of-market analysis, but also a guide to future opportunities and an indication of the better ways of realizing them.

Such a basis would provide a new approach to the entire area of marketing. It would permit a meaningful analysis, appraisal, and evaluation of marketing by truly significant and comparable segments. It becomes impossible to predict just what benefits might be derived from such an approach, but it could be the springboard from which many benefits may accrue to marketing through continued application and use. Improved marketing practice will follow improved marketing information—which comes from basic marketing research.

The development of marketing profiles involves the solution to two somewhat interrelated problems. The first is simply the identification of the criteria to be used to describe a marketing profile. What are the points needed to describe the characteristics of the market and the marketing means used to meet it—such that the total would completely describe one profile, and a major variation of any one point would provide a sufficiently significant difference to warrant a separate profile?

The second problem would be the accumulation of data based upon the identified profiles. This may at first appear to be horrendous, but experience has shown that it is not. The original reporting to the Marketing-Cost Institute of sales and marketing-cost data from 956 entities and covering $23½ billion of industrial-product sales clearly demonstrates that the needed data are available, or can readily be made available, once the criteria by which to measure such profiles are known.

The criteria to describe a marketing profile include such points as

Frequency and significance of the purchase

Relative number of customers—and of competing sellers

Degree of specialization and training of sales force

Extent of sales-service requirements

Degree of standardization and technicality of product

Whether made to order or for inventory

Channel of distribution, direct or other, used

Type of market served, users, resellers, OEMs, etc.

Price level and major criteria for purchase, quality, price, delivery, service

Market position of seller, share of market, sales volume

Corporate objectives, growth in share of market, profit, reduction in selling costs

Focus of marketing efforts on user, other

This list is suggestive, not necessarily all-inclusive. Further, there is a variation in significance between points. It may be that some can be eliminated.

There is nothing to prevent using this approach to analyze one's marketing efforts right now. The identification of the profiles in current use, together with the product groupings moving through each, at the very least can provide a new perspective of marketing. It can permit a critical examination of one's own marketing efforts based on marketing considerations—even prior to the availability of industry statistics. It is definitely a step in the right direction. Nor is industry data completely missing. See Chapter Ten for the availability of marketing-cost data tailored along these lines. See also Chapter Four for an application of this technique to the problem of selection of channels of distribution.

The use of the marketing profile as a perspective of marketing and as a basis for the analysis of marketing problems is both logical and valid. Marketing men do not market products; or, if they do, the customers do not buy products—they buy want satisfactions. Marketing problems relate to the act of marketing as it fulfills its role in providing these satisfactions in the marketing environment.

It is high time that marketing men began to review their marketing decision making from the point of view of the customer satisfactions to be created and the marketing criteria to be resolved in doing so—the marketing profile(s) to be used. Vast improvement in both the act of marketing and in customer satisfactions will follow. This is the objective of management, or it ought to be!

RELEVANT READING

Alexander, Ralph S., James S. Cross, and Richard M. Hill, *Industrial Marketing*, 3d ed., Homewood, Ill.: Richard D. Irwin, Inc., 1967, chap. 2.

Bell, Martin L., *Marketing*, New York: Houghton Mifflin Company, 1966, chap. 10.

Buskirk, Richard H., *Principles of Marketing*, 3d ed., New York: Holt, Rinehart and Winston, Inc., 1970, pp. 74–83.

Dirksen, Charles J., Arthur Kroeger, and Lawrence C. Lockley, *Readings in Marketing*, rev. ed., Homewood, Ill.: Richard D. Irwin, Inc., 1968, chaps. 22 and 23.

Fisk, George, *Marketing Systems*, New York: Harper & Row, Publishers, Incorporated, 1967, chap. 6.

Frey, Albert W. (ed.), *Marketing Handbook*, 2d ed., New York: The Ronald Press Company, 1965, sec. 27, pp. 6–13.

McCarthy, E. Jerome, *Basic Marketing*, 3d ed., Homewood, Ill.: Richard D. Irwin, Inc., 1968, chap. 13.

PART TWO

Channels of Distribution

CHAPTER THREE

Industrial Middlemen

Sound decision making involves the consideration of all the relevant data bearing on the problem. Therefore, before tackling the problem of which channel(s) of distribution to use, one should be familiar with the various middlemen, their existent services, strengths, and weaknesses. "Existent" was used deliberately. There is nothing to prevent modification of the present or development of new functional relationships. In fact, and fortunately, this is exactly what is happening.

"Middlemen," as used in consumer marketing, includes agents, brokers, wholesalers, and retailers. In industrial marketing, the retailer is eliminated as a middleman. However, there are some borderline exceptions where industrial and consumer marketing are combined, that is, where the retailer typically sells to both consumer and industrial customers. Some examples are auto-parts stores, building-supply and lumber dealers, paint stores, and plumbing-supply houses.

MIDDLEMEN AS THE MANUFACTURER'S SALES FORCE

In effect, all middlemen compete with the manufacturer's own sales force for their jobs. They exist only because they do the job better—

more effectively or more efficiently, or both. Otherwise, there is little or no economic justification for their existence. In addition, they compete with each other. Not all are equally competent, of course. This may seem to be elementary. But, it should call attention to the dual nature of the problem—first, shall we use this type of middleman, and second, which ones within that type? One should never conclude for or against a *type* of middleman because of his reactions to a few. The problem of selection is deferred to Chapter Four. Here we consider the choices.

STOCKING AND NONSTOCKING MIDDLEMEN

Merchant middlemen take title. Functional middlemen do not. The merchant middleman is sometimes viewed as the customer, since he buys and carries a stock. Actually, he is a reseller—but a step in the channel of distribution to the end user, the final customer.

Functional middlemen carry no stocks. They are compensated by commission instead of a markup. They tend to emphasize a somewhat narrower range of highly specialized services than the merchant middlemen.

AGENTS AND BROKERS

Agents buy or sell but never own the goods. Brokers buy or sell, and may do so for their own account. Each can represent either party, but not both buyer and seller in the same transaction. However, the frequency of use is most heavily to represent sellers. Major assets of agents and brokers are their skill, their specialization by broad product lines, and their knowledge of sources and outlets. Major criticisms include a willingness to take easier orders instead of pushing for sales, selling too cheaply in order to earn a commission rather than lose the sale, and a failure to represent fully the interests of the principal. If these are justified, they are in part the responsibility of the principal. To a major extent they can be remedied in defining the working arrangements in the first place.

Brokers are used in industrial marketing most heavily in basic raw materials and semifinished but standardized products, usually sold by description.

Agents and brokers are particularly suited to irregular business needs on a noncontinuous but sometimes recurrent basis, as in the case of seasonal representation. They are frequently used to either buy or sell where anonymity of the principal is desired—at least, until the transaction is completed. They can operate on a low rate of commission since their overhead is small. Specialization by broad product lines is typical. They can be a good source of market information, particularly concerning areas with which the principal is unfamiliar.

MANUFACTURERS' AGENTS

Manufacturers' agents are sales representatives, or "reps," who offer technical sales skills from an engineering background. They carry one item or line rather than the entire lines of the manufacturers they represent. They deal chiefly in hard goods and sell allied but noncompetitive items for several manufacturers—thus spreading their sales cost per call.

Their territory is limited by agreement with the manufacturer, who also sets prices and terms of sale. Thus, the reps have but limited authority. Marketing decisions are made by the manufacturer. Typically, they do not stock the goods they sell, except for quick replacement of minor needs, such as repair items, and this primarily as a service to their customers. However, there is a tendency for this practice to grow. In electronics, some "stocking reps" provide warehouse service. Obviously, this raises their costs and moves them a step closer to an industrial distributor.

The goods sold by manufacturers' agents can be divided into "bread and butter" and "gravy" lines, based on their low or relatively high commission rates. One problem of the rep is to maintain a balance between them. The "bread and butter" lines require but routine selling effort, have a reasonably high but stabilized volume (which even intensive sales push won't change much), carry a low commission, but are semipermanent. They pay the rent.

The "gravy" lines provide a real chance for a profit. They require intensive selling effort, have a low volume (at least, at the start), carry a higher commission, but may be quite short-lived. In fact, the better the job done on a gravy line, the sooner the rep may lose it—as, for example, in the introduction of a new line to open up a new territory for a manufacturer. Both parties are aware that as soon as sales permit it, the rep may be replaced by the manufacturer's own salesmen.

Manufacturers' agents are particularly suitable as a supplement to the manufacturer's sales force. They can provide inexpensive coverage to more remote areas and to areas where demand cannot sustain a full-time company salesman. They can serve to expand territories by introduction of the manufacturer's line in the preliminary developmental stage. Properly selected, they can provide both a working acquaintance with potential customers and the technical know-how to sell them. Thus, they permit expansion and growth almost on a pay-as-you-go basis, via a commission on sales made.

They can handle "special" items which require intensive selling efforts or application engineering or are different from the producer's regular lines. They require little technical or sales training, but they do require cooperative involvement by the manufacturer. They can be used permanently, or temporarily, as the situation demands. They differ significantly from wholesale distributors carrying many and often competitive lines, since their few, noncompetitive lines permit personalized attention and salesmanship for each.

Manufacturers' agents are small businesses, operating on skill and long-term personal relationships with their customers. There is, of course, a variation in such skill and relationships. Selection of the best rep for a given manufacturer can be a problem.[1] Another point may be significant—one cannot give orders to the rep as one can to a salaried salesman. Some agents may take advantage of this independence, and work hardest on the most profitable and immediate sales. Since they are compensated by commission, it is only natural that they seek out business—for their most profitable lines. It may be a false economy to pay too low a rate.

The compensation paid to manufacturers' agents should be set with an awareness of many factors bearing upon it. Among them are

1. Nature of the product, the selling skill required
2. The price and the amount of the average sale
3. Nature and extent of competition
4. The missionary work required and the potential
5. The probability of repeat business
6. The agent's travel and other expenses, particularly if special to this line
7. A reasonable profit to the agent, his incentive

When the agent has been selected, it is a mistake to hire him and forget him. He should be welcomed and made to feel a member of the team. This could involve plant visits for intimate familiarity with the goods and production processes. It could include office visits to meet and get to know the key people with whom he may have contacts. And these could very well include the advertising people, who may benefit from the agent's ideas and who should keep the agent informed in advance of promotional materials. Anything less than complete acceptance and cooperation is shortchanging both the agent's effectiveness and the manufacturer's interests.

---

[1] For one company's solution to this, see "How Jordan Found 50 Good Manufacturers' Reps," *Industrial Marketing*, October 1965, pp. 109–110.

SELLING AGENTS

Selling agents should not be confused with manufacturers' agents. Whereas they both sell on commission and may operate in the same market, as in the case of industrial supplies and machinery, the selling agents are more heavily entrenched in soft goods, linseed oil, and textiles. Selling agents handle the entire output of several directly competitive manufacturers.

The selling agents have no limitation on their territory and have full authority as to prices and terms of sale. In fact, they are the marketing department and make the marketing decisions for the small producers they represent continuously and recurrently over many years. They provide market data and product-development guidance. They do not stock goods.

Many selling agents offer financial assistance to their principals. This can assume major proportions in the relationship, as, for example, in the case of a small cotton mill operating seasonally. Heavy cash requirements at the beginning of the season and with chiefly nonbankable collateral mean that the selling agent is in an excellent position, with his intimate knowledge of both the product and the customers, to offer credit directly, or indirectly by endorsing the manufacturer's notes. This places the selling agent in a particularly favorable position to negotiate terms and influence operations of his principal. If one is in this situation and decides to use a selling agent, he should be sure it is a good one in the first place.

Selling agents become the principal's sales force, rather than supplementing it, as in the case of the manufacturers' agent. This is especially appropriate where seasonal representation is desired; where marketing and sales skill are needed only recurrently; where the major interests and skills of the manufacturer are in production; where a limited line is offered; where the market is widespread; and where financial assistance may be a factor.

INDUSTRIAL DISTRIBUTORS

Industrial distributors are resellers, stocking middlemen for industrial goods. In the earlier days it was relatively easy to distinguish between them and mill supply houses, also stocking resellers. The mill supply house selling to a wide, horizontal market added value to many products by assembly, cutting, fitting, providing engineering service, etc., while the industrial distributor was just that, a wholesaler.

More recently, industrial distributors have been adding service facilities, including assembly and repair. In steel, many perform final processing to their customers' needs. Today, for practical purposes, there seems to be no significant reason to continue to differentiate between the mill supply house and the industrial distributor.

Industrial distributors are full-service resellers. They stock, sell, deliver, grant credit, provide customer services, and are becoming highly sophisticated both as marketing experts in the field and within their own organization, even to the use of computers for automatic ordering. The sales forces are no longer order takers, but include highly trained, technical specialists—experts in both product application and customer service.

The inventories carried and the degrees of sales specialization give rise to recognition of a spectrum of types of industrial distributors. At one end is the giant with many lines, thousands of items, perhaps spread over several fields—truly a general-merchandise wholesaler. Divisionalization along specialty lines is occurring. His offerings tend to serve completely the needs of his trading area. Next, there is a recognizable specialization to one line, but with a wide stock within it. Examples of this are found in specialized machinery and supplies, such as oil-well drilling, and in electronics and steel. Further along the spectrum are specialty houses, with even more refinement of offerings, particularly where complex products are involved.

The industrial distributor has been truly the man in the middle. He has been caught between the buyer's demand for lower prices and the manufacturer's need for increased services at a lower cost. The answer has been a decision to do one of two things. One is to grow and offer maximum services by becoming more efficient, in part by virtue of size. The second, at the other extreme, is to specialize and to eliminate excess costs by virtue of the concentration provided by specialization. In both cases, services to manufacturers have not suffered. In fact, they have improved. And this to such an extent that the industrial distributor is actually increasing his bargaining power.

Some industrial distributors are going even further and starting to integrate by manufacturing one or more of their own lines. Such integration has been well established in the consumer area. It is likely to continue in the industrial.

The services performed by industrial distributors are suggested by Figure 3.1, where each line represents one call between each of eight manufacturers and eight user customers. The complexity and total cost of serving each customer once by each manufacturer is contrasted with the same task when the industrial distributor is introduced. The economic advantage is evident.

Obviously, the use of industrial distributors has its limitations. Nonstandardized, high-ticket items undoubtedly call for direct negotiation. As the goods move toward standardized products and smaller unit

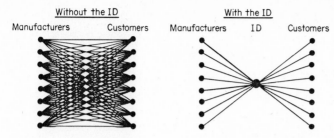

Fig. 3.1 Sales calls without and with the use of the industrial distributor. (*Adapted from Kenneth R. Davis, "Marketing Management," 2d ed., 1966, The Ronald Press Company, New York.*)

orders, the distributor becomes increasingly valuable. Smaller manufacturer-sellers; automated ordering; the need for widespread distribution, particularly if total sales volume is relatively low; specialization by product lines, particularly where the manufacturer makes part but less than all of one line; and skill in marketing, as an addition to or instead of the manufacturer's own efforts—all argue strongly for the use of the industrial distributor.

DROP SHIPPERS

Drop shippers, sometimes called "desk jobbers," do not store, handle, or deliver. The goods are shipped direct from the producer to the customer. Drop shippers operate chiefly in bulk goods where it is both unnecessary and uneconomical to handle or provide storage by a middleman. Examples are chemicals, coal, some construction materials such as lumber, and oil.

Orders are taken, frequently accumulated into carlots, and then placed with the producer, who ships directly to the buyer. The drop shipper does take title technically, but not possession. He may extend credit. However, with no handling of goods, no inventory, warehousing, or delivery expense, with orders placed after the sale is made, both his risks and operating expenses are very low.

The major function of the drop shipper is selling and economy of physical delivery. Some full-service wholesalers occasionally effect drop shipments on sizable orders and for the same reason—economy of handling, storage, and transportation costs.

MANUFACTURER-OWNED DISTRIBUTORS

Manufacturer-owned distributors are really sales branches, some with and some without stocks. Actually, they are not middlemen in the definitive sense, but a form of direct selling. However, they do represent choices in considering the channel of distribution. It is therefore appropriate to include them in a chapter on middlemen.

Manufacturers seeking both economies in and more control over the distribution of their lines may operate sales branches. This is appropriate to the larger, full-line firms, with financial strength. Sales branches with stocks operate as full-service wholesalers.

There is no question about the increased control of distribution gained thereby. There may be some question as to the reality of cost savings. This is dependent upon the allocation procedures for costs incurred by the home office as applied to the branch sales offices. General promotions, market research, cost of credit, inventory financing, and transportation charges are areas in point.

One advantage of the sales branch is partly psychological, partly real. Customers of industrial distributors may seek to obtain lower prices by buying direct on large orders. The manufacturer-owned distributor is "direct," since it is a sales branch of the manufacturer. This provides the branch increased volume with the economies of larger orders.

Manufacturers also operate sales branches without stocks. Perhaps these should be called sales offices, to distinguish them from the stocking operation. Here, the sales office obtains the orders, but has the shipment made either from a plant or a territorial warehouse. This may provide for economies in handling and transportation costs. It reduces the total investment. However, it may or may not mean somewhat slower deliveries. It is more apt to do so on smaller orders, less so on large ones.

DEALERS

Dealers are independent businessmen who are tied to the manufacturer by a franchise, at least typically. This provides for greater control over the distributional operation by the manufacturer. However, his ability to exercise it is a variable. It depends to a major extent upon the value to the dealer of the right to represent that particular manufacturer. There are two major types, exclusive and nonexclusive.

Exclusive distribution helps promote cooperative marketing. The manufacturer is assured of competent representation and the dealer of protection of his interests in the development of goodwill within his territory. Working arrangements are simplified and costs of "selling" dealers reduced. However, it is not all sunshine and roses. Some dealers may not maintain corporate standards and actually hurt the manufacturer's image. It is costly to police them, if there are very many. Some manufacturers may rely too completely on sales to "captive" dealers, and forget the ultimate customer. Production standards, quality control, and even product design may suffer. The dealers may be left holding the bag, with undesirable, unsold goods in inventory.

Nor is this all. The question of legality of any exclusive distribution structure should never be overlooked. Exclusive distribution is perfectly legal, per se. But, if it results in injury to competition, it probably becomes illegal. Exclusive dealing, not allowing the dealer to carry competitive products, and exclusive territories are two aspects of this problem. The attitude of the courts reflects a trend against the legality of both. This can bear watching if such arrangements are used.

Nonexclusive distribution is one solution to the possible legal difficulties just mentioned. However, this permits the dealer to sell whichever brand he prefers, or can. It makes manufacturers compete for preference via dealer remuneration. It increases competition all along the line, not only for the end user's patronage, but for the dealer's as well. This may be a good thing for the ultimate customer, but it is less likely to be welcomed by the manufacturers, except, perhaps, those large enough and well-established enough to have a strong brand preference. Even this is expensive to maintain.

A well-trained and effective dealer organization is a most valuable marketing asset. It can provide a high degree of cooperative control, feedback of information, and prompt communication with customers. It can assure customer and product service, both before and after the sale. There is only one thing wrong with this—it is rarely recognized as an asset on the corporate books, although it is the "firing line," the very source of both revenue to the corporation and satisfaction to the customer, a valuable property.

MANUFACTURER-MIDDLEMEN RELATIONSHIPS

No matter which middlemen the manufacturer uses, one thing is clear. There is a great need for the manufacturer to continue to be involved. He needs information, a feedback from his customers. He needs cooperation from his middlemen. And they need help from him. The manufacturer can and should provide all possible assistance. This can include such services as market research, literature, promotional aids, sales training, and even business advice. Perhaps the most essential step is the recognition of the need for this involvement. With that, the specific form(s) can be developed a la carte. With that, the efforts of both will be integrated in the teamwork which is marketing.

RELEVANT READING

Buskirk, Richard H., *Principles of Marketing*, 3d ed., New York: Holt, Rinehart and Winston, Inc., 1970, pp. 290–305.

Buzzell, Robert D., *Value Added by Industrial Distributors and Their Productivity*, Columbus: Bureau of Business Research, College of Commerce and Administration, The Ohio State University, 1960.

Diamond, William T., *Distribution Channels for Industrial Goods*, Columbus: Bureau of Business Research, College of Commerce and Administration, The Ohio State University, 1963.

Dirksen, Charles J., Arthur Kroeger, and Lawrence C. Lockley, *Readings in Marketing*, rev. ed., Homewood, Ill.: Richard D. Irwin, Inc., 1968, chap. 36.

"How Jordan Found 50 Good Manufacturers' Reps," *Industrial Marketing*, October 1965, pp. 109–110.

Rewoldt, Stewart H., James D. Scott, and Martin R. Warshaw, *Introduction to Marketing Management*, Homewood, Ill.: Richard D. Irwin, Inc., 1969, pp. 288–305.

CHAPTER FOUR

Distribution: How?
Direct, Indirect, or Both?

The problem of selection of the channel(s) of distribution to be used is secondary to the customer satisfactions to be created, and to the product(s) developed to best do so. It is, however, a good starting point for structuring the overall marketing plan, since the integration of all aspects of marketing does not establish any one as a prerequisite to the others, but permits the channel decision as a practical first step.

For most manufacturers, their channels have already been well established. So well established, in fact, that it may seem to be heresy to suggest reopening their selection, to reexamine the structure to see if it is the best one for the job to be done. We do so suggest, anyway. A critical reappraisal of the channels in use may affirm their choice, with no harm done and reassurance gained. And, it may lead to probing questions which can be a starting point for more effective distribution.

There are some very good reasons for utmost care in the selection of channel(s) of distribution. They well warrant occasional review of the channel decision periodically. In the first place, industrial marketing decision making is made with the channels in mind. Change the channels, and the whole complex of marketing decisions is affected. Second, channel decisions are by nature long term. They involve semipermanent working relationships with other firms. It becomes somewhat difficult and expensive to disrupt such working arrangements. Obviously, it should be done only for sound and serious reasons. The exercise of choice in the first place should be done with prudence. However, to stick arbitrarily to the decisions once made will not stop changes in the marketplace.

CHANNELS OF DISTRIBUTION: THE CONCEPT

Most people think words—at least most of the time. Therefore, if the words are fuzzy, so is the thinking. To sharpen our thinking, one good step is to sharpen the word meanings in our vocabulary.

To illustrate this point, a channel of distribution is sometimes referred to as a "pipeline" to provide distribution of goods from manufacturer to consumer. It implies that the goods "flow through" it. And yet, the channel of distribution relates to the path taken by the *title* to the goods, not the goods themselves. They "flow through" a pattern of *physical* distribution, which can be significantly different from the *channel* of distribution and is a complex problem in itself. Railroads and public warehouses are not in the channel of distribution, but are a part of physical distribution.

There is yet another "channel" sometimes referred to—a trade channel. This is an entirely different concept. It includes production and change in form, and covers what happens from beginning to end. There are three main types of trade channels. The *analytic* starts with one product (a pig) and ends up with many items (everything produced from a pig—bacon, ham, leather, pork, etc.). The *continuous* starts and ends with one (hardwood flooring from logs). The *assembling* brings together many products to create one end product (an automobile).

Perspective is always a most important part of decision making. It should be noted that the concept of "channel of distribution" may be an oversimplification of reality, an academic tool less used by businessmen than is implied. It implies, further, a purity of choice made by the manufacturer between eagerly receptive middlemen. Phillip McVey put it this way:[1]

> Further study of marketing textbooks may lead a reader to conclude that: (a) middlemen of many types are available to any manufacturer in any market to which he wishes to sell, and within each type there is an ample selection of individual firms; (b) the manufacturer habitually

[1] Reprinted from *Journal of Marketing*, published by the American Marketing Association, Phillip McVey, "Are Channels of Distribution What the Textbooks Say?" vol. 24, no. 3, pp. 62–63, January 1960.

controls the selection and operation of individual firms in his channel; and (c) middlemen respond willingly as *selling agents* for the manufacturer rather than as *purchasing agents* for a coveted group of customers to whom the middlemen sell.

Yet none of these conclusions is entirely valid.

Integrated action up and down a channel is a rare luxury in marketing. Why? It may be that the "channel of distribution" is a concept that is principally academic in usage and unfamiliar to many firms selling to and through these channels.

Instead of a channel, a businessman is likely to concern himself merely with suppliers and customers. His dealings are not with all of the links in the channel but only with those immediately adjacent to him, from which he buys and to which he sells. He may little know nor care what becomes of his products after they leave the hands of some merchant middleman who has paid him for them and released him to return to problems involving his special functions. A manufacturer may not even consider himself as standing at the head of a channel, but only as occupying a link in a channel that begins with his suppliers.

One further complicating factor should be mentioned. The manufacturer may not have the freedom of choice he thinks, or would like to have, in selecting his channels. With the growing acceptance of middlemen as a source of supply by their customers, the choice may well be the middleman's as to which brands he stocks. Unless the manufacturer is strong enough to penetrate that market with his own sales force, there is little he can do about it, if the middlemen turn him down.

On the other hand, the middleman can be eliminated from the marketing channel, but the functions cannot. The justification for the use of middlemen is that they do the job cheaper and/or better than the manufacturer can. This is not to say simpler. Additional problems are created—problems of selection in the first place, then problems of working with middlemen who are not employees, not under the direct control of the manufacturer. All this may add up to a very substantial reason for direct sale, even if it does cost a bit more.

Realistically, a typical situation may find a manufacturer seeking to sell the larger customers directly, the concentrations of smaller customers through distributors, and those in more remote locations through agents. Even so, there can well be areas where a key distributor has the important customers as "captives," or a key agent may control his market, or there may be some areas where customers insist upon dealing only with the manufacturer. These situations may fit the desired distributional pattern, or they may violate it. It is wrong to assume that the pattern will conform to the manufacturer's control merely because he wills it.

This is not to say that the manufacturer is completely helpless. If an ideal pattern can be found, based on a careful analysis of the best way(s) to satisfy one's customers, and considering the criteria to be resolved in doing so, the manufacturer can work toward this pattern with a definite goal in mind. A technique to implement this approach is described later in this chapter in the section "Application of the Marketing Profile."

DISTRIBUTION CHANNELS FOR INDUSTRIAL GOODS

Various authors have visualized industrial marketing channels differently. This is not surprising, because there is little overall data concerning them. Statistics assemble data on various middlemen on the basis of their *major* source of revenue with little or no attempt to trace its flow. The true picture is undoubtedly complex, far more so than a simple diagram will imply.

Nevertheless, we offer Figure 4.1 as indicative of the major channels currently in use. It may be noted that contractors are included. They are customers when they buy equipment and supplies to operate their businesses, but they become resellers of a large portion of their purchases when the materials are used in the final product delivered, whether steel for a bridge or roofing materials for a house.

It is most likely that Figure 4.1 is incomplete. Contractors occasionally buy direct from the manufacturer, for example. And, not all export agents buy only directly. A more serious error is one of degree. Any one middleman may operate in several ways, for part of his total business, or perhaps only occasionally.

One objective of the market-profile study described in Chapter Two would be the assembly of data from which modifications in Figure 4.1 could be made.

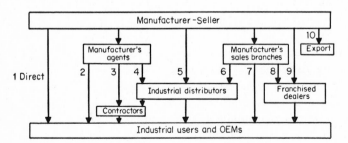

Fig. 4.1 Distribution channels for industrial goods.

PATTERNS OF DISTRIBUTION

Patterns of distribution refer to a combination of channels of distribution for a firm, or for a product. One product may be sold through one channel, or through several. For most products this depends upon the market segments to be reached, upon the type of distribution desired, and realistically, upon what traditionally has been used. It should never be inferred that there is a one best channel. The best one to use is more likely to be a pattern, a combination, and in any event, tailored to the circumstances of the firm, the nature of the product, and the market(s) to be served.

Segmentation of markets by users, OEMs, middlemen, geographical distribution, and numerous other factors as is appropriate can be very helpful. The determination of both market-segment and end-use potentials, as is discussed in Chapter Fourteen, can provide valuable perspective of opportunities—and go a long way to aid in the selection of the best means to realize them.

FACTORS IN CHANNEL SELECTION

Types of Market Coverage

There are three major types to consider: exclusive, selective, and intensive (mass) distribution.

Where selling effort is required, where full stocks are needed, where the capital investment may be large, where control of service is a factor, where goodwill of both the middleman and the brand is very important, and where dealer protection is a key factor, an exclusive arrangement becomes very practical. By this means, the manufacturer assures the middleman that no sales will be made in his territory except through him. Exclusive territories and prohibition of the middleman's carrying a second brand introduce legal considerations.

Selective distribution is the middle ground between exclusive and intensive. Middlemen are not given territorial protection, but only the better dealers are selected. One object is to preserve the corporate image while obtaining quality of representation, product service, and adequate volume from appropriate stocks. The goodwill of the dealer is important, as well as the competency of his sales force and the composition of the area as to potential customers.

There are many cases where the dealer does not matter, but maximum exposure does. On standardized products of relatively low unit cost, and particularly where the producer's brand is well accepted, little sales effort may be required. Ready availability and immediate delivery become very important. In such cases intensive or mass distribution is employed. Such a policy is one of degree, "mass" being a variable, with some efforts made to select outlets in many cases.

These three types of distribution are relative to each other, easy to distinguish from an overall perspective, and it is hard to draw precisely definitive lines between them. Exclusiveness can be accomplished by a high degree of selectivity, while some selectivity can apply to very widespread representation, indeed.

Direct, Indirect, or Both?

By far the most important decision is whether or not to sell directly, and if so, to what extent, completely or partially. This is a very moot question and the subject of much heated discussion, particularly from middlemen who would like to participate in the business they see as bypassing them. Yet, in actuality, there is no real struggle. These channels are significantly different, complementary, and each serves its own set of circumstances. However, in fairness to those middlemen who have become more proficient, who provide technical sales skills and ready delivery, and who are willing to give the attention needed to a producer's line, there is a definite growth in the lines they can handle effectively. There is less need today for a manufacturer to "go direct" in many cases than heretofore.

Direct sale provides control, not only over the selling, but also over installation and both customer and product service. Where superior and specialized technical knowledge and application engineering are important factors, direct relationships are preferred. Negotiation, particularly on large orders and national accounts, is improved. There is a partially psychological advantage to buying direct, to obtain better prices. The corporate image of the seller is enhanced. The intimate working arrangements improve the feedback both for product improvement and for market knowledge.

Whether direct selling increases or reduces marketing costs is hard to say. It depends. In many cases of direct sale marketing costs are not a major factor, anyway. Where they are, they are favored by a smaller number of potential customers, large orders or items with a high unit value, infrequent purchase, and deferred as against immediate delivery.

On the other side of the coin, direct selling means a sales force, trained, well-located, and supplemented by delivery and service functions. This takes time and money, unless it is already existent. Substantial, long-term funds are required for inventory, warehouse facilities, and customer credit. This may not be a problem for the larger corporations. It can be a real one for the many smaller manufacturer-sellers.

Further, not all industrial markets are concentrated. Where they are widely scattered, where many firms need to be contacted, where many wish to buy in small quantities, where prompt delivery of small lots is needed, where credit and open accounts are preferred on a large number of small orders, direct selling is at a big disadvantage. Goods made for inventory, as against to order, high frequency of purchase, and standardized items with many competitive substitutes also favor the use of middlemen.

In all this, it should be recognized that the interests of the manufacturer and middleman differ basically. That is not to say they necessarily conflict. The manufacturer is interested in sales of his brand; the middleman, in patronage (frequently irrespective of brand).

In addition, not all middlemen are equally aggressive. Some tend to be order takers rather than salesmen. This extends to other weaknesses—failure to seek out new customers, failure to devote sales effort to one manufacturer's line (they do carry wide stocks), and failure to offer technical sales assistance. If complacency exists in some middlemen, it is not unique to them as an institution. There are complacent manufacturers, too.

Application of the Marketing Profile

It might be illuminating to use an adaptation of the marketing-profile approach to the problem of channel selection. This would seem to be unnecessary for the extremes, but may help if the answer is not clear-cut. Suppose we plot the profile characteristics on a rating chart, with direct sales at one end, use of middlemen at the other. This is illustrated in Table 4.1.

The chart could be modified readily to permit points to be assigned to relative positions. Once the judgment is made, the resultant score could be entered in the position selected, thus plotting a profile at the same time. For instance, if position 3 were picked in favor of direct sale, with a weight of 2, the 6 might be entered in the 3 position, as follows:

Factor X (2) $\overset{\displaystyle 6}{\underset{5\ 4\ 3\ 2\ 1\ 0\ 1\ 2\ 3\ 4\ 5}{|+|+|+|+|+|+|+|+|+|}}$

Then, the sheet could be footed, as follows:

A. Total of points favoring direct sale _____
B. Total of points favoring merchant middlemen _____
C. Net, difference between A and B, favors _____
by _____ points out of a total possible points of _____, or _____ percent.

TABLE 4.1   Marketing-Profile Rating Chart for Channel of Distribution

Profile criteria	Weight	Direct sale	Merchant middlemen
Unit price	( )	High	Low
Frequency of purchase	( )	Low	High
Significance of purchase	( )	High	Low
Size of average order	( )	High	Low
Concentration of market	( )	High	Low
Proximity to bulk of market	( )	Near	Far
Number of customers	( )	Few	Many
Number of competitors	( )	Few	Many
Need for negotiation	( )	A "must"	Not required
Product	( )	Built to order	Built for inventory
Standardization	( )	Nonstandardized	Highly standardized
Technicality of product	( )	High	Low
Technicality and specialization of sales force	( )	Highly	Routine
Delivery	( )	Deferred	Immediate
Corp. finances	( )	Strong	Weak
Installation	( )	Special	Routine (not required)
Extent of sales service required	( )	High	Low
Customer preference in buying	( )	Direct	Local middleman
Focus of marketing effort	( )	User	Reseller

The smaller the difference, the less it matters which is used, or the more appropriate a dual distribution may become. The larger the score, naturally, the more persuasive it is of the indicated choice. The pattern of the profile and the weighting of the factors should not be overlooked in the total appraisal.

Even if the mathematics are not employed as an aid to judgment, the resulting pattern should help to identify the strengths and weaknesses of the channel preferred. At the very least, it will guard against factors being overlooked.

CHANNEL DECISIONS

First, of course, is whether to sell direct, indirect, or a combination just discussed—perhaps direct to the market near the plant, indirect elsewhere. The next problem, if middlemen are to be used, is the selection of the type(s). Chapter Three should help in selecting those most suited to serve best the prospective customers. The customer satisfaction should control here, too.

The selection of the specific firms should involve a painstaking analysis and evaluation of prospects. This is a two-way process, for the middleman must select the manufacturer, too. And, it is hoped, it is a long-term relationship being considered. Complete information should be exchanged, and reciprocal visiting should take place. Information can be obtained in many ways and from many sources, including professional placement firms. This should include customers, other noncompetitive manufacturers, local bankers, credit agencies, trade associations, and both the key men and salesmen of the middleman. Important points not to be overlooked are the perspective, the philosophical outlook, the goals of the middleman. The task should be thorough. Time and money spent on the final selection can be a very wise investment in the future.

COOPERATION WITH MIDDLEMEN

It should go without saying that the manufacturer should cooperate with his middlemen. The problem sometimes is not the acceptance of the idea, but the actual implementation of it. How to cooperate? Before going further, one significant point should be raised. Manufacturers who sell merchant middlemen, and view them *as* their customers, err. They are merely the next step in the channel to the end user, the ultimate customer. They frequently need help and definitely cooperation as much as anyone else. So, back to how to cooperate.

Ideally, the cooperation should be in whatever is needed to help do the job better. This is a reflection of the needs of the middleman—not merely promotional materials from the manufacturer's advertising program. They may be needed, truly. But here we should get down to cases and find out just what each middleman really needs. It may be simplification in ordering procedures, pricing, billing, or other mechanics. It may be market research, sales analysis, assistance in customer identification and potentials. It may be product education, technical assistance, training programs, or just plain business guidance. It may be in delivery, or inventory backlog available for quick delivery from the plant. Whatever it is, it should be known. And, it should be provided to the fullest possible extent.

CONTROL

When a manufacturer sells to merchant middlemen, he loses control over and frequently even knowledge of the inventories in the field. The complications from this were discussed in Chapter Two under "Industrial Demand, Variation—and Why." One of the benefits of cooperation with middlemen is that it is a two-way street. Middlemen receiving cooperation from a manufacturer are more apt to return it by providing him with reports at reasonable frequencies of data needed, including inventory levels.

There are two very good reasons for control of the channel of distribution. One is for operational efficiency and the other is to keep abreast of change. Both require a feedback of information. Both require cooperation from the middlemen. Both are essential to maximize the customer satisfactions and the efficiency of marketing. Demands on middlemen for such reporting should be simplified and of essentials only. Anything beyond that is an imposition on the middleman's limited time.

The legal aspects of distribution control have already been mentioned (see Chapter Three under "Dealers"). This is an area for involvement of the corporate counsel. Any control policy or mechanism should be thoroughly explored with him prior to implementation. It will make him happy—and it may prevent an embarrassing mistake.

PHYSICAL DISTRIBUTION

Physical distribution of goods involves considerations of plant and warehouse location; field storage in owned or public warehouses, or by middlemen; transportation; packaging and containerization; and inventories—both from an investment-cost standpoint and their availability to customers. This is an involved area, filled with almost innumerable interrelationships of factors bearing upon each segment. Fortunately, there is available today an approach to the solution to this complex problem via marketing logistics. Perhaps of even greater significance is the recognition given to the marketing concept and the need for integration of the goals with the physical aspects. Edward W. Smykay puts it this way:[2]

> The organizational question clearly relates to the orientation of goals and objectives. Physical distribution management principles merely provide an outlook which permits more appropriate construction of corporate effort to reach pre-determined goals. Of course, the most important of its influences requires orientation to the market place and, ultimately, the efficient satisfaction of consumer needs and wants.

John F. Magee summarizes today's situation quite well as follows:[3]

> To sum up, a number of pressures have piled up on today's distribution systems. As manufacturing efficiency has increased and product cost has come down, costs have grown. Physical distribution costs are a significant share of these.
>
> In the face of these trends, a number of revolutionary changes have taken place. Substantial improvements have come about in essentially all forms of transportation methods. Tremendous strides forward have been made in information-handling methods, including schemes for assimilating and processing data dealing with product demand and with the need for replenishment. Materials-handling methods, ranging from mechanized stockkeeping to extensions of the pallet concept to eliminate item-by-item handling have been gaining acceptance. Finally, and perhaps as important as improvement in physical facilities and concepts, there has been progress in ways of looking at the logistics problem and at methods for analyzing distribution systems.

The logistic approach to the problems of physical distribution makes sense. It has come a long way from the earlier days, where these matters were left to a low-paid shipping clerk to handle. Today the trend is for all related physical-distribution activities to be brought together under one authority. Cost reduction is viewed as the lowest *overall* cost, as against an attempt to minimize each one. The collective impacts of the reduction of one cost on the others is now a key factor.

These interrelationships can be somewhat segmented and formulas can be used, for example, in problems of plant location, economic order quantities, etc. This sophisticated concept integrates these mathemati-

[2] Edward W. Smykay, "Physical Distribution, Military Logistics, and Marketing Management," *The University of Houston Business Review*, Winter 1964–65, p. 8.

[3] John F. Magee, "The Logistics of Distribution," *Harvard Business Review*, July-August 1960.

cal relationships with computerization to yield most helpful information for physical-distribution decision making; and it takes into account the intangibles, corporate and marketing goals, customer satisfaction, maximization of profit, etc. But, it is a job for the specialist. Clearly, here is a case where the expertise of the specialist appears to be coupled with an awareness of the intangible significants to make a real contribution to marketing.

RELEVANT READING

Frey, Albert W. (ed.), *Marketing Handbook*, 2d ed., New York: The Ronald Press Company, 1965, sec. 20, pp. 26–40.

Gepfert, Alan H., "Business Logistics for Better Profit Performance," *Harvard Business Review*, November-December 1968, pp. 75–84.

Lambert, Eugene W., Jr., "Financial Considerations in Choosing a Marketing Channel," *Business Topics*, vol. 14, no. 1, p. 20, Winter 1966.

McVey, Phillip, "Are Channels of Distribution What the Textbooks Say?" *Journal of Marketing*, vol. 24, no. 3, pp. 62–63, January 1960.

Magee, John F., "The Logistics of Distribution," *Harvard Business Review*, July-August 1960.

Smykay, Edward W., "Physical Distribution, Military Logistics, and Marketing Management," *The University of Houston Business Review*, Winter 1964–65.

Still, Richard R., and Edward W. Cundiff, *Sales Management*, 2d ed., Englewood Cliffs, N.J.: Prentice-Hall, Inc., 1969, chap. 20.

Materials Management

CHAPTER FIVE

Buying and Managing Industrial Materials

BUYING, PURCHASING, PROCUREMENT, AND MATERIALS MANAGEMENT

The buying of industrial goods originally was done at a very low level within the corporation. It was a clerical task. Someone had to handle the paperwork involved. The heart of the matter was the negotiation, including selection of the source and agreement on price and delivery. This was an important responsibility, typically entrusted only to senior officers, or the president of a smaller corporation.

Later, roughly about the turn of the century, the specialist in buying appeared. He added perspective of planning and policy, organized the buying function, and added follow-up, inspection, and coordination with other departments. This broader concept was called "purchasing" and began to be organized into a department, headed by the purchasing agent and staffed by buyers reporting to him.

Around the time of World War II, it was but another step to broaden the concept still further, and "industrial procurement" became the proper term. This included all the activities of purchasing, but added acquisition by any means, the make-or-buy decision, more sophisticated procedures for vendor evaluation, product testing, more effective communications, information on new sources and new materials, and forecasts of supply and prices. It became a high-level, professional function. The organization for procurement extended beyond the scope of the organization for purchasing. Such areas include inventory control, scrap utilization, policy formulation in areas such as forward buying, buying jointly with a supplier, contracting with suppliers to provide parts of the productive process, legal considerations, and participation on research and development, product planning, and other corporate committees.

And so the buying operation grew into an involved complex—industrial procurement. The next step, and one still being taken, is the emergence of the materials management concept. This would bring together under one authority the full responsibility for the acquisition, availability, and control of all industrial goods, including work in process, from the recognition or anticipation of the need, through to the finished-goods inventory. Industrial procurement then becomes a part of this broadened concept. Anything relating to the smooth flow of goods from source through inventories, through the production process, and up to the point where they are ready for delivery to the customer could be included in materials management.

The object is to improve operations by bringing together under one authority all material-related considerations, to integrate and control them as a system, and to contribute to corporate welfare via economies, increased efficiency, and modernization of procedures. In some cases this even includes "automatic" ordering, by computerizing inventory control of the buyer and tying this in with the supplier's computer to provide for automatic reorders at predetermined EOQs (economic order quantities).

EFFICIENT PURCHASING PRACTICE

Vendor Evaluation

Vendors are always evaluated by their customers, in one way or another. This may be quite informal and chiefly negative, an accumulation of demerits for back orders, delays in delivery, defects, rework required, etc. Buyers are human. As industrial products become more standardized and similar, the emotional factors become more important, unless a good system of vendor evaluation is used.

One good technique is to identify the factors for evaluation, assign weights for relative significance, apply a rating to each, and arrive at an overall index for each supplier. The factors to be taken into account and particularly their relative significance can vary among buyers. The major areas for evaluation, and possible factors to reflect each, follow:

A. Capability
   1. Finances
   2. Manufacturing capacity, size
   3. Research and development
B. Performance
   1. Back orders
   2. Delivery delays, number and extent, expediting required
   3. Incomplete shipments
   4. Quality, maintenance of standards, uniformity
   5. Rejects and rework, number of and seriousness
   6. Services, product and customer
C. General
   1. Cooperation generally and in special circumstances
   2. Credit terms
   3. General reputation and prestige
   4. Price, generally high, low, competitive
   5. Trade relations

This whole process can be programmed and computerized, with the results available as desired. Current performance is continuously fed into the computer. Such a system can provide up-to-date information on suppliers when it is needed and assure completeness of reporting on the factors included.

Value Analysis

Value analysis in its simplest form is simply an examination of an industrial good to seek to determine its functional value to the buyer. The objective is to obtain the "best buy" for the function. Excessive quality features which can be eliminated to reduce costs and at the same time product improvements to do a better job are explored. The goal is the best match between the product and the quality aspects desired, at the minimum overall cost. Even a one-man procurement department can do that.

During the 1960s, value analysis grew rapidly. It became a complex, but organized, system involving physical product testing, considerations of economic substitution, cost, alternative ways of performing the function—an extensive examination to seek changes. The objective is the minimum cost for the essential functions, the value needed. It encourages product and material substitution, as well as planned obsolescence, that is, the uniformity of satisfactory performance of all elements in a component (and the elimination of excessives). It is a highly exploratory approach and a positive force for both increased efficiency and progress. It provides an incentive for innovation. So long as it is guided by a keen awareness of the customer satisfaction to be served, it is a valuable means of improving corporate welfare.

Market-Price Studies

Price is the value placed on the total product by the seller. It includes not only the industrial good, but the research and development to create it (especially if new), the product and customer services, including application engineering of the seller, use of his service facilities, his name, the packaging, delivery—everything involved in the values to be derived from the purchase. Again, it cannot be divorced from quality of the total product, including the intangibles.

At the same time, price is a variable in significance. It depends upon the values desired, including how important the intangibles may be, but even more upon the relative size of the cost, as a part of the user's total product cost. Further, cost is a variable based upon the type of product and the extent of price competition. On highly standardized, readily substitutable items, even a slight price differential can be very significant, at least to the seller.

It may be appropriate to comment on cost versus price. Obviously, they are not the same. Yet it is sometimes easy to confuse them. Price is the amount paid. Cost is the expense. For example, an automobile may be priced at $5,000 but cost $1,000 a year to own. In industrial pricing situations it may well be that cost is, and should be, the predominant consideration. It produces the savings, or fails to. Price is the amount to be invested, the finance involved. A good example of this is the consideration of the purchase of a new, expensive (in price) production tool—which is alleged to produce cost savings by its efficiency.

Market-price studies cannot guarantee minimum prices. They can aid in buying more advantageously. The same thing can be said of the stock market and studies of it. In general, the more informed the buyer is in regard to market fluctuations and the underlying causes and trends, presumably the better will be his buying decisions.

Where price is highly significant, sellers can expect pressure for price reduction from buyers. This is natural, to provide the buyer with as great a competitive advantage as possible. Hedging, offsetting a cash purchase with a future sale, is frequently used when the commodity involved is served by an exchange to provide a ready market for both cash and future transactions. Make-or-buy decisions, sometimes resulting in either contract buying or vertical integration, may be an alternative for the buyer. There is little that can be done to prevent long-range inflation and price increases. Buyers can and will do everything possible to ameliorate the impact of price increases and to seek price decreases. All this is good. The net result is to help slow inflation and to provide more value—hopefully, the value which serves the customer best.

Quality Considerations

Quality should be determined by the need, and this is determined by the function. Maximum quality is apt to be both expensive and excessive. In most cases the excess quality may produce relatively little or no increased satisfaction for the customer. If so, it is a sheer economic waste. There are exceptions to this, of course—in medicine, some pharmaceuticals, space exploration, and education. For the most part, in industrial marketing, the optimal quality to be used is the most suitable one for the need, rather than the highest possible.

This brings us right back to value analysis. The most suitable quality is the basis for the yardsticks to which the value of the offerings are compared. Yet even there, quality does not stand by itself. The actual determination of the quality specifications is apt to be a compromise between several considerations, the quality versus the price, or cost, and its impact on all other relevant considerations to yield the most suitable "mix," the best set of want satisfactions at the most favorable price. Included in this are time, life of the product, importance of the function, size and permanency of the market, and the nature of the end use served—from a basic requirement to a fad.

The Make-or-Buy Decision

There is no one answer to the make-or-buy problem, unless it be, "It depends." Each case should be decided on its own circumstances. Factors relating to this problem can be grouped as follows:

In favor of *make:*

1. To save money—it costs less.
2. To utilize unused plant capacity, machines, plant, and people.
3. To broaden the base for overhead absorption.
4. To obtain control over and assurance of supply.
5. To protect a trade secret.
6. To control the production or quality, especially if it is a complicated good.
7. To control availability and inventories.
8. To expand in the firm's area of engineering and production know-how.
9. To save on transportation costs or difficulties.
10. To enhance prestige, increase vertical integration.
11. To resell it to others, increase total volume and profit.

12. To use as fill-in work, if applicable—to even out a seasonal variation.

13. To diversify operations.

14. To serve as an object lesson to suppliers, to help keep them "on their toes" as to other items.

15. To reduce buying difficulties.

In favor of *buy:*

1. To save money—it costs less.

2. To lessen the workload—the plant is already at or near full capacity of present facilities.

3. To avoid increasing overhead. The volume may not absorb it all

4. To avoid problems of seasonality.

5. To avoid long-term commitments on a product of uncertain future demand.

6. To tap the expertise, technical skills, or production know-how of the supplier. They are not the buyer's forte.

7. To avoid paying royalties.

8. To strengthen the buyer's bargaining power with suppliers.

9. To enhance the product's image. The supplier may be very well known and respected, thereby adding prestige to the final product.

10. To simplify operations. Top management and key production men have their hands full now.

11. To provide variety. The supplier may offer several choices as standard to him, giving the buyer more flexibility.

12. To preserve trade relations with suppliers.

This list is indicative, not necessarily all-inclusive. All the considerations may not apply to every instance. But, it does suggest something of the scope and invites augmentation as is appropriate to the circumstances of a specific problem.

Relations with Other Departments and Trade Relations

No matter how the function is structured, as a purchasing department, procurement, or a facet of materials management, a free flow of needs, information, and suggestions between this function and other departments is a must. The services of the procurement function cannot be realized otherwise.

These services cover a very broad range of involvement, from participation in long-range, corporate developmental programs, to intercorporate relationships, reciprocity, buy at home, even to helping employees save money on their personal expenditures. Matters of policy are quickly raised. These broad matters of policy involve far more than materials management. They are brought together for consideration in Chapter Seventeen, "Key Services to Management."

THE BUYING PROCESS

The steps in buying, from recognition of the need through follow-up and feedback of information after the item has been in use, vary among companies. They are also a variable based on the type of purchase, from an automatic rebuy to exploration and development of a new item. The people involved and their interests also vary. Identification of buying influentials and their individual interests, together with the significance of each, becomes a problem, particularly if a new company is being approached.

There is no assurance that a specific procedure will be followed in all similar cases even within one company. Slight changes in any of the factors can introduce differences in procedure, particularly in the composition of the buying influentials involved. However, generalization within this area is possible. One excellent analysis has been made by the Marketing Science Institute.[1] It is highly recommended to those who would like an in-depth exploration of this area.

CONTRACT BUYING AND SELLING:
A DOUBLE-EDGED SWORD

(*The following material on contract buying and inventory control contains substantial contributions by Thomas F. Pray, Clarkson College.*)

In this increasingly popular practice, the customer simply lumps his requirements into as large a package as he can—usually based unfortunately on a very loose type of forecast—and places the package up for bid by all qualified manufacturers of the products involved. This is on a yearly or multiyearly award basis.

Thus, contract buying and selling is a semipermanent contractual relationship between buyer and seller. It can and frequently does include all buying entities of a firm. The seller carries nearly all the buyer's inventory and agrees to deliver within a short period of time, such as twenty-four hours. In return, the buyer guarantees the seller his business for the contracted period.

"Blanket ordering" and "contract buying" are often used synonymously. Actually, there are some differences of degree. Blanket orders

[1] See Patrick J. Robinson, Charles W. Faris, and Yoram Wind, *Industrial Buying and Creative Marketing*, Boston: Allyn and Bacon, Inc., 1967.

are normally not as long term as contract orders, have a system to reduce paperwork, and are used primarily with maintenance, repair, and operating supplies (MRO). Examples of MRO items are pencils, paper, envelopes, and cleaning supplies. Contract buying, for longer time periods, covers a far broader range of items, such as tiles, lubricants, fuels, machine tools, and other high-volume production items, and does not always reduce paperwork.

Blanket ordering involves three modern techniques: stockless purchasing, Data-Phone data transmission, and Touch-Tone pushbutton dialing. Stockless purchasing comes in many varieties, but is most often used synonymously with consignment. The buyer maintains a small inventory of material on consignment. The seller maintains the reserve.

There are two basic methods of inventory control. Under one method, the seller makes daily checks and replenishes the inventory. In the other method, a dual-card method, the seller is informed on one card by the buyer that material is needed; the other card is kept by the buyer for records. Under either method, the important aspect of stockless purchasing is that a computer is not a requisite and the number of billing invoices is greatly reduced.

The Data-Phone data transmission device is basically a telephone with a card adaptation which is connected to a computer card punch and printer at the seller's location. When inventory is at the reorder point, orders are processed instantly by placing the appropriate computer card into the Data-Phone device. The seller's electronic data processing (EDP) will duplicate the information and issue the necessary order. Paperwork is cut to a minimum; invoices are normally sent monthly. A computer is a requisite. Problems are encountered when the buyer and seller have thousands of different cards. Touch-Tone pushbutton dialing alleviates this problem.

The Touch-Tone device is similar to the Data-Phone device but is somewhat simpler. It uses a Touch-Tone telephone and a card telephone which are linked to the seller's computer. The number of cards needed is reduced to the number of means of delivery. The buyer merely types out of the part number and units needed on the Touch-Tone device. Included in the Touch-Tone method is a feedback system to indicate the use of a wrong card, and improper punching.

The Growth and Trends of Modern Contract Buying

Blanket ordering became popular as businessmen realized too much time was being spent on MRO items. The system of blanket orders helped reduce such costs.

Recent studies indicate that contract buying and selling is expanding into other industrial fields such as abrasives, metals, fuels, and even the food industry. In fact, a recent survey shows that some form of contract buying is used in just about all industrial firms.[2]

The Advantages and Disadvantages of Contract Buying and Selling

The concept of contract buying is a reciprocal relationship—a double-edged sword. There are worthwhile advantages to both buyer and seller. And, there are some disadvantages.

The buyer, utilizing a form of contract buying and selling, often gains lower prices, more valuable storage space due to the reduction in inventory, a reduction in paperwork and bookkeeping, consistency of supply, and a reduction in lead time. The seller gains all the buyer's business for the contracted goods, price stability, and a reduction in paperwork. Both buyer and seller gain improved buyer-seller relationships, a reduction in quantity of time spent in negotiation, and generally a more profitable method of buying and selling.

Disadvantages are somewhat a variable among firms. The seller could incur a high overhead cost due to the purchase of a computer and EDP equipment. Then, too, the seller utilizing a Data-Phone data transmission service leaves himself vulnerable to cut-throat pricing techniques (all the vital information that a competitor would need is on the computer card). The buyer loses his flexibility and no longer is able to take advantage of lower, on-the-spot offerings. Forecasting too high by the buyer and/or poor planning may lead to extra inventory at the end of the contracted period.

Contract buying and selling is useful in nearly all industrial fields. Its primary aim is to reduce cost of acquisition and possession. Major benefits are gained from low- and medium-priced, high-volume items. In a multiplant organization with high-volume sales, contract buying and selling techniques can be combined for various plants, so even greater savings can be made. And, this can include the low-volume divisional situations along with the others within any one firm. A company such as a specialty house, with high-price, low-volume units, would not lend itself to the modern contractual techniques.

If contract buying and selling is to be used effectively, both parties must aid each other and act in complete good faith.

[2] "More P.A.'s Turn to Contract Buying," *Purchasing*, vol. 62, no. 4, p. 49, Feb. 23, 1967.

CONTRADICTORY PRESSURES RELATING
TO INVENTORIES

Customers love to have sellers maintain a wide selection for freedom of choice and immediate delivery, as well as depth for quantity purchasing. This is fine—for the customer. And the satisfaction of the customer is the proper objective of marketing. Yet the problem of inventory management is more complicated than that. Actually, it involves sets of contradictory pressures. A gain in one is offset by a loss in the opposing one. The real problem is to decide which to adopt—or the compromise to be achieved in a middle-ground solution.

The major sets of opposing factors are:

1. Low inventory versus customer satisfaction
2. Customer satisfaction versus loss due to obsolescence (high inventory)
3. Breadth of line versus diffused marketing activities
4. Centralization versus divisionalization
5. Forward buying versus speculation
6. Gross margin versus turnover
7. Hand-to-mouth buying versus contract buying
8. One-source buying versus multiple-source buying
9. Build to order or for inventory (including repair parts)
10. Few competitors and stable demand versus many competitors and variable demand
11. Low cost of and quick replenishment versus high cost of and slow replenishment
12. Crucial nature of item, impact of a stockout, high and severe versus low and inconsequential

An awareness of these sets of circumstances will bring to attention the specifics of the various factors causative of variation within them. This is a good start for consideration of the problem of determining the level of inventory to be maintained (including the range, the maximum and minimum quantities) by item or by class of items. The attendant problem is their replacement, the frequency with which they should be reordered. This can be determined to a reasonable degree of accuracy by use of the EOQ (economic order quantity) concept. This approach introduces the cost factors bearing upon the above considerations. It can, and should, be tailored to the specifics of each item, or class of items.

However, one further point—once determined, the matter should not be forgotten. Circumstances change. All inventory decisions, maximum, minimum, EOQ, or whatever, should be considered temporary. They should be subjected to review and reconsideration periodically—or sooner, if circumstances change the key factors. This is obvious. The danger is to let day-to-day administrative detail defer this reconsideration, and perhaps, continue to do so.

INVENTORY CONTROL

Inventory provides protection against time variation in the receiving of goods and a reserve for sudden increases in production demanded by an unanticipated sales increase. When a company either stocks out because of too little inventory, or has excessive costs due to too much inventory, effective inventory control is needed.

Simple Inventory-Control Systems

A very simple inventory control is the two-bin system. This is useful for low-value goods where there is little uncertainty in demand and lead time. The items are physically put into two bins. When one bin is depleted, the second is used. When the first bin is emptied, an order is placed to replenish the empty bin and also the reserve bin. A limitation of such a system is that material must be physically separated. Control is loose. A change in physical location can cause confusion.

Another type of simple inventory control is the perpetual-inventory method (often called the "max-min system"). Under the perpetual-inventory system all inventory transactions are recorded on cards. When inventory hits a low value (min), an order is placed to replenish the inventory to the original level (max). The reorder point (min) is normally obtained from past experience. Under this system there is no need to separate stock as in the two-bin system. When a large number of different inventory items are maintained, the paperwork and cost can be very substantial. A clerk is responsible for maintaining the proper records of inventory depletion and replenishment.

Fixed-order-point systems, such as the perpetual-inventory (max-min) system, work best when the lead time and demand during the lead time can be forecast accurately.

Another simple inventory control is the ABC system. The inventory is separated into three categories, A, B, and C. Each category is established for a range of values. The items which have the largest dollar-volume value are placed in category A. The next highest dollar-volume grouping is B, and then C. The purpose of this system is to provide more and tighter inventory control for the most valuable items. Class C items might constitute 60 percent of the company's total inventory, but only 10 to 15 percent of the total value. Class A might constitute only 10 percent of total inventory, but may represent 60 percent of the total value. Normally, the class A items, while representing a much smaller proportion of inventory than C, need more control than C. Often with goods of low value, it is more profitable to carry extra inventory than to pay the salaries and other expenses needed for tighter control.

The periodic reorder system was developed to do away with some of the limitations of the fixed-order-point systems. A fixed review period is used instead of a fixed order point. Every review period, the inventory is checked and brought up to a certain limit (max). Unlike the fixed-order-point systems, there is a variable order quantity and a fixed time period between reviews. Such a system is often used when lead time and usage rates are irregular, and when it is easier to review periodically than daily, as under the perpetual-inventory system.

Analytical and Quantitative Approaches to Inventory Control

Inventory control seeks to minimize cost. This is done by finding the optimum point between costs associated with acquisition of goods and costs of possession of the goods. Problems are encountered in trying to balance the two categories of cost. As order quantities change, some cost factors are decreased, while others are increased. Figure 5.1 illustrates the favorable and unfavorable effects associated with an increase in order quantity.

The various inventory-related costs can be listed under two categories. An indicative list follows:

Cost of possession	*Cost of acquisition*
Cost of capital	Direct cost of goods
Inventory cost	Ordering cost
Deterioration	Accounting
Insurance	Clerical
Obsolescence	Inspection
Storage	Materials handling
Stockout	Receiving
Taxes	

The optimum order quantity is at the point where the increasing cost of possession (for larger orders) intersects the decreasing cost of their acquisition. This provides the minimum total cost. It is illustrated in Figure 5.2.

An example may help illustrate the relationships. Past experience shows that the demand for an industrial raw material has been 240

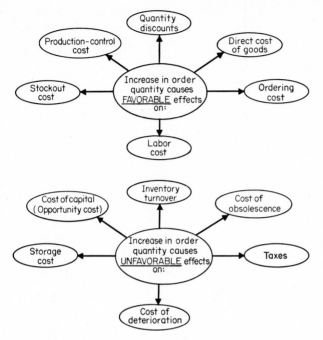

Fig. 5.1 Favorable and unfavorable impacts of an increase in order quantity. (*Source: Thomas F. Pray, Clarkson College.*)

per year. The purchase-order cost has been calculated at $10 per order. The items cost $10 each. The inventory cost is estimated at 20 percent per year. This is based on the unit cost and expresses as a percent thereof the sum of the various costs associated with possession.

When the inventory is depleted, the optimum quantity is received, and the inventory is replenished. In pure theory, the maximum inventory level could be Q units, the optimal order quantity. In practice, of course, a reserve must be added to provide for variation in usage rate and delivery time. The practical maximum is therefore the sum

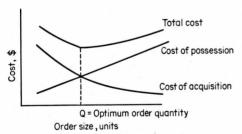

Fig. 5.2 Determination of order quantity.

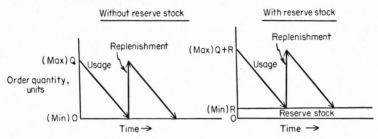

Fig. 5.3   Max-min inventory-control system.

of the order quantity and the reserve, $Q + R$ units.   Figure 5.3 illustrates both cases.

The cost of possession is the inventory rate charged applied to the average inventory. This will equal ½ the inventory (Q) times the rate (IC). The cost of acquisition is merely the number of orders placed times the appropriate order charge. The direct cost is the unit cost times the yearly usage in units.

The optimum order quantity is between 40 and 60 units. The exact figure can be obtained by following the same procedure and varying the order quantity from 40 to 60 in small increments. By inspection, it is obvious that it will be very close to 50.

U = usage = 240 units/year A = order cost = \$10 per order
C = unit cost = \$10 each I = inventory rate = 20 percent
IC = inventory charge = $(.20)(10)$ = \$2

Order quantity	Cost of possession*	Order cost	Direct cost	Total cost*
Q	$\dfrac{ICQ}{2}$ +	$\dfrac{UA}{Q}$ +	UC =	TC
10	\$10	\$240	\$2400	\$2650
20	20	120	2400	2540
40	40	60	2400	2500
60	60	40	2400	2500
80	80	30	2400	2510
120	120	20	2400	2540
240	240	10	2400	2650

* In practice, these costs would be increased slightly by the inclusion of the cost of possession for the reserve inventory carried.

The use of calculus can save much work. By taking the first derivative of the total-cost function and setting it equal to zero, the optimum order quantity to minimize costs is determined.[3]

$$TC = UC + \frac{IQC}{2} + \frac{UA}{Q}$$

$$\frac{d(tc)}{dQ} = 0 + \frac{IC}{2} + \frac{-UA}{Q^2} = 0$$

$$Q = \sqrt{\frac{2UA}{IC}} \quad \text{(where } Q \text{ is the optimum order quantity)}$$

$$Q = \sqrt{\frac{2(240)(10)}{(.20)(10)}} = \sqrt{2400} = 48.9 = 49 \text{ units}$$

Evaluation of Inventory-Control Systems and Techniques

Inventory-control systems seek to provide assurance of appropriate inventory levels, while minimizing the costs associated with acquisition and possession.

Quantitative approaches or analytical approaches to inventory control are growing, particularly in the operations research area. Elaborate operations research models and algorithms can be used effectively to describe and improve inventory conditions in many industrial areas.

Much care should be taken in planning for inventory control. The inventory model must be designed to fit the conditions of the particular industry. For more involved analysis of inventory models and assumptions used in them, see the "Revelant Reading" at the end of this chapter, and particularly Hillier and Lieberman's *Introduction to Operations Research.*

Another problem associated with such analytical approaches is obtaining accurate figures for the various costs. How does one accurately calculate the inventory-carrying cost? What exactly is included in the ordering cost? How valid is the cost figure for stockouts?

Even with such limitations, analytical approaches can be helpful in gaining insight into inventory problems. Estimations for stockout cost, inventory-carrying cost, and ordering cost can be close enough to give a figure which will decrease the total costs associated with inventory. Effective uses of analytical approaches to inventory control, along with good judgment, are often better than managerial hunches or intuition.

For such procedures, see any elementary calculus text.

RELEVANT READING

Fine, I. V., "Does Automation Affect the Purchasing Function?" *Reflections on Progress in Marketing,* Chicago: The American Marketing Association, 1964, pp. 428–431.

Hadley, G., and T. M. Whitin, *Analysis of Inventory Systems,* Englewood Cliffs, N.J.: Prentice-Hall, Inc., 1963.

Hillier, F. S., and G. J. Lieberman, *Introduction to Operations Research,* San Francisco: Holden-Day, Inc., Publisher, 1967.

Kotler, Philip, *Marketing Management,* Englewood Cliffs, N.J.: Prentice-Hall, Inc., 1967, chap. 4.

McMillan, C., and R. F. Gonzalez, *Systems Analysis: A Computer Approach to Decision Models,* rev. ed., Homewood, Ill.: Richard D. Irwin, Inc., 1968.

Miller, H. George, "The Impact of the Physical Distribution Concept on Industrial Buying Decisions," *Reflections on Progress in Marketing,* Chicago: The American Marketing Association, 1964, pp. 411–420.

"More P.A.'s Turn to Contract Buying," *Purchasing,* vol. 62, no. 4, p. 49, Feb. 23, 1967.

Rewoldt, Stewart H., James D. Scott, and Martin R. Warshaw, *Introduction to Marketing Management,* Homewood, Ill.: Richard D. Irwin, Inc., 1969, chap. 3.

Robinson, Patrick J., Charles W. Faris, and Yoram Wind, *Industrial Buying and Creative Marketing,* Boston: Allyn and Bacon, Inc., 1967.

PART FOUR

Selling
Industrial Products

CHAPTER SIX

Advertising

Why advertise at all? How can any expenditure for advertising be justified? The answer is, naturally, that there is a job to be done and advertising does it well. Then, what is this job? What are we after? Sales—yes. Profits—certainly. Satisfied customers—definitely! All are proper corporate objectives. But, they are not proper industrial advertising objectives. This is asking far too much.

It should be recognized that there are significant differences of scope among corporate goals, marketing goals, and advertising objectives. The marketing goal is its interest area within the overall corporate goal. The industrial advertising objective is a somewhat precise segment, a specific target, within the total marketing program. It is largely a refinement of a broad objective to a specific task, a step in the total attainment desired.

"To increase profits by $X per share" is an example of a corporate goal. "To increase sales by 10 percent over last year" becomes a goal of marketing. "To increase awareness of our full range of products by present customers" and "To increase by 25 percent awareness of us as a producer of our product by present nonusers with over 100 employees in SICs 34, 35, 36 within the next year" are examples of advertising objectives.

Advertising objectives identify just how advertising can be expected to assist in attaining the marketing objectives. In general, this relates to overcoming obstacles or capitalizing on opportunities in the marketplace. The tasks must be reasonable to advertising capabilities—and these are somewhat limited, particularly for industrial advertising. Let us explore this point a bit more fully.

In industry, sales come from the total corporate effort—not just from the salesman who closes the sale, and not just from any other one element alone. There are some prerequisites. The potential customer must know of us and of our product, and somewhere along the line, must develop a preference for our brand—or at least, a willingness to try it.

BASIC STEPS IN BUYING DECISION

The buying process can be analyzed into a series of steps. Robert J. Lavidge and Gary A. Steiner identify seven.[1]

Advertising may be thought of as a force, which must move people up a series of steps:

1. Unawareness
2. Awareness
3. Knowledge
4. Liking (favorable attitude)
5. Preference (first choice)
6. Conviction (desire to buy)
7. Purchase

This is a competent analysis of the steps in the consumer's buying decision. In the industrial area, we might employ less refinement and identify five major steps:

1. Unawareness
2. Awareness
3. Comprehension
4. Preference
5. Purchase

"Comprehension" means more than the awareness of a brand's existence. It means knowledge of the brand's characteristics or attributes—of its supposed capacity for giving satisfaction. "Preference"

---

[1] For a thorough discussion of these steps, see their source, Robert J. Lavidge and Gary A. Steiner, "A Model for Predictive Measurements of Advertising Effectiveness," *Journal of Marketing*, vol. 25, no. 6, October 1961, pp. 59–62. Reprinted from *Journal of Marketing*, published by the American Marketing Association.

means a favorable attitude to the degree that if the *type* of product is purchased, the *brand* will be—unless such obstacles as unavailability interfere. "Preference" may require demonstration, testing, or salesmanship to create conviction of the benefits to be derived. However, note here the fundamental importance of awareness and favorable attitude.

Psychological market knowledge is more difficult to come by than demographic knowledge. A condition of awareness is much easier to achieve than a condition of preference, or favorable attitude. Most advertising probably does not succeed very far beyond the awareness step. Awareness of brand existence is many times greater than brand preference.

Industrial advertising is far more effective in the earlier stages of this process, least so during the final stages. Obviously, then, it should be used in the early stages. It can be most effective there. It is necessary there. Its greatest contribution is there. It is hoped that increases in awareness and favorable attitude will help produce increases in sales. Yet the fact is that advertising can do all that can be reasonably expected of it without sales necessarily ensuing.

ROLE OF INDUSTRIAL ADVERTISING

At this point the question might be raised, "What can reasonably be expected of industrial advertising?"

The answer seems to be clear. One authority, Albert W. Frey, formerly Dean of the Graduate School of Business, University of Pittsburgh, puts it this way:

> . . . awareness by a potential buyer of a brand's existence, knowledge of the brand's satisfaction-giving properties, a favorable attitude toward the brand—hopefully favorable enough to induce purchase when the type of product is bought. An increase in any of these factors is desirable but particularly is "favorable attitude," for the greater the number of individuals with favorable attitudes the greater the likelihood that new and loyal customers will be created and that current customers will be held.

Thus, the role of industrial advertising is very significant. It can be a prerequisite to success in the marketplace. It is contained within the framework of reasonable capability. How could one ask for, and expect to get, more?

The refinement of industrial advertising objectives to specifics is realistic—and a long way from the theoretical "to obtain a monopoly of demand." Of far greater significance, this precision in the definition of the role of advertising can aid greatly in its implementation, budget determination, development of the copy, and selection of media and in providing a base for measuring the effectiveness of the creative advertising in the attainment of that objective.

And, of course, industrial advertising must be an integrated part of the marketing goals and strategy.

INTEGRATION WITH MARKETING

The integration of advertising objectives with marketing goals and strategy can start with the focus of the marketing effort, short or long range, immediate sales or image development, or both, and be directed toward middlemen, users, or the ultimate consumers of the consumer products from which industrial demand is derived. Some techniques follow.

PRIMARY ADVERTISING

Institutional advertising is sometimes used by trade associations as well as corporations to promote an overall goal for the industry, such as the general acceptability of a new material or product. It may be used to help change the public attitude—for example, to promote beer drinking in the home on Sunday as a socially proper concept. If successful, more beer can be sold, and more beer cans.

Push-Pull Advertising

Another technique, closely allied to this, is "pull." This directs the advertising of a component over the head of the immediate customer to the ultimate consumers, and uses consumer media to reach them. The premise is that increased consumer demand for the final product will result in more sales of the industrial component. The advertiser's participation in increasing the demand can buy him goodwill, a favorable position in selling to the industries involved.

There are many examples of this. One is that of advertising motors in consumer magazines by a motor manufacturer. Consumers rarely buy motors, per se. However, if the advertiser is successful, he impresses the customer favorably with the quality of his motors. He builds a quality image for his brand. These customers may be expected to prefer—and perhaps pay more for—a power lawnmower equipped with a motor of this name.

The essence of this technique is to "pull" one's products through the marketing channel by stimulation and expansion of ultimate consumer demand in the first place.

"Push" directs the advertising to the middlemen, to industry, to push one's products through the channel by stimulating demand of the decision makers within it. In many cases the consumers are unaware of the industrial sales or the brands of the industrial goods involved in the end product they buy, anyway. The product selection is made by manufacturers and dealers, not ultimate consumers.

IMPORTANCE OF TRUTH IN ADVERTISING

Prior to about 1400, signs and the town crier were principal advertising media. It is interesting to note that the town crier was appointed by the political entity to keep the public informed. He was empowered to "cry" the wares of merchants and to charge them a fee. The crier did so for the public good and his own remuneration. He determined what to say, and whether to say it at all. The public interest and the crier, rather than the merchant, the advertiser, controlled the advertising.

During the early printing period, from the 1400s to about 1840, advertising was characterized by long-winded copy, few illustrations, and flamboyant exaggeration. With the development of advertising agencies, which bought space at wholesale and resold it, then began to add service functions and to compete, interest in truth in advertising grew rapidly, especially after the turn of the century.

The major reason for this interest in truth in advertising is that everyone benefits from it—except those who wish to steal, to trade on the integrity of others. Unless the customer can believe the advertisement, he won't be motivated, the advertisement loses effectiveness, and then why advertise? The customer wants to be informed—he wants to be able to believe what he hears and sees. The media want that, too—for more advertising revenue. The agency wants truth, to survive. The manufacturer wants truth, if he is to advertise at all. The government wants it for the public interest. And the public confidence is goodwill and preference—without which no business will long last.

So, today, we have truth in advertising—but not completely. Copywriters and others, in seeking to be persuasive, may find themselves walking a very thin line between truth and false advertising.

Fortunately, the definition of "false advertising" as something which tends to deceive a reasonable, sophisticated adult is an excellent one. It permits mild exaggeration, some enthusiasm, perhaps beyond the literal, technical truth. As long as it does not tend to deceive, it's good, clean fun—referred to as "trade puffing." When it goes too far, it becomes false advertising.

Needless to say, there are many cases of going a bit too far. The attitude in the use of cease-and-desist orders, permitting one to agree to cease, but without admission of guilt, is realistic. It helps keep industry in line without real penalty, unless the offense actually merits more severe attention. That's there, too, if needed.

Within industrial advertising there are far fewer borderline cases than in consumer advertising. Nevertheless, there is no difference in the legality. The industrial advertisers should continue to maintain their good record, and can profit from the experiences of others who have been too enthusiastic. A good source of such situations is the Federal Trade Commission's weekly newsletter.[2]   The corporate counsel should be able to supply both copies and knowledgeable guidance.

DEVELOPING THE ADVERTISEMENT

Industrial advertising is a job for the creative artist who is also a specialist in the techniques. The decision maker is apt to be a generalist. He need not be an expert in the art of creating an advertisement. His role is to evaluate the program and the advertisements in line with their probable capacity to achieve the objectives assigned. Nevertheless, such an executive should be aware of some of the significant aspects of advertising. He must realize that an advertisement should have persuasive content and a persuasive presentation.

In the first place, the advertising must attract attention. It must be seen or heard. White space effectively used, color contrast, sex, and simulated motion help get attention. The headline, the brevity of the copy, the layout, and the reaction, the general first impression, can help guide that attention to the message conveyed by the copy.

The most effective messages can be very simple—short and to the point. They should be easy to see, read, comprehend, in a flash. Elaborate development, involved appeals, long copy, fancy gimmicks of layout or expression, all contribute heavily to losing the reader. A good message is characterized by three things: simplicity, sincerity, and suggestivity.

Appeals can be positive or negative. The former are direct, pleasant. They tend to show benefits. Negative appeals are indirect, from unpleasant to shocking. They tend to urge one to buy to avoid the unpleasant. A picture of a man being mangled by a machine, to help sell safety devices, or a snake striking a boot, to show the toughness of the material, are examples. They are very impressive. They will command attention. But too much repetition may build an unpleasant association and produce an adverse reaction.

[2] *News Summary,* a weekly publication available free from the Federal Trade Commission, Washington, D.C. 20580.

Primary appeals are used by industries and trade associations to promote a generic product—cast iron pipe, glass containers, etc.—to secure acceptance of the new. Selective appeals are those used by manufacturers to develop brand preference once product acceptance has been achieved. Patronage appeals are used largely by resellers, to persuade the customer to buy from the reseller—perhaps irrespective of brand.

One should not fall into the trap embodied by the common generalization that consumer advertising should use emotional appeals and industrial advertising should use logical-reasoning appeals. It is true that the industrial sale involves far more use of logical reasoning than does the typical consumer sale. But we are not talking sales, as such, in connection with the objectives of industrial advertising. We are working in the earlier stages of the buying process with basic motivation. One thing all industrial buyers have in common—they are human. All human beings are motivated emotionally.

If credit is mentioned in an advertisement, it must contain the full credit terms, when payment can be made without charge, and the equivalent annual interest rate of credit charges. The inclusion of a cash price only avoids this requirement. Incidentally, the required revelation of the full story, including the equivalent annual interest rate, applies to a wide range of communication devices, even a note on a salesman's calling card. This is another area for exploration with the corporate counsel, in some detail, to anticipate and prevent mistakes, even innocent ones.

FORMS OF INDUSTRIAL ADVERTISING

One reason for refinement of industrial advertising objectives is that it helps define the target audience and thereby aids in the selection of the media. As an approach to the problem of media selection, it might be helpful to list some of the various possibilities. Then a list of factors significant to the advertiser could be prepared—and each form of advertising ranked relatively to the others. Table 6.1 illustrates this. Other factors could be included, and other media. The ratings are not absolute, but relative. They represent the order of preference when considering each against a specific job requirement.

A review of this table may bring forth arguments as to the correctness of some ratings. They can readily be changed to reflect the judgment of the user. However, it is most likely that one fact will remain after any revisions. No one form is best for everything. Each has its own areas of superiority, its own strengths and weaknesses. An integrated program, bringing together the forms strongest for the most significant tasks, should give the best results.

TABLE 6.1 Relative Ranking of Various Forms of Industrial Advertising and Sales Promotion by Tasks

Rank	Credibility	Timing	Motivation	Imparting information	Audience control	Size of audience	Cost per contact
1	Technical literature	Catalogs	Trade shows	Technical literature	Salesmen	Business periodicals	Space advertising
2	Business periodicals	Salesmen	Salesmen	Direct mail	Trade shows	Space advertising	Business periodicals
3	Catalogs	Technical literature	Displays	Trade shows	Direct mail	Direct mail	Direct mail
4	Trade shows	Direct mail	Catalogs	Catalogs	Catalogs	Catalogs	Technical literature
5	Salesmen	Space advertising	Technical literature	Salesmen	Technical literature	Displays	Catalogs
6	Displays	Trade shows	Direct mail	Displays	Space advertising	Trade shows	Displays
7	Direct mail	Business periodicals	Space advertising	Business periodicals	Business periodicals	Technical literature	Trade shows
8	Space advertising	Displays	Business periodicals	Space advertising	Displays	Salesmen	Salesmen

Some leading media for consumer advertising are of questionable value to the industrialist. Media such as consumer magazines, radio, and TV are expensive. When a large consumer audience is the target, the cost per thousand contacts can be very low. But, when the target is a relatively or very small industrial audience, it can be prohibitive. There are exceptions. One is the "pull" technique to develop consumer demand, as in the power motor illustration previously discussed.

The leading media for most industrial advertising can be grouped under four headings: business periodicals, catalogs, direct mail, and trade shows. Business periodicals can be further segmented into vertical, horizontal, and general. Vertical publications serve one vertical market, one industry, such as lumber or mining. *Plastics Technology Magazine, Steel,* and *Textile World* are examples. Horizontal periodicals tend to cover all aspects of the job area selected wherever applied across industry lines. *Industrial Distribution, Modern Packaging,* and *Purchasing* are examples. The general business group tends to include a heavy emphasis on current business news and major developments over a wide range of subjects. *Business Week, Dun's, Harvard Business Review,* and *U.S. News & World Report* are examples.

Catalogs not only include the full range of product offering from the manufacturer, but also much detailed information concerning specifications. They constitute a valuable reference for the user in writing his own specifications and in product selection. They can be a very efficient source of orders, particularly for a wide line of standardized products built for inventory.

Direct mail offers excellent message control, but not readership control. It suffers from the sheer volume of such mail received daily and the high cost of maintaining a current mailing list of qualified, potential customers. On the other hand it can produce leads, convey product information, pave the way for a salesman, and help stimulate action.

Gimmicks (giveaways) are sometimes used to help get attention. They can be very effective. If the mailing list puts them in the right hands and the message is well done, a very favorable response can be obtained.

One tool, the trade show, is almost unique to industry. Strictly speaking, a trade show is not advertising. However, since it is directed to the tasks of informing and developing a favorable attitude of potential customers, it is included here. It can be very effective in introducing new developments to an interested audience. Some showmanship may be called for, but the impact created and the leads produced can be quite valuable. The composition and size of the audience together with the capacity of the attendant staff to direct attention favorably are two key variables.

Trade shows provide a good means of reaching potential customers and middlemen. New products, new features or modifications of present products, and new applications can be demonstrated to an interested and qualified audience. Trade shows vary greatly in both attendance and audience composition. They can and should be selected with care. The target market on a national or regional geographical basis is a start. Lists of attendees (when available) from past shows can be analyzed. Many trade associations sponsor trade shows and can be very helpful in providing the data with which to evaluate them.

The success of participation in the trade show rests largely upon the exhibitor, once the show to attract the right audience has been picked. Size of the exhibit is a factor, but of far less consequence than the attractiveness of it. Careful planning integrating a dramatic, hopefully unique, attention getter, with traffic control—to be inviting, provide ease of entry yet avoid congestion—and pleasingly attentive personnel are major factors in success. Handouts, literature, and request forms warrant careful consideration as to availability. Capitalizing on the interest generated by the exhibit to obtain a specific lead for prompt follow-up is a worthy and realizable goal. The volume of materials distributed, particularly if handed to visitors, is far less meaningful. But, if the visitor will react, ask questions of the persons manning the exhibit, and provide his name and address, the exhibit has been effective.

THE ADVERTISING AGENCY

Today's advertising agency has come a long way from Volney Palmer's original concept of the agency as primarily a retailer of space bought at wholesale. The fundamental responsibility of today's advertising agency is to produce advertisements (to implement the advertising program already sold to the advertiser). Perhaps the greatest prerequisite to doing this job most successfully is creativity. And this creativity needs to be soundly based upon knowledge—of the want-satisfying characteristics of the product, the market, the company, and the advertising objectives. To conceive of the idea in the first place, and then to implement it in creative advertising, are most valuable skills.

In addition, advertising agencies provide other specialists' skills relating to construction of the advertisement, as well as guidance in timing, media selection, and placement. Many offer much more, including research facilities and business advice relating to many aspects of corporate performance. This is a natural development, an outgrowth of the addition of more and more services to the agency as time goes on. For some situations this may be very desirable. For many, it is going too far.

In the first place, research, if needed to help define the market, to aid in media selection and placement, or to aid in the construction of an advertisement, can be a valuable service. But if the research results are to be used to evaluate the agency's work, to demonstrate the need for additional advertising or an increased budget, or any such purposes, they are misapplied. One of the most difficult hurdles to be overcome by any research is bias. It becomes even more difficult to do so when the researcher is a party at interest in the results.

Next, the role of the agency as envisioned by some advertising men, and supported by the services they offer, may be excessive to the need. Some agencies want to participate in many of the major decisions of their client's operations all the way, from planning to end sales. On the other hand, all too many corporations want to approve and to improve every aspect of the agency's advertising program and minute detail of every advertisement.

In such situations both the agency and the corporation are guilty of each trying to tell the other how to do his own job better. And they do a beautiful job of getting in each other's way and stifling creativity. The advertising agency is not in a position to run the client's company. The client is not in a position to tell the advertising agency how to advertise. Each can be a topflight expert—in his own business.

About all that's really needed to demand the best of both is to redefine somewhat the responsibilities of both agency and client. The company should be responsible for the product, its functional performance, and its improvement to maximize its ability to satisfy customers. The agency should be responsible for telling them about it, for developing preference as much as possible, and for the attainment of the mutually agreed objectives of advertising. The best agency will gladly accept full responsibility for creativity in its advertising. The best client will provide all the help the agency wants—and keep his hands off the result.

An excellent description of how to attain such a relationship is related by Robert Townsend in his refreshing and realistic book, *Up the Organization.*[3] He tells it this way:

> Fire the whole advertising department and your old agency. Then go get the best new agency you can. And concentrate your efforts on making it fun for them to create candid, effective advertising for you. Unless you've just done this, the odds favor that you have a bunch of bright people working at cross purposes to produce—at best—mediocre ads. We started at Avis by asking a few people for a list of the hottest agencies. Then we called on the creative heads of those agencies and tried to interest them in the rent a car business. Ultimately we stumbled

[3] From *Up the Organization,* by Robert Townsend. Copyright © 1970 by Robert Townsend. Reprinted by permission of Alfred A. Knopf, Inc.

on the right question: "How do we get five million dollars of advertising for one million dollars?" (our competition has five dollars for each dollar we have, and yet we have to pay the same price for cars, insurance, rent, gas, oil, and people).

Finally, Bill Bernbach heard the question and answered: "If you want five times the impact, give us ninety days to learn enough about your business to apply our skills, and then run every ad we write where we tell you to run it. Our people work to see how effective their ideas are. But most clients put our ads through a succession of Assistant V.P.'s and V.P.'s of advertising, marketing and legal until we hardly recognize the remnants. If you promise to run them just as we write them, you'll have every art director and copywriter in my shop moonlighting on your account."

We shook hands on it.*

Ninety days later, Bill Bernbach came out to show Avis his recommended ads. He said he was sorry but the only honest things they could say were that the company was second largest and that the people were trying harder. Bernbach said his own research department had advised against the ads, that he didn't like them very much himself—but it was all they had so he was recommending them. We didn't like them much at Avis either, but we had agreed to run whatever Bill recommended.

The rest is history. Our internal sales growth rate increased from 10 per cent to 35 per cent in the next couple of years.

Moral: Don't hire a master to paint you a masterpiece and then assign a roomful of schoolboy-artists to look over his shoulder and suggest improvements.

* To keep people at Avis and at Doyle Dane Bernbach from violating Bernbach's vision of the ideal account, I wrote "The Avis Rent A Car Advertising Philosophy," had it framed, and hung it in everyone's office (at both client and agency). It reads:

Avis Rent A Car
Advertising Philosophy

1. Avis will never know as much about advertising as DDB, and DDB will never know as much about the rent a car business as Avis.
2. The purpose of the advertising is to persuade the frequent business renter (whether on a business trip, a vacation trip, or renting an extra car at home) to try Avis.
3. A serious attempt will be made to create advertising with five times the effectiveness (see #2 above) of the competitor's advertising.
4. To this end, Avis will approve or disapprove, not try to improve, ads which are submitted. Any changes suggested by Avis must be grounded on a material operating defect (a wrong uniform for example).
5. To this end, DDB will only submit for approval those ads which they as an agency recommend. They will not "see what Avis thinks of that one."
6. Media selection should be the primary responsibility of DDB. However, DDB is expected to take the initiative to get guidance from Avis in weighting of markets or special situations, particularly in those areas where cold numbers do not indicate the real picture. Media judgments are open to discussion. The conviction should prevail. Compromises should be avoided.

Perhaps the most significant factor in this entire relationship is the pinning down of the responsibilities for decision making and performance—each to his own, with no fudging. Cooperation was encouraged. Impediments to creativity were removed. An atmosphere of challenge, demanding the best of both agency and client, was created. Who can ask for more?

EVALUATION

Industrial advertising can and should be evaluated as evidenced by its performance against objectives. In most cases this does not mean sales results, directly. Its job was defined when the advertising objectives were set. So, let's start with them. What progress has been made in their attainment—and at what cost?

Basically, this is apt to wind up as a value judgment. However, there are measures that can be made to assist in reaching that judgment. Each specific objective—degree of awareness, etc.—can be analyzed as to its status before and after the advertising. Progress is reflected by improvement, measured by the difference in status. Research can assist. This is discussed in Chapter Thirteen.

One point should be made here. Industrial advertising *results* indicate effectiveness. The *cost* to achieve them reflects efficiency. These are separate concepts, usually intermingled in the evaluation. Marketing costs, including advertising, possess a high degree of substitutability.[4] This introduces yet another perspective—is there another way to achieve this result by substitution of one form of marketing effort for another? Perhaps not. But it's still a good question, and should call for a carefully considered reply, as part of the evaluation of the advertising.

THE BUDGET

This has purposely been left to the last, where it belongs. Advertising decisions should not start with the budget and be tailored to it, but with the job to be done. The budget should be a function of that— never sales, or some arbitrary allocation from the corporate controller as to how much can be afforded, industry statistics on average expenditures, or the pressure from an agency for more. If the cost to do the job is higher than the budget permits, increase the budget—or revise the job.

Advertising is unique in one respect. If it is mediocre, if it is some-

[4] For further discussion of marketing costs, see Chapter Ten.

thing less than the best, it becomes very expensive with relatively little results to show for it. The best advertising (not necessarily the most expensive, but best in such factors as creativity, simplicity, uniqueness) by the very preponderance of its results becomes very effective and efficient at the same time. Anything less than what is needed to achieve this result becomes highly questionable as a sound investment.

A sound approach to the budget allocation for industrial advertising is to start with the goals of the corporation and identify the objectives advertising may be expected to serve, such as long-range image building. Next, the marketing goals provide the source of identification for specific additional long-range immediate tasks. This set of objectives can then be the basis for the development of the advertising program in full detail and the budget needed to implement it.

Further, if the funds available for advertising are limited, starting with the tasks permits relative evaluation and selection of the most essential. This changes the budgetary requirements, but provides assurance that the funds available are being put to the best use. Any variation should be in the budget, never in the quality of the advertising itself. If the budget must be less than optimal, cut the jobs, not the quality. This also promotes integration of the approved advertising with the marketing program. If any advertising tasks are to be dropped, consideration of the impact of this on marketing and possible other action to be taken can be given promptly.

RELEVANT READING

Backman, Jules, "Is Advertising Wasteful?" *Journal of Marketing,* January 1968, pp. 2–8.

Elling, Karl A., *Introduction to Modern Marketing,* New York: The Macmillan Company, 1969, chap. 11.

Freeman, Cyril, "How to Evaluate Advertising's Contribution," *Harvard Business Review,* July-August 1962, pp. 137–140.

Frey, Albert W., and Jean C. Holterman, *Advertising,* 4th ed., New York: The Ronald Press Company, 1970.

Lavidge, Robert J., and Gary A. Steiner, "A Model for Predictive Measurements of Advertising Effectiveness," *Journal of Marketing,* vol. 25, no. 6, pp. 59–62, October 1961.

Messner, Frederick, *Industrial Advertising,* New York: McGraw-Hill Book Company, 1963.

News Summary, Washington, D.C.: Federal Trade Commission.

Townsend, Robert, *Up the Organization,* New York: Alfred A. Knopf, Inc., 1970.

CHAPTER SEVEN

Selling and Sales Management

THE ART OF SALESMANSHIP AND THE INDUSTRIAL SALESMAN

One of the greatest salesmen of all times, if not *the* greatest salesman, was "Diamond Jim" Brady. He earned his living selling, and enjoyed the living fabulously. He epitomizes the art of salesmanship. Yet today, there are many who could easily outsell him.

The art of salesmanship is still needed, and at an extremely high level. Yet salesmanship alone is not enough. The days of the glad-hand showman are gone. Science, a technological background, and application engineering are now essential for most industrial sales jobs. They are an addition to the art of salesmanship, not a substitute for it.

It is still the same job—only now far more complex, demanding, and technical. The salesman must still please, convince, motivate, and secure action. But, in doing so, he must help the customer solve his problems. This frequently calls for technical skills to convince today's sophisticated buyers—and their buying influentials. Add to this a perceptive and pleasing personality (and let's include a big dash of empathy) together with reasonable amounts of ambition, self-discipline, and tact, and we have a good start. Given some experience and perseverance, a good man may develop.

All this adds up to a rather impressive set of qualifications. Nor are they merely idle words. It is what the industrial salesman will face in his competitors—and the trainee had better realize it. Education and intelligence, art and science, character and personality, courage and responsibility combine to create a highly competent man. He earns the respect of others for what he is. And, he continues to learn and thereby continues to improve his ability to keep on demonstrating his capabilities before hard-nosed customers. He must, if he is to continue to obtain their goodwill and patronage. He is a match for "Diamond Jim" anytime.

These requirements are high. The man should be selected with great care. The good salesman's contribution as a member of the corporate team is high. He should and will be well paid. If the present employer doesn't pay him well, a competitor will be glad to.

TYPES OF INDUSTRIAL SELLING

Industrial selling is done for the manufacturer, for the reselling middlemen (industrial distributors, dealers, and contractors), and by an agent or broker. The sale can be direct to user or to reseller. See Figure 4.1 for an overall perspective of these various selling situations.

Types of industrial selling can be structured by products, customers, territory, and functions. On highly technical items, product specialization can be a must. If the seller offers a wide line, additional salesmen are used for other items. This means two or more salesmen cover the same territory and call on a given customer, each one representing his product line(s). This duplication is costly. But it may be necessary. It can be far more productive than for one man to try to cover everything.

Where the need for product specialization is less, division of the selling task by customer groupings offers several advantages. The personal relationships between salesman and customer are given a chance to mature. Goodwill is enhanced. This representation of the full line saves on selling costs and on customers' buying costs. And, perhaps most important, the salesman learns the problems of his customers and can become an expert in helping to solve them.

Such a personalized, cooperative relationship provides yet another valuable benefit to the seller—information. He can receive a prompt feedback of changing conditions in the field, including competitive activities. He may obtain advance notice of anticipated changes in customer requirements. At the very least, he has assurance of firsthand field information.

Geographical segmentation is a variable in significance, depending upon the section of the country and the size of the segments. It can be very appropriate. In addition to the expected economies in time and travel expenses, it can permit matching the salesman to the customer, psychologically and sociologically. A Yankee is not the most suitable man for the South; the West Coast prefers a Westerner; and industry in the Northeast prefers metropolitan types. Obviously, geographical segmentation is least applicable to home-office specialists who cover the nation as needed on major transactions.

Functional subdivision of the total selling job and specialization within each function has been one answer to the increased demand for top technical expertise. This has proved to be particularly effective even on a national scale in some major situations. One illustration is of an order placed by the home office in New York, as a result of a sale made to the buying influentials in Chicago, for an installation to be made in Texas. Application engineering and postsale follow-up will be in Texas. The key decision makers will continue to be in Chicago and New York. Three different men, each a specialist in his own aspect of the total task, can readily be involved.

OBJECTIVES OF SELLING

Recognition of the objectives of selling is a prerequisite to the most successful performance and to the evaluation of it. Not all selling is directed to obtaining the order. Yet, orders obtained are frequently the basis for both compensation and evaluation. This is unfair to the salesman and to the corporation. It frequently results in a misdirection of sales efforts and somewhat lopsided results. Worse, such results continue to be accepted because traditionally they have been so.

It is only natural and human for the salesman, aware that sales volume is the basis for his compensation, recognition, and possible promotion, to concentrate on just that—getting more orders. He cannot be blamed for shortchanging anything else. The error lies with his sales management, in structuring his job and its measurement of performance in the first place. For a discussion of measuring men, see Chapter Fifteen.

The objectives of selling are a variable. Some are inherent in the overall sales task. Some are additions to it. And some are instead of orders. Inherent objectives include such things as identification of buying influentials; the obtaining of information, including specifications; data for competitive bidding; changing field conditions (including activities of competitors); changing customer requirements (including advance notice of any anticipated changes in nature or volume of requirements); and other data to provide a feedback for better forecasting. Objectives sometimes added to the normal sales task include rendering assistance to middlemen, perhaps even making some sales for them; handling of customer-service requirements (including postsale follow-up); handling of complaints; field interviewing for corporate research studies; participation in trade shows to help develop leads, perhaps for other salesmen; and many forms of long-range goodwill development.

Objectives which obtain instead of orders, rather than as a part of or in addition to the selling task, suffer most if not given full recognition. Typically, the work is spread over months or years without immediate sales being made. Here we refer to such things as the steps to be taken toward an ultimate sale, particularly on very high-ticket items, multimillion dollar installations, for example. Sales are made very infrequently. They may develop only after months or years of work. Another example is the obtaining of new accounts as against repeat orders from present customers. To do this successfully may take much time, effort, and concentration. Shall the salesman do this in his spare time, fit it in somehow, when and if opportunity occurs—but be paid for the orders he turns in? How much value is inherent in new accounts versus calls for repeat orders? It can be argued that the good salesman will do this anyway. However, it is a long-range development. To expect the salesman to do it on his own, and at the probable sacrifice of current income, is expecting a lot. If the job is to be done, it should be recognized. It can very well constitute a functional specialty as a special assignment to a man or a group.

Systems Selling

A primary objective of industrial sales has been the sale of a product to create customer satisfaction. For many firms, this is fast becoming a secondary, almost incidental, objective. Products are no longer sold, as such—systems are.

A system is simply an interrelated group of components to perform a complete function or service for the customer. This means that the seller develops lines of products which can be marketed in one package. Unrelated products can be continued, or dropped. It gives guidance to corporate growth by product development and by acquisition. The sale becomes a big one, of the entire package rather than of bits and pieces. The competitive advantage is obvious.

This raises the requirements for the industrial salesman. It fosters cooperative specialization and the development of sales teams. The customer's problem needs to be identified and solved, and the system designed and sold. And it must work. A lot is involved. Customer satisfaction becomes a very real goal. Product orientation is replaced with customer orientation. Integration is no longer an option. It is an excellent application of the marketing concept.

Yet it is not without difficulties. Integration of production and production schedules, divisional coordination, the need for training the corporate salesmen, and often providing customer education are real problems. The big one, of course, is the task of bringing together the related products to create the system in the first place. But, if it can be done, the reward for such capability is high.

From the marketing point of view, there are several advantages. The customer's attention is on the entire package as a unit. The price is for the system. Individual components are no longer separate sales considerations, including price. The seller has another advantage if repeat sales of consumables are involved in the system's operation. In many cases, a system which works well in one location can be sold for use in some or all of the customer's other locations. The stakes are high. But the potential for creating customer satisfaction by systems selling has hardly been tapped.[1]

TYPES OF INDUSTRIAL SALESMEN

The Inside Salesman

The voice on the telephone and the man at the counter, two major duties of inside salesmen, are most significant. They, together with the outside salesman, are the firm's contact with its most important people—its customers. Yet, traditionally the working conditions for those on the telephone are anything but an aid to their morale. The inside sales job has been a training ground for outside salesmen. And the pay has not been inspiring.

The result has frequently been a loss of respect for the job. The cost in goodwill of indifference, inexperience, lack of help in special situations such as rush orders, wrong information on prices or specifications, and general lack of confidence in anyone except the boss is very hard to measure, but very real nonetheless.

Inside salesmen are important people. They spend most of their time with customers, on the telephone or face to face. They should possess the same high qualities and experience expected of outside salesmen. They are highly valuable members of the team.

Ideally, the work of both the inside and outside salesman should be carefully integrated. The inside man can perform functions to complement his outside counterpart. He can check on inventory, follow up on shipping, provide accurate data on specifications and price, and handle special requests on the spot. If assigned to his own group of

---

[1] For a good discussion of systems selling, see Thomas J. Murray (ed.), "Systems Selling: Industry's New Tool," *Dun's Review,* vol. 84, no. 4, p. 51, October 1964.

customers, he gets to know them and develops a personalized contact of great value. One of the benefits of this is vastly improved customer relations.

Such teamwork between inside and outside salesmen can create a most effective sales service. A good inside salesman should be well paid for his contribution to corporate welfare. A poor one shouldn't be paid at all.

Field Salesmen

Field salesmen perform at their customer's desk or place of business, face to face with him. They receive the full force of objections, and fail to sell more often than they succeed. Yet they do succeed. This takes something more than the personal and technical qualifications discussed at the beginning of this chapter. This "something" has been variously called ambition, courage, drive, enthusiasm, perseverance, and will to succeed.

The man must not let failures defeat him. Rather, they should motivate him to better and corrective effort. Once attained, once the salesman has proved to himself his ability to sell in the face of obstacles, he will be doubly secure. He will be confident of himself and of his job. His performance will reflect it. This man cannot be fired from his capability—from the exercise of his skill. He knows he can handle his job. He is a salesman, and proud of it.

Many companies regard field sales as an excellent background for managerial talent. Candidates for many managerial positions are deliberately given this opportunity to develop themselves, while gaining valuable firsthand experience. They develop their ability to think on their feet, to communicate effectively, to motivate others, to learn self-discipline, and to listen—to learn the other's thinking first, then take the appropriate action. It works.

Product Managers

With the development of marketing orientation, firms began to note that they had a number of successful products and some slower ones. The overall marketing effort was successful, but somehow, some items were being bypassed. An answer to this was the product manager, to provide marketing effort for a product or product line.

The product manager is in a somewhat complex position in the firm. He coordinates the efforts of others as they relate to his product. But he must do this without line authority over the others. He is staff in the development of marketing programs for "his" product. He is line in that he has complete responsibility for the product's success. This can include direct supervision of salesmen assigned to his product,

sometimes exclusively. He is accountable to the chief marketing executive for line profitability. Yet his activities rarely include authority over
production. Normally, he will have full marketing responsibility.

Missionary Salesmen

The primary task of missionary salesmen is to promote the brand of
the manufacturer. This is done through cooperation and education of
distributors' salesmen, through demonstration of product advantages in
joint calls on users, and even in making some sales for distributors. The
reaction of distributors to the use of missionary salesmen is not always
as favorable as the manufacturer might like. Such promotion through
education, when supported by a need (by distributors' salesmen or by
users) as with new features or applications to be demonstrated, can
be very well received. Under other circumstances, without a real need
to be filled, the stimulation of sales probably will not affect the total
taken, but may mean a shifting in volume from one brand to another.
This is fine for the manufacturer. It is less so for the distributor. An
exception is the exclusive distributor who carries only this manufacturer's
line.

Missionary saleswork can be very productive and helpful when technical change, major modification, new applications or uses, and territorial
expansion are involved. It is highly applicable in the introduction of
new products. But it can be overdone. Once the real need has been
filled, too much of this type of selling tends to destroy its value to
everyone.

Technical Specialists

As the economy becomes more complex, as manufacturers produce more
technological developments, as the application and uses become more
involved, the required technical capabilities of the salesman to help
market the products are increased tremendously. In fact, in many cases,
the customer must be taught the use and inherent possibilities. This
need has stimulated the development of technical specialists to work
with salesmen. This support can create an effective sales team.

The need for technical specialists is a variable by industry. The trend
is for it to continue to grow. In some cases one such man is needed
for every two or three field salesmen. He provides the technical information needed by the customer. This has two results. One is more
profit from more closed sales. The other is in building the image and
goodwill of the firm as a reliable source of help.

Such technical specialists become very conscious of the need for the
firm's products to create customer satisfaction. This is the essence of
their field duties, to demonstrate that in providing their counsel. This

perspective from a technically knowledgeable point of view can be very helpful to the seller in product planning, R&D, advertising, and marketing. It becomes an excellent source of specifics for further implementation of the marketing concept.

IDENTIFICATION OF BUYING INFLUENTIALS

Except for semiautomated rebuys, the buying decision is apt to involve several people. Each one influences the decision from the point of view of his interest area. The problem is to identify each one of them, the relative significance of each in the final decision, and the nature of each one's interest. In general, the greater the significance of the purchase to the buyer, the higher the level and the more widespread these influentials will be.

There are two major difficulties in the identification of buying influentials. One is that the composition of the influentials will vary considerably from one firm to another. The second is that job titles alone can be very misleading. There is a noticeable lack of uniformity in the use of titles for a given job function among various companies, even within the same industry.

In short, awareness of this problem can be helpful in pointing up the need for careful exploration and analysis of each buying situation. Time spent in doing so can be very productive in guiding the marketing effort and in ensuring that as many as possible of the influentials are included.

One illustration of the analysis of people, their impacts, and behavioral patterns was compiled several years ago. It is still most appropriate to visualize the involvement today. This is presented in Table 7.1.[2]

SALES MANAGEMENT AND SALES SUPERVISION

Industrial sales management, whether at a corporate-headquarters level or on a divisional basis, is typically responsible for planning and the control of sales operations. This involves the type of sales coverage; territories; sales controls and reporting; compensation; promotion; meetings; direction of selling efforts; evaluation; and trouble shooting.

Sales supervision is apt to be more of a field job. Whereas there is a variation by size of firm in the allocation of responsibilities to sales supervision, they usually include selection of salesmen; training; motivation; personal selling; direct supervision of performance; account

[2] Reprinted by permission from *Sales Management, The Marketing Magazine,* copyright 1953, Sales Management, Inc.

TABLE 7.1   Analysis of Customer Buying Behavior

This table shows how Amercoat Corp. isolated the group of men who may exert buying influence on the corrosion-control plan they sell.   Correlated paragraphs summarize each man's job influence, his knowledge and interest in corrosion control, his knowledge and interest in control methods, and his buying habits. The same technique can be used by any company that sells to the industrial market, working, of course, with its own key men.

Key men	Contributor factor rating	Job influence	Knowledge and interest in corrosion control	Knowledge and interest in control methods	Buying habits
General manager	"A"	Primarily interested in results. Likely to leave details to others.	Limited knowledge. May have active interest in obtaining better results.	Little knowledge. Interest likely to be in anticipated results only.	May make final decision. Likely to leave details to others.
Manufacturing director	"A" or "B"	Primarily interested in results. Likely to be important factor in obtaining action.	Knowledge likely to depend on size and nature of the company. Should have active interest if aware of own hazards.	Knowledge probably limited. Should have active interest in best methods.	May have authority to place or initiate order. Important factor in any case.
Plant manager or superintendent	"A" "B" or "C"	Degree of importance depends on size of company and operating practice.	If operating in place of manufacturing director, likely to have above-average degree of knowledge and interest in both subjects. Otherwise, may be figurehead. His goodwill, however, is important.		Unlikely to have authority to buy. Recommendation or requisition may be important.
Maintenance or corrosion engineer	"B"	Important factor in companies where charged with responsibility for maintenance costs.	Likely to have both interest and knowledge particularly if operating as corrosion engineer.	Should have active interest and some knowledge. May be prejudiced regarding some methods of control.	Unlikely to have authority to place or initiate order, but recommendation important.
Purchasing agent	"C"	Negative rather than positive, but in many companies must be seen first.	Limited, if any.	Limited, if any.	Close buyers, but largely influenced by other department heads and by top management.
Research department	"B"	Negative as regards operating costs. Positive as applied to products and testing.	Knowledge and interest may be purely "scientific," rather than from dollars and cents viewpoint.	Knowledge and interest likely to be "scientific" and possibly prejudiced.	Usually have no authority to place or initiate orders. Tests likely to be important.
Plant engineer	"B" or "C"	Degree of importance depends on size of company and operating practice.	If operating in place of maintenance or corrosion engineer, likely to have most of his knowledge and interest in both subjects. Otherwise, important only from standpoint of goodwill.		May have authority to "requisition"; otherwise recommendation may carry some weight.
Paint foreman	"C"	Usually follows "line of least resistance." Interest and pride need to be stimulated, especially if new method involves extra effort.	Neither knowledge, nor interest except in rare cases.	Except in rare cases, no knowledge beyond methods now using and no active interest except in easier ways to do the job.	Usually have no authority to place or initiate orders. Goodwill and willingness to handle products properly are important.

Key to Contributor Factor Rating:
"A"—The men who must make the final buying decision and who have the authority to authorize the expenditure.
"B"—The advisory, intermediate or subordinate men who must also be sold; otherwise the "A" men are likely to withhold approval.
"C"—Other men who may influence the buying decision. As a rule, these men have no authority but can block the sale by direct opposition or a negative attitude.

responsibilities; preliminary evaluation; and liaison between customer, salesman, and the home office.

Selection of Salesmen

The selection of salesmen should be done with great care. Much is involved. The cost of hiring, training, and expenses in the field until the man develops his performance to a profitable level is high. To this can be added the numerous fringe benefits now automatic upon employment. But, unless the man is a permanent success, he will incur another loss in his turnover, that of customer goodwill. Frequent changes in sales representation mean redevelopment of valuable personal relationships—and the development of a feeling of unreliability in sales representation by customers. This is a real loss in goodwill.

The selection of salesmen is an art of prediction. The problem is to select those with the best combination of personal characteristics, education, and experience for the particular job.

Probably no one will be perfect. The judgment of the candidates most likely to succeed can be aided by a comparison between the characteristics most needed (derived from the job description) and the characteristics possessed by the man. The application blank can be designed to weed out the obvious misfits. Testing and personal interviewing become the crucial factors—with far greater weight on the interviewing.

Tests are sometimes used, in part because they are an easy way to avoid the harder job—in-depth exploration via interviews. Test results are indicative only. High scores are inconclusive. Low scores need not be preclusive. They do form an aid to the interviewing. They can indicate areas for further face-to-face explorations. They should never be used as a substitute for a considered value judgment.[3]

Motivation

This is an area of sales management where many mistakes have been and continue to be made—yet where it is relatively easy to be quite effective. The difficulty lies not in the implementation, but in the assumptions commonly made, whether realized or not.

At the worst, it is assumed that people hate work, are lazy, have no internal motivation, and need to be driven to do a job. This philosophy existed for centuries. It should have been abandoned long ago—yet it still persists in many forms of regimentation and policing of people. (How many calls did Bill turn in last week?)

[3] For a practical and thorough treatment of the key characteristics of individual salesmen, recruiting, knockout factors, testing dos and don'ts, and interviewing, see Henry R. Bernstein (ed.), "How to Recruit Good Salesmen," *Industrial Marketing*, October 1965, pp. 70–77.

Far better, it is assumed that people love their work, are ambitious, have needs and wants which they will work to satisfy, and welcome an opportunity to do a good job. This is a big step in the right direction—but not quite far enough. It permits the further assumptions that everyone will work harder for more money; that a specific reward will motivate all salesmen—and those that aren't so motivated probably are just lazy and should be fired; and that motivation is something external to the man, to be done by the manager. These are half-truths—dangerous in that the man gets blamed for motivational failures, when it really is the manager's lack of appreciation that is faulty.

Man works to satisfy his needs, true. But motivation comes from within. It is the internal drive which stimulates the man's performance to attain the goals he seeks. These goals vary from one individual to another at any one time. Yet they can be grouped into a series of steps, levels of attainment. Man starts with the lowest. When that is attained, he moves up, and he is no longer motivated by the needs of the first step. These steps are survival, security, stability, success, and satisfaction, in that order. Man will work hard for food, when he is hungry. Once survival is assured, he works for security, and so on. In today's economy, at least the first three levels have been accomplished by most employed persons.

This means that money to attain a satisfactory standard of living, success, will be a powerful motivating force—but only to those who have not achieved it. Even though the standard of living is a variable, once it is attained, additional money loses most of its power to motivate (especially with income taxes where they are). Other symbols of success, personal recognition, any of various ways of providing even intangible ego satisfactions will become more effective.

Motivation is a personalized, internal matter. The reward to produce the motivation desired varies among different people and their levels of attainment. This calls for individualized attention, but the effectiveness to be achieved can be well worth it.

Job reassurance and money can be very effective to the young beginner. Given the help he needs, the opportunity, and a chance at a sizable reward, he is apt to push himself far beyond where anyone could drive him. If he succeeds and earns the reward, perhaps a big bonus, he should get it. Let him taste blood. And the signals should not be changed because his total compensation is getting too high. Many good salesmen earn more than their sales managers—and should.

At the other extreme is the low producer. If training, helpful supervision, and positive motivation do not increase his productivity, there is one tool left. It is negative, to be used only in special cases, but powerful—job insecurity. If used, it should be absolutely private between the man and his supervisor. One way is to place the man on probation for a year. At the same time, every assistance tailored to his needs should be given. But, if this does not work, if the man cannot or will not respond, he should be terminated. Perhaps he is a misfit, and a transfer is in order. Perhaps he is an error in selection. The original error is made worse by keeping him in a hopeless situation. Proper, humanitarian considerations appear to argue for it. In some cases a weak manager uses this as an excuse to avoid an unpleasant duty. It may be better for the man, and it certainly is better for the morale of the rest of the sales force, to cut the deadwood, and promptly. The manager who procrastinates confesses his own shortcoming.

SALES TERRITORIES, POTENTIALS, QUOTAS, AND SUCH

The sales manager needs much detailed information to permit him to reach decisions in these areas. Essentially, he is a line officer. Providing the data he needs is a task for staff, frequently given to market research.

It is an important job, with a broad scope of information, and with sophisticated techniques. Further, the state of the art is changing rapidly. In fact, so much innovation and progress has been made in recent years that refresher courses, participation in professional conferences, and current reading are essential, if one is to be kept up to date. These matters occupy a special section in this book, Part Six, "Measurements of Marketing, Markets, and Men."

PLANNING AND CONTROL

In addition to sales management's planning responsibilities, which relate to the attainment of corporate marketing goals, there is a set of responsibilities which relate to control of the sales force. Whether done directly by the sales manager or with the help of sales supervisors (as in larger situations), the sales manager has primary accountability for the results. Involved are the development and motivation of salesmen, their evaluation, compensation, direction of effort, territories, and the quality of their performance.

Since the sales manager cannot be in all places at once, he must rely heavily upon sales reports and his system for obtaining, interpreting, and using them. This is a serious matter, involving both quantitative and qualitative information. It is well worthy of careful study and implementation.

**TABLE 7.2 Files Available for Order
Entry/Sales Reporting System**

MASTER FILES

Customer Master File	*Product Master File*
Customer Number	Part Number
Billing: Address	Product Structure Code
City & State	Standard Cost
Shipping: Address	Selling Price
City & State	Inventory Data:
SIC Code	Quantity on Hand
State & County Tax Codes	Reorder Point
Salesman Responsible	Lead Time
Forecast	
Prior Years' Purchases	
Calls ⎫ Summary	
Orders ⎭	
Amount of Billings	

Open Order File	*General Ledger*
Customer Number	Account Number
Order Number	Dollars
Product No. (Part No.)	Salesmen Expense $
Quantity	Salesmen
Price	Reimbursement $
Cost	
Salesman	
Territory	
Order Date	
Delivery Date	

The Ferry Cap & Set Screw Company, through the continued efforts of Dan J. Cantillon, has developed an integrated program directed to improvement in this involved area. It works. Dan describes it this way.[4]

Sales and profit data are not sufficient for management to intelligently evaluate the effectiveness of an entire sales program. Other tools must be made available to provide sales and marketing personnel with meaningful information for day-to-day, and short and long-range decision-making and control.

An indepth study was made to completely isolate Ferry Cap management's thinking regarding its sales objectives, and an improved marketing information and reporting system was developed to reflect these require-

[4] Used with permission of Dan J. Cantillon, Vice President, Ferry Cap & Set Screw Company, Cleveland, Ohio.

ments.   The first step was to tailor some of the details and summaries of current reports to meet the specific needs of various managers.   Then, an integrated and automated system was designed to obtain better control, report consistency, and exception-type processing.

There are four master files involved in this system—customer, open order, product, and general ledger or expenses (planned and actual).   A brief description of the content of these files is shown in Table 7.2.

The system begins with updating the customer file with name and address changes, credit, and other code changes, and updates of salesman call reports.   This data is run through a maintenance program to update the customer master file and create an activity journal for reference and audit trail purposes.   Similar maintenance type runs are made to the product file for such changes as standard cost, selling prices, etc.   An open order file is set up to capture the initial order immediately upon receipt.   When all orders are captured through this single entry point management can exercise true control over the selling and marketing process.   An illustration of the single entry point is shown in Figure 7.1.   From the entry of a customer order, all data files and subsystems can be updated with this single input document.

It is this basic file that provides the data for all periodic and regularly scheduled reports and analysis.   Manufacturing receives production requirements; demand history permits the inventory function to establish lead times and quantities to be stocked; while sales and financial data

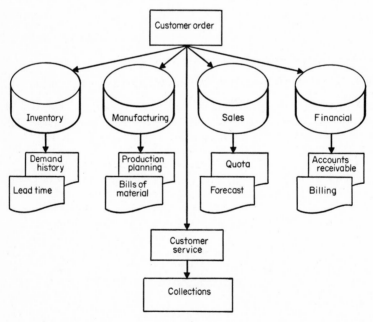

Fig. 7.1 Order entry information flow.

is furnished for product/customer analysis, sales analysis, and forecasting. An outline of three basic and significant sales reports follows:

REPORT NO. 1
PROFITABILITY ANALYSIS BY TERRITORY

This report shows the following elements of information for each territory for the current quarter.
1. PRESENT—Present Year
   (a) Sales—Sales this quarter
   (b) Cost—Cost this quarter
   (c) Sales Exp.—Sales Expense includes salaries, commission, travel and entertainment. All expenses are pro-rated on the basis of calls.
   (d) Margin—Sales minus the sum of Cost and Sales Expense.
2. LAST YEAR—The same information displayed under PRESENT is found here for the corresponding quarter of the previous year.
3. CALLS—Sales Calls
   (a) All—Total sales calls (Ferry Cap & Divisions).
   (b) FER—Ferry Cap sales calls only.
4. SALES/CALL—Sales per call, Item 1(a) divided by Item 3(a).
5. PROFIT/CALL—Profit per call, Item 1(d) divided by Item 3(a).
6. % OF SALES—The underlying elements are all calculated as a percent of PRESENT SALES, Item 1(a).
   (a) Cost—Item 1(b) divided by Item 1(a) times 100%.
   (b) Expense—Item 1(c), Expense, divided by Item 1(a) times 100%.
   (c) Profit—Item 1(d), Margin, divided by Item 1(a) times 100%.

REPORT NO. 2
ANALYSIS OF GROUP A, B, C, D, E ACCOUNTS BY TERRITORY

On this report all data is shown on the basis of territory and group. The information for each territory is printed on a separate group of paper so carbon copies can be distributed to the salesmen. The following definitions are used for the groups.

Group	Definition
A	The six largest accounts in sales for this quarter in the territory.
B	The next fourteen accounts.
C	The next twenty accounts.
D	All remaining accounts with sales this quarter.
E	Calls on accounts with no sales this quarter.

The following information is displayed on this report.
1. GROUP SALES—Total sales to a group as defined above and indicated on this report line.
   (a) NOW—Group sales this quarter.

(b) LAST YR.—Group sales for the corresponding quarter last year.

2. % OF TERR.—Current sales for this group, Item 1(a), as a percent of total sales within the territory.

3. AVER./ACCT—Current sales for this group, Item 1(a), divided by the number of accounts within this group.

4. CALLS—Sales calls.

(a) No.—The number of calls made on customers in this group.

(b) %—The number of calls made on customers in this group, Item 4(a), as a percent of the total number of calls made within the territory.

(c) AVER. SALES—Group Sales, Item 1(a), divided by the calls made in this group, Item 4(a).

5. SALES EXP.—Sales expense for this group. (Sales expense is the total of salary, travel, entertainment, commission and bonus for the whole territory pro-rated to groups on the basis of number of calls.)

(a) NOW—Sales expense this quarter.

(b) LAST—Sales expense for the corresponding quarter last year.

6. EXP./CUST.—Sales expense, Item 5(a), divided by the number of accounts in this group.

7. EXP./CALL—Sales expense for the territory divided by the number of calls. (This is the standard for pro-rating sales expenses as defined in 5.)

REPORT No. 3
TWENTY LARGEST ACCOUNTS

This report is a simple listing of activity by account for the twenty largest accounts within each territory. A report for each territory is printed on a separate sheet of paper with the territory name printed at the top so that carbon copies can be given to the salesmen. Following is an explanation of the data elements of this report.

1. CLASS—Either a one or a two. One signifies a distributor, and two represents manufacturers.

2. SALES—Sales this quarter.

3. CALLS—Sales calls.

(a) No.—The number of sales calls.

(b) %—The percent of total sales calls for the territory made on this account.

(c) AVER. SALES—Sales, Item 2, divided by calls, Item 3(a).

4. SALES EXP.—Sales expense for this account pro-rated on the basis of number of calls.

5. SALES/EXP.—Sales, Item 2, divided by sales expense, Item 4.

6. MARGIN—Total profit realized on an account.

7. MARGIN/EXP.—A rough measure of return on sales expense (Item 6 divided by Item 4).

FERRY CAP AND SET SCREW COMPANY
REPORT NO. 1
PROFITABILITY ANALYSIS BY TERRITORY

QUARTER ENDING 06/30/66

TERRITORY	PRESENT SALES	PRESENT COST	PRESENT SALES EXP.	PRESENT MARGIN	LAST YEAR SALES	LAST YEAR COST	LAST YEAR SALES EXP.	LAST YEAR MARGIN	CALLS ALL FER	SALES/CALL	PROFIT/CALL	COST	PCNT OF SALES EXPEN	PROFIT
BAKER	239,252	154,811	5,254	79,187	198,356	145,422	3,578	49,000	307 241	992.75	328.58	64.7	2.2	33.1
FERIS	254,803	161,879	4,423	88,501	206,356	165,422	4,578	36,000	335 221	1,152.95	400.46	63.5	4.1	34.5

FERRY CAP AND SET SCREW COMPANY
REPORT NO. 2
ANALYSIS OF GROUP A B C D E ACCOUNTS BY TERRITORY

QUARTER ENDING 06/30/66

TERRITORY	GROUP	GROUP SALES NOW	GROUP SALES LAST YR	AVER/ ACCOUNT	PCNT OF TER.	CALLS NO.	CALLS PCNT	AVER SALES	SALES EXP NOW	SALES EXP LAST	EXP./ CUST	EXP./ CALL
BAKER	A	153,705	145,000	25,618	64.2	23	9.5	6,683	394	264	66	17
	B	68,633	52,000	4,902	28.7	42	17.4	1,634	719	683	51	17
	C	15,337	11,342	766	6.4	26	10.8	590	445	432	22	17
	D	1,577	1,000	87	.6	12	5.0	131	205	152	11	17
	E					138	57.3		2,361	1,452		17

FERRY CAP AND SET SCREW COMPANY
REPORT NO. 3
TWENTY LARGEST ACCOUNTS BAKER

QUARTER ENDING 06/30/67

CUSTOMER	CLASS	SALES	CALLS NO.	CALLS PCNT	AVER SALES	SALES EXP.	SALES/ EXP.	MARGIN	MARGIN/ EXP.
ACE BRASS AND COPPER CO	/	46,087	3	1.0	15,026	51	885	5,324	104
ROYAL SCREW AND BOLT	/	25,697	5	1.1	5,139	85	501	1,036	12

The data contained in these and other reports is used to control and review operation results as it relates to Ferry Cap's marketing plan and profit goals, and is used effectively in sales meetings and management. Action reports on individuals or products are received that prevent or remedy various problems before serious damage has been done.

The managers receive reports summarizing progress to prior years and plan, by product line, territory, and significant changes in the "A" and "B" customer sales figures. The summarized reports received by the managers are another step in the exception-reporting principle. However, the managers have the ability to see any salesman, product, or even specific customer activity in detail, upon request. Consequently, each level in the Ferry Cap organization is concerned with summary and highlight information on a regular basis (Table 7.3).

The comparison of actual sales by territory and product line to budget volumes, as well as prior years, facilitates the spotting of trends within a given salesman's territory that may be indicative of a situation requiring corrective action by marketing management.

Salesmen's quota figures for the next year are set up and sales forecasts by product line are established. A detailed report is sent to each salesman on a monthly basis to inform him of progress and to make him aware of several significant factors. A listing showing his sales by customer for the present period and year-to-date, contrasted to the same

TABLE 7.3   Report Structure by Use

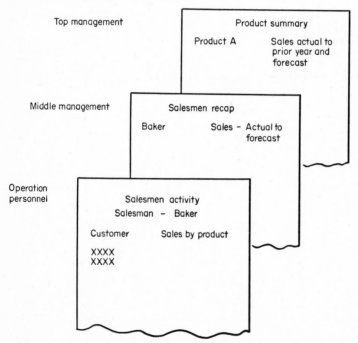

period in prior years, permits him to analyze or at least be aware of changes in customer buying habits or modify his own selling plans. In addition, the amount of quota points ahead or behind his forecast are also shown. The salesmen respond on a quarterly basis and explain deviations from the marketing plans. The salesmen then are in a position where they must use the information we are furnishing them. This type of "action" report is very useful to help call attention to possible shifts in suppliers on the part of a customer. It also forces salesmen to keep closer contact with key accounts. Further, it is useful to receive information regarding changing requirements or specifications by the customers and may help uncover price changes or other marketing indicators as well.

Perhaps the most significant aspects of this system are its thoroughness and its adaptability. The essentials are readily capable of being incorporated into a similar system for other industrial-selling situations. The improved communication of essential data should improve the manager's decision making and the effectiveness of his control. The benefit should show where it counts, in improved sales performance consistent with the marketing goals.

RELEVANT READING

Bernstein, Henry R. (ed.), "How to Recruit Good Salesmen," *Industrial Marketing*, October 1965, pp. 70–77.

Compensating Field Sales Representatives, The National Industrial Conference Board Studies in Personnel Policy, no. 202, 1966.

Dolson, Arden J., "Making the Most of Inside Salesmen," *Industrial Marketing*, October 1965, pp. 83–85.

"Fauver Finds a Cure for Chaos," *Industrial Distribution*, January 1966, pp. 60–61.

McMurray, Robert N., "Sell More with Fewer Salesmen," *Nation's Business*, June 1966, pp. 96–100.

"What Are the Best Sales Aids for Industrial Salesmen?" *Industrial Marketing*, October 1965, pp. 96–98.

CHAPTER EIGHT

Governmental/Defense/ Space Marketing

(Four businessmen, experienced in this area, joined forces with the author to create this chapter. Their combined knowledge and thinking produced this realistic treatment. They are: Gordon W. Benoit, Manager—Marketing; John F. McNeill, Manager—Sales; William W. Poorman, Manager—Contracts; and Norman J. Cardinal, Specialist—Marketing Planning, all of the Undersea Electronics Programs, Heavy Military Electronic Systems, General Electric Company.)

It is expected that there may not be complete agreement with the separation of governmental/defense/space into a third major segment of marketing, as was discussed in Chapter One. The problem similarities within, but differences between, segments as a basis for such segmentation is completely valid; it is the application that can produce a range of differing conclusions.

The reason is that the governmental market should never be envisioned as a special entity, characterized by a special set of problems. It is, in fact, a broad spectrum of environments, considerations, reasons for purchase, and products. Even the significance of the major marketing factors is a variable within it.

At one end of the spectrum one sees a very close similarity to a duplication of industrial marketing. For example, in selling standardized hardware products, and in selling highly standardized equipment such as trucks and air compressors to political entities below the federal level (to counties, cities, or towns), the involvement approximates very closely an industrial sale. Specifications, price, availability for prompt delivery, service, and personal salesmanship are key factors, as in an industrial sale.

When one refers to the governmental market, even the military portion, part of the uses for a good can be for special purposes and part for routine, industrylike purposes. For example, a truck for combat use will be designed to cover rough terrain. A truck for routine hauling of supplies from warehouse to depot will be standard, except for the coat of paint.

At the other end of the spectrum, there exist highly specialized circumstances, a completely differentiated set of conditions. Here one finds defense marketing. In between are many other entities, with considerable variation not only in what they buy, but in the considerations for purchase, in the composition of the buying influentials, and in the many intangibles involved in the purchase decision. This variation in total involvement, both among major governmental entities and also within each, presents a problem in depth to learn the ramifications and complex of variables appropriate to each.

A major objective of this chapter is to identify and discuss the key factors of this total involvement. As a start, Table 8.1 has been prepared to help show some of the differences in procurement by selected major governmental entities.

This table is intended to be indicative of the wide range of products and services sold to the government. At the same time, it suggests that, to a major extent, but not completely, a given type may be purchased by only one or two entities. The table is not complete—it is but a start. However, it does form an approach. The blanks mean that either this is a relatively minor activity or that type of purchasing is handled through the General Services Administration. A seller might expand the list of governmental entities and place his own products where they fit in the matrix. Once so completed, it would provide a guide to the specific entities to be approached, as well as an indication of both competitive and noncompetitive products being sold. This is but a start, a broad perspective, but it is a start toward the identification and appreciation of the involvement of his governmental marketing situation(s).

A DESCRIPTION OF THE MARKET

Taken as a whole, the government as a customer is by far the largest procurer of goods in the world. There is almost no commodity, product,

TABLE 8.1 Examples of Product Groups Purchased by Selected Government Entities

Type of product/ services \ Governmental entities	Dept. of Defense	National Aeronautics & Space Admin.	General Services Admin.	Dept. of Transportation including U.S. Coast Guard and FAA	Dept. of Commerce	Depts. of Health, Educ., & Welfare and Housing & Urban Develop.	Many other diverse procuring agencies and authorities
Commodities	Food, basic metals, petroleum products	General supplies	Paper, chemicals, lumber	Petroleum products	Paper		
Low technology	Shoes, clothing		Small hand tools, elec. appliances, services: guards, janitors, etc.				
Standard	Noncombatant materials-handling equip. and vehicles	Parts	Office equip., automobiles, trucks, commercial vehicles	Airport lighting, fire-fighting equip.		Financial aid	Medical supplies
Specialized	Operational vehicles, military computers, engineering consulting	Parts, engineering consulting	General-purpose computers, machine tools	Communication equip.	Printing presses	Modular housing	Power generation equip., medicines
High technology	Combatant aircraft and ships, scientific research, radar, sonar, weapons	Spacecraft, communication equip., scientific research	None	SST, high-speed ground transportation, airspace, marine navigation equip.	Oceanographic devices, weather satellites	Medical research, environmental research	Atomic energy research

or service which is not purchased by some branch of the government—and usually in substantial quantities. This means that every manufacturer has an opportunity to sell to the government if he chooses. However, it is not the standard commercial product purchased by the government which makes governmental/defense/space marketing deserve special treatment. That is not far removed from industrial. It is the specialized and high-technology products and services, covered by detailed government specifications, that differ. Their procurement is regulated by untold numbers of laws and regulations, oftentimes contradicting and confusing. Even their sale is rarely of a finished product as much as it is of an acceptable capability to produce one.

The governmental market is large. Just how large can be quantitatively evaluated by referring to Figure 8.1. This shows the total actual expenditures of the federal government over the period 1960–1970 and estimates the expenditures for the period 1970–1975. The four groupings of functions, human resources, physical resources, national defense, and other, are the groupings used in constructing the budget for fiscal year 1971.

As a rough approximation it may be assumed that presently about 25 percent of this $200 billion is spent for goods and services as opposed to transfer payments, grants-in-aid, subsidies, interest, and salaries and wages paid to its own employees, both civil and military. This, then, is the size of the federal government market. It can also be assumed that state and local governments would expend an equal amount, thereby

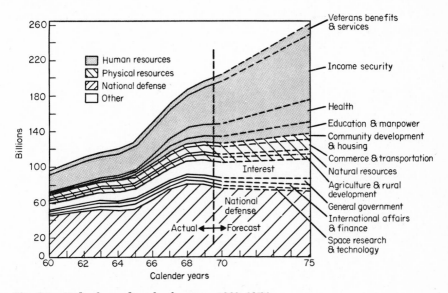

Fig. 8.1 Federal spending, by function, 1960–1975.

setting the total governmental market in 1970 at approximately $100 billion.

Figure 8.1 also shows that between 1960 and 1970 federal spending increased by 198 percent. During the same period, growth in spending for national defense was 64 percent. Health expenditures, though relatively small in 1960, increased by 1,631 percent, and education and manpower spending by 462 percent. It may be noted that even though the projection from 1970 to 1975 indicates an increase to $263 billion in 1975, national defense spending is expected to be lower. The large increase over this period is expected to be in human resources—from $79 billion to $122 billion in 1975, an increase of 57 percent.

In theory, the federal government is a monopsony, a single buyer. In practice, the "customer" is many people, representing diverse interests, differentiated organization and procedures, and with the implemental entities a completely separated structure from the financial. Then, too, they are constantly changing, in part a result of shifting political influences; also, reorganizations and changing philosophies of operations occur as top men change.

From the standpoint of doing business with the federal government, it is a vast structure, so vast as to be awesome. It is organized, on paper. It is confusing, with a myriad of intertwining and frequently overlapping interests. Beneath the surface a well-oiled machine might be expected to be uncovered, once one penetrates the confusion. This is false. The confusion is the reality.

There is no effective centralization of authority. There are many people who can kill a procurement, but no one man who can cause it to happen. It is essential to know who the key people are, to attempt to influence them before the cutoff time, and this calls for considerable lead time, or a continuous operation. The most powerful man is the one who initiates. Others simply impede or promote it—and an unidentified impediment can be fatal. Therefore, it is essential to have friendly relations, coupled, it is hoped, with confidence and respect, at all levels.

In much industrial marketing, and in governmental below the federal level, many sales are made on a personal basis to but one person, or at the most, a small number of people. Pricing, low bidding, specifications, past performance, and so on are involved. But the determination is in the hands of a few key men, who tend to remain fixed in their positions of influence over a considerable time period.

The problem in defense marketing is that the organization is so complex, there are so many more persons to be identified, the influentials and decision makers are more diffuse, their influences are more pervasive, and there are almost constant changes within the organizational structure.

All this is to say, know your customer. This is fundamental. In governmental marketing it is simply more involved. To complicate matters further, it is also necessary to learn how each individual and organizational group operates—not how the book says they operate, but how they really do.

The major governmental entities differ materially in the various organizations within the services, in the way they operate, in their emphasis upon different interests, and therefore in the effectiveness of a given approach. This needs to be tailored by a current awareness of the customer's objectives—frequently a multifaceted set of criteria.

DEPARTMENT OF DEFENSE (DOD) PROCUREMENT

Phases

Until such time as a worldwide arms ban is effectively implemented, the Department of Defense must have the best weapons and advanced systems our economy can produce for our national security.

Such weapon systems do not come into being overnight. They require time, substantial financial investment, research and developmental capability, productive and managerial capability, and a fantastic ability to estimate costs several years in advance in the face of unknowns. These unknowns encompass technological developments anticipated and planned to be resolved—and the unanticipated unknowns, those which are not or cannot be foreseen at the inception of the task, but which are bound to occur in reality.

A major problem in estimating cost is the potential existence of the unknowns, the unanticipated, the problems which cannot be foreseen in the conceptualization stage of development. Add to this competitive bidding, a fixed-price contract for the total system's package, and the prime contractor is in a position of assuming great risks, with but a limited profit. The Renegotiation Board takes care of that, in its recovery of any profits it deems to be excessive.

The DOD procurement process is divided into four phases. Hudson B. Drake identifies them as[1]

1. Concept Formulation.
2. Contract Definition.
3. Engineering Development.
4. Production and Operation.

[1] Hudson B. Drake, "Major DOD Procurements at War with Reality," *Harvard Business Review,* January-February 1970, pp. 127–128.

The most critical juncture between these arbitrary phases, so far as unanticipated unknowns are concerned, is the one between Contract Definition and Engineering Development, hence I shall be most concerned with this juncture and with the contract signed immediately after it— namely the fixed-price contract for the subsequent Engineering Development and Production & Operation phases. To appreciate the forces that operate at this juncture, one must understand exactly what information this contract is supposed to contain. Succinctly, it is the documented performance requirements and/or physical characteristics which define a system and its hardware end items. This documentation constitutes the technical requirements to be written into the contract.

The AIA group developed its findings about unanticipated unknowns by identifying all the basic steps involved in the development of weapon systems. That is, drawing on direct experience with real programs such as Minuteman, C-5A, T-38, and the VELA spacecraft, they identified the activities that were common to all of them. The study also reached two conclusions:

Industry handles the anticipated unknown well. It has well-developed procedures for analysis and planning, determination and allocation of system and subsystem performance parameters, error budgeting, scheduling, and so forth.

Unanticipated unknowns are another matter. Many factors affecting system performance and schedule cannot be forecasted at all, or cannot be forecasted with adequate confidence on the basis of paper designs and analytical studies. For example, hardware performance is seldom, if ever, absolutely certain until after the hardware has actually been built and tested. There are many causes for this: mutual interference (aerodynamic, electronic, and so forth), environmental conditions (especially in combination), sequence-sensitive effects, combined stress, and others.

He concludes:[2]

What is really needed is reformed policy that includes viable estimating procedures and a procurement policy for major-system acquisitions that is consistent with the technical development process and the evolution of a sound technical baseline on which to formulate realistic estimates of cost and schedule.

This problem of packaged procurement and contract applicability is recognized. It will continue to command attention by both government and contractor. One thing is certain—there will continue to be changes, revisions, and it is hoped, improvement.

[2] Ibid., p. 140.

Regulations

Another characteristic of the defense market which differs sharply from the industrial is the wide variety of contracting regulations used by the government agencies. These have been instigated to develop the facts, in order to be sure of the complete legality of every transaction. Many regulations provide for fine or imprisonment of any individual who actually does something contrary to what he has certified. By requiring certifications of fact, the offender can be prosecuted under federal law, not only for violating the law, but also for fraud.

General government procurement is governed by the Federal Procurement Regulations. Department of Defense procurement is governed by the Armed Services Procurement Regulations (ASPR). Space procurement is governed by the National Aeronautics and Space Administration Procurement Regulations. DOD's regulations (ASPR) are actually a series of fairly large volumes—about 3 feet of linear bookshelf space.

Figure 8.2 indicates some of the representations to be made. Note, for example, number 3 relative to payment to others to help obtain the business involved. This seeks to prevent the use of the "5 to 10 percenters," the influence peddlers. There are many other representations required relative to the accuracy of cost information submitted.

Methods of Procurement by Federal Agencies

Formal Advertised Procurement The congressionally specified preferred method of procurement is by formal advertising. This can be a misleading term. It refers to a specific method of procurement and does not include other procurements, even though they may be advertised.

In a formal advertised procurement, the government issues an IFB, or Invitation for Bid. This requests a fixed-price bid and does not require any breakdown of costs or supporting data. On the standard government bid form there are two blocks, one, RFP or RFQ (used interchangeably), if the procurement is to be negotiated, and the other, IFB, if the procurement is "advertised." If checked IFB, the sealed bid will be opened publicly. To be acceptable, one must comply in every respect with the bid request with no deviations as to delivery or to the product delivered. It may not be qualified in any way, or it will be rejected as nonresponsive. At the public opening, anyone present may examine any or all bids and may request copies of them as well. Procurement on a formally advertised basis accounts for 11 percent of the Department of Defense's total dollar volume.[3]

---

[3] *Defense Industry Profit Study,* a report to the Congress by the Comptroller General of the United States, B-159896, Washington, D.C., Mar. 17, 197', p. 3.

F42   30 September 1970, Rev. 8

ILLUSTRATIONS OF STANDARD AND DEPARTMENT OF DEFENSE FORMS REFERENCED IN ASPR

F–100.33 *Standard Form 33: Solicitation, Offer, and Award*—Continued

REPRESENTATIONS, CERTIFICATIONS, AND ACKNOWLEDGMENTS

The Offeror represents and certifies as part of his offer that: *(Check or complete all applicable boxes or blocks)*

1. SMALL BUSINESS *(See par. 14 on SF 33–A.)*
He ☐ is, ☐ is not, a small business concern. If offeror is a small business concern and is not the manufacturer of the supplies offered, he also represents that all supplies to be furnished hereunder ☐ will, ☐ will not, be manufactured or produced by a small business concern in the United States, its possessions, or Puerto Rico.

2. REGULAR DEALER—MANUFACTURER *(Applicable only to supply contracts exceeding $10,000)*
He is a ☐ regular dealer in, ☐ manufacturer of, the supplies offered.

3. CONTINGENT FEE *(See par. 15 on SF 33–A.)*
(a) He ☐ has, ☐ has not, employed or retained any company or person *(other than a full-time, bona fide employee working solely for the offeror)* to solicit or secure this contract, and (b) he ☐ has, ☐ has not, paid or agreed to pay any company or person *(other than a full-time bona fide employee working solely for the offeror)* any fee, commission, percentage, or brokerage fee contingent upon or resulting from the award of this contract; and agrees to furnish information relating to (a) and (b) above, as requested by the Contracting Officer. *(For interpretation of the representation, including the term "bona fide employee," see Code of Federal Regulations, Title 41, Subpart 1–1.5)*

4. TYPE OF BUSINESS ORGANIZATION
He operates as ☐ an individual, ☐ a partnership, ☐ a nonprofit organization, ☐ a corporation, incorporated under the laws of the State of

5. AFFILIATION AND IDENTIFYING DATA *(Applicable only to advertised solicitations.)*
Each offeror shall complete (a) and (b) if applicable, and (c) below:
(a) He ☐ is, ☐ is not, owned or controlled by a parent company. *(See par. 16 on SF 33–A.)*
(b) If the offeror is owned or controlled by a parent company, he shall enter in the blocks below the name and main office address of the parent company:
Name of Parent company and main office address _____
(include ZIP Code)_____
(c) Employer's identification number *(See par. 17 on SF 33–A.)*_____
                    (Offeror's E.I. No.)   *(Parent Company's E.I. No.)*

6. EQUAL OPPORTUNITY
He ☐ has, ☐ has not, participated in a previous contract or subcontract subject either to the Equal Opportunity clause herein or the clause originally contained in section 301 of Executive Order No. 10925, or the clause contained in section 201 of Executive Order No. 11114; that he ☐ has, ☐ has not, filed all required compliance reports, and that representations indicating submission of required compliance reports, signed by proposed subcontractors, will be obtained prior to subcontract awards. *(The above representation need not be submitted in connection with contracts or subcontracts which are exempt from the clause)*

7. BUY AMERICAN CERTIFICATE
The offeror hereby certifies that each end product, except the end products listed below, is a domestic source end product *(as defined in the clause entitled Buy American Act")*; and that components of unknown origin have been considered to have been mined, produced, or manufactured outside the United States.

EXCLUDED END PRODUCTS	COUNTRY OF ORIGIN

8. CERTIFICATION OF INDEPENDENT PRICE DETERMINATION *(See par. 18 on SF 33–A.)*
(a) By submission of this offer, the offeror certifies, and in the case of a joint offer, each party thereto certifies as to its own organization, that in connection with this procurement:
(1) The prices in this offer have been arrived at independently, without consultation, communication, or agreement, for the purpose of restricting competition, as to any matter relating to such prices with any other offeror or with any competitor;
(2) Unless otherwise required by law, the prices which have been quoted in this offer have not been knowingly disclosed by the offeror and will not knowingly be disclosed by the offeror prior to opening in the case of an advertised procurement or prior to award in the case of a negotiated procurement, directly or indirectly to any other offeror or to any competitor; and
(3) No attempt has been made or will be made by the offeror to induce any other person or firm to submit or not to submit an offer for the purpose of restricting competition.
(b) Each person signing this offer certifies that:
(1) He is the person in the offeror's organization responsible within that organization for the decision as to the prices being offered herein and that he has not participated, and will not participate, in any action contrary to (a) (1) through (a) (3) above; or
(2) (i) He is not the person in the offeror's organization responsible within that organization for the decision as to the prices being offered herein but that he has been authorized in writing to act as agent for the persons responsible for such decision in certifying that such persons have not participated, and will not participate, in any action contrary to (a) (1) through (a) (3) above, and as their agent does hereby so certify; and (ii) he has not participated, and will not participate, in any action contrary to (a) (1) through (a) (3) above.

9. CERTIFICATION OF NONSEGREGATED FACILITIES
(Applicable to (1) contracts, (2) subcontracts, and (3) agreements with applicants who are themselves performing federally assisted construction contracts, exceeding $10,000 which are not exempt from the provisions of the Equal Opportunity clause.)
By the submission of this bid, the bidder, offeror, applicant, or subcontractor certifies that he does not maintain or provide for his employees any segregated facilities at any of his establishments, and that he does not permit his employees to perform their services at any location, under his control, where segregated facilities are maintained. He certifies further that he will not maintain or provide for his employees any segregated facilities at any of his establishments, and that he will not permit his employees to perform their services at any location, under his control, where segregated facilities are maintained. The bidder, offeror, applicant, or subcontractor agrees that a breach of this certification is a violation of the Equal Opportunity clause in this contract. As used in this certification, the term "segregated facilities" means any waiting rooms, work areas, rest rooms and wash rooms, restaurants and other eating areas, time clocks, locker rooms and other storage or dressing areas, parking lots, drinking fountains, recreation or entertainment areas, transportation, and housing facilities provided for employees which are segregated by explicit directive or are in fact segregated on the basis of race, color, religion or national origin, because of habit, local custom, or otherwise. He further agrees that (except where he has obtained identical certifications from proposed subcontractors for specific time periods) he will obtain identical certifications from proposed subcontractors prior to the award of subcontracts exceeding $10,000 which are not exempt from the provisions of the Equal Opportunity clause; that he will retain such certifications in his files; and that he will forward the following notice to such proposed subcontractors (except where the proposed subcontractors have submitted identical certifications for specific time periods): *Notice to prospective subcontractors of requirement for certifications of nonsegregated facilities.*
A Certification of Nonsegregated Facilities must be submitted prior to the award of a subcontract exceeding $10,000 which is not exempt from the provisions of the Equal Opportunity clause. The certification may be submitted either for each subcontract or for all subcontracts during a period (i.e., quarterly, semiannually, or annually.) NOTE: *The penalty for making false statements in offers is prescribed in 18 U.S.C. 1001.*

ACKNOWLEDGMENT OF AMENDMENTS ⁝g offeror acknowledges receipt of amendments • the Solicitation for Offers and related documents numbered and dated as follows:	AMENDMENT NO.	DATE	AMENDMENT NO.	DATE

NOTE.—Offers must set forth full, accurate, and complete information as required by this Solicitation (including attachments) The penalty for making false statements in offers is prescribed in 18 U.S.C. 1001

15129   REVERSE OF STANDARD FORM 33, NOVEMBER 1969   ⋆ U S GOVERNMENT PRINTING OFFICE 1970 OF—390–455 (11X)

Fig. 8.2 (*Source: F-100.33 Armed Services Procurement Regulation.*)

Negotiated Procurement The second major category of procurement is negotiated. This may or may not be competitive. It will probably be publicized in that almost all procurement actions under any federal agency are publicized in the *Commerce Business Daily*, a newspaper issued by the Department of Commerce.

In negotiated procurement, cost and pricing data must be submitted, and most often, certified. The terms and conditions of the contract may be negotiated, provided the essential purposes of the procurement are maintained and there is no significant deviation in the time of performance. The specifics of the product may be varied during the negotiation, if the technical groups within the government and the contracting officer wish to allow it.

Whenever a negotiated procurement is competitive, the government must state the evaluation criteria which will be used to determine the successful bidder. The successful bidder need not have submitted the lowest price. In negotiated procurements there are many types and subtypes of contracts. The two principal types are fixed price, with its variations, and cost reimbursement, of which there are also several variations. Cost-reimbursement contracts provide for government reimbursement of the contractor's actual direct and indirect costs, as such costs are defined and allowable according to the Armed Services Procurement Regulations (ASPR).

Variations of these contain additional incentives for meeting performance criteria. The first government incentive contract relative to performance was written with the Wright Brothers. The government paid a stipulated number of dollars per mile for every mile per hour the airplane flew faster than specified and penalized them so many dollars per mile for every mile per hour the airplane performed under its specified speed.

In cases where the government and the contractor feel that it is virtually impossible to measure the contractor's performance in terms of any kind of a predetermined formula, a cost-plus-award-fee contract (CPAF) may be used. The dollar limits of the award fee to be paid are pre-established during the contract negotiation. In this case the government evaluates the contractor's performance after the fact in terms of his responsiveness, his ability to meet the original requirements of the contract, his management efficiency, and his cost efficiency. Although there are predetermined ground rules established as evaluation criteria, there is no rigorous formula to apply in making the award determination. There is also no appeal from the ruling.

Some fixed-price contracts utilize escalation clauses in determining the final price to be paid. In this way the contractor may be insulated from the economic fluctuations of price changes of a commodity he cannot control, such as steel. The escalation provisions may also be made to apply to fluctuations of labor costs.

If the contractor is an industrial concern as opposed to an educational or a nonprofit institution, the government will pay a fee for his efforts in addition to reimbursing him for his actual costs. This may be a fixed-dollar fee which will not vary regardless of the costs incurred in the performance of the contract. Or, it may be an incentive fee, where the fee will be diminished as the costs of performance go up, and increased as performance costs go down from some preagreed target cost. The former are called "cost-plus-fixed-fee" (CPFF) contracts, and the latter are called "cost-plus-incentive-fee" (CPIF) contracts.

In the fixed-price category, the firm-fixed-price contract is the simplest. A specified price is paid for the work performed regardless of the contractor's actual costs. A variation of the firm-fixed-price is the fixed-price-incentive contract, wherein the government will share the overrun, or underrun, if any, from the estimated and agreed target-cost figure. The essential difference between the FPI (fixed-price-incentive) and the CPIF contract is that the FPI contract has a ceiling beyond which the government will not share any of the additional costs. Generally, FPI contracts have a nearly equal sharing of over- or underrun costs between the contractor and the government. In CPIF contracts the share ratio places the largest share with the government, which may pay 90 percent of the overrun with the contractor paying 10 percent. If there is an underrun, the contractor would get 10 percent and the government would keep 90 percent.

In the incentive form of contracts, delivery is frequently used as a base for some of the incentive. The contractor is paid a reward for early delivery or suffers a penalty for late delivery. The government may, when delivery is very important, invoke a predetermined penalty in firm-fixed-price contracts for late delivery. This provision is generally referred to as a "liquidated-damages clause." Although this provision can cause a loss to the contractor if he delivers late, it should be noted that it does establish a limit on his liability and protects him from being sued for actual damages, which could be significantly greater.

Still another form of contracting used in the scientific area is very close to a research-type grant. In this case the government may buy the services of a group of engineers or scientists for a fixed dollar amount for a specified period of time to investigate some particular subject. This is usually a short-term contract, but on a fixed-price basis for ease of administration. The commodity being bought is simply scientific effort.

Another contract variation is a cross between a fixed-price contract and a cost-reimbursement contract. It is the labor-hour-time-materials contract. Fixed-price labor rates are set forth in the contract. The contractor is paid at this fixed-price rate for the effort worked. This kind of contract is used when the amount of time and the amount of material to be used is not, or cannot be, predetermined. Since the risk to the contractor is low, the profit rate is also commensurately low.

In a negotiated procurement, as opposed to an IFB or formal advertised procurement, the type of contract is also negotiable. Although the selection of the contract type is supposed to reflect the proper risk and should relate to the ability to accurately estimate the cost of performance, there are often political and competitive pressures which have an influence on the selection. If, for instance, a competitor is willing to assume a high risk and accept a fixed-price contract, this may make it impossible to win if you are willing to accept only a cost-reimbursement type.

The general rule in negotiated procurement is that the type of contract should be consistent with the party's ability to foresee costs and problems that will be encountered in the performance of the contract. The government, as a matter of policy (which it sometimes violates), generally takes the attitude that the contractor should not be given a contract form that would make him responsible for risks that he cannot control or cannot reasonably foresee. Therefore, contracts for something of a highly developmental nature, requiring invention or a large amount of innovation, would probably be of a CPFF or CPIF type. If, however, the contract were for a repeat production of an item that had been previously produced, even though it is a highly complex item, it would probably be of a firm-fixed-price or fixed-price-incentive type with a high share ratio and a low ceiling price. The contractor's ability to accurately predict the cost of the item is a factor, probably the determining factor, in the type of contract that will be used. Along with the contractor's ability to forecast his costs is the credibility of those costs to the government auditor. If the government auditors don't feel the cost forecasts are supportable, they will probably object to a type of contract under which the contractor might make a windfall profit. In the absence of strong effective competition, the government is generally very concerned about its ability to recapture anything which it considers to be a windfall or excess profits.

A popular misconception of a negotiated procurement is that it is done in secret. In fact, it is almost always publicized in the *Federal Register* or in the *Commerce Business Daily*. Another fallacy is the feeling that it is always of a cost-reimbursement type. Cost plus percentage of cost is an illegal form of contract, including any contract that takes on the aspects of cost plus percentage costs—that is, when the contractor's profit actually increases when additional costs are incurred. Such a contract, if discovered, will be declared nul and void and abrogated by the Comptroller General. The consequences of an illegal contract such as this would be no reimbursement of cost to the contractor.

The Armed Services Procurement Regulation sets forth a detailed

TABLE 8.2

SOURCE: *Armed Services Procurement Regulation.*

list of clauses for use in drafting contracts.   These are grouped by type of contract and list both those required and those for use when applicable.   Table 8.2 illustrates one page of the index of the ASPR.

SUBCONTRACTING

Selling to prime contractors who are dealing with the government is, in most respects, very similar to selling to a large industrial customer who is not a prime to the government.   However, in "subcontracting," where the goods involved become a part of the prime contractor's sale to the government, the contract will contain many of the same terms, conditions, and restrictions by which the prime contractor is bound.

This happens in part because the prime contract with the government states that certain conditions will be passed down to subcontractors. Another reason, and perhaps the major one, is that the prime contractor does not want to assume a responsibility for the subcontractor's non-compliance. To protect himself, the prime inserts the same provisions in the subcontract that are placed on him in the prime contract.

Thus, some of the conditions imposed on the subcontractor are absolutely mandatory, and some are a result of the prime protecting himself—which he will surely do, if he has any sense.

Sometimes the selling by the subcontractor is actually done directly to the Department of Defense, even though the purchase will be made by a prime contractor. The subcontractor seeks to create a demand for his goods or services by the final customer. If the "selling" is successful, the government may request or direct the prime contractor to subcontract to the "preferred" supplier.

It is almost always advantageous to be the prime contractor. However, because of facility limitations and other such considerations, there is frequently a sharing of a major contract between leading competitive firms by subcontract. This is advantageous, both for the government in expediting delivery and for the firms. An example might be the subcontracting of a fuselage section by one airplane manufacturer to another.

Another aspect of subcontracting is in the creation of teams. For example, ABC electronics might team with aircraft manufacturer X to supply the electronics as a package for their aircraft, whereas MNO electronics might team with aircraft manufacturer Y to do the same thing. If X gets the job, so does ABC, and MNO is out.

It is, of course, very desirable to be in the position of being the only supplier of a particular product, perhaps because of some unique feature. In such a case, regardless of who obtains the prime contract in which this product is used, the subcontract would be awarded to this "sole source" supplier.

PRICING

In the case of the formal advertised procurement, the contractor can price at any level of profit he wishes. Of course, if the price is too high, he won't receive the order. In fact, competitive bidding is quite effective in driving the price down, unless the bidder has a unique product.

In the case of the negotiated procurement, there are fairly restrictive regulations and measures that the government employs to restrict profit. On any procurement over $100,000 the contractor is required to set forth in great detail his predicted, estimated costs and to certify the accuracy of the cost and the pricing data on which the costs are based. The contract will then contain provisions which state that if any misrepresentation or error is found to exist, the government will reduce the contract price by the amount of that error or misrepresentation. The government is not even required to go into court to recover from such errors, since the data has been previously certified. The government also has definite guidelines which it applies in setting acceptable profit rates, and these are comparatively low.

In addition to the 11 percent of DOD procurement covered by formal advertising, negotiated procurement using price competition amounts to 27 percent.[4]

ADVERTISING

Advertising is a basic tool for developing awareness, at least, by most industrial manufacturer-sellers. In the governmental area it is less valuable and is officially discouraged. Even though this does not alter the basic need to develop both awareness and a favorable attitude, advertising suffers in that it is considered to be a nonreimbursable expense, and it cannot be included in allocated overhead. If used at all, it must come out of profit. Advertising expense to recruit personnel is the one exception which is allowed as a legitimate expense.

Even though the Internal Revenue Service recognizes advertising as a legitimate business expense, the military disallows it in any contract which is subject to audit or cost reimbursement.

Interestingly enough, in spite of this accounting restriction, the government indirectly requires the contractor to advertise. This comes about through mutuality of interest in public acceptance of defense programs. For example, describing the merits of a sonar in advertising would be highly questionable as to its effect on producing sales; but the message conveyed to the public is institutional and seeks to develop better public relations for both the customer, the government, and the firm. However, this in no way changes the fact that the cost is disallowed as a business expense.

The 5 to 10 Percenters

Not too many years ago, a firm seeking to find entrance into government business might have employed a professional to provide guidance to the right people, open doors, and aid in persuasion. Such professionals

---

[4] Drake, op. cit., p. 3.

peddled influence as well as knowledge, and typically charged 5 to 10 percent for their services. It was a way of becoming known, obtaining identification of buying influentials, and getting one's story told.

Today, the influence-peddling business, at least on a contingency-commission basis by professionals, not full-time corporate employees, is far less. Its use is not prohibited, but, if it is used, a full disclosure to the procuring agency of the individual, the circumstances of his retention, and the amount he was paid must be made. A bona fide, full-time employee of the corporation can be paid on a salary or commission basis. Any manufacturer who seeks to do much business with the government will have on his payroll people whose job it is to gather information needed for corporate planning, to help identify buying influentials, and to help get the firm's story across. This is perfectly legitimate, and necessary.

PLANNING IN GOVERNMENTAL MARKETING

Marketing planning with respect to governmental marketing is just as important to business success as marketing planning in industrial endeavors. However, in governmental, it tends to be done on a more informal basis than is usually the case when dealing in strictly industrial products.

One reason lies in the very nature of the marketing task, with more face-to-face confrontations and more oral communication. Another factor is the difference in involvement and performance of marketing functions. While these functions retain the same titles, they differ so significantly from their counterparts in the consumer and industrial areas as to be almost unrelatable. For example, service becomes logistics, sales become almost exclusively application engineering, and order service becomes contract administration. Market research involves itself in geopolitics, military missions, war, defense and space budgets, and the latest technological developments of the enemy.

In defense marketing, the requirement to sell the latest technological developments introduces a corollary—very rapid obsolescence. Marketing is most intimately related to the future, as against simply present products. This is to say that research, development, product planning, and technological capability are the critical forces to keep the firm competitive.

An illustration of the reality and significance of this intimate relationship between marketing and the future-oriented forces of research, development, product planning, and technology, formulated into a long-range strategy, may be helpful. This is a case of a company which recognized a future need and the fact that there might not be very much competition in that particular market. In the early days of the threat of Russian missile firing, it was determined that an intercontinental ballistic missile could be fired from Russia to the United States. Obviously, the problem of detection of such a missile after it is on its way was a severe but most important one. At the time, it was likened to looking for a golf ball 3,000 miles away. This analogy was drawn from the facts that the nose cone of a missile is very small, and its vast speed requires detection a long ways away—if anything is to be done about it in time.

Marketing planning recognized this as a really serious problem. The General Electric Company, on its own, decided to study the problem. The first step was to try to relate as best it could all the known technology relative to radar and the physical phenomena. It assembled a large group of capable individuals to do this study. It contracted with the government to do this for $1—in order to establish credibility for the work and to tap whatever classified information that might be available.

As a result, GE became a leader very early in the game and eventually sold and installed high-power radars in the North looking toward Russia to detect missile firing.

Identification of Needs: The Customer's Problems

In industry, it is not uncommon for customers to cooperatively provide sellers with data on the nature, quantity, and performance characteristics of their future needs. Similarly, in the defense business, if we were trying to sell antiballistic-missile defense systems, for example, ideally we would like to go to the Russians, the Chinese Communists, or whomever, and find out their deployment system, the technological facets, and performance characteristics of their ballistic-missile system. Obviously, this kind of cooperation is not available, as it would be industrially to help design a new power plant for a public utility.

So, the task of defining and projecting today a product that may be needed some years in the future is much more difficult. Implicit in this is security, even in our own country. One must safeguard such developments, even though they are a long way from production.

These, then, are some of the problems and attendant responsibilities of the market researcher and product planner in the defense area. Realistically, the demand for defense goods is derived from the needs of the future. The sonars and radars to be put on ships projected to be built in the future are somewhat a function of the type of ship, large and multipurpose, or small, swift, and specialized. And this, in turn, is a function of both the military and political analyses of future military missions.

The researcher must postulate what the outside threat to the United States is and will be. Then, the determination of how best to counter that threat must be made. The range can be all the way from guerrilla warfare to atomic missiles. In short, the problem starts with the knowledge of war—and particularly, war in the future.

The next step is to attempt to analyze what the military problems are going to be. Does the military already have the devices necessary to solve the problems that will be posed to it by the enemy or the threat? And if not, what are all the alternative approaches that could be used to solve these problems? With that as part of the input, the next step is to make an analysis of what the customer's resources are going to be, his likely budget. There's no point in devising a $10 million solution if he's only going to have half a million dollars to spend. This requires a knowledge of national priorities and resource allocation.

Approaches to Problem Solutions

Once the potential seller has postulated the military missions of the future, the problems to be faced, and their potential alternative solutions, then he must make a decision as to his approach to filling that need. Because of the substantial costs involved, it becomes most impractical to pursue all the different possible solutions at the same time. So, a choice must be made. He must pick his horse and ride it—put his money and effort on it. This provides the direction for the firm's research and developmental effort. It is hoped that the result will enable the firm to compete successfully. It cannot be a "so-so" solution to be sold via promotion and salesmanship, as might be done to ultimate customers. Here, it just won't be good enough. And financing this effort is apt to cost the firm a great deal of money.

Sales Planning

As part of the preparation for sales planning, the person or office which officially established the customer requirement needs to be identified. This is but a start. One entity will officially establish the requirements, but there are many other persons or organizations which will influence the final decision. These need to be identified, too, for they are a significant part of the total sales picture.

Ultimately, once the solution has been picked and the buying influentials are known, the strategy to be followed to convince the customer must be planned. It might be decided to present the firm's solution as the best—most competent—one, in the area of performance. It might be because it is unique. Or, it might be decided to sell the firm as the best source. It might be presented on the basis of a proved and credible solution as against something else perhaps more unique, but only on paper. Fast delivery may be a factor, if the problem is immediate. And, of course, the old price game may be played. These possibilities all interact. It is hoped the best combination will be selected and implemented.

In sales planning, two conflicting tendencies within the governmental complex (the customer) need recognition. One is a conservative group which does not want to use anything that has not been previously proved. The extremists within this group may demand such proof over a considerable period of time and under all possible circumstances. They would still be fighting wars with muzzle loaders, since such weapons cannot jam. Then there is the opposite group which always sees something better on paper. This group will always be working on the latest fantastic device, designing and redesigning, but never producing a product. The practical contractor cannot afford either extreme. He must produce a working product, incorporating reasonable progress and having a high likelihood of success while avoiding stagnation of the tools of warfare.

Another major facet in product and sales planning is the impact of political change within the time period involved. The administration can change readily after an election. Although procurements are most often implemented on a five-year defense program, and a contractor may be working on a product that takes four years to develop, a change in administration may negate the need for that product entirely. For example, for many years large surface ships were demanded. Equipment must be designed and built for such vessels. Now, with a change in administration, the smaller, faster ships are wanted. One administration may prefer reliability and effective performance. The next may want to emphasize low cost and be willing to accept somewhat lower performance levels as adequate to the probable need. No one wants the highest-cost solution. But there can be a great difference in opinion as to what constitutes the lowest-cost solution without sacrifice of capability. One aspect of this is the struggle between the multipurpose versus the specialized airplane. Which design is really better or cheaper in the long run is a rough problem to resolve to everyone's satisfaction, if, in fact, it can be resolved at all.

In short, and perhaps most fortunately, we have an extremely dynamic environment. The ground rules can change drastically and quickly. The demands upon the businessman include his ability to recognize and adapt quickly to change. Basically, this does not differ from the industrial environment. The real difference is in the degree. In the governmental environment the changes can come far faster and be more drastic. It is one way to remove the complacent—and quickly.

The Small Company

It should not be inferred that only the large, well-financed conglomerate can compete for government business. It is true that it has an advantage in being able to underwrite developmental costs. However, except for possible economies of scale, the advantage largely stops there. The smaller firm which keeps abreast of the technological developments can still compete for sales of the end product with its own capability.

The Department of Defense encourages such competition. It seeks to prevent any one firm from obtaining a monopoly in a given area. It can be, and has been, helpful to another company, large or small, to help that company become a viable competitor. The interests of both parties are served thereby.

Market Research

Market research in governmental marketing differs significantly from that in the industrial area. It is heavily desk research of secondary data. The problem is to obtain, recognize, and analyze the multitude of data available relative to potential purchases by the federal, and other, governmental entities. Knowledge of the sources becomes a very valuable asset to the researcher in this area. Even the *Congressional Record* can be of help. Some companies assemble and publish selected data as a service. A start and an indication of the scope of such sources are found in the "Relevant Reading" at the end of this chapter.

THE SALESMAN

There is no significant difference in characteristics between salesmen in the governmental area and their counterparts in the industrial. Both require skill in communication, empathy, capacity to motivate people, and the ability to command respect. The art of salesmanship does not differ.

The technological background and skills required of the industrial salesman have increased vastly over recent years. So, too, have they for the governmental salesman. There is little doubt but that this requirement is at its highest level in selling today's high-technology goods to industry or to the government. The salesman must not only know, but be able to communicate, comprehend, explore change in, and actively work with technical modifications on a par with his customer's specialist. Unless the salesman is capable of talking to the customer on equal terms with him, he will rapidly lose credibility with the customer.

Beyond this is yet another requirement. In defense marketing, the salesman is selling munitions, devices—the tools and equipment of war.

In order to discuss the uses and applications of such goods, the salesman must understand war.

The governmental salesman must be capable of rendering a service, not only to his customer, but also to his employer. He is, in effect, a communication link between them. Rarely is the sale one of a finished good, well established and with well-known characteristics which need simply demonstration and application. Particularly in the defense area, it is most apt to start with a concept on paper. This must be effectively communicated to the customer—and the customer's message, the customer's problems, effectively communicated to the company. This frequently involves communication not only with the customer's professional engineer, but also with the professional operator—for example, aeronautical engineers and fighter pilots.

In defense marketing, this selling of capacity and skills (including management as well as engineering or technical), as well as the ability to develop and actually produce a product, is perhaps the major difference between governmental and industrial marketing. It is very seldom that the industrial customer is primarily interested in his supplier's skills, as against the factors relating to the product, its cost, performance, etc. The military is often more interested in the contractor's skills than in any other factor.

Compensation of Salesmen

By far the most popular compensation plan for salesmen selling to the government is straight salary. There are many reasons for this. In the first place, the ultimate sale of a $100 million contract may have begun, really, with the $100,000 research contract, years before. Even the people may have changed in the meantime. To provide a commission or such on the big contract to the salesman writing it would be to reward him for the work of others—many others.

Selling to the government is teamwork, today. It calls for varying effort by different team members, depending upon the specifics of a situation. A lot of people are involved. Salary determination from evaluation of performance is fair to everyone concerned.

Further, there are external influences totally beyond the control of the entire team. Congress may decide to effect a change, for example. To reward or penalize for this would be unfair.

Since the governmental salesman's efforts cannot be tied directly to his closed sales, and since many other factors are involved, salary is preferred. The range in salary should provide a financial incentive. Evaluation of his performance, in terms of his effectiveness—and not merely his effort—provides a sound base for recognition and, it is hoped, raises.

GETTING ACQUAINTED: AN APPROACH TO GOVERNMENTAL/DEFENSE/SPACE MARKETING

What might the new man to this area do to become acquainted with it? How can he find his way around, develop a "feel," see where his interests fit, and learn enough to plan effectively? How long will this probably take?

Anyone new to governmental/defense/space marketing might contemplate with a feeling of trepidation the seemingly horrendous task of getting "in" in Washington. Admittedly, it can be extremely frustrating to merely knock on doors to try to learn the ropes. This will produce results—in development of patience, self-control, and an appreciation of the meaning of perseverance. Fortunately, there is a better way.

A good start is a little advance information, coupled with intelligent planning. The local library or the Government Printing Office can provide a handbook, about 1 inch thick, entitled *U.S. Government Organization Manual.* This is published annually. It describes in detail virtually every agency and department of the United States government—the role of each, their activities, and what their authority is. This can be put together with the government's budget (also obtainable from the Government Printing Office) and the congressional hearings. This should enable one to determine in a preliminary way which entities might represent a market for his goods.

The entities so identified can be the target for further, in-depth exploration and study. It should be noted that this should be done for each one, since they are very apt to differ considerably. It is almost impossible to characterize the buying habits of the government in any kind of standardized form, they differ so. They are only characterized by having a more or less uniform set of procurement regulations. Beyond that, how they buy, where they buy, and whether they buy locally or centrally vary as much as American industry's practices do. The Navy buys significantly differently from the Air Force or the Army.

Perhaps the next thing to do is to subscribe to the *Commerce Business Daily.* This is published by the Department of Commerce. It contains a synopsis of all contemplated government procurement, except a very few so highly classified that they are kept secret. Even records of classified contracts are published.

After a month's reading of the *Commerce Business Daily,* the potential salesman should be able to discern where the buying activities are located and which type of activities are buying commodities or products or services he is interested in selling. He must realize that the procurement agency that is shown as letting the contract is not necessarily the same group which established the requirement. It may be necessary to track it back further to determine that. As a start, the procuring agency, that is, the contracting officer, the negotiator, or the buyer, can be asked about the agency for which he is making the procurement. Travel will be involved. Individuals need to be seen and developed, as in any selling. But direction of effort, advance identification of people, can be very helpful. A full-time representative in Washington probably is not needed at the start. The important thing is to get acquainted with the key people in establishing the requirements to begin with and then those who influence the decision. Once this has been successfully accomplished, perhaps the next time around, he'll have the advance notice that is often so necessary to successfully sell to the government.

If the new man is based primarily in one geographical area, he can very often get help from his congressman. This should be used with care. If the congressman seeks to be an influence peddler for the firm, it may rebound to the firm's disadvantage. The working-level troops will probably react against that, and at the first opportunity, get even with the contractor. The congressman can help, and legitimately, by advising as to the people to see and in what agencies, and perhaps give him a boost by making an appointment for him.

Some congressmen in various areas hold symposiums in which they bring in government procurement agencies to tell small-business associations about pending procurements. These are listed in the *Commerce Business Daily*.

RELEVANT READING

Aerospace Daily, Washington, D.C.: Ziff-Davis Publishing Company. A daily publication of pertinent news reports for the aerospace and defense industries.

Camp Reports, New York: Frost & Sullivan, Inc. These are reports of market segments consisting of history and limited forecasting.

Commerce Business Daily, Washington, D.C.: U.S. Government Printing Office. This is a daily list of United States government procurement invitations, subcontracting leads, contract awards, sales of surplus property, and foreign business opportunities.

Defense Market Measures System, New York: Frost & Sullivan, Inc. This is a quarterly report of contract awards by contractors with cross-references available by type of equipment, awarding agency, or geographical area.

DMS (Defense Marketing Service), Greenwich, Conn.: McGraw-Hill Publications. This service consists of Defense Market Intelligence Reports compiled in the following titled volumes:

> *Defense Market*
> *Aerospace Agencies*
> *Missiles/Spacecraft*
> *Ships/Vehicles/Ordnance*
> *Electronic Systems*
> *AN Equipment*

These reports are updated on a monthly basis.   They contain funding and program history, and in some cases forecasts.

Drake, Hudson B., "Major DOD Procurements at War with Reality," *Harvard Business Review,* January-February 1970, pp. 119–140.

The Journal of the Acoustical Society of America, New York: American Institute of Physics.

Pace, Dean Francis, *Negotiation and Management of Defense Contracts,* New York: Wiley-Interscience, a division of John Wiley & Sons, Inc., 1970.

Research & Development Directory (annually) and *R & D Contracts Monthly,* Washington, D.C.: Government Data Publications.

The following are all government publications available from the Superintendent of Documents, U.S. Government Printing Office, Washington, D.C.

1. *Armed Services Procurement Regulations* (ASPR)
2. *ASPR Manual for Contract Pricing*
3. *Commerce Business Daily*
4. *Defense Posture Statement to House Armed Services Committee on Defense Programs by Secretary of Defense,* annual
5. *Defense Procurement Circular* (DPCs)
6. *Department of Defense Appropriation Bill,* fiscal year
7. *DOD/NASA Incentive Contracting Guide*
8. *Federal Register*
9. *Hearings before Subcommittees of the Committee on Appropriations.   Subject: Department of Defense Appropriations*
10. *Navy Procurement Directive* (NPD); similar for Air Force and Army
11. *Annual Presidential Reports to the Congress.   Subject: U.S. Foreign Policy for Calendar Year*
12. *The Budget of the United States Government and Appendix*
13. *U.S. Government Organization Manual*

CHAPTER NINE

International Marketing of Industrial Goods

SPREAD OF INDUSTRIALIZATION

Since the beginning of the eighteenth century, there has been a relatively rapid spread of industrialization over the world. It is far from over. The growth of industrialization has been spotty and at differing rates. Some areas of the world have hardly been touched. Those that were have varied recognizably in rate of progress.

For the most part, the leading countries had achieved their economic "takeoff" points by the end of the nineteenth century. Once this level is attained, the economy is capable of providing for its own future growth. Table 9.1 documents this general observation.

It is interesting to note that the "takeoff" period lasted about twenty to twenty-five years, with full maturity attained approximately thirty-five to fifty years later—at least for those nations whose development started in the nineteenth century.

THE UNDERDEVELOPED COUNTRY

The underdeveloped countries do not represent a great international market—yet. The ultimate potential is there, but it begins to be realized

TABLE 9.1 The Rostow Timetable: Tentative, Approximate Takeoff Periods and Maturity Dates

Nation	Takeoff period	Maturity
Great Britain	1783–1802	1850
France	1830–1860	1910
United States	1843–1860	1900
Germany	1850–1873	1910
Sweden	1868–1890	1930
Japan	1878–1900	1940
Russia	1890–1914	1950
Canada	1896–1914	1950
Argentina	1935–	Not yet
Turkey	1937–	Not yet
India	1952–	Not yet
China	1952–	Not yet

SOURCE: "Takeoff, Catch-up, Satiety," *Business Week*, no. 1597, Apr. 9, 1960, p. 100, reproduced with special permission.

only as development progresses.   The impediments are real.   The problems are just beginning to be understood.   One conclusion is certain—the task is not easy and it takes time.   However, the economic, political, and human benefits of developmental success are great.

Marketing can aid in economic development.   It would be extremely naïve to assume that it alone can create it.   It is an important factor, but only one of many important factors in the total required.[1]

The evolution of the marketing process through various stages of economic development from mere self-sufficiency through mass distribution and consumption is presented in Table 9.2.

Interest in the progress of the most recently developing countries has been growing rapidly and from at least three major points of view. There are those whose interest is primarily political.   They seek to make friends of these countries and by spreading capitalism to fight the spread of communism.   Others are primarily humanistically inclined.   They seek to aid the "less fortunate."   Then, the third viewpoint is interest in foreign markets as an outlet for goods, our surplus productive capacity.

But, no matter the reason, political, social, or economic, to achieve the goal, they all must contribute.   In order for the underdeveloped country to be a customer, a friend, and hopefully a political ally, it is first necessary that it be physically able to buy and use products

[1] For a good discussion of the problems and marketing's role in underdeveloped economies, see Robert J. Holloway and Robert S. Hancock, *Marketing in a Changing Environment*, New York: John Wiley & Sons, Inc., 1968, chap. 20.

TABLE 9.2 Evolution of the Marketing Process

Stage	Substage	Examples	Marketing functions	Marketing institutions	Channel control	Primary orientation	Resources employed	Comments
Agricultural and raw materials (Mk.(f) = Prod.)	Self-sufficient	Nomadic or hunting tribes	None	None	Traditional authority	Subsistence	Labor Land	Labor intensive No organized markets
	Surplus commodity producer	Agricultural economy—i.e., coffee, bananas	Exchange	Small-scale merchants, traders, fairs	Traditional authority	Entrepreneurial Commercial	Labor Land	Labor and land intensive Product specialization Local markets
Manufacturing (Mk.(f) = Prod.)	Small-scale	Cottage industry	Exchange Physical distribution	Merchants, wholesalers, export-import	Middlemen	Entrepreneurial Financial	Labor Land Technology Transportation	Labor intensive Product standardization and grading Regional and export markets
	Mass production	U.S. economy from 1885–1914	Demand creation Physical distribution	Merchants, wholesalers, traders, and specialized institutions	Producer	Production and finance	Labor Land Technology Transportation Capital	Capital intensive Product differentiation National, regional and export markets
Marketing (Prod.(f) = Mk.)	Commercial—Transition	U.S. economy from 1915 to 1929	Demand creation Physical distribution Market information	Large-scale and chain retailers increase in specialized middlemen	Producer	Entrepreneurial Commercial	Labor Land Technology Transportation Capital Communication	Capital intensive Changes in structure of distribution National, regional and export markets
	Mass distribution	U.S. economy from 1950 to present	Demand creation Physical distribution Market information Market and product planning, development	Integrated channels of distribution Increase in specialized middlemen	Producer Retailer	Marketing	Labor Land Technology Transportation Capital Communication	Capital and land intensive Rapid product innovation National, regional and export markets

SOURCE: Reproduced with permission from Hess and Cateora, *International Marketing* (Homewood, Ill.: Richard D. Irwin, Inc.), 1966 ©, page 172.

profitably. Its own productivity must increase. It must have the income to pay for imported goods and have the desire for them in the first place.

In short, the country's standard of living must be raised, and the people must want this badly enough to accept the changes necessary to achieve it.

The impediments to economic development are sometimes very strong and very deeply entrenched. Involved are religious beliefs, taboos, traditional ways of doing things, and attitudes. Such things are very difficult to alter for any reason, in anyone. The total problem is far more complex than that. It takes a real understanding, but understanding is not enough. This solves nothing. It is but a first step in adapting economic development to the customs, the total environment of each nation.

Marketing can play a major role in this process. Once trade is established on a mutually profitable basis, the political barriers are apt to be amended or removed. In short, marketing through mutually profitable trade can produce real benefits, which become a powerful force to improve political relationships.

Along similar lines, the role of the multinational corporation as an aid to development well warrants recognition. An editorial in *Fortune* concisely describes it:[2]

Smaller, poorer nations have more reason perhaps to be worried when they are confronted by huge international corporations, whose annual turnover sometimes exceeds their own G.N.P. Yet they recognize that they cannot afford to close the door on foreign investment, as the Japanese did. So, they welcome investment, but when it generates viable enterprise they hem that in with restrictions and threaten it with expropriation. The result is that further investment is discouraged.

The tragedy here is that the real losers are the backward nations themselves. For the multinational corporation offers the best hope of bringing them out of their backwardness. It is the most economic medium for spreading technology, management skills, and capital around the world. It is a far more effective force for development than government-to-government aid, which often gets dissipated in politics and bureaucracy, and in any event represents only the transfer of money, with little accompanying knowledge about how to put it to work and make it productive.

Among the more advanced nations, the multinational corporation is a great equalizer. The notion that it widens the management and technology gaps has got things turned upside down. The subsidiaries of

[2] Courtesy of Fortune Magazine, editorial, *Fortune*, vol. LXXX, no. 3, August 15, 1969.

worldwide corporations are not autonomous enclaves, isolated from the mainstream of their host country's economy. They hire and train local managers, engineers, and lab workers, and not just for the sake of public relations but because it makes good business sense. They also stimulate the growth of local suppliers and marketers and research facilities.

It is significant that I.B.M., which symbolizes what many Europeans find most fearsome about multinational corporations . . . , developed two of the ten models in its 360 computer series in Britain, and one in Germany. In all of Europe, it employs 65,000 people, of whom only about 200 are Americans. Though many of those European employees may stay with I.B.M. all their lives, many others will surely go off to local companies, carrying with them the knowledge and training that will help power the Continent's advance into the computer age.

MARKETING ABROAD

Fundamentally, the economic theory of absolute or comparative advantage explains international trade. It is a cost-oriented approach. As such, it is significant, but incomplete. Cost is important domestically, too—but it is far short of the total involvement. This same total involvement, though augmented by national differences, applies internationally.

From a marketing point of view, the competitive satisfaction of customers is still the goal. International marketing is simply done on a broader base. Competition is on a larger scale. But, cost, or even price, is not the sole determinant. A high price can be coupled with superior quality. Other factors—availability, credit, customer and product services, etc.—continue their roles internationally just as they do domestically.

The significant difference between international and domestic marketing lies not in the customer satisfactions to be created in the face of competition. It lies in the environmental conditions. These do differ. They must be known, understood, appreciated, and respected. These differences are real. That they differ from one's own does *not* make them "inferior." The businessman abroad is the foreigner—not the people of the nation he is in. If he can adjust successfully, he is apt to be welcomed. If not, he is the one to suffer most. The adjustment—or lack of it—is his responsibility.

There is no real difference in people from one nation to another. It is, again, the environment which is different. This creates differing values, goals, concepts, traditions, laws, and customs. Once the need to learn them is fully appreciated, and once this has been achieved, the resultant action becomes relatively easy. An intelligent application of common sense with respect for others, their concepts, and their way of life will go a long way to developing friendly relationships among people. Successful business is still based on goodwill of people—everywhere.

In working abroad, little things make a big difference in goodwill. Many people watch the newcomer most carefully. They are very quick to react unfavorably, although not obviously (they are too polite for that), to his mistakes. Etiquette, choice of words, addressing a man by his first name too soon, even where one sits, opening the door of an automobile for a male guest (or failure to)—such things are interpreted as good manners or lack of them. They are important. The informality of our way of life in dress, manners, and general behavior is not accepted as good conduct in many nations of the world.

Regimentation and patience are greater abroad. At the same time, special treatment for the privileged—the political, social, or economic leaders—is the way of life. Nor does this include the American salesman. The proper conduct can be learned quickly, from someone who knows and from observation—if one seeks to learn.

On a corporate level, the multinational company should consider carefully the needs of people in each nation. It should be a reflection of their wants, not an imposition of ours. In organizational structuring to do business abroad, the creation of an atmosphere of partnership in the total enterprise, rather than that of an aggressive foreign firm, can help significantly. Gene E. Bradley identifies seven key points in this connection as follows:[3]

> Most Americans would oppose arbitrary organizations or codes of good behavior which some Europeans propose.
>
> But Americans should not dismiss lightly the seven criteria for multinational operations which summarize many European proposals heard to date:
>
> - Management by host-nationals.
> - Stock acquisitions by employees.
> - Stock acquisition within the host country.
> - Joint ventures (not complete U.S. ownership).
> - Local capital participation in the subsidiary.
> - Personnel policy of bringing top men to the world headquarters based on greatest ability, not nationality.
> - Decentralize research and development into the countries where subsidiaries operate.
>
> Valuable corporate examples can be cited of companies building success stories on criteria such as these—Ford, Upjohn, Chase Manhattan, J. Walter Thompson, Eastman Kodak and Esso, to mention just a few.

[3] Gene E. Bradley, "We Must Heal U.S.-Europe Rift," *Nation's Business*, vol. 56, no. 2, p. 80, February 1968.

The marketing concept has universal applicability, but it is far more accepted in the United States than abroad. In Europe, workers were viewed as a labor cost until the European Economic Community began to change this to regard them as consumers. Such changes will continue. The application of the marketing concept must depend upon the environmental conditions of each nation. These do differ. The principle does not. Another very significant difference between international and domestic marketing lies in relationships between governments. Such things as the creation of the European Economic Community, the treatment of important exports via tariffs, and political affiliation and attendant restrictions are unique to international marketing. The act of marketing, with special emphasis upon the knowledge of the market, is the same. The forms of its application will be both similar and dissimilar to domestic, because of their adjustment to the environmental differences.

Can marketing strategy be standardized on an international basis? If the forms differ for environmental causes, need this prohibit a unified approach to them? One authority, Robert D. Buzzell, does a thorough job of appraisal of this problem and concludes:[4]

> Traditionally, marketing strategy has been regarded as a strictly local problem in each national market. Differences in customer needs and preferences, in competition, in institutional systems, and in legal regulations have seemed to require basically different marketing programs. Any similarity between countries has been seen as purely coincidental.
>
> There is no doubt that differences among nations are still great, and that these differences should be recognized in marketing planning. But the experiences of a growing number of multinational companies suggest that there are also some real potential gains in an integrated approach to marketing strategy. Standardization of products, packages, and promotional approaches may permit substantial cost savings, as well as greater consistency in dealings with customers. The harmonization of price policies often facilitates better internal planning and control. Finally, if good ideas are scarce, and if some of them have universal appeal, they should be used as widely as possible.
>
> All of this adds up to the conclusion that both the pros and the cons of standardization in multinational marketing programs should be considered, and that a company's decisions should be based on estimated overall revenues and costs. Obviously, each case must be considered on its own merits—slogans and formulas are not very helpful guides to intelligent planning.

[4] Robert D. Buzzell, "Can You Standardize Multinational Marketing?" *Harvard Business Review*, vol. 46, no. 6, pp. 102–113, November-December 1968.

If marketing strategy is to be designed with a multinational perspective, then the firm's organization must make provision for line and staff marketing positions at appropriate levels. Space does not permit a full discussion of the organizational issues here, but it may be noted that there is a clear trend among leading companies toward establishment of marketing coordinators, international committees, and other mechanisms for at least partial centralization of marketing management. Hoover, Singer, General Electric, Eastman Kodak, and many other companies have recently made changes in this direction.

Finding the right balance between local autonomy and central coordination is not an easy task, any more than is balancing the gains of standardized marketing strategy against the needs of heterogeneous national markets. But it is an important task, with high potential profit rewards for management. Finding the best solutions to these problems should be high on the priority list for every multinational company.

COMPETITION INTERNATIONALLY

Evidence that competition on an international scale is growing is not hard to find. The long-term trend toward free trade is obvious. The development of the European Economic Community is a major step in that direction. The growth in both our exports and imports means more competition, abroad and at home. The international firm faces it in selling abroad. The domestic firm faces it in selling in the United States in competition with imported products. This is likely to be a continuing and growing problem for American manufacturers of industrial goods in the future.

It should be noted that not all of the imports are from foreign corporations. Many United States corporations have expanded their operations overseas to compete better in the foreign market and to manufacture abroad for sale or rental in the United States—to compete better at home.

Statistical data on United States manufacturing abroad for sale or rental in the United States are extremely hard to find—if, in fact, they exist. It is even more difficult to attempt to compile such data on industrial versus consumer goods.

This development makes sense. It strengthens the economy abroad while at the same time providing a better value here. Nor is it mere theory. The trend is well established with proved profitability. It is but a natural development, triggered by a desire for competitive advantage. It is most likely to continue to grow in both volume and scope.

J. Frank Gaston, Economist for The Conference Board, recognizes the lack of information and the need for further study in this area. He states:[5]

> As a result of major changes in the position of the United States in the world economy a more thorough analysis of our export and import trade is sorely needed. Among the factors that need more systematic examination are:
>
> 1. The pace of price and cost inflation in the United States in contrast to that of other industrial nations.
> 2. The impact of the industrial capability of Western Europe and Japan both on export potential and on the establishment of overseas operations by U.S. corporations. Connected with this aspect of foreign competition is the role of the foreign operations of American affiliates in providing an industrial base for competition in third markets as well as in the United States.
> 3. The effect of further economic and political integration of the European Economic Community. The importance of this entity will grow considerably if the United Kingdom is successful in its bid to become a member.

Note particularly his number 2, above.

In fairness to those who face and resent the competition from imports, whatever the source, let us recognize that this is a natural and logical reaction. It is natural for the businessman to love to sell abroad, but to seek protection from competition from imports in his domestic market. However one feels about it, competition is most likely to increase. The effects can be painful. Temporary measures to alleviate the pain are not apt to be long-run solutions. Facing the problem squarely and planning for the best overall solution in the long run may be difficult, but it, too, makes sense.

United States manufacturing abroad helps nations to develop. This is a major contribution to international goodwill and to world peace. In order for people to become customers, they must represent effective demand. This means both the desire and the ability to pay. And this comes from earnings, productivity. It is no different abroad. If we are to make customers of foreigners, we can do well to help them become earners, to help increase their productivity—their standard of living. As this happens, their prices are apt to rise, thus evening out economic differentials. The principle of absolute or comparative advantage, recognized years ago, still applies.

In spite of the difficulty of obtaining statistics to measure this trend, it is not at all difficult to find examples to illustrate it. Many major United States firms have been manufacturing abroad for sale or rental

---

[5] J. Frank Gaston, *The Vanishing American Trade Surplus,* The Conference Board, Worldbusiness Perspectives, no. 1, New York, November 1970, p. 4.

in the United States for some time.   Others have been expanding their international activities in this manner over the more recent past.   These firms deserve the profits they have earned and should be lauded for the steps they have taken.   Yet they (for the most part) do not mention it in their advertising.   The goods are correctly identified as to the source—in fine print.   They seem content to permit the source to pass unnoticed.   It may be that the general public is deemed not to be ready for this knowledge, yet.   It may also be that the time is rapidly approaching for public recognition of the economic, social, and political responsibilities being served by such firms.

Someday this may become a plus feature, enhancing the price-quality relationship of the good and the prestige of the corporate name.   About all that is needed to achieve this result right now is the right sort of publicity, built on the facts.   The public already has a high regard for the superiority of many quality imports.   There seems to be nothing to preclude a favorable reaction, acceptance, and probable preference for the satisfaction-giving capabilities of many more—and for the development of much corporate goodwill at the same time.

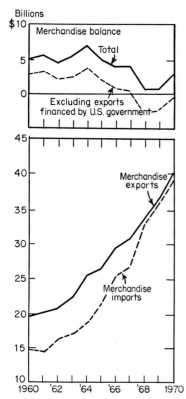

Fig. 9.1 Export-import merchandise trade balance. (*Source: J. Frank Gaston,"The Vanishing American Trade Surplus," The Conference Board, Worldbusiness Perspectives, no. 1, November 1970, p. 2.*)

UNITED STATES EXPORTS, IMPORTS, AND FOREIGN INVESTMENT

While total exports and imports increased quite rapidly during the decade of the sixties, the United States trade surplus decreased. Figure 9.1 vividly illustrates this.

TABLE 9.3   United States Manufacturing Exports and Imports, 1969
(Figures in millions of dollars)

Industry	Exports	Imports
Primary and Fabricated Metals	$ 3,248	$ 5,050
Machinery, Except Electrical	7,461	2,624
Electrical Machinery	2,678	1,947
Transportation Equipment	6,242	5,198
Chemicals	3,383	1,232
Paper	585	1,081
Rubber	335	422
Food and Beverages	4,446	5,309
Other Products*	9,066	13,189
All manufacturing	$37,444	$36,052

* Fuels, crude materials, and miscellaneous manufacturing.
SOURCE: *Statistical Abstract of U.S., 1970*, 91st ann. ed., U.S. Bureau of the Census, 1970, pp. 779–782.

TABLE 9.4   Sales of Foreign Manufacturing Affiliates by Industry and Destination, 1968
(Figures in millions of dollars)

Industry	Total sales	Local sales	Exported to: United States	Exported to: Other countries
Primary and Fabricated Metals	$ 4,666	$ 3,437	$ 398	$ 831
Machinery, Except Electrical	8,192	6,165	338	1,689
Electrical Machinery	5,298	4,655	90	553
Transportation Equipment	14,522	10,402	2,485	1,635
Chemicals	10,215	8,497	189	1,529
Paper	2,534	1,420	745	369
Rubber	2,126	1,948	30	148
Food and Beverages	5,366	4,593	211	562
Other Products	6,757	5,348	255	1,154
All manufacturing	$59,676	$46,465	$4,741	$8,470

SOURCE: *Survey of Current Business*, U.S. Department of Commerce, October 1970, p. 20.

**TABLE 9.5 Sales Expectations of Foreign
Manufacturing Affiliates**
(Figures in millions of dollars)

Industry	Estimated 1969	Expectations		
		1970	1971	1972
Primary and Fabricated Metals	$ 5,480	$ 6,357	$ 7,311	$ 8,042
Machinery, Except Electrical	8,839	9,458	10,498	11,548
Electrical Machinery	5,813	6,743	7,957	9,389
Transportation Equipment	16,043	17,487	18,711	20,208
Chemicals	11,341	12,815	14,609	16,362
Paper	2,701	2,890	3,266	3,658
Rubber	2,238	2,462	2,684	2,926
Food and Beverages	5,280	5,808	6,389	7,028
Other Products	7,376	8,409	9,502	10,737
All manufacturing	$65,111	$72,429	$80,927	$89,898

SOURCE: *Overseas Operations of U.S. Industrial Companies, 1970–72*, a research study made by McGraw-Hill Department of Economics, Aug. 14, 1970, table 4.

**TABLE 9.6 Planned Overseas Capital Expenditures for
Manufacturing by American Companies**
(Figures in millions of dollars)

Industry	Estimated 1969	Planned		
		1970	1971	1972
Primary and Fabricated Metals	$ 553	$ 871	$1,000	$ 636
Machinery, Except Electrical	910	1,010	1,081	962
Electrical Machinery	390	558	435	496
Transportation Equipment	800	1,046	1,002	961
Chemicals	1,120	1,501	1,531	1,378
Paper	156	320	282	285
Rubber	155	153	159	172
Food and Beverages	185	229	222	235
Other Products	371	397	397	380
All manufacturing	$4,640	$6,085	$6,109	$5,505

SOURCE: *Overseas Operations of U.S. Industrial Companies, 1970–72*, a research study made by McGraw-Hill Department of Economics, Aug. 14, 1970, table 1.

Table 9.3 provides the data on our 1969 exports and imports by major industries.

Then, by these same industry breakdowns, Table 9.4 indicates the 1968 sales of foreign manufacturing affiliates—and their destination.

The sales expectations of these foreign manufacturing affiliates over the next few years by industry is shown in Table 9.5.

**TABLE 9.7 Planned Total Capital Expenditures
for Manufacturing by Regions**
(Figures in millions of dollars)

Region	Estimated 1969	Planned		
		1970	1971	1972
Canada	$1,109	$1,411	$1,313	$1,134
Latin America	653	740	789	653
Common Market	1,426	1,835	1,789	1,817
Rest of Europe	667	845	864	789
Oceania	388	562	648	526
All Other	397	692	706	586
Total	$4,640	$6,085	$6,109	$5,505

SOURCE: Derived from *Overseas Operations of U.S. Industrial Companies, 1970–72*, a research study made by McGraw-Hill Department of Economics, Aug. 14, 1970, table II.

The planned overseas capital expenditures for manufacturing purposes by American companies is shown in Table 9.6 for these same years. Investment in petroleum and mining, while available in the source, has been omitted here.

The allocation of these planned capital expenditures for all manufacturing to major economic regions for these same years is tabulated in Table 9.7.

ORGANIZATION FOR INTERNATIONAL MARKETING

If we project the evolutionary development of marketing, together with the marketing concept, into the future, we might visualize the ideal marketing organization. This would not be simply a market-oriented firm doing business internationally. It would be a world corporation. The headquarters location would not be important. That could be anywhere. The important aspect would be that its top management would have a worldwide perspective and worldwide responsibilities. Their thinking, planning, and direction of corporate effort would be worldwide. This corporation would optimize the location and use of its resources tǫ serve best its customers in the markets of the world.

Such an entity would be big. It would become a powerful force for world peace. It would provide the best price-quality relationship available. It would be tough competition to beat. It would argue strongly for the removal of trade restrictions as an impediment to economic development. It would be local in its operations within any one nation, but worldwide in its total marketing. It would help raise the standard of living wherever it operated. It would be a living example that free enterprise really works everywhere. Such corporate enterprises are coming. It is merely a question of how long it will take for them to evolve.

Structurally, one could visualize middle management being segmented by major geographical regions. There might be a director of marketing for Europe, the Americas, etc. National responsibilities would be subordinate to regional. The market complexity and level of economic development within each area become limiting factors. Further refinement along specialized product lines or product systems is feasible, wherever appropriate—very much the same as now. Local management would handle local problems—but accountability and perspective, integration of effort, would not stop there. It would be a facet of the total perspective—the world market.

A major prerequisite to the attainment of this status lies in the capacity and interest of top managers to accept the vast responsibility of operating a world enterprise. The ramifications are far greater than running a multidivisional, yet national conglomerate—even with some foreign affiliates (typically under nearly independent control).

Such world corporations would not pose a threat to the little companies. They would enhance the opportunities for the entrepreneurs, as they have been doing for some time. The present distribution and preponderance of small corporations overall and by industry in the United States attests to this. All our largest corporations are served by great numbers of small business enterprises. On an international scale, the world corporation could be a powerful force to encourage the initiation of hundreds of such businesses. And this can be a potent start toward more rapid economic development on the same scale.

We do not have this as yet. But some of our leading firms are coming very close. One example is the IBM World Trade Corporation, a subsidiary of International Business Machines, with a separate corporate location and structure charged with the responsibility for all of IBM's international business operations. This corporation, while subordinate to IBM domestically, encompasses the worldwide perspective, crucial to the world corporation. And it is this perspective which is a prerequisite to this level and scope of operations.

Foreign-Subsidiary-Controlling Corporation

Actually, this is the proper classification for the IBM World Trade Corporation—along with several others. This is the first step below the world corporation just envisioned. It is a very practical and realistic structure. Foreign operations are centralized for control purposes, yet implemented somewhat a la carte to the nations involved. It is really but a question of perspective. So long as the United States market dominates the operations, the subsidiary or international-controlling corporation is very suitable. When, and if, the international markets begin to dominate, then the world corporation would seem to offer the better approach to total operations, planning, and control.

Foreign Subsidiary

The foreign subsidiary is very popular. It is a semiautonomous corporate entity, usually located in the foreign nation. It is owned largely or entirely by the United States parent. Periodic visits and meetings, heavily informative in nature, help determine policy. Typically, it is held accountable for earning a profit, but management and control of operations are chiefly local.

Thus, this lacks the continual world perspective and supervision of the foreign-subsidiary-controlling corporation. It is but one step below that stage of development. The major weakness is in effecting integration of resource use and marketing among various nations. If but one major foreign nation is involved, this point is not significant. It becomes very much more so as additional markets, additional nations, are added.

Joint Ventures

The joint venture helps to overcome the image of the foreign firm exploiting the nation. It is joint ownership in a local enterprise. Thus, foreign investment is coupled with local. Local management provides an intimate working knowledge of the market and business practices. The local partner offers other advantages, some psychological, some legal. In many nations foreign operations face all sorts of local laws which can be real impediments. The joint venture through its local partner can obtain very practical aid.

Licensing

This requires no foreign capital investment. The manager of the local firm takes full responsibility for manufacture and sale. Carefully selected, he adds his local prestige to the product's. He assumes the task of handling any local legal matters. And this may be the only way of entry into his market if the government does not permit or penalizes foreign ownership.

These advantages offer relatively easy entry into foreign markets. The real price for them is loss of control over both manufacturing and marketing. This can be very significant. At best, the foreigner is at a disadvantage to police his agreement. Local courts may not help him much. The licensee may become powerful enough to decide to be a competitor on his own. Currency regulations and exchange rates vary from time to time. Getting one's money out of a nation can sometimes be a real problem.

USE OF MIDDLEMEN

Middlemen offer the same advantages abroad that they do here. They provide ready access to the markets they cover and reduce the investment required to establish one's own selling organization. They may or may not take title, depending upon whether they operate as merchant or functional middlemen as in the United States. They vary more in effectiveness, primarily due to variation in customary business practices and attitude toward aggressiveness. Salesmanship is not an honorable profession everywhere. Tradition may impede operations, especially in regard to time.

Thus, foreign middlemen operate essentially the same as the domestic counterparts. The major difference is in the variation in their effectiveness as marketing representatives coupled with the loss of control. It is simply more serious abroad—and more frustrating.

Import and Export Agents

Such firms are functional middlemen who represent their principals internationally. They offer specialized knowledge of materials, sources, and the foreign nations involved. In addition, they can be very helpful in expediting shipments across national boundaries. Because they do not take title and assume little or no risk, their operational expenses and compensation rates are low.

Intermerchants

One functionary, unique to international marketing, is the intermerchant. The need for his services arises when one seeks to arrange payment from a soft-currency country to a hard-currency one. This is not easy directly without a prohibitive loss of value. The intermerchant typically operates to arrange a three-way deal, involving a third country. In theory, the intermerchant should not exist. In practice, he will continue to be needed until such time as foreign exchange of all trading nations becomes far more readily acceptable at or near par.

Export Merchants

Export merchants maintain selling organizations in the foreign markets they cover and buy goods to serve those markets. Popularly referred to as "trading companies," they are apt to be large, powerful, and both politically and traditionally well entrenched. Tradition is important—far more so abroad than here. As such, they possess a high level of bargaining power in selecting the lines they wish to carry, and in price negotiations. However, since they buy domestically, the selling costs of firms doing business with them are nominal.

AIDS TO INTERNATIONAL MARKETING

An article, "Tips on a $50 Billion Market," in *Sales Management* does a good job of summarizing many sources of specialized help and information on international marketing. It covers activities of the Department of Commerce and ten other key organizations. This summary is included at the end of this book, in the Appendix.

CARTELS, COMPETITION, AND WEBB-POMERENE

Congress passed the Webb-Pomerene Act in 1918. This permits firms to join in combinations and monopolies in export trade. One objective was to increase the power of United States firms to compete in foreign markets. Banks which engage in such overseas activities are controlled by the Edge Act of 1919.

The international cartel seeks to avoid the duplication of effort of competition. It may strive to maintain prices, allocate markets to members, establish quantities for each, and even operate as a selling agent for them. These actions would be deemed to restrict competition or tend to create a monopoly in the United States.

Different governments view cartels differently. Some oppose them; others support them, in varying degrees. The rapid growth of both our exports and United States–owned subsidiaries abroad has augmented the problem of the relationships of competition-oriented firms and cartel operations. "If you can't lick 'em—join 'em" may be an apt phrase in this connection. To the extent that it applies, a current problem of jurisdictional reach is involved.

Raymond Vernon identifies the theoretical and practical aspects of jurisdictional reach. He states:[6]

> Successful extraterritorial application depends on effective jurisdictional reach. Such effectiveness has both a theoretical and a practical side.
>
> In theory, when parties plot to restrain U.S. trade in ways that the Sherman Act or its augmenting statutes absolutely proscribe, the parties may be violating provisions of the act even though they never actually set foot on U.S. soil. However, the detection and prevention of a con-

[6] Raymond Vernon, "Antitrust and International Business," *Harvard Business Review*, September-October 1968, pp. 84–86.

spiracy on the part of companies located abroad is difficult, even when one or more of the companies is controlled by a U.S. parent.

First, there is the problem of gathering evidence. When the evidence lies physically in the jurisdiction of another country, the country has been known to prohibit enterprises from producing the evidence. Situations of this sort have occurred in Canada, The Netherlands, and U.K.; and more can be expected in the future.

Secondly, there is the question of remedy. When the remedy for any conspiracy requires some act to be undertaken in another country's jurisdiction, such as the sale of stock or the licensing of patents, the other country has sometimes prohibited its nationals from acting as directed by the U.S. courts.

For those that are concerned with the practical power of the law, therefore, rather than with the hypothetical reach, the jurisdictional issue involves still another dimension of considerable uncertainty.

And further:

Another area of ambiguity that will surely take on magnified importance is the area of transactions between parents and their subsidiaries. The general rule about agreements between parents and subsidiaries is not clear. There is fairly wide agreement in the legal fraternity that an agreement is illegal if it is intended to achieve some coercive restraint on the trade of a third party—that is, a party outside the corporate family. The mere fixing of a subsidiary's price by a parent, when this is not intended as a means of coercing a third party, is usually construed as being outside the scope of the law's prohibitions. In practice, the application of such a rule leaves large areas of uncertainty.

The law on parent subsidiary relations is uncertain enough when corporate structures are contained within narrow geographical and functional limits. It becomes even more uncertain as the intercorporate structure becomes more complex and crosses international boundaries.

In conclusion, he says:

There are times in the affairs of men when problems worth worrying about do not have quick and easy solutions; this is such a case. The best that business can hope for is a complex process of reconciling national jurisdictions in ways that are acceptable to the governments concerned, while still leaving the businessman with scope for his creative skills in moving money, ideas, people, and goods across international boundaries.

This is no simple job. One has to find a formula that will accommodate the antitrust preferences of the United States with the indicative planning preferences of France, the nineteenth-century laissez-faire liturgy of German business, and the export-cartel proclivities of the Japanese bureaucracy.

Up to now the solution that most U.S. businessmen have been inclined to support has been a very simple formula: "Let antitrust stop at the water's edge." At first glance, this formula has a certain beguiling plausibility. If each country limits its reach to its own jurisdiction, how can any clash occur?

A little reflection, however, shows why the formula is naïve. By their very nature, importing and exporting involve the jurisdictions of more than one country. If the United States were to apply a self-denying ordinance on the application of antitrust to conspiracies that were entered into beyond the water's edge, it would simply be throwing away the right to protect itself from arrangements by foreigners that it thought harmful to its national interests. Some nations have taken such a step; but the wisdom of the step is doubtful.

INTERNATIONAL MARKETING: A VAST OPPORTUNITY FOR ECONOMIC, HUMAN, AND POLITICAL PROGRESS

Clearly, the potential for future growth and development of industry is gigantic on a worldwide scale. International marketing can help in this. Mutually profitable international business relationships become a most powerful argument for the removal of impediments, legal and political. They can lead, rather than follow. There are problems to be faced, but nothing to preclude their solution—so long as people want the improvement badly enough to try. Adjustments to international differences in environment can mean more tolerance, a broader outlook, and more goodwill. Goodwill is at the very root of economic, human, and political progress. It truly is a goal worthy of our very best efforts in attainment.

RELEVANT READING

Drucker, Peter F., "Marketing and Economic Development," *Journal of Marketing*, vol. 22, no. 3, pp. 252–259, January 1958.
Elling, Karl A., *Introduction to Modern Marketing*, New York: The Macmillan Company, 1969, chap. 13.
Frey, Albert W. (ed.), *Marketing Handbook*, 2d ed., New York: The Ronald Press Company, 1965, sec. 28.
Grimes, Arthur L., "International Marketing: Opportunities and Problems," *Financial Executive*, November 1965, pp. 58–63.
Holloway, Robert J., and Robert S. Hancock, *Marketing in a Changing Environment*, New York: John Wiley & Sons, Inc., 1968, chap. 21.
Westing, J. Howard, and Gerald Albaum, *Modern Marketing Thought*, 2d ed., New York: The Macmillan Company, 1969, chap. 24.
Worldbusiness Perspectives, a new quarterly, New York: The Conference Board. Each issue deals with one topic. Charts and text emphasize analysis, interpretation, and implications.
Yoshino, Michael Y., "Marketing Orientation in International Business," *Business Topics*, vol. 13, no. 3, pp. 58–64, Summer 1965.

PART FIVE

Costs, Pricing, and Financing

CHAPTER TEN

Marketing Costs

Basic to a consideration of marketing costs is the definition of "marketing" itself. If there is to be comparability of marketing costs, whether by firms, products, or sets of marketing circumstances, the base must be uniform. The detailed definition of "marketing," set forth in Chapter One, originated in research to create such a base acceptable to practitioners. The premise is that all moneys spent to accomplish the marketing task become marketing costs—no matter who spends them.

Marketing costs have sometimes been referred to as "distribution costs." This is acceptable—to those who accept the acts of distribution as a definition of "marketing." Obviously, this omits many significant aspects of marketing as it is currently viewed. Headquarters-support activities, the cost of determining needs and wants of customers, aid in product development, aid in production planning, and varying degrees of several other aspects are overlooked.

It is not important that the definition of "marketing" in Chapter One be generally adopted. It is important that some definition be adopted. Because the definition of Chapter One was derived for these purposes, and since it has proved to be workable in practice, it will be used in this discussion of marketing costs. It is repeated from the cost viewpoint, and to facilitate review of content.

MARKETING COSTS DEFINED

"Marketing costs" are all expenses incurred to determine the needs and wants of customers, develop new markets, aid in product development, estimate potentials, forecast, and aid in production planning; to operate a marketing organization, determine marketing strategy, select channels of distribution, inform and motivate customers, price, sell, provide marketing services including order entry, customer financing, credit and collection, and both customer and product services; to provide for physical distribution, including packaging, transportation, field warehousing of finished goods, and delivery; to contribute to overall corporate planning and to plan and control this entire operation.

This means that marketing's share of top-management expense and similar appropriate allocations should be made. Marketing, integrated throughout the firm, incurs costs wherever it is a factor.

It should be kept in mind that the *manufacturer's* marketing costs are but part of the typical *product's* marketing costs. All the middleman's expenses (and his profit) are marketing costs. This is not contradictory. It is simply that marketing costs are assembled by and for the use of firms. One should simply remember that it is just that, the firm's marketing costs—not necessarily the total for the want satisfaction (or for the product which creates it). Both are valuable perspectives.

DIFFERENCES BETWEEN MANUFACTURING AND MARKETING COSTS

Manufacturing and marketing costs differ significantly in many respects. Historically, manufacturing costs have been deemed to create assets. The products of these costs, from opening inventory through work in process, up to and including finished goods, are reflected as asset items in the inventory accounts of a firm. On the other hand, marketing costs have been deemed to create expenses—even when the real task today is to market rather than to make. Major marketing assets are almost never reflected on the books, are rarely measured, and seem difficult to appraise. The value of an established dealer organization, marketing's impact on customers' preferences, goodwill, the value of a new account, and the many intangibles of the marketing structure are most difficult to reflect in dollars and cents under present circumstances. Yet, which contributes more to corporate welfare—an inventory of unsold goods and work in process, or an inventory of dealers and the goodwill of customers? Which would be the greater loss?

Manufacturing develops product costs. Marketing costs frequently are treated as period costs rather than product costs. This remains true even though it is most difficult to determine which periods are actually benefited by which marketing-cost expenditures—to say nothing of the relative degrees of impacts as between periods. A determination of the actual cost of the revenue produced becomes a major problem.

Manufacturing costs are relatively easy to identify. They generally originate in a plant and are accumulated by cost centers, departments, processes, and product units. A high degree of control is exercised over each. Marketing costs, on the other hand, originating both in the office and in the field, come from many locations and may be accumulated by groups of customers, products, salesmen, sales territories, and type of middlemen. To a major extent the customers, competitive action, and other uncontrollables in the field affect marketing expenditures. This frequently means that there is a far lower degree of control over the need for such expenditures than exists in manufacturing.

The efficiency of manufacturing becomes a reflection of decreasing unit costs. The point of optimal level of production is readily determinable. Even beyond this point, the increasing unit costs are easily measured and known. Efficiency in marketing is frequently a reflection of increasing sales volume, which may or may not mean increasing profit. The optimal level of sales volume, maximum marketing efficiency, is far harder to determine.

Cost-reduction programs for manufacturing costs are desirable. They can increase efficiency. But reduction of marketing costs may decrease efficiency. For many marketing expenses, greater efficiency may follow an increased expenditure. For example, a mediocre advertising program on a limited budget is not improved by a further budget cut. It might be improved by an increase. The maximum efficiency in most marketing costs is not necessarily at the minimal expense level.

Yardsticks, standards for cost analysis and comparison, are highly developed and readily available within manufacturing. They have been practically nonexistent within the area of marketing costs.

TYPES OF COST ACCOUNTS

In the area of marketing-cost accounting, there are many paired approaches to costs and cost accounts. The accounts reflecting marketing-cost data as carried on the books of most firms today are typically an adaptation of one or both of two bases, natural and functional. The natural basis accumulates cost by the object of the expenditure; for example, salaries, supplies, and travel. The functional basis recognizes a major marketing activity for which costs are accumulated; for example, physical distribution may include transportation, storage, materials handling, and field warehousing. Either of these bases may be broken down further by sales territories, branches, channels of distribution, classes of customers, methods of sale, sizes of orders, or products.

Other bases for the assembly of cost data are

Direct versus indirect
Fixed versus variable
Short term versus long run
Average versus marginal
Imputed versus outlay
Common versus separable
Substitutable versus nonsubstitutable
Product versus time segment
Corporate versus total product marketing
Assets versus expenses

Each of these approaches provides its own perspective and for a specific purpose. These complement each other, rather than conflict or duplicate. In the assembly of marketing-cost data, one could deal with dollars or percentages. Percent of net sales enhances comparability.

There is one weakness in most accounting systems from the marketing-cost point of view. They were originally designed to provide information for control of operations and for tax reporting. Current operational costs are charged to the appropriate expense accounts and become income tax deductions. No real attention has been provided to the true nature of many marketing expenditures. It is highly doubtful if it will be for some time to come. The inherent problems of proper allocation are great. Yet the solution could provide a far more meaningful report of both corporate assets and the expenses of marketing operations. Consider, for example, advertising. To what extent is this a current operational expense or a long-term investment in goodwill? If measured by its impact, in which time periods should the expense be recorded? What about the recruiting and training of salesmen? Or the cost of obtaining new dealers and new accounts? The solution to such problems, while difficult, could vastly improve the measure of marketing's contribution to the firm—an area which can stand much improvement.

A MARKETING-ORIENTED P/L STATEMENT

The typical profit-and-loss statement starts with the firm's gross receipts and ends up with net profit after taxes. It encompasses the seller's revenues and expenses, but not the middleman's. Yet, viewed from the perspective of the costs involved in creating the want satisfaction the product produces, they are a part of this total picture.

A profit-and-loss statement including the costs of middlemen may provide a better picture of the total marketing costs. It might start with the revenue received from the final purchaser, the end user, then subtract the costs involved at each step in the distributional channel. This would provide a valid base for comparing the total marketing costs of selling through different channels of distribution, direct sale versus through distributors, for example. It becomes an interesting approach, and one which reflects the manufacturer's marketing costs in their true light—as a step in the total involvement. If used, it is not suggested as a replacement of the present profit and loss statement, but rather as a supplement to provide an additional perspective.

REFINEMENT AND SEGMENTATION

"Refinement" of marketing costs refers to the base for compilation—by industry, corporate size, product line, channel of distribution, or any major factor causing a market or marketing difference. "Segmentation" refers to the breaking up of total marketing costs into significant items— advertising, field-selling expenses, management, research, etc.

The problem is simple to state. What are management's real needs for improved analysis, decision making, planning, and control? In theory, almost infinite combinations of refinement and segmentation—and subsegmentation—are possible. In practice, it becomes necessary to strike a balance between what one might like to have ideally and the capability of industry to provide it—with sufficient representation to make the results meaningful.

The Segments

Determination of the segments presents no real problem. Basic research produced the reactions as to what industry wanted, what they felt to be most meaningful. This breakdown has been used successfully several times in assembling marketing-cost data by the Marketing-Cost Institute, Inc., now a division of The Conference Board. It follows:[1]

    A. Marketing Management and Services
       1. Marketing Planning, Administration & Product Management
       2. Advertising and Sales Promotion
       3. Marketing Research
       4. Pricing, Estimating, Quoting
       5. All Other Marketing-related Costs
         Subtotal—Marketing Costs

[1] Used with permission of The Conference Board from the Marketing-Cost Institute's data-reporting form, 1970.

B. Selling
1. Sales Management
2. Outside Salesmen
3. Inside Salesmen
4. Field Services
5. Compensation to Agents or Brokers
6. All Other Selling-related Costs
    Subtotal—Selling Costs
C. Physical Distribution
1. Field Storage and Warehousing
2. Delivery and Transportation
3. All Other Distribution-related Costs
    Subtotal—Distribution Costs
D. Total—All Marketing Costs

Since no two firms keep their books in exactly the same way, a list of what is in and out of each category is needed. The compilation of the cost data has presented no real problem, once the definitive structure became available. This is a testimonial to the capability of the accounting and data processing people. That such information was not furnished marketing management sooner is simply a reflection of marketing's failure to request it.

Table 10.1 identifies the content of each of the cost segments. It may be noted that this is, in effect, an even finer breakdown of the definition of marketing on which it was based.

The Refinements

The determination of the refinements of marketing-cost data seems to be no real problem, at first. It is obvious that the costs should be accumulated to reflect the seller's situation. Corporate size, product line, and channel of distribution become a good start. But it is quickly realized that *any* factor causative of a significant difference in the cost structure needs to be identified and used. Whether the goods are made to order or for inventory, whether the sale represents a major purchasing consideration for the buyer or a routine rebuy, the degree of technicality—many such factors become involved. The computer can be used to determine the significant differences. Hence, this task rapidly assumes major proportions.

The marketing profile, already discussed at the end of Chapter Two, answers this problem by bringing together the key factors of marketing and the market. A major change in any one means another profile. But, for the goods using the *same* profile, the marketing costs can be readily assembled—and for the different profiles of the same goods. This provides realistic comparability for marketing costs—and based upon the uniformity of the circumstances of the market and the act of marketing. It represents a giant step forward in providing truly meaningful data to aid in marketing decision making.

THE NEED FOR MARKETING COSTS

As our economy moves further from one of scarcity to one of surplus (characterized in a rapidly increasing number of cases by surplus productive capacity), as differences in productive efficiency tend to narrow (with increased automation, advantageous location, and a relatively uniform awareness of technology), efficiency in marketing, particularly in the face of vastly increased competition at a high level, becomes a must. Knowledge of marketing costs, the allocation of marketing expenditures to provide a minimum cost per unit of revenue produced, an identification of strengths and weaknesses in the marketing area, the establishment of yardsticks to aid in this identification, to guide remedial action, attention and control—all become increasingly important. Today, efficiency in marketing may well represent the greatest opportunity for increased profits to the manufacturer-seller. The attainment of such efficiency should be greatly facilitated by the development and use of appropriate cost data and yardsticks as a factor in marketing decision making.

In this connection, one point should be emphasized. There is no one best set of marketing costs. But, for any one marketing profile, that is, one set of market and marketing circumstances, whereas the costs will not be identical, they should present a similar pattern. Any significant deviation should be a red light. This simply calls for further examination, to determine whether or not it is justified. It may well be. Or it may not—and thereby point the way to still further exploration, perhaps remedial action. Identification of the deviation is but the first step. The justification and any subsequent action becomes the responsibility of the manager. If improvement results, he has earned the credit for it.

Accurate marketing-cost data can help determine the correct total cost, as a factor in price setting. Even though prices are not set on cost, evidence of a high margin can provide more freedom for competitive pricing decision making.

In addition to the foregoing analysis, which should contribute to improved current operations, there is a more fundamental use for marketing-cost data. There are many major problems within marketing which can be effectively approached via such data. Some examples are:

1. What significant interrelationships exist within marketing expenditures and how are they related? For instance, is there a relationship

TABLE 10.1 Cost Categories

The following definitions and code numbers refer to the cost categories shown on the cost tables:

MARKETING MANAGEMENT AND SERVICES (A)

Marketing Planning, Administration and Product Management (A-1). Includes costs of all activities and the time of all personnel concerned directly with the planning, administration and coordination of the unit's over-all marketing effort, and of marketing programs for its individual product lines. Excludes any costs relating to the planning, administration or coordination of other specific functions, such as sales management, covered in other categories.

Advertising and Sales Promotion (A-2). Includes costs of all advertising and sales promotion efforts developed and carried out at any level in the company in direct support of the sales of the unit's products, including compensation of personnel, media expenditures, promotional allowances to dealers, direct mail promotion, displays, product publicity, catalogues, trade shows, and the like, as well as an appropriate allocation of the unit's share of any group or corporate advertising from which it directly benefits. Excludes the costs of public relations personnel and activities, as well as the costs of strictly "institutional" advertising.

Marketing Research (A-3). Includes costs of all marketing and sales research pertaining to the unit's products and markets, including the compensation of research staff, the purchase of outside marketing research services, and an appropriate allocation of the costs of any marketing research carried out elsewhere in the company from which the unit benefits.

Pricing, Estimating, Quoting (A-4). Includes costs of developing prices, price lists, price quotations and bids, including pricing research and the preparation of estimates, drawings and the like in support of sales proposals. Includes time spent by staff personnel in these activities; but excludes such time spent by members of the field sales force, which is covered in B-2 below.

All Other Marketing-Related Costs (A-5). Includes any additional costs relating strictly to the unit's marketing staff activities and support services not included elsewhere. Excludes costs more directly related either to sales-related activities or to physical distribution, which are in categories B or C below.

SELLING COSTS (B)

Sales Management (B-1). Includes all costs incurred in the management, direction and supervision of the unit's *sales* effort, including compensation and expenses of sales managers both at headquarters and in the field, as well as any other expenses incurred in training members of the unit's sales organization or its resellers or other selling agents. Excludes costs relating to *nonsupervisory* personnel in the field who are engaged primarily in selling activities (B-2), or to the time of managerial personnel more directly related to *marketing* planning and administration (A-1, above).

Outside Salesmen (B-2). Includes compensation and other expenses incurred in maintaining the company's sales representatives in the field who sell the unit's products and who contact and service present and potential accounts that are users or resellers of these products. Excludes costs of inside salesmen (B-3, below), as well as of field personnel who are strictly concerned with supervisory duties (B-1), or with field services (B-4) rather than with selling. Excludes entirely any costs reflecting any

TABLE 10-1   Cost Categories (Continued)

portion of salesmen's time spent in selling products and accounts of units in the company other than the one for which costs are reported.

Inside Salesmen (B-3).   Includes compensation and all other costs relating to work of any inside salesmen for the unit who have no assignments in the field and very little face-to-face dealings with customers, prospects, or resellers.

Field Services (B-4).   Includes compensation and all other costs relating to the pre-sale and post-sale work of field service personnel in providing sales and technical services directly related to the potential or actual sale of the unit's products—e.g., engineering, application, installation, merchandising, and other sales service assistance to the unit's customers, potential customers, and resellers.   Includes also costs of servicing under warranty.   Excludes costs of salesmen's time spent on field service work (which is covered under B-2).   Excludes any costs relating to technical services that are provided on a contractual basis and for which the company is specifically compensated.

Compensation to Agents or Brokers (B-5).   Includes compensation and other actual monetary payments to agents, brokers and similar types of outside representatives who sell the unit's products but do not stock or take title to them.   Excludes costs relating to assistance and support of stocking resellers.

All Other Selling-Related Costs (B-6).   Includes any costs directly related to the selling operations of the reporting unit not included elsewhere.

Physical Distribution Costs (C)

Field Storage and Warehousing (C-1).   Includes all costs relating to the physical storage of the unit's products, including *all* the related costs of company-owned warehousing for the products and/or rental charges for use of public warehousing facilities.

Delivery and Transportation (C-2).   Includes all the unit's costs relating to the movement of its products at any and all stages from factory to customers or to stocking resellers, including movement of the products to and from field warehouses.

All Other Distribution-Related Costs (C-3).   Includes any costs relating to the physical distribution of the unit's products not included in the two previous categories.

source: The Marketing-Cost Institute's data-reporting form, The Conference Board, 1970.

between field-sales costs and advertising expenditures?   Do the firms with the largest advertising budgets enjoy the lowest sales costs?   If so, is this particular to certain sets of circumstances or relatively uniform across the industrial board?   Can it be shown that there is no such relationship?   Would the answers to such questions be of interest and value to manufacturer-advertisers, advertising agencies, media, and marketing management?

2. Is there an optimal range for marketing costs—in total or for any one segment?   That is, is there a high point beyond which one is probably wasting money, or a low, below which one is not spending enough to do the job?

3. What are the relative costs and efficiencies of various marketing mixes? Are the more efficient ones augmentative, or merely efficient by contrast with others less so? What happens to overall efficiency if the latter are reduced or eliminated?

4. To what extent are marketing costs and efficiency of results really substitutable? And are there attendant sets of circumstances which impact on the degree of freedom to substitute without loss of result?

5. Are there significant variations in marketing costs? Are there trends? If so, do they relate to economic trends or particular industrial conditions, and how? Are they predictable?

No one can foresee just what might come from application of such data. The unknowns predominate. The potential for learning more of the act of marketing, of the differences between associative and causative factors, and of in-depth exploration of the efficiencies and the identification of relevant circumstances well warrant continued attention to this area.

AVAILABILITY OF MARKETING-COST DATA

It is logical to expect trade associations to provide marketing-cost data, at least from the more market-oriented firms of their membership. Some do an excellent job of assembling cost data from their members. Even with sophisticated reporting, it is rare to find such data assembled by marketing significants, by channel of distribution or specific product groupings. Trade-association membership is structured along broad industry lines of somewhat nonhomogeneous firms. Nor do all firms in each industry belong to an association or the same association. Other trade associations have made little or no attempt to compile such data.

As a result, such information from trade associations is a variable. Many trade associations, in recognition of the need for and value of this information, have been cooperating with The Conference Board to help bring the marketing-cost data service to the attention of their members.

Most corporations have been making marketing-cost analyses and comparisons for some time. The basis for this has largely been performance to budget. The budget has been a competent projection of their historical costs, adjusted for future plans and expectancies—all their own. Intercompany and interindustry yardsticks for the costs of marketing under similar circumstances have been missing.

The Marketing-Cost Institute

During the 1960s preliminary research into the area of marketing costs was conducted. This led in 1967 to the creation of the Marketing-Cost

Institute as a research entity to receive, process, and distribute market-ing-cost data.   The initial response demonstrated the reality of manage-ment's interest and the availability of the prerequisite data on a uniform basis to permit comparability.[2]

In 1969 the Institute became a division of The Conference Board.   Par-ticipation in the Institute's service is open to all manufacturer-sellers, both consumer and industrial.[3]   This research service provides manage-ment with not only meaningful yardsticks but also unique information never before available on the relationships of marketing factors to costs.

Earl L. Bailey, director of the Marketing-Cost Institute, reports on some of the results of the Institute's research in his article, "Manufac-turers' Marketing Costs," in The Conference Board *Record*.   Excerpts from that article follow.[4]

Despite management's concern, comparative marketing costs have never been satisfactorily explored.   The lack of reliable, comparable data on companies' cost experiences is now being remedied by the Marketing-Cost Institute, a division of The Conference Board.   Its cooperative Market-ing-Cost Service keeps participating managements informed on prevailing patterns of marketing expense in their respective industries.   In addition the Institute carries on a broader, continuing program of cost research.

Some of the Institute's latest findings . . . shed light on important factors associated with differences in manufacturers' marketing costs.

In a recent year, one of the principal marketing units of Company A, a well-known multidivisional manufacturer, spent 36% of its sales income just to maintain its marketing effort.   In the same year, com-parable expenditures by marketing units in manufacturing Companies B and C amounted to 12% and 6%, respectively, of their sales.   What is of greatest interest in retrospect—as it was to each of the managements concerned—is that in none of these instances was the total expenditure for marketing in relation to sales seriously out of line.   Evidence suggests that the cost/sales ratio for each of the three units was probably very close to average *for its particular kind of marketing operation* that year.

There are, of course, many reasons why all manufacturers do not spend exactly the same proportion of their sales dollars on behalf of marketing.   For one thing, no two marketing operations share exactly the same strengths and weaknesses.   They vary as to relative market

[2] For highlights of this development, see "Marketing-Cost Research Takes a Giant Step," *Industrial Marketing*, November 1968, copyright 1968 by Advertising Publica-tions, Inc., Chicago, Illinois, pp. 56–62, and "Marketing-Cost Data," *Sales/Marketing Today*, January 1969, pp. 22–23.

[3] Detailed information on the availability of marketing-cost data may be obtained from the Marketing-Cost Institute, Division of The Conference Board, 845 Third Avenue, New York, N.Y. 10022.

[4] Earl L. Bailey, "Manufacturers' Marketing Costs," The Conference Board *Record*, October 1971.

share, reputation, quality of product, quality of management, quality of field representation, market coverage, and the like. As a result, no two operations are likely to achieve the same degree of marketing efficiency. One will probably be able to generate relatively more sales than the other for the effort and money expended.

Even if the aggregate budgets of two marketing departments were of similar size, their managements might allocate their resources in different ways.

Key Factors Related to Marketing Costs:

The following characteristics of manufacturers' marketing units and product lines are significantly related to the ratio of their total marketing costs[5] to their sales:

A unit that markets consumer products:

- Type of product market.
- Sales volume of the unit.
- Number of reseller accounts serviced for the line.
- Amount of sales service extended to reseller accounts.
- Significance of the product's purchase to the consumer.

A unit that markets non-consumer products:

- Type of product market.
- Sales volume of the unit.
- Number of customer or reseller accounts serviced for the line.
- Frequency of the product's purchase.
- Whether line is sold from inventory or manufactured on order.
- Distribution channel by which product reaches the user.
- Number of competitors for the line.

There are still other factors that might be expected to influence comparative marketing expenditures, but which apparently do not. Thus, there is no evidence that differences in the degree to which manufacturers' products are standardized, or the degree of specialization of assignments within their sales forces, contribute in any significant way to differences in their *total* marketing-cost ratios.

While research now confirms that certain characteristics of manufacturers' marketing operations have an important influence on the ratio of their total marketing costs to their sales, there remains some variation in such ratios still not accounted for by these characteristics. It is reasonable to assume that some of this unexplained variation is attributable in part to management decisions and other internal influences within companies. To put it another way, although the cost ratios of a large number of marketing units sharing the same cost-related characteristics

---

[5] This excludes another major category covered in the Marketing-Cost Institute, physical-distribution costs, which are subject to other influences.

can still be expected to vary, there is a tendency for their ratios to converge on an average.   If the ratio for one does not conform very closely to that average, an obvious possibility is that there may be something unusual about its basic operating style or the efficiency with which it exploits its market opportunities.

With further study, no doubt, will come more precise knowledge of the determinants of marketing costs, as well as their relation to sales—the causative and the effective.

RELEVANT READING

Bailey, Earl L., "Cost Guidelines for the Marketer," The Conference Board *Record*, vol. 6, no. 12, pp. 42–44, December 1969.

Hudig, John, "Marketing Costs and Their Control," *The Financial Executive*, July 1963, pp. 16–20.

Jones, Manley Howe, *The Marketing Process*, New York: Harper & Row, Publishers, Incorporated, 1965, chap. 3.

Kotler, Philip, *Marketing Management*, Englewood Cliffs, N.J.: Prentice-Hall, Inc., 1967, pp. 585–592.

"Marketing-Cost Research Takes a Giant Step," *Industrial Marketing*, November 1968, pp. 56–62.

CHAPTER ELEVEN

Pricing

The concept of price as the key factor between buyer and seller—as the value of the total satisfactions received by the buyer from the seller and therefore of prime importance—is well established. So well, in fact, that it is commonly viewed as the nexus between them, the connecting link in their relationship. That this is not true in actual practice, at least in most cases, seems to detract but little from the belief.

WHEN PRICE IS, AND ISN'T, IMPORTANT

It is true that price is important and that the pricing decision is very significant; but it is not true that the significance of price is a top-level constant to purchasing considerations across the board. Rather, it is a variable.

When goods are priced above the market, price tends to lose significance, except to help imply the quality, and nonprice quality considerations dominate. When goods are sold at the market, with no serious price difference between highly competitive substitutable items, price per se washes out. For practical purposes it is the same for all. Other, nonprice factors, such as product and service differences, dominate in the purchase decision. When goods are sold below the market, the price appeal is strong. It may imply a "saving." It may seek to obtain high volume with a reduced margin. It may be an indication of a lower level of quality. It may be a caution signal—a new supplier trying to get "in" through an opening low price, or a strong hint that something is out of line, somewhere. It may be a very strong appeal, particularly if it constitutes a bona fide reduction from the competitive level.

In competitive bidding, unless one has a unique product, price is apt to be quite important. But even here, it is not always the major determinant. Not all such contracts are awarded to the lowest bidder. The actual selection most frequently involves consideration of many other factors, technical excellence and both product and customer service, for example.

In industrial marketing, price is used far less as a competitive weapon than it is in consumer marketing. Industry is more knowledgeable. Industrial customers are far more interested in delivery, service, and general capability and reliability of the seller. Vendor evaluation is a serious consideration in industrial buying. Quality of both the product and the application engineering, both product and customer service, and the capability of the seller to work cooperatively with the buyer to maximize his satisfaction all tend to sublimate price both as a strategic tool and as a buying consideration. This is not to say eliminate. Rather, it is a question of degree. Nonprice factors are growing, while price is declining in significance—relatively.

Cost versus Price

The distinction between cost and price is sometimes overlooked. Price is the amount to be paid for a good. Cost is the expense incurred in its ownership and use. Price measures the amount of the capital investment. Cost is a reflection of its efficiency. A high price can be offset by cost saving in use and operation. A low price may mean higher operational expenses, a shorter life, or other increased costs but be accompanied by lower depreciation and interest charges (cost of capital). In some cases, machines completely written off are still in use, even though relatively inefficient, for a la carte orders and short runs. There, the somewhat higher costs of operation, when coupled with a zero price, cost of capital, and depreciation, still provide an attractive net cost for such business.

ORGANIZATION FOR PRICING, AND A FEW OTHER THINGS

As corporations grew and segmentation became necessary for operational efficiency and better control, divisions were created. The basis for this divisionalization was products, heavily dominated by manufacturing and geographical considerations. This made sense and worked very well. With the exception of the major division of operations between industrial and consumer, only a few firms, at the start, created divisions based on the market to be served. Many of these were in consumer marketing, mail order versus retailing, for example. More recently, and primarily since World War II, governmental divisions were created.

So, we have a start. In considering pricing as a major function of marketing, our attention is directed toward the market. Where more than one market is served, the prices and, in fact, the underlying price policies are influenced by the nature of the markets. They can differ significantly. A different pricing policy can be used for each one. Thus, pricing decisions become a reflection of the markets, rather than the manufacturing.

Add to this the simple fact that price does not stand alone. It is but one factor in the total marketing strategy. This strategy is (or ought to be) adopted to a major extent as a result of the nature of each market.

Let's go one step further and consider the marketing concept, the integrated goal of customer satisfactions. Add this to the picture and we can begin to perceive a new approach to corporate organization, with divisionalization based on the markets being served, instead of the products being manufactured. This is really not "new"—it is but a further refinement. It recognizes the impact of market demands, and tailors the firm to meet them by adjustment of the corporate organization based on market and marketing considerations.

The value of this approach lies in the market orientation as a guide to concentration and integration of corporate efforts for the attainment of corporate goals. It will create new problems. It will also create a new level of customer satisfactions. The implementation should not be dismissed because of the problems. Rather, it should be given serious consideration wherever present or future volume in more than one differentiated market permits it. If such an organization provides a more uniform administration and attainment of policy, if it is (or can become) more efficient, if it lessens the problems of dealing with customers, and most important of all, if it tends to increase customer satisfactions—it is worth a second thought. The increase in customer satisfactions by such an approach can be a lucrative reward for the effort.

This organization is not proposed for all situations. There are many reasons, heavily traditional, to deny it. Production could remain specialized, but feed more than one division if the products are sold in more than one market. However, there are many situations where it is appropriate. In such cases, it offers an integration of pricing, marketing strategy, customer service, and all the attributes of the implementation of marketing, under a set of circumstances directed toward the attainment of the basic goal, maximization of customer satisfaction at a profit.

Technological specialization, instead of being impeded, might even be augmented. The specialist would become even more expert in the problems of his market and better known to his group of customers.

Therefore, it is suggested that in those cases of multidivisional firms, with several product lines serving more than one market, right down to the smaller company with but a few profit centers, a critical appraisal of their situations from this point of view can do no harm, and may open the door to moving in the direction of improvement in marketing.

POLICY

Price policy provides the framework for pricing decisions. The selection of the price policy is guided by the corporate goals and the circumstances of the market. Since many firms serve more than one market, the difference between markets may call for a different price policy in each, as was noted above. On the other hand, it may be entirely feasible to adopt a uniform price policy for an entire company. This decision comes from an awareness of the applicability and the likelihood of one or various policies to serve best the corporate objectives in the face of variable market circumstances.

The major price policies in common use, their goals, and significant factors involved in each follow.

Market Share

Market share is a measure of the firm's relative penetration of a market, expressed in dollars, units, or percent of total industry sales. This aids in evaluation of one firm versus its competitors. For this purpose, i.e., relative, competitive performance, it is far more valuable than return on investment (ROI), absolute sales, or profits.

A pricing policy using market share as its objective places the emphasis on volume. This, in turn, tends to seek more volume through lower prices, perhaps coupled with aggressive selling effort. It may succeed, even in highly competitive situations.

Perhaps the biggest danger in this policy is the very emphasis on volume, and deemphasis on profit. A point can be reached where additional volume can be attained only at a cost greater than the additional profit generated from that increased volume. If this volume is attained through a price reduction, the net result can readily be reduced total profit. Even in cases of reasonably high elasticity, where a price decrease produces a proportionately greater demand and where revenue is increased thereby, there is no assurance that profit is increased. The crucial point lies not in the elasticity or the increased revenue alone, but also in the costs—and specifically in the ratio of fixed to variable costs. The higher the percentage variable costs are of total costs, the greater must be the elasticity for a profit to be derived from a price reduction. Perhaps an example may help clarify these relationships. Clare E. Griffin provides an appropriate one:[1]

> Let us consider in some detail the automobile industry which, in many ways is fairly representative of American heavy industry. It will be illuminating if we work out the implications of the studies of demand mentioned by John Blair, which indicate a price elasticity for new automobiles ranging from 1.2 to 1.5. These studies seem to imply that this would justify a price reduction. What the 1.5 figure means, for example, is that the increased demand will be one and one-half times as great as the decreased price, or that a 1.0% decrease in price would produce a 1.5% increase in demand. (Strictly speaking, the coefficient is a minus quantity, for the quantity bought varies inversely with price. However, it seems easier to neglect minus signs and this fairly common practice will be followed here.)
>
> Let us accept for the moment the largest of these figures as an indication of the reaction of demand to a price change and ask whether it would be profitable for an automobile manufacturer to reduce the list price of a line of cars by, say, $100. Assuming that the average price of the line is $2,500, let us place the anticipated sales volume at this price at 1,000,000 cars. We will also assume that a price reduction by one producer will be met by others, so that we are not considering a relative price advantage but the effect of a general price change. How will volume and revenue be affected? Consider this:
>
> A price reduction from $2,500 to $2,400 is 4%. With a demand elasticity of 1.5 this would indicate a resulting increase in sales of 6% (i.e., 1.5 × 4%). So volume would be increased from 1,000,000 to 1,060,000 cars, and sales and revenue would be affected as follows:
>
> At price of $2,500, 1,000,000 cars × $2,500 = $2,500,000,000
> At price of $2,400, 1,060,000 cars × $2,400 = $2,544,000,000
>
> Thus, we would have increased revenue by $44,000,000. This is where much popular reasoning, as well as that of some economists, ends. The conclusion is hastily drawn that if the manufacturer really recognized the degree of elasticity, or if he were not overly cautious or just plain stupid, he would seize this opportunity to increase revenue.
>
> Of course, revenue alone is not the objective; rather the maintenance of profit is the ultimate goal, and to estimate this we must consider costs as well. This is the point often overlooked by those who criticize business, especially the mass-production industries. Over-estimating the role of increased volume in reducing unit costs, they forget that the

[1] Clare E. Griffin, "When Is Price Reduction Profitable?" *Harvard Business Review,* September-October 1960, pp. 126–128.

true effect on total costs of producing the additional 60,000 cars will depend on the ratio of fixed costs to variable costs.

In the automobile industry, my own interviews indicate that the ratio would be on the order of 15% to 20% for fixed costs and 80% to 85% for variable.

In order to consider what happens to cost in our illustrative case, let us accept for purposes of our analysis, a fixed-variable cost ratio of 20 to 80, thus taking again the upper limit of the estimated range which would be most favorable to the price reduction proposal.

We assumed as our starting point a price of $2,500 and a volume of 1,000,000, thus yielding a revenue of $2,500,000,000. Now if we assume that unit costs are $2,300, there is a total cost of $2,300,000,000 and a profit of $200,000,000. If the 20 to 80 ratio of fixed to variable costs exists, this total cost then breaks down to fixed costs of $460,000,000 (20% of $2,300,000,000) and variable costs of $1,840,000,000 (80% of $2,300,000,000), or $1,840 per car.

If we reduce the price to $2,400, revenue will, as indicated before, become $2,544,000,000, but the number of cars produced and sold is increased from 1,000,000 to 1,060,000. Costs will become:

Fixed Cost	$ 460,000,000
Variable ($1,840 × 1,060,000)	1,950,400,000
	$2,410,400,000

Profits can be determined thus:

Revenue	$2,544,000,000
Costs	2,410,400,000
Profit	$ 133,600,000

Thus, while the price reduction produced an increase in revenue of $44,000,000 (from $2,500,000,000 to $2,544,000,000), it reduced profits by $66,400,000 (from $200,000,000 to $133,600,000). Expressed in unit terms, the price reduction led to reduced revenue per car of $100, and to reduced cost per car of only $26.42. Cost at the larger volume, therefore, would be $2,273.58 instead of $2,300 at the old volume. Obviously, the additional cars are not free goods, and anyone who makes recommendations as to price policy on the basis of revenue only—or on the assumption that the reduction in revenue per car will "naturally" be offset by the larger volume—is being decidedly unrealistic.

Target Pricing

This price policy places the emphasis on a measure of profitability instead of volume. Various measures are used, depending on the preferences of the management. Return on investment (ROI), return on sales, maintained markup on cost, and return on capital employed are some. In essence, they are cost plus. The price is determined by adding to estimated standard costs an average margin to produce the desired return. Variation in markups between products is discretionary. It is hoped that the overall results will be "on target." Realistically, the target could be a range from unsatisfactory, through varying degrees of desirability, to optimal.

Inherent in this is the determination and accuracy of the estimated standard costs. This involves allocation to each product. And this is not easy to do accurately—under conditions of varying utilization of plant and equipment as well as variation in other cost items. It can produce too high a price for some products, once the markup is added. Competition is still a factor in most price setting.

Some managements have used this approach to supervise their divisional operations. The division is granted wide latitude in its operations and decision making. It may be provided with additional capital as requested. All that is required is that the division provide the minimum return on investment, or better. If the divisional manager overextends himself, or fails to produce the targeted result, perhaps a new one will do better.

Setting the target return in the first place is crucial. It involves a high degree of discretion, past performance of the division and the industry, industrial potentials, and knowledge of reasonable expectancy of what the market will bear. Although the range varies significantly among industries, target returns of 14 to 20 percent after taxes are not unheard of.

Fair Prices

The concept of "fair prices" raises the immediate question of "fair to whom?" Many companies accept fair prices as a more reasonable and practical goal of pricing than an arbitrary percentage—such as a return on investment of X percent. The difficulty is to define "fair"—and to determine this from three points of view: the manufacturer's, the middleman's, and the customer's.

A firm might be viewed as "entitled" to a "reasonable" profit. Practical competition denys this. It is "entitled" only to such reasonable profits as it can earn competitively. A fair price based on inefficiencies in cost will not survive long in a competitive economy.

A price policy which attempts to earn a reasonable profit—a fair profit—must be set on the cost structure of the firm and incorporate a "reasonable" return. This is essentially the same as target pricing, with, perhaps, some modification in the rate of return acceptable as "reasonable" or "fair." In target pricing the primary emphasis is the average return to the firm. In fair pricing, the considerations are broadened to include the others involved, and the price is set to serve best the interests of everyone.

Price Leadership: Avoid or Seek?

Price leadership introduces a keen awareness of the prices set by competitors. The price leader is the one to introduce a price change, which is followed by others. In the long run, only the most efficient firms can afford to struggle for price leadership.

Obviously, the best position to take, assuming efficiency permits, is a bit below the competition—but not so far below as to cause retaliation. Industrial price changes are quite frequent, but usually in small amounts—at least, as compared to consumer pricing. Taking this pricing position permits the firm to maintain its prices for longer periods. Even if the firm does not enjoy an advantage in efficiency, and such a price position means a somewhat reduced margin, the probable increased volume and ease of selling may be well worth it.

If the cost structure prohibits selling a bit below, or at the lower end of the market-price range, the next higher position is to price at the market. This means that the market prices control the firm's. The "market" can be either the price leader, the major competitor, or several firms which price very closely to each other. Under such circumstances, price is no longer a major factor in selling. Sales are made on product and service differentiation, goodwill, and other nonprice factors.

Selling above the market is not necessarily a sign of further inefficiency. Rather, if it can be done successfully, it means that some aspect of superior quality or service is the basis for sales. A truly unique product or feature may substantiate this position. Or, the firm may be able to offer an exceptionally high level of technological assistance. Another justification can be simply in the difference between cost and price. The high market price might be coupled with a better operational cost to the user.

Whether to avoid or seek price leadership is, therefore, not the major question in pricing. Rather, the pricing position is more soundly determined from an analysis of the firm's competitive advantages and position, the major factors involved in the customers' decisions to buy, and the marketing strategy of the firm. Whether or not this results in becoming a price leader is almost incidental as long as the underlying factors support the position taken. To seek price leadership per se, say, for prestige, can be a very dangerous and self-defeating tactic, except for the firm in the optimal situation of a significant advantage in efficiency, an equal or superior product, and the capability of maintaining this position for some time.

Protection from Competition

If the cost of entry to a market is relatively low, it will be easy for competition to enter. High prices may provide high profits, and this is readily discernible to competition. They are well aware of the costs, too. Under such circumstances, about the only protection a firm has is the time advantage before competition can become effective.

To dissuade competition, if this threat is real, and particularly in introducing a new product, lower prices may be used.

Another consideration is the size of the potential market and the capability of the firm to serve it. Competition may not seriously impede sales, anyway. This merely lessens the threat; but, at the same time, it permits somewhat higher prices. A danger in this is overpricing. The competitor may enter the market at significantly lower prices, force a price reduction on the original seller, and cost him goodwill as a result.

One further point might be mentioned here. The opening price might be set as a function of full cost. If it happens that considerable R&D expenditures are included, the rate of recovery is crucial. It can raise the full costs, and consequently the prices, substantially. A competitor may be able to introduce a competitive substitute without extensive R&D expenditures. The answer to this might be to either avoid full-cost pricing or to substantially lower the rate of recovery of R&D expenditures. The resultant lower price may lengthen the time required for a competitor to recover its investment, particularly if new plant and equipment are required.

Guarantee against a Price Decline

A guarantee against a price decline isn't a guarantee that the seller won't reduce his prices. In fact, when used, it is under conditions which provide a high likelihood that prices will be reduced.

In prosperity, with gradually increasing price levels and very little probability of a price decline, such a guarantee is seldom used. Under conditions of recession, with actual or anticipated price reductions, the buyer may start buying hand to mouth. He reduces the size of his normal orders and seeks to follow the price decline, to buy more heavily at a lower price later on. The seller, faced with this action by his larger customers, may seek to maintain production levels by offering a guarantee against a price decline, to obtain the normal, larger orders.

The guarantee simply states that if the seller reduces his price, the buyer will be reimbursed for the reduction. This protects the buyer from a cost disadvantage, when his competitors buy later at the lowered price. With this protection, the buyer does not suffer if prices are lowered. He can buy in the normal quantity preferred by both buyer and seller.

Such guarantees must contain a time limit, obviously. One problem for the seller who uses them is whether to have them all expire at the same time or to stagger the expiration dates. If the former, and if prices do in fact decline, he can probably defer his reduction to avoid reimbursements, but obtain business only with additional guarantees during the guaranteed period. If staggered, the price cut will call for varying reimbursements, but the pressure to defer the price cut is far less.

In addition, problems of determination of the amount of the reimbursement are involved. The basis could be time. In this case, the time remaining as a percent of the total time involved could be applied to the amount of the reduction, to determine the reimbursement. Or, the reimbursement might be of the full reduction, applied to the number of units on hand at the time of the reduction. This involves the buyer's inventory-accounting procedures, lifo versus fifo (last in, first out, versus first in, first out). Other equitable bases can be determined. The guarantee should spell them out in detail to avoid any misunderstanding with its attendant risk to goodwill.

FACTORS INVOLVED IN THE ACT OF PRICING

The total involvement of factors in the act of reaching a price decision is tremendous. Even the listing of all the factors bearing on the decision seems almost endless. They could be grouped under major headings such as costs, product, stage in product life cycle, services, corporate goals, channel considerations, credit, demand, type and reaction of competition, market share, economic, geographic, image, social, ethical, and legal as a start. Under each one of these would be several to many variables—some controllable, some not.

To further compound the problem, costs and sales results are historical. Pricing is for the future. Problems of forecasting and all its uncertainties become involved.

Economics provides an in-depth analysis and study of pricing theory. This is excellent background for a broad perspective. Mathematical models and sophisticated quantitative approaches can be employed. All aid—none solve. When it comes right down to the "nitty-gritty" of it, the price is a discretionary value judgment of a manager. And this introduces the man and his experience, intuition, foresight, and human biases.

Discretionary Range

The discretionary range available to the industrial pricing executive is a variable. It is minimal under conditions of keen competition and standardized items. It is perhaps greatest on high-ticket capital installations, high-technology items built to perform to an exacting set of specifications. In between is a wide range of product and market considerations which offer various degrees of freedom in price setting.

In some situations, the market price is established through varying degrees of open competition. The price is frequently published daily, and both public and private transactions are apt to be made at a price very close to that figure. This is particularly true for agricultural products, basic raw materials, and commodities. Here, both the pricing executive and the buyer can do very little about the price except to try to anticipate future changes. This discretion in price setting by the individual seller approaches zero.

Competitive Situation

The varying degrees of competition, all the way from monopoly, with one seller and perhaps many buyers, to monopsony, with one buyer and many sellers, have been adequately discussed and explored, and generalizations have been reached, in basic economics texts. More sophisticated treatments are readily available in more advanced texts. Some of the more explicit are included in the "Relevant Reading" at the end of this chapter.

One point to be included here is not theory, but reality. The competitive *situation* is one thing—the competitive *reaction* is another. And the competitive reaction to a pricing decision is both uncontrollable and highly important (at least when price is important). It may, or it may not, follow along predictable or theoretical lines. That decision rests with the competitive managements, their goals, and what they deem to be in their best interests in the face of each one's own total circumstances.

In general, most industrial marketing is in the middle ground, a variegated area with a high level of competition, typically many buyers and sellers (although this is a great variable), a high degree of product differentiation, reasonable ease of entry into the market, heavy use of nonprice competitive weapons, and a high level of sophistication of buying influentials. No one firm can control the market for long, although a few large sellers acting in concert might. Governmental policing of competitive activities is strong and is a potent factor in fostering a high level of competition.

Costs

Revenue minus costs equals profit. It is obvious that to be sure of a profit, revenue must exceed total costs. On an aggregate basis this is not hard. The weakness lies in attempting to do so on an individual-product basis. Here, cost determination presents a major problem.

A variation in costs affects cost-oriented pricing decisions and/or profit. But cost is, to a frequently unrealized degree, discretionary. Let us examine the composition of a cost figure. It includes direct labor and materials—readily ascertainable. No problem there. It also includes factory burden, depreciation, general administrative overhead, and marketing costs. These are very heavily allocations. And allocations, however accurately computed, are based on discretionary judgment. In no way is this a reflection on the logical applicability or fairness of the base used, the time periods involved, the rate or method of depreciation used, or any other such determination. That must be done. Typically, it is most competently done. The point lies not in the technique employed or the reasoning involved. It lies in their nature—allocations are based on judgments. Change the circumstances, or even the attitude of the man in charge, and the judgment can change, the allocation can change, the cost can change. So the price and/or profit can change.

The use of tax-oriented data for cost determination is quite common. It should be realized that costs determined for tax purposes, for example, where accelerated depreciation is involved, should not influence cost for current pricing purposes. The cost accountant should not be too tax-accounting-conscious. These are two different cost determinations for two different purposes. They need not match.

Price has been deemed to be a function of cost in many instances (cost-plus pricing). Could it not be possible to work the other way around, and make the allocated cost a function of the price? Is the allocated cost figure an immutable result—or is it an amendable one, based on market considerations, as well as tax accounting or production considerations? It is submitted that there are circumstances where the flexibility which could be utilized in costing (as a result of discretionary judgments, soundly based) might permit far more price flexibility and/or profitability in competitive marketing.

Demand

The demand for industrial goods possesses some significantly different characteristics from consumer-goods demand. These are contained in Chapter Two, to which the reader is referred since they are significant to the pricing consideration.

Basically, industrial demand is derived rather than autonomous. As such, the industrial buyer does not face the question of whether or not to buy; rather, the question becomes, buy from whom, when, and how? The goods must be acquired, some way. They are needed to satisfy the demand he faces. The make-or-buy decision is an outgrowth of this.

There is, then, far less need for persuasion to create or stimulate demand than is common in consumer marketing. There is a far greater need for an effective influencing of the existent demand to the individual seller. This produces a keen awareness of the buyers' needs, rapid advances in technology to better serve them, and a high degree of interdependence and cooperation between buyers and sellers. Pricing tends to be sublimated to such considerations. Reliability, delivery, appropriate quality, service, and order processing (including automated rebuys) are very significant. All tend to influence the selection of the source of supply.

The total amount is determined by the derived demand to be satisfied. The behavior of the demand for the goods of the individual firm well warrants careful consideration of the characteristics of industrial demand discussed in Chapter Two.

Geographical Location

Geography presents no problem in pricing industrial diamonds, or goods with a relatively high unit value and with transportation charges a minor portion of their total cost. However, on many basic raw and semiprocessed materials, the unit price per pound is low, and transportation costs loom large in the total paid. In such cases, geographical location, proximity to or remoteness from the source, involves major differences in total delivered cost and thus becomes a factor in the price-policy decision.

When transportation charges are minor or negligible, f.o.b. origin is frequently used. The goods are placed free on board a carrier at the point of origin. The buyer pays the transportation. The seller is simply paid for the goods. Price discrimination is avoided. Postage-stamp pricing is used for many such items. This is simply "free" delivery, effected through a uniform delivered price, regardless of location. Whereas, in theory, the near help subsidize delivery to the far, in practice the involvement is very small or trivial. The convenience in billing to both buyer and seller well warrant its use.

When transportation charges become significant or large, f.o.b. origin tends to restrict the seller's effective sales area to a reasonable distance from his location(s). To enlarge the trading area, f.o.b. destination is used.

The "Pittsburgh-Plus Plan" started the basing-point system. This is simply quoting prices competitively, f.o.b. Pittsburgh, with transportation charges from Pittsburgh to the buyer's location added. Buyers no longer need compute and include transportation from the location of each of serveral competitors to arrive at a delivered cost. They now pay the same transportation charge, irrespective of the actual distance the goods travel. The next step is to add more basing points, thereby creating a multiple basing-point system.

When the actual charges paid the carrier are less than the freight collected, the difference is phantom freight. When the actual charges are greater, the seller absorbs them. The profits of phantom freight from the nearby customers used to offset the costs of freight absorption to the more removed customers can permit quite extensive interpenetration of markets. This subsidy of one group of customers by another is illegal, if it results in unfair competition. This can happen if the buyers are in competition. It does not mean that the basing-point system is illegal, per se. Its *use* becomes so, if it results in unfair competition.

Zone pricing is done to simplify handling transportation charges by the use of an average transportation charge to any location within one zoned area. To avoid embarrassment by two different effective prices to customers located on each side of the zone boundary line, state lines, rivers, etc., should not be the boundary lines. "East and west of the Mississippi" splits St. Louis; and a look at the map, particularly at the North, can demonstrate the impracticality of its use. A major trading area should be entirely in one zone, with the boundaries running through "no-man's land."

Governmental

Any pricing executive should be thoroughly familiar with the Robinson-Patman Act of 1936, an amendment of the Clayton Act of 1914, and with the interpretations and trends since then. Add to this the Federal Trade Commission, also created in 1914, as an arbiter, and the impact of the governmental influence on pricing decisions can be seen to be both profound and realistic. Here is an area for involvement of the corporate counsel, particularly in the contemplative stage of any corporate price-policy considerations.

In brief, price fixing and price discrimination are illegal; the latter is illegal if it results in unfair competition or if it tends to lessen competition or create a monopoly. Legal price discrimination can and does exist in many situations. Some are in the absence of competition; based on time, as different admission charges for matinee and evening theater tickets; based on geography, with no competition between such areas; based on use, as in electricity; and based on quantity, as in cost savings of quantity discounts.

The identical price to two different, competitive buyers is not conclusive of no price discrimination. It must be for the same goods—not for two different degrees of refinement, for example. Cost and price differentials must be substantiated, if challenged. Even though this has given a boost to cost accounting, particularly since 1936, it still may be difficult to satisfactorily demonstrate cost savings to permit pricing differentials, even today. Pricing to meet competition is legal, provided it is "to meet" and is bona fide. There are strict limitations applicable to such pricing. Among them are the timing, location, and the customers involved, as well as prevention of any reduction below the price being met, or the use of the reduced price to gain new customers. These, of course, do not apply to general price reductions to everyone.

There are special circumstances which are exempt from the general rules. Some examples are bona fide closeouts of a permanently discontinued line; reductions to move a highly seasonal item before the end of the season; legitimately going out of business at a location; and need for an immediate sale in the face of real and imminent economic or physical obsolescence or spoilage.

Marketing Objectives

In addition to the obvious need to integrate the pricing decision with the attainment of the marketing objectives, some special situations can become involved in pricing. One item might enjoy a low price, in order to penetrate a market, and thereby provide increased demand for other items commonly used with it. Tie-in product sales are a good example, and particularly if such products are not highly standardized. A slightly less obvious tactic, but one equally applicable, is to seek increased sales by lowering the price of the good, in order to increase the granting of credit—which may enjoy a rate of return substantially greater than the profit on the item sold. In essence, pricing can be a powerful tool to aid in implementation of the marketing goals, both generally and in special situations.

TERMINOLOGY: MATHEMATICAL
INTERRELATIONSHIPS

Figure 11.1 has been prepared to illustrate graphically the relationships and relative values of the basic pricing terms.

"List price" is rarely a price at which an item is intended to be sold. Rather, it is a mathematical base from which other prices are computed. In catalogs, where description and specifications change far more slowly than price, the list price can be printed on the page. Readily replaceable trade-discount lists, perhaps a different one for each stage in the distribution channel, can provide the information needed to determine cost. This greatly prolongs the life of the catalog, saves money, and preserves the confidentiality of cost. To do this, the list price should be set originally at a level somewhat above the highest intended resale price by any middleman and for a reasonable time in the future.

"Trade discounts" (TDs), sometimes called "functional discounts," are given to middlemen for the performance of their functions. The TD is written in the form of a chain discount, 40, 20, 10 percent, for example. This is not a 70 percent discount from list. Rather, 40 percent is first taken, then 20 percent is taken from the remainder, then 10 percent from that remainder, and so on. With a list price of $100, 40 percent off leaves $60; then, 20 percent of $60 is $12, leaving $48; then, 10 percent off the $48, or $4.80, provides a cost of $43.20. Thus one moves downward from list, via TDs, to cost.

"Cost" can be the cost of an item to the reseller. This diagram is equally applicable collectively. "Cost" would then become cost of goods sold.

"Markup," or "mark-on," is the difference between cost and the original marked price (OMP). This is the price first placed on the price ticket. On any one transaction it may be the sales figure. Collectively, it is somewhat higher than sales, or sales receipts, which are the actual receipts for the goods sold. The difference is an aggregative term, "retail reductions" (RR's), which include all such items as stock shortages, pilferage, breakage, spoilage, discounts to employees or special groups of customers, and markdowns.

"Margin," the difference between sales and cost, should not be confused with markup. Margin covers two items, expenses of operation and profit. Margin, retail reductions (including its subdivisions), and markup can be expressed in dollars or percent. When percent is used, it is very important to recognize that there are two—and only two—bases for the percent calculation. One is cost. The other is sales. The origi-

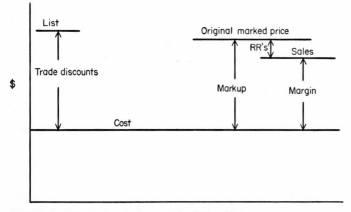

Fig. 11.1 Pricing terminology and relationships.

nal marked price is never a base for anything. In fact, it is not added up or recorded on the reseller's books. His cost and sales are. During recent years, percent of sales has been growing rapidly in popularity, so much so that it is the common assumption as to what is meant if the base for a percentage figure is unidentified. If one means percent of cost, one would be wise to say so to avoid confusion.

It may be helpful to further illustrate these relationships with the use of some simple mathematics. For example, a "10 percent discount to employees" is not a retail reduction of 10 percent, but 11.1 percent (*of sales*). If an employee buys an item priced at $100 with this discount, he would pay $100 less 10 percent, or $90. The 10 percent discount, as a percent of sales, is 11.1 percent ($10/90 $\times$ 100 = 11.1 percent).

A similar instance relates to markdowns, another element of the retail reductions. If a 25 percent markdown is to be taken, i.e., the price is to be reduced by 25 percent of the *sales* to be received after the markdown, a $10 item should be repriced at $8—not $7.50. (The $7.50 results from a 33⅓ percent markdown—$2.50/7.50 $\times$ 100 = 33⅓ percent.)

There is a practical way to convert a percentage margin based on sales to the equivalent margin based on cost. Consider this:

Selling price	$1.00
Margin	.25
Cost	$ .75

It is obvious that this margin is 25 percent of sales, 33⅓ percent of cost. Consider further:

Margin, based on:

Cost	Sales
33⅓%	25%
⅓	¼
¼	⅕
½	⅓
⅜	3/11

If we convert the percent to its equivalent fraction, then ⅓ of the cost is seen to equal ¼ of the sales. It may be noted that one can convert from one column to the other (from one base to the other) very readily. The numerator goes across, unchanged. The denominator of the fraction sought is obtained by adding the numerator to the denominator of the cost fraction to obtain the denominator of the sales fraction. Or, by subtracting the numerator of the sales fraction from its denominator, the cost fraction is computed. A little experimentation will demonstrate how easily this can be done. And it works irrespective of the numerator, which need not be 1, as, for instance, in the last set of fractions illustrated. In working with this conversion, it should be remembered that cost gets the larger fraction, sales the smaller.

Said much more simply, once the concept is visualized: Carry the numerator across unchanged. Add or subtract the numerator to/from the denominator, such that cost gets the larger, sales the smaller fraction.

The original marked price required to anticipate the retail reductions involved in all reselling operations, cover cost and expenses, and yield a net profit of X percent can be calculated from the foregoing diagram logically. Expressed as a formula, it becomes

$$\% \text{ markup} = \frac{\% \text{ margin} + \% \text{ retail reductions}}{100\% + \% \text{ retail reductions}}$$

DISCOUNTS

There are numerous special discounts provided by sellers to stimulate business. Most are classifiable into three major types—trade, cash, and quantity, of which there are two types, cumulative and noncumulative.

Trade discounts were discussed above.

Cash discounts are closely allied to credit terms. They are discussed in the next chapter.

Noncumulative quantity discounts are based on the size of each individual order. Cumulative quantity discounts introduce time. They are based on the total volume purchased over a time period, such as a month, or six months, etc. Noncumulative quantity discounts are designed basically to pass on to customers economies of maintaining a desired minimal order size. Cumulative quantity discounts seek to capture the buyer's business for a period of time. They do not relate to individual order size. Both are legal, provided the cost savings to substantiate them are real. Obviously, noncumulative quantity discounts are far easier to defend.

Quantity discounts have not been declared legal or illegal. That is, the law neither permits nor prohibits their use. It is inconceivable to believe that the lawmakers were not well aware of them in passing the Robinson-Patman Act. Therefore, they are legal by tradition, but without compulsion. If used, the onus for demonstration that they are fair, that they are substantiated by cost savings to justify the discount structure, is on the seller. As long as this can be done, they are a legal and fair means of price reduction to seek more business. Arbitrarily reducing prices to the small number of large buyers, at the expense of the larger number of small buyers, by a biased discount structure invokes the "most favored buyer" concept—and this is strictly illegal for lack of substantiation of the cost savings behind it and for the unfair competition it creates.

BREAK-EVEN ANALYSIS

One concept, deeply ingrained in the minds of many businessmen, is that more sales mean more profits. This is perfectly true in many circumstances and within limits. The trouble is that the change in circumstances or the exceeding of the limits goes unrecognized. In fact and in practice, the basic concept is so strong that all too many businessmen forget, overlook, or have lost completely the awareness that there *are* limits or changes in circumstances under which the concept is no longer true.

To say that increased sales always mean increased profits is absurd. Or, put another way, to say that to obtain the increased profits we desire, we *must* increase sales, is equally absurd. Most businessmen would agree with this—in theory. But, with rare exception, they will then continue to bend every possible effort to improve their own businesses by increasing sales. In short, whereas there may be agreement on an academic—or theoretical—notion, the businessman continues to operate his business on the basis of his better judgment, giving very little attention to the concept he professes to believe in.

Straight Line

Let us take a look at a basic tool which has furthered the concept of more sales meaning more profits. This is the break-even analysis. In the more popular form, it is the straight-line, break-even analysis.

The diagram in Figure 11.2 is structured from cost and sales data. Costs are divided into fixed and variable. Those expenses, including sales salaries but not commissions, which will remain constant for a certain period of time, such as a year, are accumulated and plotted parallel to the base line as fixed cost. These remain unchanged, irrespective of volume.

Then, the variable costs are accumulated as an amount *per unit*. They are plotted as an addition to the fixed cost, thereby producing the total-cost line.

The revenue line is the price of the product times various quantities. The break-even point is readily determinable. To the left of it, of course, is a loss where costs exceed revenue, and to the right of it is profit. By substituting various prices, one can add other revenue lines, to visualize the impacts of such changes on the break-even point and profit.

This is a very readily constructed and useful tool—within limits. The fallacy is that the workable limits for the use of this tool are very narrow. They exist plus or minus a reasonable quantity from the present level of operations only! Yet, by looking at this diagram, it would *seem* apparent that *the greater the quantity sold, the greater the corresponding profit and without limit.*

It becomes appropriate to recognize the underlying causes for the limited applicability of the straight-line, break-even analysis. In the first place, the cost data undoubtedly came from current records at the present level of operations. Change that level very much and the variable costs will change, too. The diagram assumes that variable costs are a straight line, the same per unit at all plotted quantities.

The fixed costs may change, too, and particularly for any substantial departure from the current level of operations.

The revenue is plotted as a straight line. There is no recognition of demand. There is no assurance that the needed or desired quantities can be sold at the price assumed and for the costs employed.

However, if common sense is employed in the structuring, and if the application is confined within reasonable limits, this is an excellent first step in a cost-oriented approach to pricing.

One further application of this technique is somewhat negative in nature. Reasonably accurate determination of costs can be of help during periods of recession to determine the point to cease operations while

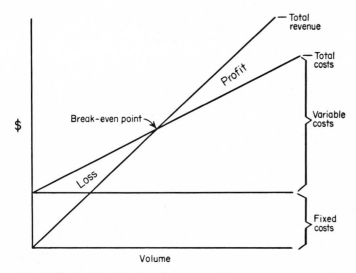

Fig. 11.2 Straight-line, break-even analysis.

minimizing loss. Under conditions of decreasing demand and gradually declining prices, operations could continue as long as price is greater than or equal to variable costs. The reasoning behind this is that the fixed costs are sunk. They must be paid anyway. Any excess of variable costs over revenue thereby increases the loss. This is a highly theoretical observation. In practice, all items of fixed costs may or may not be "fixed" under such conditions. Production may or may not be for immediate sale, as against for inventory in anticipation of future rather than current needs. And there are many other factors involved— labor relations, industrial relations, the responsibilities of corporate citizenship, and the probable duration of the recession, to mention a few.

Break-even-Point Curve

One application of this technique is to substitute various reasonably possible prices and then to plot the resulting break-even points on a separate diagram. This is illustrated in Figure 11.3.

The curve results from a smoothed connection of the break-even points plotted. It provides a picture of the quantity needed to break even for any price within the range.

It is actually a series indicating the change in break-even points as different prices are considered. For example, at price A, quantity M must be sold to break even. Any additionals sold beyond M start showing a profit.

If demand is deemed to be somewhat inelastic, another use of this curve is to indicate the minimum price required to break even. If N units might be sold, they must be priced at $\$B$ to break even. If they can be priced higher without loss of volume, a profit is indicated.

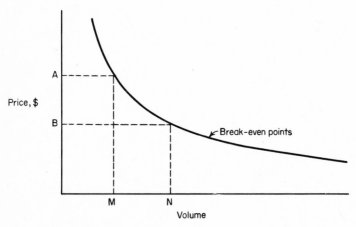

Fig. 11.3 Break-even-point curve.

Another practical use of these data might be to assume a return on sales or investment of X percent as a minimum. This could be incorporated as an additional "variable cost," or it could be an additional consideration, as an addition to total costs. The points of intersection of this revised "total cost" figure with the revenue lines could be plotted instead of—or in addition to—the break-even points. This would indicate the various price-quantity combinations needed to achieve the objective of a minimal required return. A judgment of feasibility of attainment should be aided thereby.

Now, consider adding demand. For any price selected, what is the quantity level with the highest probability of being sold? This answer may well be a range, but probably a relatively narrow one. It provides a guide as to probable results, while recognizing the degree of uncertainty of the demand judgment. This is a far sounder position to be in than ignoring the demand because it is hard to measure accurately or because it is simply overlooked. For a good, concise, and practical article on the introduction of demand, see Bill R. Darden's "An Operational Approach to Product Pricing" in the April 1968 issue of the *Journal of Marketing*.

Curvilinear

The curvilinear break-even analysis is the same tool, from a slightly more sophisticated and realistic approach. The results are depicted in Figure 11.4.

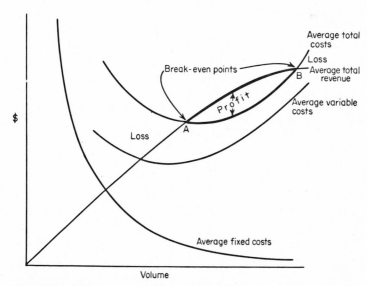

Fig. 11.4 Curvilinear, break-even analysis.

Here the approach is to determine average fixed costs instead of the absolute sum of fixed costs. This is obtained by dividing the fixed costs by various sales volumes. The shape of the average-fixed-cost line shown in Figure 11.4 is typical. As a constant number is divided by ever-increasing quantities, it falls off very rapidly at the start, then more slowly, continuing to decrease but never meeting the base line.

The variable costs are not a constant for all levels of production and sales. They start relatively high with too low a volume for efficiency, move downward as efficiency increases, and beyond the point of maximum efficiency start upward again with overtime, excessive use of plant and equipment, and so on.

The average-total-cost line (ATC) is the combination of these two costs. This starts downward where average fixed costs and variable costs are decreasing. It is flat where there is no change (where the decrease in average fixed costs is exactly offset by an increase in variable). It starts upward again when the increase in variable cost is greater than the continued decrease in fixed.

The average-revenue line is curved, too, at least in most circumstances. It comes from the fundamentals that greater sales for a firm normally are made at lower prices and a lower price affects all units sold. If the average-revenue line is now superimposed on this diagram, it can be seen that there is not one break-even point, but *two*.

Between the break-even points A and B there is a profit. To the left of A is a loss, and to the right of B, again there is a loss. In which direction should the firm seek to move—to the right, to the left—to decrease sales or to increase them? Obviously, the answer depends upon where it is now. The profit (or loss) is measured vertically by the distance between the average-total-cost and the average-total-revenue lines.

This same result could be obtained by use of marginal-cost and marginal-revenue curves. However, for practical purposes it adds little to the determination already made. It is another approach. The danger then exists of misinterpretation of the mathematical precision of the result for accuracy of fact. It is rarely possible to determine costs by individual products, or to control sales, that accurately.

This approach can be applied to total corporate operations, to divisional, or to a major product or product line. It illustrates the point that increased sales do not always mean increased profits. It is indicative, primarily. The cost data may well be estimates. The inherent assumptions of demand persist. Used with a keen awareness of the limitations, it can be a valuable aid to, but not a substitute for, discretion in the pricing decision.

RELEVANT READING

Buggie, Frederick D., "Lawful Discrimination in Marketing," *Journal of Marketing,* April 1967, pp. 1–8.

Buskirk, Richard H., *Principles of Marketing,* 3d ed., New York: Holt, Rinehart and Winston, Inc., 1970, chaps. 17–18.

Colberg, Marshall R., Dascomb R. Forbush, and Gilbert R. Whitaker, Jr., *Business Economics,* Homewood, Ill.: Richard D. Irwin, Inc., 1970.

Darden, Bill R., "An Operational Approach to Product Pricing," *Journal of Marketing,* April 1968, pp. 29–33.

Griffin, Clare E., "When Is Price Reduction Profitable?" *Harvard Business Review,* September-October 1960, pp. 125–136.

Lanzillotti, Robert F., "Pricing Objectives in Large Companies," *American Economic Review,* December 1958, pp. 921–940.

McCarthy, E. Jerome, *Basic Marketing,* 4th ed., Homewood, Ill.: Richard D. Irwin, Inc., 1971, pp. 632–661.

Oxenfeldt, Alfred R., "Multi-Stage Approach to Pricing," in Edward C. Bursk and John F. Chapman (eds.), *Modern Marketing Strategy,* Cambridge, Mass.: Harvard University Press, © 1964 by the President and Fellows of Harvard College.

Udell, Jon G., "How Important Is Pricing in Competitive Strategy?" *Journal of Marketing,* January 1964, pp. 44–48.

CHAPTER TWELVE

Credit and Finance

ROLE OF CREDIT

Our economy runs on credit. Credit cards—plastic money—are rapidly replacing even cash for innumerable small transactions, both consumer and industrial. Their convenience and stimulus to the economy are desirable. Credit has come into its own as big business—and very profitable big business, to finance business across the board, all the way from convenience purchases to financing war.

The role of credit as used by industrial sellers is a variable. Some use credit and selling terms as a competitive weapon. When credit is so employed, it becomes a selling aid. Competition in credit terms can be a potent weapon to the salesman. Credit considerations as a factor in deciding from whom to buy can be very persuasive to the buyer. The net cost, if any, of liberal credit terms becomes a cost of marketing—perhaps a very effective marketing expenditure.

Credit can also be a necessary evil. In some industries, sales are traditionally made for cash. Yet, at the same time, competitors have learned that the availability of credit increases sales, so credit is made available to customers. In such circumstances credit is compulsory, if the seller wishes to do any business. Here, the credit operation, granted in the first place because competitors traditionally do so, becomes a financial operation. Its control is vested in the financial segment of the business, and the usual friction between salesmen who want liberal credit and a credit manager who wants minimal bad debts exists.

In the third instance, credit is regarded as an independent, profit-generating center. Here, sales are for cash, but credit is made available to finance them. This may be through a credit corporation owned by the seller, or it may be through a separate credit corporation. This credit corporation accepts the notes of the buyers, pays cash for them to the seller, and collects the principal plus interest from the buyer. Installment financing is a good example of this type of operation. The effective annual interest rate charged can provide a very lucrative reward. The ready availability of the credit helps in the selling, particularly on high-ticket items to the many smaller corporations that may be short of ready cash, yet in a position to benefit from the use of the product.

TERMS OF SALE

The three elementary terms of sale are CWO, CBD, and COD. At first glance, it may appear that no credit is involved in any of these terms. Actually, CWO, cash with order, so qualifies. Cash before delivery, CBD, and cash on delivery, COD, involve credit to the extent that the seller performs prior to being paid. If an item, a machine tool or a suit, is built for a sale on CBD or COD terms, and the buyer fails to pay, the seller is out the costs incurred up to that point, less any salvage. In cases of questionable credit, or where the cost of checking credit is excessive to the sale, terms such as $X down (CWO) and the balance COD are used. The amounts are set so that the risk to the seller is minimized.

Cash discounts have been used traditionally. They offer a reward via a price reduction for payment within a limited time period. Obviously, this avoids carrying charges for accounts receivable beyond the discount date and prevents all bad-debt losses on such discounted invoices. The value of these savings to the seller is unquestioned. On the other hand, the discount not taken can be viewed as a charge for credit from the last day to take the discount until the invoice is due in full, without the discount. From this point of view, the charge can be quite high. Conversely, in such cases, taking the discount can represent a substantial reduction in net cost.

Examples of various terms of sale incorporating a cash discount are

2/10 n 30, 2/10 EOM (or Ult, or Prox) n 60, and 1/10 ROG n 30. 2/10 n 30 means that the buyer may deduct 2 percent from the invoiced price of the goods if he pays within ten days from the day the invoice is dated. This invoice is due in full thirty days from the date of the invoice. These terms are strict in interpretation. Large amounts can be involved. The day the invoice is *dated* is the starting point, not the day it is mailed, or received, or the day the goods arrive, or the tenth of the following month. The figure 30 means exactly that, not one month. In practice there may be a variation in leniency in enforcement between sellers. This does not change the interpretation of the terms.

Variations of 2/10 n 30 merely change the amount of the discount or the length of time between the discount date and the due date. Examples are 1/10 n 25, 3/10 n 60, etc.

It should be noted that cash discounts apply to the goods only—not to prepaid transportation charges if they are included. These have been advanced by the seller as an agent for the buyer, and the seller expects this cash reimbursed in full.

EOM stands for "end of the month." "Ult" for *ultimo* and "Prox" for *proximo* are identical in meaning. They are used more frequently abroad.

2/10 EOM n 60 would be read to mean a discount of 2 percent is available if paid within ten days from the end of the month in which the invoice is dated. The bill is due in full at the end of the second calendar month following the month in which the invoice is dated. For example, an invoice dated September 15 with 2/10 EOM n 60 terms gives the buyer until October 10 to pay it and earn the discount. It becomes due in full on November 30.

These terms provide liberal credit, and their interpretation is less strict than the net terms just described. The percentage rate is occasionally varied. The time to due date is commonly 30, 60, or 90 days (read as the end of the first, second, or third calendar month, following the end of the month in which the invoice is dated).

Seasonal dating provides an interesting variation of EOM terms. Suppose a manufacturer faces a seasonal demand, high in the fall, minimal in the summer. In order to obtain orders in May to maintain productivity during his slack season, he might offer 2/10 EOM n 60, as of October 1—a postdating of his invoice. If he receives the order in May, he can produce it over the summer and deliver in September or October, as the customer prefers. The bill is due with a cash discount November 10, and in full December 31. It has cost the seller some interest on a good account, but he has enjoyed production economies and an advance order a competitor cannot take away from him. The cost of the additional credit may be well offset by these economies and the competitive advantage gained.

ROG terms, i.e., 1/10 ROG n 30, mean a 1 percent discount if paid in ten days from the receipt of the goods, net 30 days (literally) from the receipt of the goods. This is used when the transmittal time of the invoice may be far faster than delivery of the goods. Many people like to earn cash discounts, but hesitate to discount a bill until after the goods are received, inspected, and approved. Literally, the time starts from the day the goods are first *available for delivery*, when the freight car is spotted, the ship docked. Delay in unloading does not defer the start of the 10-day period. Large sums may be involved.

Anticipation is an additional incentive to prompt payment. It provides for a discount, typically at 6 percent per year, for payment in advance of the due date—applicable to the net due on the discounted amount—or, if that is missed for any reason, to the full amount of the invoice. It is computed as a straight discount at 6 percent per year for the number of days involved between the date of payment and the appropriate due date. The objective is to obtain earlier payment. Without it, payment would normally be received close to the due date, rather than in advance thereof.

Rarely does the casual buyer seem to appreciate the true value of a cash discount. Let us analyze this with reference to the typical 2/10 n 30 terms. The question might be raised as to the value of this discount. Why discount it by the tenth day?

Two percent earned on the tenth, versus no discount on the thirtieth, is 2 percent for 20 days, the amount of time of the earlier payment to qualify for the 2 percent discount, between the tenth and the thirtieth day. Two percent for 20 days is 36 percent per year—effectively earned for a period of 20 days. Failure to take advantage of this discount is, in effect, borrowing money for 20 days at an interest charge of 36 percent per year.

Should this happen monthly, it can become extremely valuable. Let us suppose a small firm buys at the rate of $10,000 per month, on 2/10 n 30 terms. If it pays its bills on the tenth, it earns at the rate of 36 percent per year, for the time period between the tenth and the thirtieth, two-thirds of the time, or effectively, 24 percent per year. On each invoice it keeps 2 percent of $10,000, or $200. This times 12 months accumulates to $2,400 cash in the bank for the year. And $2,400 is 24 percent of the $10,000 of monthly purchases. Many businesses fail to earn 24 percent per year on operations. Discounting one's bills can contribute materially to corporate welfare. Even if the firm must borrow the $10,000 and pay 7 percent thereon for a year, the net is still a healthy 17 percent profit for so doing.

FINANCING THE INDUSTRIAL SALE

Open-Account Credit

Open-account credit, sometimes incorporating a cash discount, sometimes not, but due on a monthly basis, is used industrially in the same manner as consumer charge accounts. The cost to the seller is offset by the added convenience to the buyer, the ease of purchasing, and the expectancy of more of the customer's business as a result. It is highly applicable to frequent purchases of relatively small dollar amounts.

Installment

Installment sales become appropriate for less frequent purchases of higher-priced items. The seller receives his cash promptly. The buyer is granted credit on the item purchased. He need not disrupt his normal borrowing procedures with his bank or others. The cost of installment credit can run quite high. A mathematical illustration may help one visualize the key point involved—and the resultant effective annual interest rate. Consider this:

Let us suppose that an item is offered for sale at a cash price of $2,000, with 25 percent down and the balance payable at $118 per month for fifteen months. The *amount* of the credit is $1,500, the cash price less the down payment.

The *cost* of the credit is the amount to be repaid less the amount of the credit. $118 per month for 15 months equals $1,770 to be repaid. Subtracting the $1,500 yields a cost of credit of $270.

The nominal interest rate is the cost of the credit divided by the amount, $270 divided by $1,500, or 18 percent—for the life of the contract, fifteen months. This becomes 14.4 percent per year (18 percent divided by 15 equals 1.2 percent per month, or 14.4 percent per year).

Note that an installment loan differs from a straight loan, which provides full use of the principal with interest accumulated as time goes on. In installment loans, the interest and carrying charges are added at the inception. In our example the face of the note becomes $1,770 (not $1,500) and is decreased by $118 monthly.

The effective annual interest rate in this case is 25.7 percent per year. This is to say that financing this transaction by installment credit is, in effect, borrowing money at straight interest at the rate of 25.7 percent annually.[1]

---

[1] This can be verified by starting with the $1,500, adding one month's interest at 25.7 percent per year, subtracting the $118 payment, and so on to the end of the 15 months. The total interest so added will be $270. The 25.7 percent

Consignment

Consignment selling places an inventory in the hands of the buyer. Title remains in the seller. Periodic review or replacement provides the current billings. This may be for the goods actually used, or it may be a function of time, on a prearranged schedule. The risk of obsolescence remains in the seller.

Consignment provides for ready availability of goods, while minimizing the investment of the buyer. In the absence of competitive substitutes owned by the buyer, this works well. However, the investment for the goods delivered but not yet billed can earn very little. Credit charges cannot be made on the seller's property. In effect, consignment involves increased risk through increased investment in inventory, located elsewhere.

The primary advantage to the seller is in placing his goods where they are readily available for use, in economical quantities as to shipments, and in the ease of selling because of the billing system. Under circumstances of continued use of somewhat standardized items, this competitive advantage may be well worth the risk.

Leasing

Leasing, as against ownership, offers several advantages to the user. Without the investment required for outright purchase, working capital requirements are lowered. There may be some tax advantage to fully deductible lease payments, although the accelerated depreciation now permitted largely offsets this. Operational efficiency can be high by the use of the newest equipment. Service and maintenance problems can be minimized as a part of the lessor's responsibility.

Leases are for a limited term and may or may not include an option to buy. Some leases permit application of a percentage of the rental toward the purchase. The lease may be based on time or on operations, such as units produced.

Equipment-leasing companies have been created to purchase equipment for a lessee, who selects both the equipment and the seller and negotiates the price. He then pays the leasing company for its use, under a lease. Typically, after the expiration of the first lease, it is renewable at reduced rates, or the equipment can then be purchased.

---

can be computed mathematically or interpolated from interest tables. It can be approximated by use of the formula $R = 2rn/n + 1$, where R is the effective, annual interest rate sought, r is the nominal, annual interest rate, and n is the number of payments in the contract. This formula does not yield precise results. It errs slightly on the high side, but it is reasonably close if an overall approximation is all that is required. In this case it yields 27 percent, instead of the 25.7 percent, an error of 1.3 percent.

Care should be exercised to prevent the purchase clause from creating a conditional sales contract out of the lease. If so, the Internal Revenue Service will require capitalization and depreciation instead of a rental expense.

FINANCING THE INDUSTRIAL SELLER

Sale and Leaseback

Another form of leasing of special interest to the industrial seller is sale and leaseback. It continues to grow in popularity. It is a way of increasing working capital by selling equipment, a building, or other physical assets, receiving cash, and then leasing them back for continued use. This converts the fixed asset of property ownership to a liquid asset, cash, with the lease payments a write-off as operational expenses charged to current revenue.

Many entities are entering the leasing business as professional lessors. The Conference Board states:[2]

> Leasing used to involve a direct relationship between the user and the owner of the facilities. But now there is a host of intermediary professional lessors. They include: independent leasing companies that provide specialized operating or financial services or act as brokers; specially constituted agencies likes trustees, dummy corporations and "captive" leasing arms of manufacturers; major financial institutions such as banks and insurance companies; pension trusts, industrial development agencies, foundations, and universities; and individuals in high tax brackets. Among some of these intermediaries, moreover, striking changes have occurred. For example, there has been considerable attrition of small, thinly capitalized independent leasing companies. And a number of major banks have in the past five years begun to function as direct lessors, instead of merely acting as third parties in lease transactions.

Factoring

Factoring involves checking the credit of customers, guaranteeing it to the seller, and collecting the accounts receivable. In this sense, the receivables are sold to the factor. This is done for a commission, usually between 1 and 2 percent of the receivables.

Advances may be made against future receivables with interest charged. Other loans, secured or unsecured, are available from factors. Some operate as export factors, doing the same job abroad, and assuming the full risk of credit, including any political hazard.

In recent years, factoring has expanded through the addition of

[2] *Leasing in Industry,* The Conference Board, Studies in Business Policy, no. 127, 1968, p. 1.

supplementary services. The larger factors offer financial advisory services and nonbankable loans. The rates are high, but so is the risk. Smaller businesses are the major source of business for factors. Obviously, as soon as the firm can qualify for straight loans from a commercial bank, it will do so. The cost is less, but again, so is the risk.

Factors earn interest on their loans. Their commissions are another matter. It may be an economy to use them. The value to the firm for credit checking, guarantee against bad-debt losses, and bookkeeping expenses saved in collection can be compared directly with the cost of the commission. If this is favorable to the firm's doing these things, and yet it needs loans, commercial financing may be the answer.

Commercial Financing

Commercial financing is very close to factoring in its operations. The significant differences are that the seller checks his own credit, obtains no guarantee of it, and collects directly from the customer, who will not be aware of the existence of any commercial financing arrangement.

Loans are made on a revolving basis, with new accounts receivable added as matured ones are removed. Such loans are frequently short term and at rates above unsecured bank loans. Financial assistance is available from commercial finance houses for other forms of loans secured by inventories, equipment, and other collateral.

RELEVANT READING

Bartels, Robert, *Credit Management,* New York: The Ronald Press Company, 1967.

"Guide to Management Services," *Dun's Review,* 2d Annual Report, Special Supplement, part II, pp. 119–124, January 1966.

"Guide to Management Services," *Dun's Review,* 1st Annual Report, Special Supplement, part I, pp. 154–155, January 1965.

Leasing in Industry, The Conference Board, Studies in Business Policy, no. 127, 1968.

Maddock, Sydney D., "Industrial Financing: Its Role in Distribution," *Advanced Management,* February 1957.

PART SIX

Measurements of Marketing, Markets, and Men

CHAPTER THIRTEEN

Industrial Market Research and Measuring Marketing

DATA GATHERING VERSUS RESEARCH[1]

Data gathering is typically the process of obtaining various bits of information—usually unrelated—from a variety of sources. The act of gathering data, unless it is defined and directed, is useless. And this is a long way from research, in the practical sense.

Admittedly, "research" is a very ambiguous term. It is used to mean everything from highly sophisticated and scientifically controlled laboratory procedures seeking new truths, to random scanning of books in a library. In the latter case, one of the reasons for the use of the term "research" is to upgrade the prestige of the reader, by the inference.

In business, there are significant differences of degree between research and data gathering. They are at opposite ends of a scale. Data gathering is frequently haphazard in both results and technique. It may be an accumulation of information for information's sake, such as creating a library. There may be a central topic to provide some guidance to the selectivity, such as compiling data for a speech.

[1] Substantial portions of this chapter were contributed by A. P. Moran, Manager, New Products, Electrical Components Division, The Bendix Corporation, Sidney, N.Y.

Research adds depth and discipline to the process. It is noncursory. The techniques are a variable. But, they are scientific in the control of bias, in the promotion of objectivity while seeking truth. The product of market research is data. However, it is a special set of data—that which is relevant to a problem. Research is guided by the relevancy. The objective of market research is aid in problem solution or decision making. The value of such research is the ability of the data to contribute to better solutions of problems or to reduce the risk in decision making. It is the applicability and usefulness of the data, the results of research, which are of value—not the process, per se.

Market Research Defined

"Market research" is systematic procurement, organization, and interpretation of facts and opinions to aid in improving the quality of marketing decisions or solutions.

The Market-Research Function

Typically the market-research *function* includes, or should include, far more than the mere providing of data. The interpretation, integration with other factors relating to the problem, and its effective presentation to management—both orally and in a summarized report—are most significant responsibilities. These are far beyond the scope of data gathering, obviously. Nor is this all. In many cases, although it is not research, per se, the function includes the researcher's responsibility to make recommendations to management based on his findings—and to defend them.

Decisions or solutions—both are contained within the framework of adjusting corporate effort to market opportunity. The contribution of the market-research function to corporate welfare lies in the ability of its data to improve the quality of this adjustment.

Any market researcher who contents himself with producing scientifically correct data and submitting it in a voluminous, detailed report is most seriously shortchanging the most crucial aspect of his job. Any management which does not expect, yea demand, an effective presentation and application of the data is shortchanging itself.

The ability of the researcher to make defensible recommendations makes a problem solver out of a data provider—a manager out of a technical specialist. It should be welcomed by both the researcher and his management. The keen awareness of the use of research results in the assumption of this responsibility will vastly improve both the research and the contribution of its results to decision making.

It might be interesting to abolish all jobs entitled "director" or "manager" of market research.   The implication inherent in the position title is that the executive is in charge of market research—an expert in the techniques.   This is not wrong, but it is a misplacement of the emphasis.   It is suggested that a vast improvement might obtain if the emphasis were where it belongs—on the information.   Let's replace those jobs with directors or managers of market information and with appropriate changes in the job description.   This should imply that they need to be expert in the information relevant to decision making—however obtained.   It might even reduce the staff of some market-research departments, but, at the same time, increase the effectiveness thereof.

DATA SOURCES

Data sources are divided into primary and secondary categories:[2]

> Primary sources are: a. internal and external confrontations, e.g., interviews with marketing, engineering, management, and specific consumers; b. internal records (How often company files are ignored!   They are a mine of valuable data!); and c. customers' planning documents.   Secondary sources of material and data are various published materials, hearings, trade journals, etc.
>
> Nothing can replace current, fresh intelligence and customer-originated planning information.   Those data gatherers whose prime data source is voluminous, self-augmented and self-originated clipping files eventually learn that 90% or better of what they have clipped and filed are useless in a given instance.

The United States government is one of the largest data gatherers in the world.   Although accumulated on a gross basis, these data are used in most instances as the foundation, or limit setters, on the data needed for a defined subject of interest to industrial or governmental planners.

In almost every case of United States government data gathering, the reason for obtaining the data and its intended use are clearly stated.   As with all "data banks" the information can be combined, extrapolated, or otherwise manipulated to fit the purpose of the user.   Data on contract awards and other matters relating to analysis of governmental markets are set forth in Chapter Eight.

Industrial trade publications in the United States contribute many data bits as a result of surveys of their industry areas, analysis by their experts on segments of markets, or estimates by large industrial contributors of quantitative or qualitative bases for their markets.   These data

[2] Derived from Pat Thomas, "The Market Analysis Report," *Data on Defense and Civil Systems,* Data Publications, June 1962, pp. 25–29.

are usually subdivisions of gross data reported publicly by United States government sources. Often they are highly reliable because of the insight provided by people very familiar with methods of data reporting and their ability to interpret it wisely for their segment of industry participation. This is often done because of increasing realization that SIC codes are too gross to provide usable planning information directly.

Although there appear to be many data sources, it is usual for most industrial companies to find little or no definitive data to fill their needs to support new product development, open new markets for present products, or determine exact market penetration relative to their competitors. Therefore, most companies perform their own data gathering from both the plant and outside, and combine it with other information to formulate their own market intelligence base.

Early evaluation of available data relating to the problem indicates the "holes" that must be filled with additional specific data. Market research then determines what data is yet needed to resolve the required answers, and the mechanisms and techniques to be used to gather it.

ROLE OF INDUSTRIAL MARKET RESEARCH, OBJECTIVES, AND LIMITATIONS

Fundamentally, the role of industrial market research is to help management adjust corporate effort to market opportunity in order to increase customer satisfactions from the firm. This is achieved by providing data to aid in problem solving, decision making, planning, and control of operations.

> The degree to which market research can contribute to the direction given an industry by its managers is proportional to the size of the decisions those managers must make in product planning or marketing. There is usually very little market research and planning done in a steamship company because it doesn't cost much to send a ship into a new port on a trial basis. But building a new turnpike or laying a new ocean cable has generated geographic studies of unbelievable depth. The investment is simply too great to allow any more risk than necessary.[3]

Until 1950, industrial market research was largely a casual review of previous forecasts relative to sales results. Government and its large industrial contractors then started to develop separate research departments. This form of market measurement was fully accepted in the 1960s, with recognition that it was an important part of business, market,

---

[3] "Market Research and Planning in Industry," *Defense Market Measures Users Manual*, New York: Frost and Sullivan, Inc., Nov. 1, 1966, p. 1.

and product planning.   Today's industrial market research is a keystone of corporate marketing planning.

Normally a function of the marketing department, market-research results are used (or should be used) by all line and staff functions.   The results are used to develop the flexible short- and long-range plans necessary to keep all the firm's diverse functions "on target" to profitably reach the agreed-upon goals.   They can help to organize priorities and provide emphasis for key programs.   Market research can save time and money by indicating programs and products that should not be considered for development for any of many reasons.

> Measuring markets by market research is an irreplaceable segment of the marketing cycle.   Without research there is far less basis for future action, much less basis for judgment of current efforts and effectiveness. The role of market research in the whole marketing cycle is illustrated in Figure 13.1.[4]

The prime objective of market research is to provide a core around which other marketing and management intelligence can be used to fashion a resilient but sturdy and virile program.   A golf ball illustrates this point by being able to perform its intended function in quickly adapting to the environment even though deformed by sudden events. An overall business plan must have this same sense of direction, yet be able to accept unexpected market changes without excessive deviation from the goal.

All market research must be user-oriented.   Since market development relies heavily on research to determine the possible options and the priority of choices, the research and sales plans must mesh closely and

[4] From the Introduction to *Defense Market Measures Users Manual*, New York: Frost and Sullivan, Inc., Jan. 1, 1963, p. 2.

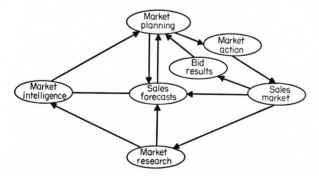

Fig. 13.1   The role of market research in the marketing cycle. (*Adapted from: "Defense Market Measures Users Manual,"* *New York: Frost and Sullivan, Inc., Jan. 1, 1963, p. 3.*)

clearly outline the user or consumer pulse, trends, attitudes, and prohibitions. A loose estimate of these critical market factors can doom an otherwise well-organized program.

Specific objectives of market research are to determine:[5]

> That a product has a market.
> What and where the markets are.
> Whether a market can be penetrated by the firm's capabilities.
> What the firm's penetration is or can be—by product type, quantities, and dollars.
> Whether it is worthwhile to pursue a particular program.
> Priorities among program possibilities.
> Detailed information on customers and competitors.

Implicit in these objectives is the need for an unbiased plan with suitable alternatives to assure reaching the firm's objectives on time, within costs, and with a clear statement of the rewards expected.

Because the research results are the core of so many business decisions, they must be completely objective. An accounting-oriented researcher may reach different conclusions from his interpretation of data than an engineering-oriented one, for example. This means that the training of the researcher is important. Objectivity is needed, along with ingenuity, intelligence, and a capacity to see both the forest and the trees. The researcher does not first find out what management wants to hear, then seek data to fit a preconceived conclusion. To guard against bias caused by "Not Invented Here" (NIH) comments relative to data easily available in one's own plant, Delphi techniques are proving to be very valuable in gathering information from a variety of experts.

The Delphi technique is a systematic method of obtaining a consensus of expert opinion while avoiding limitations of polling and panel methods. It is a program of sequential questionnaires, the answers to which are assembled as distributions, stated in terms of means and quartiles. These findings, along with comments and arguments, are returned to the respondents to the first questionnaire, with a request for any revisions in opinion in the light of this new data. This procedure is repeated by two more successive rounds, which converge and narrow the results.[6]

Any market-research program is limited by the current data that can be gathered in time to answer a specific need. In the usual case, management must make a decision in less time than it takes to run a good

[5] A. P. Moran, Manager, New Products, Electrical Components Division, The Bendix Corporation, Sidney, N.Y.
[6] For a good description of the Delphi technique, see J. C. Van Pelt, "Technological Forecasting," Perspectives in Defense Management, Washington, D.C.: Industrial College of the Armed Forces, Fort Lesley J. McNair, January 1971, p. 47.

market-measurement program. In all such cases, research results are potentially inaccurate and should be confirmed afterward. However, the research report can and should include an estimate of the confidence level in the data presented.

Even with the best of quantitative data available, market-research results are limited if the sales department does not contribute "real world" qualitative data to provide information on the numerous intangibles which affect the expected reaction of the marketplace.

If planning is a once-a-year project rather than a continuing one, confidence and accuracy of market research suffers. If research is needed at all, management should accept the need for a continuing market-research function, and fund it reasonably. By doing so it will get the results it should have—knowledgeable, usable, oriented, on-time market information with which to make decisions.

Use of Results: Errors by Management and Researchers

In today's quick-action organizations market-research results must be keyed to the needs of the prime user. Too often market research is rendered useless because it did not bring clearly to the fore the key information to be used in decision making. It is not the manager's job to understand the market-research problem; it is the function of the market researcher to understand the manager's requirements and to satisfy them. If market research does not perform properly, the manager will reach his objectives in another way.

At times management has jumped the gun in basing decisions on research results before they have been thoroughly verified. If wrong, research is blamed—not management.

There has been too little realization of the value of marketing measurements, of how they can contribute to decision making. Perhaps this is a carry-over from previous failures, blamed on research, either for earlier incompetence of the research or for too heavy a reliance by management on the data provided. All research has not always been competent, and a tendency of reading too much into the results has existed.

There has been too little integration of the use of the information by both marketing and nonmarketing executives. This is in part a failure to integrate marketing, itself, into the corporate organization as it should be.

Some managers have felt that marketing success depends more upon creative and aggressive personalities than it does upon careful collation of facts and cautious investigation of alternatives—in short, that research, being historical, is opposed to creativity.

Management's attitude concerning the use of the results of the research is often wrong. There is a tendency to rely very heavily upon the skills and discretion of management, and to give too little significance to anything opposing what management may have already decided should be done. And, along this same line, many managers choose to misinterpret research data because it does not conform to a "seat-of-the-pants" estimate formed years ago when they were in the field. This danger is ever present, and managers must be prepared to accept that the field changes.

Some managers may expect a research report to make a decision for them. In many cases this is true—the report indicates the decision. The manager, however, must have a bigger picture in mind, the business plan. Knowing the goals and objectives, the manager must make the tactical and strategic choices and set priorities on the allocation of resources to achieve them.

Management must accept that not all problems have satisfactory answers. Managers should know that ability to forecast certain elements of the environment which are important to the future of business is at best limited. Therefore, options, flexible plans, or alternatives are as important to consider as the program preferred by a research report.

Truly, one of the more important criticisms of the researchers is their emphasis upon techniques, rather than upon the information provided and its application. Researchers early learned that the quality of their results was a function of the quality of their techniques. Their attention and effort has been to better the techniques, to improve the quality of the result. They have succeeded in this to a great extent. This emphasis upon techniques is not to be deplored—it is needed. It should continue. The error is to fail to give sufficient attention to the need for, the practical value and effective contribution of, the results produced.

There has been a failure of communications. Researchers have not developed skill in effective presentation of their results. A chart is an aid to, but not a substitute for, an effective presentation. Researchers are frequently guilty of very poor salesmanship. They have often failed to sell their own management upon the value of their contribution.

Marketing research is too often concerned with bits and pieces and not enough with relationships and the requirements of the whole program. It has often been too narrow and myopic in seeking the information. Too often it does not probe deeply enough.

Research results may be fragmented, or presented as "one plan at a time," which poses an all-or-nothing decision to management. This is to be avoided. All plans must be cohesive and provide viable alternatives to be acceptable.

When the research department has freedom to investigate new markets, it often looks at new glamour markets rather than mundane products which are within present company capability and could contribute profit sooner.

Marketing research tends to be more descriptive than analytical. Confusion between descriptive information and causative impact exists. Cause-and-effect relationships tend to be minimized.

Marketing researchers too often neglect the profit viewpoint, a charge somewhat related to that of overconcentration on procedures and techniques and underconcentration on decision making.

A much more basic criticism of marketing research bears on its emphasis on the immediate and the current, and its lack of concern for the long terms and the fundamental. It attempts to provide assistance in solving each individual problem as it arises and does too little toward building principles out of these single-shot experiences, which can facilitate the solution of future individual problems.

It is relatively easy to be critical. However, if improvement is to result, it is appropriate to be equally constructive. The following is submitted to that end.

1. When any research is proposed and before it is undertaken, put it to the simple test of whether it gives promise of abetting a better decision, enough better to warrant the effort and expense.

2. Make sure that interest in and fascination for techniques for techniques' sake do not get in the way of a full return on each research dollar expended. The expenditure is for information, not for techniques.

3. Combat the notion that research inherently is an obstacle in the way of creativity. Creativity thrives on knowledge.

4. Promote better communication on research among all executives who have any voice in its use; try to eliminate areas of ignorance, misunderstanding, and prejudice.

5. Encourage experimentation with the new analytical tools with the view of speeding adoption of the useful ones, and speedy elimination of those which cannot contribute profitably.

6. Bend every effort to hasten the day when marketing management and marketing research information are inseparable.

7. Join in the organized efforts to raise standards of research and to eliminate the shoddy and the deceptive.

8. Give support—moral and/or financial—to basic research aimed at building a useful body of marketing knowledge and theory. Advances in sound marketing theory and in marketing knowledge will be followed by advances in sound marketing practice.

Criteria for Good Research

Management expects the market-research department to do an outstanding job in all the areas where it has determined that the department should be involved. Therefore, a prime criterion of good research is to give management what it needs, based on knowing what management expects and wants.

Not all research is good. There are times when no research at all is better. Research is expensive, and it must be a part of a company plan for progress and profit. Many companies and industries are not technology-based and are dollar-limited. They need guidance to determine where their growth should be. Research must be customer-oriented and largely based on trends of the industry and needs of specific customers. The test to apply to these programs is whether the product or market being researched is relevant to the industry and customer needs.

The criteria for good results are that all these areas be clearly and accurately defined:[7]

1. The research to be done is clearly defined.
2. The plan of attack is understood by all participants.
3. All internal and external sources of value have been exhausted and will be referenced in the final report.
4. The scope of the total market has been dimensioned, the company share determined—and forecast.
5. The company goals, strengths, and weaknesses have been considered.
6. The state-of-the-art of the marketplace is defined, and trends identified.
7. The customers have been defined.
8. The competition has been analyzed, together with any other threats.
9. The long- and short-range goals are accurately established using #4 and #5, and a path defined to reach these goals.
10. Alternatives have been provided for strategic and tactical plans.
11. Acquisition or licensing has been considered, if appropriate.

When these elements are available, a report is prepared. It should contain the authoritative base and built-in cross-checks of data. To complete the task, it must then be competently and effectively presented. The application of the research results, indicated by the presentation, is the heart of the job.

[7] A. P. Moran, Manager, New Products, Electrical Components Division, The Bendix Corporation, Sidney, N.Y.

SAMPLING INDUSTRIAL VERSUS
CONSUMER MARKETS

There are two basic questions involved in any market research. The first relates to the validity, the truthfulness of the results—"Did we find out the facts?" The second relates to its reliability, the representativeness of the respondents—"Is this result from the right people?" These questions apply to both consumer and industrial market research. The answers involve an awareness of some significant differences between the two areas.

Major differences between industrial and consumer research are in the size, distribution, and composition of the markets. In the consumer area, there are, literally, millions of individuals and families. All are small purchasing units. Subsegments by age, geographical location, income, and other factors still contain large numbers of the population. Even though some skewing occurs, as in distribution of population by income brackets, in many other cases the distribution of their characteristics tends to approach the normal curve. Random-sampling techniques are usually appropriate. Statistical measures and interpretation therefrom are highly applicable.

However, the industrial market presents an entirely different picture. This has been described in Chapter Two. The size and distribution of firms, together with the great concentration of purchasing power in the relatively few largest firms, means that the industrial market is highly skewed. Thus, the use of any random-sampling techniques will produce its results from the least meaningful respondents.

One major exception obtains if replies from the total *firms*, irrespective of size, are desired. If the data sought relates to the companies involved, completely independent of their sales volumes, random sampling becomes appropriate.

If one seeks answers relative to the total market or marketing involved, then a few selected respondents (who are doing most of the business) may provide them. This statistically indefensible sample may furnish far more reliable and practically usable results than would a technically perfect sample of all the firms. This becomes even more important if the answers are significantly different between small and large firms. Further, it can be obtained far quicker and cheaper than conducting a major survey. The contribution of the results to decision making is enhanced both in timeliness and reliability—provided the selection of the firms and the research procedures used are competently done.

An even better approach to this sampling in the industrial area can be by stratification of respondents. All the largest firms could be covered, and then a sample of the remainder. Or, the firms could be stratified by various size brackets. The sampling could be a variable between brackets, ranging from 100 percent coverage of the top few to a small percentage of the relatively large number in the smallest bracket.

Even in cases where the circumstances of the population to be surveyed are somewhat randomly distributed, the circumstances of the *respondents* may not be. The danger of this happening is far greater in industrial market research—again, because of the skewed distribution of sales by firms in the first place. A good test of the actual representativeness obtained is a weighted comparison between the respondents and the universe. The weighting factor could well be relative sales-size brackets. Preferably, this should be done by division or product groups involved. Some large firms are quite small as to one particular division.

The Use of Statistics

Statistics can change raw data from a relatively meaningless assembly to a most meaningful source of information. Statistical techniques, including statistical inference, can develop the significant aspects and interrelationships of data. They thereby contribute heavily to decision making, by vastly enhancing the quality of the information presented to the decision maker. This relates to the validity, the truths contained within the data.

But the use of statistics cannot in any way change the reliability, the representativeness of the respondents. The mathematical precision of a result must never be confused with its accuracy—in the sense of the facts of the universe. *If* the respondents are representative, then their response can be projected to the universe. But if they are not then statistical inference will not improve this lack of reliability.

Thus, in industrial market research, statistics applied to a truly representative sample (and this eliminates a random sample in almost all cases) constitute an effective working team to produce the best results. If the decisions utilizing these results are of major significance, every attempt should be made to increase both the validity and the reliability of the research. Usually this is not difficult. In most cases it is not a question of capability—it merely takes more time and money.

MARKET RESEARCH ABROAD

A key problem in market research abroad has been the general lack of published data either by governments or private sources. Few countries have required reporting of information usable to establish a gross national product. Those countries that do attempt to establish reporting procedures meet with reluctance on the part of manufacturers to comply.

Additional problems are related to the backgrounds of adjacent nations. In Europe as an example, one product may be usable in ten nations, but it is probable that shape, color, merchandising methods, etc., must be different for five of the ten countries. Therefore, the market-research problem is compounded in defining the differences.

When a United States firm attempts to do marketing research in offshore areas, it invariably meets these problems:

1. High to excessive costs.
2. Language barrier.
3. Companies contacted are reluctant to reveal any information that can be related to the financial affairs of that company.

> In recent years McGraw-Hill has been attempting to overcome some of these deficiencies. David Strassler, market research manager for *Electronics Magazine*, points out that European respondents for data, once they know and have confidence in your company, are truly more responsible and willing to collaborate than many U.S. sources. He stresses that the company with which one is associated is very important. Most European companies know their own markets very well. Industry information is spread at higher management levels through private organizations.[8]

During recent years, several entities have been compiling data for their own needs. Problems of reliability and lack of comparability, primarily a reflection of variation in reporting and in the bases used, exist. However, they represent a significant step forward in the availability of basic information for research purposes.

Charles C. C. Smith, vice president of IBM World Trade Corporation, first identifies the United Nations, with its flock of international agencies, commissions, and organizations, as a good start. He then adds:[9]

> Here is a list of agencies publishing their own statistics, all of which my company uses at one time or another:
>
> ECE (The Economic Commission for Europe);
> ECA (The Economic Commission for Africa);
> ECAFE (The Economic Commission for Asia and the Far East);
> ECLA (The Economic Commission for Latin America);
> ILO (International Labor Organization);
> FAO (Food and Agricultural Organization);
> UNESCO (United Nations Educational, Scientific, and Cultural

---

[8] Used with permission of David Strassler, Market Research Manager, *Electronics Magazine*, McGraw-Hill, Inc.

[9] Charles C. C. Smith, "Improved International Data Sources and Facilities," *Research Support for Global Marketing*, The Conference Board, Experiences in Marketing Management, no. 10, 1966, pp. 16–18.

Organization);
ICAO (International Civil Aviation Organization);
IBRD (International Bank for Reconstruction and Development);
IMF (International Monetary Fund);
WHO (World Health Organization);
UPU (Universal Postal Union);
ITU (International Telecommunication Union).

You will notice that this group of agencies spans a great deal of the marketplace and many of the applications in industry in which multinational corporations are interested.

Other multinational organizations, such as OECD (Organization for Economic Cooperation and Development); EEC (European Economic Community); GATT (General Agreement on Tariffs and Trade); UCI (International Union of Railways); and IATA (International Air Transport Association) also gather and publish extensive and very valuable international data.

We use, in addition, some excellent information sources, both commercial and noncommercial ones. The U.S. Department of Commerce offers the World Trade Information Service. The International Statistical Institute in The Hague, Netherlands, and The Pan American Statistical Institute in Washington, D.C., are excellent information sources. *Business International*, published in the United States, and *Informations Internationales*, published in Paris, are excellent professional services.

Beyond these well-known services are a host of services provided by manufacturers' associations and banks—for their members and their customers. A good example is the service offered by the Chase Manhattan Bank.

Marketing research agencies are available for special market surveys. The major agencies in this country have built up international organizations, and most of them can tackle almost any global job. Among foreign-based marketing research agencies, we think one of the best is probably The Intelligence Unit of *The Economist*, which is located in London. No long list of international data sources would be complete without *The Statesman's Year Book*, which is published by Macmillan & Company in London. This work contains highly comprehensive information about virtually every country in the world.

FORECASTING AND RESEARCH

Research and forecasting differ significantly. Research develops the facts of today and yesterday—historical data only. Forecasting predicts the probabilities for tomorrow—the future. No matter the means, no matter the sophistication of the techniques, forecasts are always made in the face of uncertainty. And the uncertainty is a variable. It can be high or low—but it is always present to some degree.

Good forecasting starts with historical data. Research contributes the launching pad. These data can be provided to a high degree of accuracy and refinement. Forecasts into the future, properly launched, can be remarkably close to performance, in the short run. In the long run the errors are far greater, but generally of far less significance and easily corrected en route.

From the standpoint of sales forecasting, the basic problem is to find one or more measurable and highly predictable factors which are causative of and vary with (in either direction) sales results. In consumer marketing this can be comparatively easy. The sales of many products are affected by and vary with changes in such factors as population, per capita buying power, etc.—which change relatively slowly and predictably. In the industrial area, the problem is compounded by the very nature of industrial demand, discussed in Chapter Two, and by a more rapid and violent reaction to both real and anticipated change in any of the factors from which the demand is derived. This can make life most interesting for the industrial forecasters. It will keep them up to date on economic, political, and environmental, as well as technological, forces.

Forecasts and research results are exactly alike in one respect—they both serve to provide information for improved decision making by the manager. They both, it is hoped, tend to reduce somewhat the uncertainty present in decision making. They are essential ingredients in planning.

Since the future is the only time period the businessman can control, forecasts of probable results must be made in one way or another. They can be hunches or other "feelings" about the future in the mind of the decision maker—all the way to the most highly sophisticated projections of data. The techniques of forecasting from the exercise of judgment, through line projection, extrapolation, derivation, correlation analysis, econometric analysis, and probability approaches, would and do fill many books. References to some selected and more concise sources are included in the "Relevant Reading" at the end of this chapter.

MARKETING MEASUREMENTS

The interest in marketing measurements varies among companies. This may well be a reflection of a similar variation in the interest in marketing, the variation in the adoption of the marketing concept itself.

Marketing measurements are any quantitative data relating to an aspect of marketing—as against the market. They can serve management by providing data for three purposes: general information, decision making, and evaluation of marketing (in whole or by segments).

There is a wide range in terminology among firms in referring to marketing measurements. However, the essence seems to be contained in the following six categories.

1. Forecasts. Included here are sales, annual, long-range, quarterly, monthly, economic, product, and other special types.

2. Performance-evaluation reports. These include customer-attitude studies, product margin, expense statements, territory profit margins, various operating reports, sales versus budget comparisons, expenses versus budgets, sales versus potentials, historical comparisons, personal contacts, etc.

3. Sales reports. This involves a wide range of reporting—daily, weekly, monthly, product sales, territory sales, call reports, sales by customer, sales by salesperson, sales by distributor, sales backlogs, and shipments.

4. Market-share indicators. These are reports of market penetration, company versus industry statistics, association statistics, industry sales, competitive action, and quotation-activity reports.

5. Budgets. Here a wide range in degree of refinement exists.

6. Quotas. If used, they are chiefly sales quotas. Budget and activity quotas are rare.

Accuracy Requirements

The more accurate the research results, the better—within limits. Obviously, accuracy is a highly desirable characteristic. However, it is also expensive. It can be overdone. Increased accuracy of the results can be obtained in most cases very simply. It merely means substantial increases in sample size, with attendant expense increases.

Accuracy should be appropriate to the need. The total involvement, the significance of precision in the result, and the purposes of the study become key factors. There is a great range in use of results, from a decision concerning a multimillion-dollar investment in new facilities, to an indication of relative potentials to help define an opening sales territory for a new man. Accuracy excessive to the need is a sheer waste of time and money.

In industrial market research, indicative results may be all that are needed. To improve them by making them both statistically defensible and highly accurate may not contribute materially to the quality of the decision to be reached. The point is that the intended use and significance of the results should control—not the desire of the researcher to do a more "perfect" job.

The degree of accuracy appropriate to the need should be defined in the first place. Then, tailoring the job to that level of accuracy is relatively simple. This can provide for economy in the cost of the results in cases where accuracy requirements are relatively low. It can provide for anticipation of the needed expenses for the job in cases where accuracy requirements are high. In both cases, the time and money spent on the research are being used more effectively.

EVALUATION OF MARKETING

Clearly, the historical yardstick used to evaluate marketing is sales. This continues, in spite of an awareness that the firm does not control sales results; that many uncontrollable factors in the environment including competitive activities combine in various ways to affect sales; that sales cannot be attributed to the marketing function alone, but, if anything, are attributed to the efforts of the entire firm; that there is a significant difference between the performance of the marketing function, integrated throughout the firm, and the performance of the marketing *department;* and that more sales do not necessarily mean more profits.

All these points are known to management. Most managers will not only readily agree with them, but insist upon their truthfulness. Yet, all too many continue to exert their every effort for more sales and to measure the success of their results in more sales—really giving but lip service to that in which they profess to believe.

A major reason for this is the ease of obtaining the sales figure, its variability, and the inherent and powerful association of sales revenues and profit. "The greater our revenues, the more we make!" Obviously (and in spite of the foregoing). Further, most firms in this country have long equated size with success. It is almost a fetish. If one is successful, one grows—and the big money comes from bigness—the bigger the firm, the greater the profit. Nonsense!

If this were true, then the permanency and success of the larger firms should be a function of their size. The larger the firm, the more the profit, the more funds management has to work with to assure continued growth and even more profit. It just has not worked out that way. Does it imply that it would have, except for one thing—incompetency, or complacency, perhaps with a lack of perspective, in the management? In short, would it have been the case except for management's shortcomings and errors?

Do we excuse management for being blind to change? For being product-oriented in a highly competitive situation? For viewing themselves as being in the railroad instead of the transportation business? For adherence to that which made them successful twenty years ago? For stubbornness in refusing to give up the obsolete and embrace the new? For using the wrong criteria to evaluate, to measure progress? For the wrong goals in the first place?

History is replete with innumerable cases to illustrate the results of such an approach to business. This need not be belabored. Instead, how might the job be improved?

In the first place, all evaluation of marketing should be a measure of the degree of success in attainment of the objective(s) assigned to it. So, the start comes from the objectives. They need to be determined, and agreed upon, with most careful consideration of the total situation, the firm's capabilities, and reasonable expectancy. Once the long-range corporate goals are established, they can be broken down into bites for shorter terms, and the specific goals for the next year or so—the short term. This permits ready identification of the marketing goals, both short and long range. And this permits assignment to the various key functions of marketing specific goals for short-range attainment.

Starting with the goals can broaden the perspective as to how best to attain them. Growth, for example, can be in sales size and under essentially present circumstances. It could be by territorial expansion. It could be by new products. It could be by acquisition. Or, it could be growth in profitability versus growth in size, or both. Should we seek a greater share of market, or perhaps give up some market share, emphasize for reduction the cost of selling, and thereby increase profitability? What is our relative competitive position now—and what do we want it to be? How fast do we wish to progress? How much risk can we afford? What are the reasonable limits to our capabilities?

Once the goals have been adopted, the direction provided, the alternative choices of action considered, and the specific targets set for next year, a base is created for evaluation. This act of evaluation is relatively simple. It is merely a question of comparing results to the reasonable, planned for, expectancy. Progress toward the goal becomes the crucial point. The data to measure this progress must be tailored to the situation. Obtaining it is not really hard, once the need for and use of the specifics are known.

The danger at this point is to resort to sales, again, and to let the more appropriate measures slide. True, it may require some new data to provide the measures of progress toward the identified targets. However, it is a viable and useful evaluation geared to the desired progress to provide crucial control that is sought. What more justification is needed? Data should contribute to better analysis, decision making, and control. Data needed for progress-toward-objective evaluation does just that.

In each of the action chapters in this book the basis for evaluation of performance is given. (See the chapters on advertising, selling and sales management, marketing costs, and the others in this section.) A major point is that assembling the data for evaluation is not a simple task. It requires an in-depth analysis of the performance versus expectancies of each area. However, if one measures actual progress toward identified goals in appropriate detail, the results in improved control can be a most valuable contribution to corporate welfare via improved future decision making.

RELEVANT READING

Eschenfelder, A. H., "Creating an Environment for Creativity," *Research Management*, vol. 11, no. 4, July 1968.

Feder, Richard A., "How to Measure Marketing Performance," *Harvard Business Review*, May-June 1965, pp. 132–142.

Green, Paul E., and Donald S. Tull, *Research for Marketing Decisions*, Englewood Cliffs, N.J.: Prentice-Hall, Inc., 1966, pp. 454–459.

Keane, J. G., "Some Observations on Marketing Research in Top Management Decision Making," *Journal of Marketing*, October 1969, pp. 10–15.

Redmond, John C., "A Discussion of Research," *Research Management*, vol. 12, no. 6, November 1969.

Schlaifer, Robert, *Probability and Statistics for Business Decisions*, New York: Mc-Graw-Hill Book Company, 1959, chap. 1.

Thomas, Pat, "The Market Analysis Report," *Data on Defense and Civil Systems*, Data Publications, June 1962, pp. 25–29.

Tilles, Seymour, "How to Evaluate Corporate Strategy," *Harvard Business Review*, July-August 1963, pp. 111–121.

Wolfe, Harry Deane, *Business Forecasting Methods*, New York: Holt, Rinehart and Winston, Inc., 1966, pp. 70–89.

CHAPTER FOURTEEN

Measuring Markets: Past, Present, and Future

CONFUSION IN MEASURING MARKETS

In the basic research on market measurements, marketing managers were asked how they determined their potentials, what measurements they used, and how they used them. One vice president's reply is typical of many.

> Well, first of all, we're in a unique situation—there are only a few other major firms making our particular product. We know our customers. We know our industry. So, we start with last year's sales, amend them for what's most likely to happen, and this gives us our forecast. That's used to help prepare our budget. Then, the budget is approved by the Board.
>
> So, we have a very accurate yardstick to control our operations and to measure our performance. Once the budget has been approved by the Board, everyone involved knows exactly what's expected of him. And, if anyone comes up with a serious departure from his budget, he'd better have a real good reason for it. It works very well.

This man is convinced his firm is doing a good job. The budgeting is accurate—that's proved by the performance. The performance is good—that's right on target to the budget. Everyone is happy. Sales and profits are over last year's. Raises are forthcoming—and everyone becomes more and more complacent every year.

Such a situation is a very desirable one to find—in a competitor. Let's examine what is happening a bit more closely.

First, the firm uses past performance as a basis of planning for tomorrow's. The budget comes from a projection, perhaps a highly sophisticated projection, of the past. The plans are geared to the budget. The performance is geared to the plans. Then, when the performance matches the prediction, each tends to prove the other right.

This firm does not realize it, but it is not measuring potentials at all, merely present customers. Every error of poor salesmanship and misdirection by sales management in the past is projected into the future—undetected, unidentified. The future is, to this firm, merely more of yesterday, not an unrealized opportunity for tomorrow.

Robert K. Heady, in his account of one firm's outstanding success, writes:[1]

> Tremco's "glowing picture" for the future, in the minds of its executives, is based upon the marketing experience Tremco has gained since 1963.
>
> To put it bluntly, Tremco has learned what some other companies selling in the construction field have failed to discover: The importance of (1) identifying a market, (2) establishing its size, (3) calculating its potential, and (4) determining the feasibility of serving that market—profitably.

The greatest obstacle to effective measurement of markets does not lie in the techniques to do so. It lies in the mind of the complacent manager who "knows" his market. If he is right, to the extent that he is right, no market measurement is needed. But, if he is wrong, to the extent that he is wrong, market measurement is needed. The prerequisite is simply the recognition of the need—if for no other purpose than to prove the manager was right in the first place. If the measurement fails to do that, it can open the door to future opportunities, truly unrealized opportunities.

CORPORATE USE OF MARKETING MEASUREMENTS

It is easy to confuse the meaning of various terms, such as "sales goal," "sales potential," "market potential," "sales estimate," and "quota." Table 14.1 indicates the use and relationships of the more basic ones.

[1] From "Tremco: A Marketing Success in the Construction Industry," by Robert K. Heady, *Industrial Marketing*, July 1967, copyright 1967 by Advertising Publications, Inc., Chicago, Illinois, p. 77.

TABLE 14.1 Marketing Concepts in the Firm

Objective	Primary responsibility	Marketing concepts	Source
Long-range planning	Top management Board of directors President Executive committee	Sales goals	Long-range forecast and executive discretion
Short-range planning	Management: Top Financial Production Marketing	Estimated sales	Short-range forecast and executive discretion
Market perspective	Marketing management	Potentials: Market End use Market segment Sales	Market measurements and demand estimates
Sales performance	Sales management	Quotas	Measurements of markets and men plus discretion

Corporate Sales Goal

The "corporate sales goal" is an integral part of long-range corporate planning. It can be defined as a long-range sales objective typically for a product or product line. It is an expression of where we seek to be, regarding sales, five to ten years hence. It should be somewhat optimistic. It need not be highly accurate.

A sales goal can be expressed in dollars or units, as a share of market, or as a percent of market potential to be attained. It could be for the entire market or refined by segments thereof. It is a product of anything from a dream to a competent, long-range forecast. It can be broken down to annual steps (and frequently is). Its purpose is to provide a guide to progress and bench marks for evaluation of progress en route.

The goal may well be in excess of the estimated sales, the quotas, and the sales potential. It could not correctly be in excess of the market potential.

Sales Estimate

This measurement should be neither optimistic nor pessimistic. Rather, it should be as realistic as possible. A reasonably high degree of accuracy is both needed and obtainable from the short-range forecast.

The sales estimate is the sales revenue expected to be realized during a given time, such as a year, for the company as a whole and for divisions and major products or product lines. Sales estimates are refined by quarters, months, and in some cases, even weeks or days.

The sales estimate becomes the revenue side of the budget. It is heavily used to serve the short-range planning needs of the corporation in allocation of funds, production scheduling, sales promotion, and sales management. Even though the short-range forecast is the primary source of this estimate, the involvement includes not only the forecasters, but also marketing, production, and financial executives, as well as top management—not only for final approvals, but also to provide for complete integration of all the factors bearing upon the sales estimate.

Potentials

The corporate sales goal spells out what we would *like* to accomplish. The sales estimate identifies what we *expect* to accomplish. But, omitted so far, is a most essential ingredient of effective planning—the *opportunities* for improvement. It should be emphasized that this information should not be an afterthought, something separate and apart, nice for information's sake but of little practical value. Rather, a complete integration of this information from the very beginning is most essential to competent corporate planning. It should be the starting point for both the corporate sales goal and the sales estimate.

Potentials exist in possibility. They are unrealized, future opportunities, not past accomplishments. Yet, common business usage of the term rarely gives more than lip service to the latent, undeveloped future possibilities. Typically, past performance, either company or industry, is used as the starting point with an adjustment added for next year's growth. The result is treated as the potential. Such usage very deftly directs the attention to preserving the status quo, to the complacency of normal growth as the limit of possibility, and away from the perhaps jarring realities of potential markets.

A Market Potential[2] A "market potential" can be defined as the total sales of a product, within a given period of time and for a given geographical area, the world or a trading area. This would be the optimum figure of total sales, if all who could *reasonably* use the product were to do so. It should be noted that this would be the total reasonably possible sales for a *product*, irrespective of seller. This figure, for any given period, would be higher than total realized sales for that period, unless the market is actually at a complete saturation point. If so, no new opportunities for further growth exist, product substitution is

[2] The following material is adapted from "A Basic Guide to Measuring Markets," by George Risley, *Industrial Marketing*, June 1961, copyright 1961 by Advertising Publications, Inc., Chicago, Illinois.

impossible, no new applications are conceivable, and interindustry competition can open no new doors. Progress is indeed limited. This may be true, but if so, it is rare.

The major use for a market potential is perspective. It provides a bird's-eye view of industrial welfare, progress, and possible turning points. It contributes to trend analysis and visualization of the impact of interindustry competition. This bird's-eye perspective is an excellent start from which to approach the further segmentation of the market.

End-Use Potential   A second concept is an "end-use potential." This differs from the market potential in that it refers to one specific end use, rather than the sum of all end uses. It would represent the optimum, total sales for all products by all sellers serving this specific end use. Again, the share of any one seller is unidentified.

Market-Segment Potential   The "market-segment potential" offers another approach. The attention is now directed to the total possible sales for any one segment of the total market. Rarely does a seller serve one market exclusively. This refinement could begin by distinguishing governmental marketing from industrial and from consumer. It could go further and create a market segment for each major channel of distribution involved. A most interesting application of the market-segment potential might be to develop it for the various market profiles for a market.

These three potential measurements are optimal figures for all sellers. They do provide a very valuable base for share-of-market analysis. Identification of one's strong and weak points is almost indispensable to a determination of the basic causes of both favorable and unfavorable deviations and a prerequisite to remedial action.

Sales Potential   A "sales potential" is that share of a potential (market, end use, or market segment) which can be allocated to a firm. This figure, too, would be somewhat optimistic.

The sales potential can be expressed in dollars or units, or as a percent of the total, the company's potential market share. As with the market potential, it is for a given period of time and for some defined geographical area.

Quotas

To serve the objectives of increasing sales efficiency and effectiveness, a "quota" is frequently used. The primary area of responsibility for the implementation of quotas rests with sales management. This need not be exclusive to sales management, but clearly it is most directly involved. Properly constructed, quotas can serve many purposes and be very valuable tools to aid in attaining these objectives.

Basically, a "quota" may be defined as a fair share of the overall sales task allocated to a salesman or a territory or other marketing segment, for one or more specific purposes and expressed for a definite time period.

Quotas have been determined in many ways, but all of them have in common some degree of managerial discretion applied to some base. This involves both the selection of the base to be used and the identification and weighting of the factors to be taken into account. Two salesmen in different territories, each having the same potential, could have different quotas, quite properly.

We now have four concepts, four tools to aid management: the corporate sales goal, the estimated sales, potentials, and quotas. It might be noted that these four measurements are four different sets of figures and serve four different sets of objectives. With an awareness of the identity of each, together with each one's capacity to contribute to management's problems in a given situation, the selection of which to use is facilitated.

MEASURING TECHNIQUES

Estimating Demand

Techniques to measure markets assume the existence of a market. But, suppose it doesn't exist? Consider the problem of a generic product, for which no market now exists, but which will create its own new market. This introduces the problem of estimating demand as opposed to measuring markets.

In approaching this task we have one positive advantage. We are most apt to interpret market potential in its true sense. And this points the way to the solution to the problem. We can borrow from the techniques available to measure markets those which apply to the measurement of a true market potential, the unrealized segments.

One good approach is functional. An identification of the functions of the product leads immediately to consideration of who performs these functions, in what volume, and where. Measurement of the capacity of the product to perform its functions and computation, even approximately, of the functional totals involved can provide an approximate size of the market potential. The estimate of demand must then be some portion of this total. It will be affected significantly by the introduction and effectiveness of the promotional efforts to be used, as well as the complex of decisions on all the other key controllables involved, timing, price, availability, etc. This simply reinforces the fact that marketing does not stand alone, but to be effective must be completely integrated into the corporate decision-making structure.

Another approach to estimating demand is the broad economic one. The techniques and skills of econometrics can be very helpful. It may be necessary to involve the market-research people to obtain the data in the first place. Such a combination of skills, intelligently used, may provide a very appropriate and practical solution to this problem.

Test marketing can be employed. This is without doubt the most accurate means, but it is time consuming. Risk of revelation to competitors exists. On balance, the decision as to the procedure to be followed is most likely to be a function of the total involvement, the seriousness of the impact of a major error in the estimate of demand, and the lead time over competition available.

Measuring Potentials

Market Potentials   Under this category, there are two recognizable techniques. The first is called "usage rate," and the second, "total market measure."

The *usage rate* identifies potential customers by creating a list of all users of the product. Ideally, this should be done by identifying the functions performed by the products and listing all those users whose operations include these functions.

Once the functional applications are determined, a measure of maximum volume by the various customer categories is made. This is neither easy nor impossible. Criteria can be developed, depending upon the particular situation, to do this quite accurately.

Historically, many sellers have used employment data, because of its availability. This is far short of a perfect indicator. Usage rate should be correlated with the factors which cause its variation from one industry to another, perhaps one company to another, such as the varying degrees of automation, make-or-buy decisions, possession of captive plants, and production technique differentials as they apply.

The market potential is simply the sum of the various applications times the usage rate in each case for all known users. Viewed in this light, it represents the total sales, if all potential customers used this product.

In some industries value added correlates very closely with consumption of industrial materials and supplies. Where this is true, this can form a second set of data for these purposes. Obviously, it is less appropriate to sellers of major installations and capital goods generally.

The *total market measure* uses consumption data of product by industry and by company. Statistical series data are used to measure consumption. Field surveys are sometimes used to check this.

The market potential is the present total consumption by industry from all suppliers. This differs from the usage-rate approach in that this measures total actual current consumption, whereas the usage rate measures potential consumption, if all who could use the product did so.

Trends can be measured and industry growth or stagnation identified. A careful analysis of customer welfare and future growth possibilities can be significant to the selling industry. At the very least, attention is directed to the bird's-eye perspective in total, both currently and in the future.

End-Use Potential The "end-use potential" involves a possible ambiguity of definition. It might be taken to mean all end uses of a given product, or it could mean all products for one end use. Probably the better answer is to use both approaches. Using one end use and accumulating the total for all products serving this particular usage will provide a good perspective of the extent of competition. On the other hand, the individual seller is undoubtedly concerned with total uses served by his product. These may well be more than one. If this is the case, then the total for each end use is computed and accumulated to the sum of all the uses for a product (which would equal the market potential for that product). This means, then, that both the usage-rate and the total-market-measure techniques can be used to compute the end-use potential.

Market-Segment Potential The "market-segment potential" directs attention to the identity of the customers and how best to reach them. For any one product there may well be more than one market. One good way to approximate this is to start with past sales records, which may be readily available by these different segments. A sales analysis of such records could very readily produce the historical patterns. These market-segment potentials, coupled with the market-profile approach, could produce a most enlightening and critical appraisal of the effectiveness of each profile.

Sales Potential In the category of "sales potential," one finds many techniques. Actually, very few of them measure a potential. In most cases, they do a competent job of measuring relative potentials of various marketing subdivisions, such as territories, each to the other. The end product is frequently expressed as a percent of total, but the total comes from elsewhere.

Four divisions are discernible. They are identified as "sales projection," "potential allocation," "correlation," and "share of market."

Sales projection computes a potential by projecting past sales into the near future. There are three methods.

The first assumes that past sales have equaled the potential sales. Projection of past sales gives the future potentials.

The second projects the past sales of a corollary product to obtain the potential for one's own product. It assumes that the sale of two commodities parallel each other. A measure independent of one's own sales efforts is obtained, if the base product is sold by another company, as may be the case.

The third method is based upon the assumption that sales parallel employment and that company purchases do not vary much from the average. Sales are classified by industry, usually using SICs (Standard Industrial Classifications) to establish the categories. Employment data are used to compute average sales per employee for each product line. This average applied to the employment in a company yields that company's potential.

The inherent assumption that past sales equals the potential probably is not true. Further, the application of an average to measure a potential in a specific case is open to question as to accuracy. There is no recognition of intercompany variations or of the many other factors affecting sales. Many companies compute potential from past sales adjusted by a figure for their industry. It is not always recognized, but they are not measuring potentials, merely present customers.

Projection of past sales carries with it all the errors of the past. The real danger in this is that such errors are unrecognized. Attention is directed away from their existence. Complacency is encouraged.

But these techniques are a step in the right direction. They look reasonable to salesmen and are easy to understand. They are inexpensive. A highly trained staff is not needed. If accuracy requirements are not high, they may serve the purpose.

The *potential allocation* division is by far the largest. There are ten major subdivisions, depending upon the data and technique used.

All allocate a given potential in proportion to some factor or combination of factors. They produce relative potentials (usually expressed as a percent of total) with varying degrees of accuracy. If the factors bearing on the sales of a given product are correctly identified and properly weighted, a competent relative potential results. It is reasonably easy to understand, and can be done by a clerical staff guided by a competent director.

The ten subdivisions of potential allocation are (1) past sales, (2) estimated sales, (3) market factor–single, (4) market factor–multiple, (5) SIC-employment, (6) SIC–purchase index, (7) usage rate, (8) index-company-single, (9) index-company-multiple, (10) index-published.

Past sales as an allocation technique is similar to the projection technique, but here a previously established potential is allocated to subdivisions (areas, salesmen, etc.) in proportion to the relative distribution of past sales. It assumes that past sales performance is equally satisfactory in all areas. Reflection of adjustment toward company goals is missing.

Estimated sales allocates sales potentials in proportion to the estimates of them. These estimates may come from the salesmen or be negotiated through managers and supervisors to salesman. In either case, once established, they form the base for the potential allocation. This assumes competency of the knowledge of the estimator, and, especially if it be the salesman, his objectivity.

Both the market-factor techniques use personal judgment rather than scientific methods in factor selection and weighting. The factors are set up in terms of percentage of total units for a given market, are weighted, and averages are struck. The result is the percentage of total sales possibilities assigned to each territory. Total anticipated sales applied to this produces the potential for each area.

This procedure takes into account conditions peculiar to each product. It is easy and inexpensive. It is one way to compute an individual measurement without past sales figures. However, it is arbitrary. What is called "judgment" is often guesswork, a "guesstimate." How to combine the factors and determine their relative weights to provide the best measure of regional demand is not determined.

These techniques assume that the sales for a product correlate favorably with the variation in the factors selected. Further, they assume that the true relationships between the factors selected and the sale of the product are the same as the apparent ones. They may differ appreciably, or in some cases, be reversed in varying degrees. They stress description and largely ignore cause.

The development of standardized industrial classification systems, such as SIC, has been of great assistance to industry, in spite of its shortcomings. It is used together with employment data in the SIC-employment method and with an index of purchases, in the SIC–purchase index. In the former, company or industrial sales are classified by SIC. An industry weight, computed as a percent of sales per category, is applied. Production employment times the industry weight gives the relative potentials as a percent of total.

The SIC–purchase index is similar to the above, except that a purchase index for each SIC classification is computed. This is the relationship between the buying industry's total purchases of the product being measured and the industry's total sales of its products. This $X of purchases divided by $Y of sales equals the purchase index for each SIC classification. In some cases, particularly end-user industries, capital expenditures for plant and equipment have been used in lieu of sales, to get a similar index.

Both of these techniques assume that the sales for a product parallel the sales for a classification and that the product usage rate parallels some single factor—either employment, customer sales, or capital expenditure—irrespective of type of operation, degree of automation, and make-or-buy decisions.

The techniques do not identify reasons for sales variations not accounted for by the one factor used. They assume that all companies in an industrial classification perform the same operation as to usage of one's product. This may or may not be true, or it may be true with widely varying degrees of usage. The factors determining the usage rate may be far more complex than is reflected by any single measure.

However, the two techniques are objective and eliminate arbitrary judgment. They may be sufficiently accurate to the needs. They are somewhat involved, but not overly so. They represent a big step forward over the use of a company's past sales.

The usage-rate method develops a "user's index" of normal product usage by operation performed. This is obtained from a direct survey. It is then weighted by the relative volume of each industry. The result is expressed as a percent of total and is readily allocated to territories.

It is easy to sell to salesmen, easy to understand. Its use is somewhat restricted, being most applicable to direct selling, least to marketing channels containing middlemen.

The usage-rate technique does not seek out the reasons for, or the extent of, usage-rate variations. Judgment is required in weighting. Current data may be available or may not. The basic assumptions here are that the historical usage rate can predict future sales potential and that the usage rate is reasonably constant for various companies within an industry.

The last three potential-allocation techniques use index numbers. In some cases a single market factor is used to develop the index for a company's product (index-company-single). Sometimes a combination of market factors is used (index-company-multiple). Others use a published index. All these use some statistical data, alone or in weighted combination, to indicate purchasing power as a basis for measuring potential. The result is expressed as a percent of total.

They are readily available and offer simplicity of use. They are easy to understand. Their use offers one way to compute an index of potential independent of one's own past sales. Most published index numbers are well suited for use in measuring potentials of consumer goods and somewhat less so for industrial, unless the industrial product is directly tied to a consumer counterpart.

However, one index may not measure differences in sales among markets for a given product. General buying power may not be the all-important element in quantitative analysis. Index-number techniques assume that some general indicator of purchasing power will reflect market potentials. It is somewhat naïve to assume that any single index can reflect accurately the complex influences which combine in various ways to influence sales.

Any good index number should possess at least three basic factors, weighted by their relative impact on sales. These three are measures of ability to buy, willingness to buy, and an economic factor to reflect current and local business conditions. It may take more than one market factor to reflect properly any one of these three.

Correlation is the third category of techniques to measure sales potential. This is one of the most recent developments and easily one of the most complex. It is highly accurate.

The approach uses scientific procedures (mathematical and statistical tools) instead of the usual arbitrary "better judgment" to determine the factors to be selected. The variation in sales is analyzed. The collective impact on sales of the intangible market factors is recognized and measured.

If maximum accuracy is desired and the staff to do the job is available, or the firm is willing to hire others who are competent to do so, this technique would seem to be superior to the others. Once done for a company or industry, it is simple to use and keep up to date.

The basic assumption is that those market factors which make for best sales have been operating in the past, and that the relationships true in the past will continue to be true in the near future. Then, an accurate determination of the best combination of these factors can measure a sales potential in the near future (and in the past, to see what a company's sales should have been).

This technique uses multiple-series correlation to seek out, select, and weight the optimum combination of factors bearing upon the industry's sales of a product. The accuracy of this result is measured with mathematical precision. This procedure is complicated, but can be done simply (graphically).

It may be difficult for the sales force to understand, unless they are properly informed of it. Spurious correlations of casual relationships are possible, unless prevented by competency of the correlator. Lack of confidence in this method exists, primarily due to an inability to understand it.

It can measure a potential, rather than merely allocate one. It is objective. Past sales are not used to measure the potentials. The potential so determined reflects the buying habits and other factors by their impact, as well as the known factors. The direction and effect of any one factor on sales can be isolated, studied, and determined.

It eliminates the multiplication of the same influence in two or more factors. It permits testing and discarding of irrelevants. It sets up normals for each area and takes into account conditions therein. It makes possible the use of intangible factors not otherwise employed, such as variation by area in prices, type of competition, and sales effort. The accuracy of the result is known and thereby controllable within predetermined limits.

Share of market, the fourth category, starts with a determination of the total usage for a product for all users and from all suppliers. Averages are avoided.

Surveys are often used to obtain the necessary consumption data after the industries are identified. This is done for individual companies within each industry to identify users from nonusers and varying consumption levels among companies.

These data are then expressed by geographical area, counties, and major plants. Comparisons with company sales determine the share of market. The degree of variation can then be analyzed and expressed in controllable and noncontrollable factors for executive guidance and remedial action.

The basic assumption is that consumption patterns and rates operative historically will continue into the near future. Changes can be forecast quite accurately, especially in the short run. However, it may need research to obtain consumption data. This has been done quite completely and relatively inexpensively in several cases, at least. It is a task of major proportions for some products, admittedly.

This technique measures a potential and provides a bird's-eye perspective. It is completely objective. It permits identification of overlooked prospects and provides information as to missed orders—even of present customers. It points to analysis of causes of good and poor results and thereby to specific remedial action.

ANTICIPATING THE MARKET

It is appropriate to recognize that most companies share a desire to anticipate business trends. The theoretical ideal is to enter growth markets early and to anticipate fading markets in time to shift to more profitable areas. To the extent that this can be done in practice, general business indicators are very valuable. Imports and exports should be included. Econometrics can make a most valuable contribution to complement the measurement of current market potentials. It helps maintain the long-range perspective so essential to continued success.

THE IDEAL PROGRAM

There just isn't a one-best technique, suitable for any or all sellers. The best technique is the one most suitable to the many factors involved in its selection, such as the need for and use of the results, the accuracy required, the type of product, channel(s) of distribution, managerial support available—to list a few. It is a tailor-made task for the specific circumstances of the seller, including personnel and budget, as well as the willingness of management to use the results.

RELEVANT READING

Appraising the Market for New Industrial Products, The Conference Board, Studies in Business Policy, no. 123, 1967.

Hawkins, Edward R., "Methods of Estimating Demand," *Journal of Marketing*, April 1957, pp. 428–438.

Hummel, Francis E., *Market and Sales Potentials*, New York: The Ronald Press Company, 1961.

Pessemier, Edgar A., "An Experimental Method for Estimating Demand," *Journal of Business*, October 1960, pp. 373–383.

CHAPTER FIFTEEN

Measuring Men

All managers evaluate performance of their men, one way or another. The evaluation of sales performance must be done in the face of changing market conditions and of individuals who differ in their personal characteristics, skills, and backgrounds. The corporate sales goals become involved. So does the discretion and capability of the manager.

The major tool to improve the quality of this task is a quota.[1] Properly implemented, a quota can stimulate salesmen, provide direction of effort, and furnish the basis for both evaluation and control of sales performance.

OBJECTIONS TO THE USE OF QUOTAS

It would seem that such a tool would be widely used and immensely popular. It isn't. There are two reasons for this. The first is emo-

---

[1] Substantial portions of this chapter are from "A Basic Guide to Setting Quotas," by George Risley, *Industrial Marketing*, July 1961, copyright 1961 by Advertising Publications, Inc., Chicago, Illinois.

tional. There has been considerable prejudice in connection with the use of quotas. This gives rise to criticisms which erroneously blame all quotas for the weakness of one. For example, overemphasis on sales may be a valid criticism of a sales quota. It fails completely as a criticism of all quotas. This may not be fully appreciated. There may be a lack of awareness of the other types of quotas.

The second reason for the nonuse of quotas is the conclusion that quotas cannot reflect accurately the seller's particular situation. This comes from the difficulties envisioned in obtaining the data, a lack of confidence in the mathematical techniques, and an acute awareness of the "special" circumstances faced by the firm. That these were valid objections to quota setting in the past is not denied. That they continue to be valid objections to a properly designed quota system today is strongly denied.

It is submitted that a clear visualization of the role of quotas—their integration into the corporate pattern; a knowledge of how to set them; their strengths, weaknesses, and limitations; their adaptability and the purposes they serve—can permit one to reach a valid decision as to whether or not to use them. This can aid in determining how to go about obtaining the quota most suitable to the need, as against something which is much less effective.

DEFINITION

In common usage a "quota" is a proportion, an allocation to a segment. Business usage embodies both elements. The "proportion" implies some accuracy of measurement. "Allocation" implies managerial discretion, taking into account other factors.

For business purposes, "quota" should be defined as a fair share of the overall sales task allocated to a salesman, territory, or other marketing segment. It is the product of managerial discretion applied to a base, for specific purposes, and expressed for a defined time period.

Quotas should never be confused with a sales goal, a sales estimate, a market potential, or a sales potential. These have been discussed more fully in Chapter Fourteen.

In summary, the sales goal is a long-range, corporate objective. The sales estimate is the probable sales for a certain period, often used as a base in budgeting. The long-range forecast helps provide the former; the short-range forecast, the latter. The market potential is the total reasonably realizable sales of a product by an industry. The sales potential is the total of such sales for a company. The quotas may use a sales estimate or a sales potential as a part of the base figures, but discretion usually varies the quota from the base used.

USES OF QUOTAS

Quotas are used most frequently for evaluation of performance. However, it should be remembered that performance typically includes more than just sales.

If other factors of performance are important to the job, a quota designed to measure sales alone is a poor yardstick. The resultant objection from the salesman—and one shared by intelligent management—is not to the use of quotas, but to the inadequacy of the type of quota selected. Obviously, a quota should be designed to measure all the major factors of performance, if it is to be used to evaluate that performance.

There are two significant aspects of quotas as a yardstick for evaluation. The first is management's evaluation of the man, as an aid to helping in his improvement and to taking other appropriate remedial action. The second is the man's self-evaluation. He will evaluate himself, anyway. The bias sometimes present in self-evaluation is replaced by a competent yardstick. It makes it far easier for the man to be his own best critic. Let him spot his own weaknesses. He'll improve them. Let him enjoy his own successes—he's earned them.

A second use of quotas is to provide an incentive. This can be done annually or for shorter periods, or for a special period such as the duration of a contest. Nothing prevents the use of both at the same time. In fact, it may be desirable, if contest quotas are used, to have an annual quota too, broken down by months, to help prevent overselling during a contest at the expense of the previous and succeeding time periods.

If incentive quotas are used, they need not be closely related to either the estimated sales or the sales potential. Their purpose is to inspire. To be effective they cannot be too low, nor can they be unattainably high. They must be attainable, with an adequate reward for success.

It should be noted that quotas can measure the performance of and provide incentive to two groups of men—both salesmen and their sales managers. Some sales managers have been lukewarm toward quotas because of this very point.

Quotas are an effective device to aid in directing the efforts of the sales force. This is particularly important where selected items are to be pushed and where "nonselling" tasks need more emphasis.

Quotas are sometimes used as a basis for compensation of salesmen. Here the quota might be set at the break-even point, with increased compensation for exceeding it, or at the point of a fair measure of the job, and again with incentive pay for exceeding it. In either case, the sum of these quotas need not match the sales potential or the estimated sales. Every salesman could be expected to exceed his quota.

There has been a growing trend to divorce compensation from quotas. Straight salary is used, with or without quotas. Part of the reason for this is the failure of many quotas to measure total performance. In such cases, management substitutes its discretionary judgment in recommending merit raises and promotions. Occasionally, this may be justified. Generally it is, in effect, recognition of a need for better quota setting—an admission of a lack of appreciation of what a good quota can do to aid in this.

In addition, quotas can be used to aid in other aspects of corporate operations, such as production planning, inventory control, facility location studies, rationing of scarce goods to customers under conditions of a sellers' market, allocation of advertising, and expense control to achieve minimal distribution costs.

The quota may serve all these purposes at the same time. This is a matter for decision by management. The identification of the purpose(s) to be served becomes a factor in the selection of the type of quota to be used.

THE CONSTRUCTION OF A QUOTA

Figure 15.1 illustrates the ingredients and process of quota setting.

Corporate Sales Goals

An ideal starting point for the construction of a quota is to use the long-term forecast as the source of the first data. From this we extract the corporate sales goal, the sales segment of the long-range corporate goal refined to annual bites. This is where management would like us to be next year.

Types of Quotas

Typically, or invariably, when one mentions a quota, it is a sales quota. There seems to be a profound lack of recognition of the other types. They differ completely in specific objective, in their computation, and in the basic data employed. A glance at Figure 15.1 will indicate that three major ones are a sales quota, a budget quota, and an activity quota. The fourth type is even more important in application, but is simply a combination of the first three.

Sales Quotas Sales quotas can be classified into two groups, those which reflect a hoped-for performance and those geared to actual expectancy. The difference lies in the discretion applied to the base figure used, not in the measurement of that figure.

There are four bases for sales quotas: a sales estimate (from the short-range sales forecast), sales potential (from any of several research

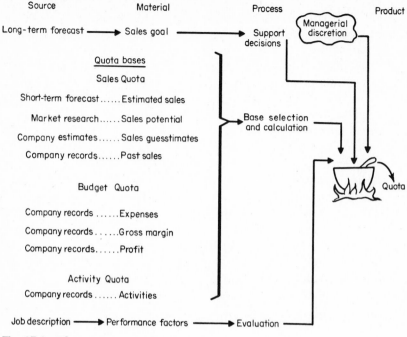

Source   Material   Process   Product

Long-term forecast ⟶ Sales goal ⟶ Support decisions   Managerial discretion

Quota bases

Sales Quota

Short-term forecast......Estimated sales

Market research......Sales potential

Company estimates......Sales guesstimates   Base selection and calculation

Company records......Past sales

Budget Quota   Quota

Company records ......Expenses

Company records........Gross margin

Company records......Profit

Activity Quota

Company records ...... Activities

Job description ⟶ Performance factors ⟶ Evaluation

Fig. 15.1   The construction of a quota.

techniques), a sales "guesstimate" (either management's or the sales-man's), and past sales.

Past sales have been used frequently as a base and extended by adding either a percentage or an arbitrary amount as an increase for the next year's quota. This method is simple. It is inexpensive. It is easy for the salesman to understand. It appears to be geared to progress.

However, it assumes that a close relationship exists between past and future sales and that past sales have been satisfactory. This may be true, or it may not. In any event, it projects any errors of the past into the future. It tends to direct attention away from poor salesman-ship and fosters complacency.

It protects both the salesman and the sales management from any embarrassing truths of any aspect of poor performance. If such cases exist, ignorance is often preferred over accuracy. It sets a quota based on whatever the past has been, irrespective of the potential for expan-sion. Two salesmen with similar past sales histories are given the same quota, even though one may be selling 50 to 60 percent of his potential and the other 10 percent. The real error is that such differentials are not known.

However, past sales should not be ignored. If a more accurate base figure is used, any major deviation from past sales cannot be expected to be accomplished overnight—nor is the fault necessarily the salesman's. If he has been doing a good job of achieving whatever quota he has been given by management, he cannot be blamed because that quota is wrong. Past sales do become a valuable factor in realistic quota setting. Corrective action can then be taken in reasonable bites, with both the salesman and sales management aware of the facts and the opportunity for improvement.

A *sales "guesstimate"* is one step in the direction of a more accurate base figure for quota setting. This is an intelligent guess as to future sales. It is not restricted to a mere projection of past sales. It takes into account local conditions and the various intangible factors influencing sales.

It can be of high quality, depending upon the capacity of those who do the job. If the salesman is responsible for it, it assumes the competency of his knowledge of all the factors and his objectivity. If management does it, it assumes an awareness of the changing conditions in each sales territory as well as the broader factors which influence future sales and a fair consideration of the causes for a lower quota, when called for. A tendency to be overcome is that of always expecting more and of minimizing any factors opposing this.

The *sales potential* measurement and the *sales estimate* derived from a short-range forecast offer the highest degree of accuracy for the base figure. The sales potential, if completely done, provides a yardstick as to what the sales opportunities really are.

There are four major categories of measurement of sales potential: the sales projection, potential allocation, correlation, and share-of-market techniques. Very frequently, the potential-allocation group, including index numbers, either company or published, is used as a base in quota setting.

If the impact of corrective action to be taken by management to achieve sales improvement is taken into account in forecasting sales, then the sales estimate provides the probable sales base. It can be used with a minimum of adjustment if the quota is to be one of actual expectancy.

Actually, all four bases make a contribution to the base figure to be used in setting a sales quota. Probably the ideal is to include past sales for realism, the sales "guesstimate" to reflect probable change, the sales estimate to reflect the impact of company corrective action, and the sales potential to reflect the relative share of market and the sales opportunity.

The selection of the best combination of these factors and the weight to be given each represents a task, truly. However, the task is identified. Better sales performance and lower selling cost can be valuable rewards for attempting the task and for continued efforts toward its improvement.

Budget Quotas   A budget quota is used to shift the emphasis from sales to a reduction in the cost of selling or to an increase in the profit. It is particularly suitable if a seller is facing a market near its saturation point, or where a given seller has achieved his maximum practical share of market. More sales can be made only at great expense. Therefore, it seems wiser to protect one's sales position and stress selling efficiency.

There are three bases for budget quotas: expenses, gross margin, and profit.

Expenses are often used as a base, and one common procedure is to estimate the salesman's expenses for the future period. This can be expressed in dollars or as a percent of sales. The budget is then set in some relationship to this figure. Incentive can be provided for expense reduction, or for achieving or being under budget, by additional compensation, either directly or as a bonus. An expense quota can be used alone. It can be combined very easily with a sales quota.

One caution seems appropriate here. As salesmen become cost-conscious, a tendency to overdo expense reduction can be created. If the salesman starts to patronize cheaper hotels, avoid necessary social responsibilities in the field, and so on, a false impression can be created in the customers' minds and the results can be detrimental. This danger may not be great, but it should be watched.

The *gross-margin* basis for the budget quota places the emphasis upon selling those items with the highest margin, rather than the easier-to-sell and less profitable low-margin items. This is particularly useful if the margin varies significantly among different items or classes of items in a line.

Profit is another aspect of this same sort of emphasis. Items with the highest margins may represent the greatest profit. If they do not, or if margin differentials are minor and yet profit varies appreciably among different items, then profit may be used as a base.

The problem here is to define profit and to measure it. The calculation may become too involved for salesmen to understand. The detail and record keeping needed may make this procedure expensive. The cost and many expense factors are not subject to control by the salesman. However, where feasible to use, it does tie the salesman's performance and his reward directly to the profit of the employer.

Activity Quota   A major criticism of quotas is that they tend to overemphasize sales. This may be true of sales quotas. Clearly, it is less true of budget quotas. It is not at all true of activity quotas.

An activity quota uses as a base any one or a combination of many

factors, each of which is a part of the desired performance. Such factors include the number of calls made (for sales, service, or missionary
work), new or reactivated accounts, prospects, demonstrations, displays
secured, progressive steps toward order placement, bids made—and any
other units of measurement of activity. It permits recognition of day-
to-day, nonselling activities, as well as steps achieved in long-range development of accounts which buy infrequently but in large amounts.

Activity quotas can be a booby trap for the unwary. Used alone,
they can reward salesmen for quantity of work, irrespective of quality,
for a dangerously long time. Adequate supervision and close contact
with salesmen to be sure of the quality of performance are an obvious
necessity.

Combined Quota   The combined quota is merely a combination of
two or more of the above. It is especially helpful when sales management wants to achieve a proper balance between emphasis upon sales,
costs, profitableness, and other activities important to be performed,
yet not measurable in dollars or units sold.

The factors to be measured from sales, budget, and activity bases
are listed, then weighted by relative importance. The extent of attainment of each factor is multiplied by its weight. The total measures
the relative position of each man to his quota. A point system is sometimes used for the weights.

This becomes a precise tool to measure performance. It can include
incentives. It can be used readily as a base for a compensation plan,
with or without bonus payments. However, it is complex. Keeping
and computing the necessary data may be somewhat costly.

If the salesman questions the result, it may be time consuming and
perhaps difficult to audit. Yet, making the audit is necessary to convince
him of its accuracy, especially if the computations are done in the home
office and he is in the field. Most of such difficulties can be prevented
by proper orientation in the first place.

Once the type of quota has been selected and the base for it obtained,
the base figure can be computed. It is recognized that much care is
involved in reaching a sound, workable base for quotas. It means work.
It should be kept as simple as possible, consistent with a reasonable
degree of accuracy. However, once properly set up, and with appropriate reporting forms designed, subsequent calculation becomes routine.

Errors of computation of the base are to be carefully avoided. Such
errors have caused the quotas to be unrealistic. This is not a criticism
of quotas, as such, but a criticism of the quality of the base figure
used and the technique used to measure it. Fortunately, techniques
are available today to do just that, to have the probable error of measure
ment known and hence controlled within predetermined limits.

Factors of Performance

A significant omission can, and frequently does, occur in quota setting. This is to omit proper consideration of the factors of performance. All too frequently there is little or no attempt to identify or measure them.

The first step is to recognize the factors which are involved in the salesman's performance of his total task. This would seem to be so obvious as not to merit mentioning. However, very rarely is it done. Typically, the executive exercises his discretion without ever clearly identifying the considerations or attempting to measure the total for each man. An accurate list of all the pertinent factors, prepared from the job requirements, is a good start. Each item on this list should then be weighted for each one's relative significance to the rest. Then each man's situation can be rated for each factor. The collective total for each man becomes the factors of performance to be taken into account together with support decisions and the base figure in the application of managerial discretion to arrive at a quota. It is submitted that this procedure is not a substitute for, or a restriction of, the exercise of judgment by management. Rather, it is an aid to better judgment by providing more accurate data.

The factors to be considered include (but are not limited to) the man, the product, the channel(s) of distribution, the territory, the job, the company, and the psychological impact of the quota on the man. By "man" is meant his personal data—his age, experience, ability, special skills, job attitude, family attitude, personal goodwill, everything bearing upon his ability to perform. The product includes the type of selling required, end user versus OEM, service needed, price, competition, acceptability, and other factors. The job can be divided into activities and can vary appreciably even within one company. The company image, developmental plans, position in the industry, degree of support, facility locations, and so on may vary from one territory to another. This list is meant to be suggestive, not inclusive.

These factors are intangible for the most part and are somewhat difficult to measure accurately. This is not to say that no attempt need be made to do so. On the contrary, a serious attempt to refine the measurements is called for. Evaluation charts can be used. The man may be asked for his own judgments. A supervisor may be asked for his. A committee can be set up to assist or to determine the values. Top sales management can participate, of course.

Ideally, a job-evaluation plan could be used. This could be done by the company staff, if qualified. An outside consultant could be employed to set up the task in the first place. Thereafter, the company staff can use it, usually with only minor refinements needed for several years.

Such a procedure does result in one very valuable benefit, particularly if the man participates. The human relations can be greatly improved. It tends to convince the man that management is trying to measure honestly the factors of his job, rather than asserting the yardstick by which he is to be judged. It fosters acceptance of the quota. This is a prerequisite if the quota is to provide incentive. The effect of this upon the salesman's morale, loyalty, and enthusiasm is profound.

It is appropriate to comment here that anything ratable or measurable can be used as a factor in quota setting. The techniques to do this are well established and readily tailored to the task. It is simple to convert the rating of an intangible characteristic through a point system to a mathematical symbol or scale which reflects it. The relative importance of various characteristics can be provided by weightings. The total points achieved can become an element in the quota. A change in points can be appropriately recognized as improved performance. The basic thesis involved is that improved performance will follow from improvement in the man.

Quota-Setting Process

We now have three basic elements for our quota: the corporate sales goal, the quota base, and the performance factors. The decisions of management in the actual allocation of manpower and money to aid in reaching next year's sales goal should be determined. These support decisions and the extent and impact of them upon next year's performance must be taken into account in the final determination of the quota. The quota base calculated is the next item. The third is the result of the evaluation of the man himself. These three elements are now brought together in a weighted combination to reflect their relative significance to each other. We might now put them into the pot. However, we are still missing one important ingredient.

Managerial Discretion

Up to this point we have been, it is hoped, as impersonal as possible. The data accumulated and the treatment should not include any "adjustment." This means we provide the facts. Nor is this an impediment to executive discretion. Rather, it is a way of placing the opportunity and responsibility for such discretion right where it belongs—on the executive exercising it.

This discretion provides the actual consideration and integration of the management support decisions, the factors of performance, and the base calculated. It is an essential ingredient in quota setting.

This application of discretion is not to be criticized. It is not a weakness in quota setting. It permits negotiation of the quota with the man and others involved. It provides freedom to adjust the quota for any intangibles present.

The power to exercise this discretion is placed at varying levels in various companies. The range is from the immediate sales supervisor upward through sales management to a special executive committee created for the task. Such committees sometimes include the comptroller and the production man as well as sales executives. The product of this is the quota. It could be expressed in total for the company, by products or product lines, by sales territories, and by customers, and refined as necessary to permit adequate application.

Accuracy Requirements

In quota setting one should keep in mind the purposes of the quota. It is not necessary that the quota be matched by sales, or that the sum of the quotas equal the sales estimate or the sales potential or any other figure.

It is desired that the influence of the quota on sales be felt in proper places and in the right direction. Errors of salesmanship often run quite high. No discretionary judgment is perfect. If the results are more of the desired performance and less of the least desirable, it would seem that quotas are doing their job.

Accuracy of the base used for quota setting can be quite high. Forecasts within 5 to 10 percent of actual sales are common, and forecasts within 1 to 2 percent are not rare. Research can measure sales potentials to a high degree of accuracy—or to a lower one. It is a function of the time and money available and the accuracy needed for interpretation and application of results. A lower standard, a greater degree of inaccuracy, if satisfactory to the task, is a better job than expensively realized, excessive accuracy.

Flexibility

Quotas need not be 100 percent accurate, but they should be reasonably so. As time goes on, conditions change. If automatic adjustment to this change is included in the base figure, the quotas are adjusted accordingly, periodically.

Flexibility is not a sign of weakness. Even a perfect quota today, maintained dogmatically, can lose its impact tomorrow. Inflexibility of quotas does not prevent changes in the field. A reasonable balance is necessary between complete flexibility to every slight change and inflexibility regardless of changes. This should present no serious problem once the need for reasonable flexibility is recognized. This is particularly true of industrial quotas, where conditions can change more frequently and far more drastically than in consumer-goods selling.

SECURING ACCEPTANCE

This is *the* most essential step in implementing a new quota system or a change in one. Quotas, to be effective, must be *truly* accepted, not only by the salesmen, but by management. What the man says across a desk to his boss may not be significant. What we are after here is what he really thinks after he has left the office—what he says when he is having a beer with the boys.

The application of scientific techniques to sales management is sometimes resented. There is a real danger of showing up any lack of skill on the part of both the salesman and sales management. It is easy to get by, to impress the boss, by absolute increases. Income may be satisfactory, so incentive to change is lacking. Further, if there is anything about the creation of a quota which is not understood, it becomes head-office "gobbledygook." This is feared and resented, even by the most competent.

Therefore, the first step in securing acceptance of quotas is to have a sound overall plan. This plan must be competent. It must be fair. It must be understood. A less accurate, simpler plan, readily understandable, may be a better choice, at least at the beginning, than a more complex plan yielding higher accuracy but harder to comprehend.

Whatever system is used, it should be explained thoroughly to both management and the salesman—every salesman. A complex plan can easily be used, if it is understood. The explanation and acceptance are the vital criteria, not the degree of complexity, per se. Good salesmen are reasonable and intelligent. If the plan is basically sound, this will be recognized and a big hurdle is immediately passed.

Participation in the quota setting by those involved is a sound technique in securing acceptance. This should not be mere lip service. The result may often be a compromise. That is far better than an arbitrary overruling by authority. The loss of favorable impact of the quota on the man is too big a price to pay for the privilege of assertion. Reasonable compromise, with the basis for adjustments identified, is most apt to be convincing, once the compromise has been made. This applies to both parties, equally strongly.

Salesmen should be kept informed of their progress at frequent intervals. This permits identification of strong and weak points quickly. An analysis of the causes of both strengths and weaknesses can be made by both the salesman and his manager. Decisions for remedial action can be reached quickly and corrective action instituted promptly.

EVALUATING PERFORMANCE

Quotas are not absolute standards of performance, even if evaluation of performance is the major reason for their use. Deviations from quota should be expected. The significance is not great if the percentage is reasonably low. The real value in such deviations is to use them to identify the causes of both favorable and unfavorable deviation for remedial action. It should be remembered that the quota itself may be wrong.

It is equally fair to ask which is nearer right, the quota or the performance. If the quota is soundly conceived, fair, and reasonable, it is also attainable. Then, the significant point is the difference between it and the performance, the direction and the extent.

Both favorable and unfavorable differences should be analyzed carefully and from two points of view. One is to help the salesman by identifying the causes of the exceeded quotas, to obtain more, and the causes of the deficiencies, to seek to minimize or eliminate them. The second is to seek improvement in the quota setting itself. Probably both factors are present, if the differences are great. Open-mindedness is a valuable asset in such analysis. Improvement of both the future quotas and performance is aided thereby.

SUMMARY

In recapitulation, how does one build a quota? Undoubtedly, the first step is to decide upon the objectives to be served with an awareness of the possible uses to which a quota can be put. This may, but need not, be integrated with a compensation plan. Obviously, it would be better to do so if motivation is significant. Next, select the appropriate type and make the computations. One should not overlook the vital necessity of presenting the system to everyone involved and securing acceptance. While this is in process, the performance factors can be evaluated. The result is integrated with the managerial support decisions and the calculated base. Managerial discretion is then exercised to arrive at the quota. The men should be kept informed of their progress in sufficient detail and at reasonably frequent intervals in order to permit prompt evaluation of performance by both the man and his supervisor as a basis for prompt remedial action.

Science can measure the base, but quota setting is an art, a skill of management. Because it is an art is no reason to fear it. The benefits are great. A good quota system can aid in progress through motivation, evaluation, direction of effort, and remedial action. It must be soundly conceived, fair, reasonably simple, reasonably accurate, and reasonably timely. It should provide for automatic correction of variables from the field. It should involve participation of the salesmen in a feedback of factors arguing for less as well as of factors arguing for more. But the creation of a good quota system is not enough. It must be properly presented and accepted. An open-minded attitude in the interpretation of deviations from quota and an unbiased seeking of the causes thereof are vital. Experience can show much improvement, not only in the act of quota setting, but also in the sales results, in both their effectiveness and efficiency.

RELEVANT READING

Frey, Albert W. (ed.), *Marketing Handbook*, 2d ed., New York: The Ronald Press Company, 1965, sec. 13, pp. 21–41.

Measuring Salesmen's Performance, The Conference Board, Studies in Business Policy, no. 114, 1965.

Still, Richard R., and Edward W. Cundiff, *Sales Management*, 2d ed., Englewood Cliffs, N.J.: Prentice-Hall, Inc., 1969, chap. 16.

"The Controversy in Sales Quotas," *Dun's Review*, May 1966, pp. 47–78.

Townsend, Robert, "Incentive Compensation and Profit Sharing," *Up the Organization*, New York: Alfred A. Knopf, Inc., Copyright © Robert Townsend, 1970, pp. 75–82.

PART SEVEN

Industrial Marketing Management

CHAPTER SIXTEEN

New Products

WHAT IS A "NEW" PRODUCT?[1]

"New" products differ significantly in "newness." This is important since the involvement and the attendant risk in new-product introduction parallels very closely the variation in the newness.

The range is from a major modification of an existing and well-established product all the way to a completely new development, a generic product. A new product can be new to the seller only, but have been marketed by others. Or it can be new to one group of customers, a new market, but sold successfully elsewhere by the firm. It can be new to both the firm and the market. It can be new, yet competitive with existing products. It can be new and create its own new market. Obviously, there are many degrees of newness—and equally, many degrees of risk.

This range in newness—from something that has not previously been conceived for a market that does not yet exist, to a minor modification of a standard product (and in consumer marketing, the change may

[1] Substantial portions of this chapter were contributed by A. P. Moran, Manager, New Products, Electrical Components Division, The Bendix Corporation, Sidney, N.Y.

be confined to the package, instead of the product)—calls for appropriate variation and flexibility in the firm's product-planning responsibilities.

New products will continue to be a most significant factor in economic development. Their role in corporate planning cannot be long ignored by any firm. Those that do are simply inviting competition to make them obsolete and are without the means for survival by prepared adaptation to change.

There is nothing new in this. The process has been going on since the beginning of the barter system. The real change is in the time element. Today, the life cycle of a product is much shorter; change is much more rapid. And there are more changes being made in many different directions.

We seem to be compressing events into ever-shorter time periods in our generation.

> It took 65 years from the time it was invented for the electric motor to be applied . . . 33 years for the vacuum tube . . . and 18 years for the x-ray tube. But it took only 10 years for the nuclear reactor . . . only 5 years for radar . . . and less than 3 years for the transistor and the solar battery.[2]

LIFE CYCLE OF PRODUCTS

Products are not forever. They have a life cycle. See Figure 16.1. Position in this cycle produces varying degrees of profit. Profits increase relatively rapidly during the growth phase, but fall off rapidly under competitive pressure during maturity. Very few firms have figures on

[2] Reprinted from *Journal of Marketing,* published by the American Marketing Association, Leo Burnett, "Marketing Snags and Fallacies," vol. 30, no. 3, July 1966, p. 1.

Fig. 16.1 Basic life cycle of products. (*Source: "Management of New Products," Chicago: Booz-Allen & Hamilton, Inc., 1968, p. 4.*)

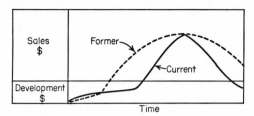

Fig. 16.2 Comparison be-
tween former and current
product life cycles. (*Source:
Pat Thomas, "Removing the
Black Art from Product Planning," "Data on Defense and
Civil Systems," Data Publications, December 1963, p. 41.*)

profits by products available to them. However, if available, profits
by products become a far more valuable planning tool than sales by
products.

Obviously, the time period and dollar values vary among different
products. Nevertheless, the cycle does exist. Some products merely
take longer to die.

This lovely curve is artistically smoothed for graphic impact. This
in no way lessens the truthfulness of the great variation in the profit-sales
ratios as products move through their life cycles. A more realistic por-
trayal of today's high-speed business rate is shown in Figure 16.2, where
the former and the current product life cycles found in today's real
world are compared.

Because of competition, market saturation, and technological obsolescence (and perhaps industrial espionage), sales volume and duration
become misshapen. More time is required in development, so developmental costs are rising and claiming a greater share of profit margins.
Therefore, more total profit is needed. This can be provided by successful new products.

It is obvious that industry needs the profits from new products. The
value of new products to various industries is indicated in Figure
16.3. In this group of industries it is clear that new products are
planned to account for the bulk of the contemplated growth.

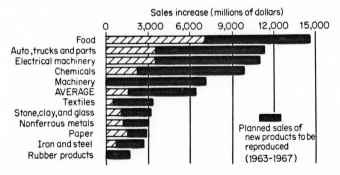

Fig. 16.3 Planned contribution of new products to expected
sales growth, 1963–1967. (*Source: "Management of New Products," Chicago: Booz-Allen & Hamilton, Inc., 1968, p. 5.*)

IS IT REALLY AS RISKY AS THEY SAY?

No one really knows the facts. It is most probable that there has been exaggeration by writers. In the first place, firms do not keep statistics on failures and are reluctant to admit them. And, "failure" is a very ambiguous term. There are degrees of failure, from a flop after introduction to a dropping en route, prior to introduction. Time and money will have been spent, even in the earliest phases. If successfully introduced and profitable, the product might have been phased out because the profit return was unsatisfactorily low.

It is quite probable that the introduction of new products to an industrial market is less risky than to the consumer market. Industrial needs are easier to identify and tend to be more specific, the market is better known, channels of distribution are more direct, and the number of customers is smaller. All these tend to lessen the risk.

Yet, the risk in the introduction of new products is clearly very high. It is definitely not a standard high risk simply because it is a new product. Undoubtedly, it is far more of a variable among different situations—and with involvement in far more than the product, per se. If any one factor is to shoulder the blame for new-product failures, it is the management. Managerial errors are far more prevalent than product errors. In the past, management has often assumed that the prerequisite to success in the marketplace is technical superiority. This is always a desirable characteristic, but it does not provide assurance of economic success, or even feasibility. A new product could be demonstrably superior in performance, but the requirement that it fill a real market need and sell in sufficient quantity at a profitable price has been more often assumed than explored. It is only natural for a product-oriented engineer-manager to assume that a technically successful product will automatically be an economically successful one.

And this danger is especially insidious if this was the basis for the development of the firm's business some years ago. It tends to be most convincing to the manager. His firm's and his personal history prove he has been—and therefore is—right. The error is in his failure to recognize change in the total involvement, and the extent of that involvement in the first place.

Figure 16.4 attempts to portray the range in risk as different factors in this involvement vary. Each of the factors might be visualized as a scale, with the extremes identified. Each could then be rated for any one new-product situation. The total applied to the failure-rate line might indicate the relative hazard.

It is most likely that relatively few new-product introductions face exactly the same situation or have the same rating. It seems safe to

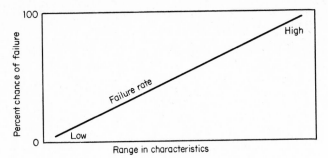

Fig. 16.4 Risk as a function of change in characteristics of total involvement.

Low chance of failure	*High chance of failure*
Economy:	
Scarcity	Surplus
Seller's market	Keen competition
Firm:	
Finances sound	Finances weak
Well known and established	New to potential customers
Management:	
Customer-oriented	Product-oriented
Product planning well organized	Product planning a la carte
Marketing concept integrated	Marketing concept left to marketing/sales
Spare managerial capacity	Fully occupied
Marketing:	
Market potentials known and forecast	Logical market assumed
Sales to present customers	Sales to new customers
Uses present channels of distribution	Uses new channels of distribution
Product:	
Standard	New technology
Production procedures well known	New production techniques
Technology:	
Known to management	New to management

say that the risk of failure varies among new-product situations and is a reflection of the variation in the factors impacting thereon.

While this list is not presented as all-inclusive, it does indicate something of the scope of the total involvement. Augmentation and refinement become perfectly appropriate. For any one product situation, there may well be a variation in significance of the factors from that of others. The value of such an approach is to call attention to the total factors involved and their impacts on the risk. It should be noted that most of them are controllable, at least to some extent. Awareness of the least controllable, such as the economic, can help measure the risk, at the very least.

How Many Eggs for One Bird?

Figure 16.5 emphasizes the mortality of new-product ideas by stages of evaluation or action, and introduces time spent (or lost) in culling out unacceptable product ideas. This figure indicates that fifty-eight ideas fed into the hopper generated two commercial products, one of which became entirely successful.

COST OF NEW-PRODUCT FAILURES

The lack of records, and the almost impossible task of allocation to create them, prohibits an accurate measurement of the cost of new-product failures. It is likely that if such data were compiled, it would not add significantly to what we already know—that this cost is very high.

Part of the job of product planners is to reduce the risks and the attendant costs of product failures. A look at the accumulation of cost as an individual product passes through the stages of a new-product program may be of interest. Figure 16.6 may help to visualize this.

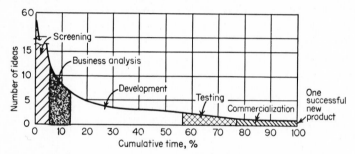

Fig. 16.5   Mortality of new-product ideas (by stage of evolution—fifty-one companies). (*Source: "Management of New Products,"* Chicago: Booz-Allen & Hamilton, Inc., 1968, p. 9.)

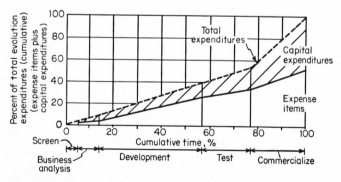

Fig. 16.6   Cumulative expenditures and time (by stage of evolution—all-industry average). (*Source: "Management of New Products,"* Chicago: Booz-Allen & Hamilton, Inc., 1968, p. 10.)

It can be noted that development takes about 50 percent of the time and 30 percent of the cost. During commercialization the costs rise rapidly. Therefore, competent feasibility studies and market testing as early in the game as can be may help to cut expense by permitting prompt and ruthless elimination of the least likely. They may also serve to increase efforts on those most likely to be successful.

> Of all the dollars of new-product expense, almost three-fourths go to unsuccessful products; about two-thirds of these waste dollars are in the "development stage." Thus, about eight out of ten development scientists and engineers may be said to be working on projects that will not be justified in terms of commercial usefulness (basic research is not included here).
>
> If management could decrease this waste only slightly, it would in theory—and often in fact—greatly enhance its effective manpower in the new-product process.[3]

Once the new-product idea has been approved for commercialization, its chances of success are quite good. Not many got that far, but of those that did in fifty-four prominent companies, two-thirds were successful. See Figure 16.7.

This is to say that the great expense and the chance of failure lie in the developmental stages, prior to commercialization. Once the product is commercialized, even though this involves reasonably heavy capital and expense outlays, the likelihood of success is favorable. Obviously, the quality of the decision to commercialize, or not to, is a key factor.

[3] *Management of New Products,* Chicago: Booz-Allen & Hamilton, Inc., 1968, p. 11.

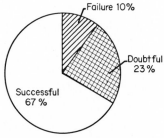

Failure 10%

Doubtful 23%

Successful 67%

366 new products recently marketed

Fig. 16.7 Success of new products commercialized (fifty-four prominent companies). (*Source: "Management of New Products," Chicago: Booz-Allen & Hamilton, Inc., 1968, p. 11.*)

THE WHY OF SUCCESS OR FAILURE: KEY FACTORS

Why is new-product introduction such a risky business? Why is the failure rate so high? What can be done to weed out the failures sooner, to enhance the likelihood of success of those introduced, and to lower the risk in the entire process? In fact, can it be done?

Success in new-product introduction might be likened to a batting average or a golf score. The question then takes on a more realistic aspect. It becomes, How can our batting average be improved, or our golf score lowered? This seeks improvement over present performance as a goal, rather than the ultimate. And this is readily possible, if attention and effort are conscientiously applied toward that goal.

Reasons for Failure

The Conference Board reports on the results of its 1971 survey of 125 members of its Senior Marketing Executive Panel. This survey refers only to the success of *major* new items marketed—not mere improvements or minor additions to a company's line. It states:[4]

> Post mortems on some of these failures revealed that a combination of factors was responsible. In other cases, company spokesmen say that just one factor or one serious miscalculation led to a product's downfall.
> The most important reasons given for disappointing results after the release of new products or services to market are summarized as follows:

Cause of failure	Percent of companies citing
Inadequate market analysis	45
Product problems or defects	29
Lack of effective marketing effort	25
Higher costs than anticipated	19
Competitive strength or reaction	17
Poor timing of introduction	14
Technical/production problems	12
All other causes	24

The foregoing is based on reporting of both manufacturing and service companies experiencing failures. Data relate to factors contributing to the disappointing performance, in some important respect, of major new products (or services) introduced during the previous five years. Percentages total more than 100% because some companies reported on multiple causes of failure.

[4] David S. Hopkins and Earl L. Bailey, "New-product Pressures," The Conference Board *Record*, June 1971, pp. 16–24.

Causes of failure are not much different from one industry to another. Nor are they markedly different from those cited by companies participating in another Board survey (of manufacturers only) six years earlier. In both instances, inadequate appraisal of the market in advance was the most frequent reason. Next most common: defects or limitations that turned up in the product itself. Again in both instances, the reaction of competitors to the new entry—or the misjudging of this reaction—was fairly well down the list of reasons for failure. In short, as managements are frank to acknowledge with hindsight, when a new product goes wrong, the fault often lies largely within the company itself.

Ways to Reduce Failure

Management has been giving high priority to finding ways of reducing the chances of future failure. By far the largest number of resulting actions are organizational changes aimed at strengthening the planning, coordination and control of the company's new ventures.

Over the years, there is often much reshuffling and experimentation as management tries to find the most effective ways of organizing the company's new-product activities.

Among multidivision companies, the coordination of new-product projects is carried out wholly at the divisional level by 39%; wholly at the corporate level by 16%; and at both levels by 45%. Factors affecting preference include management's commitment to decentralization, the relative homogeneity of product lines among the company's divisions, the importance of a particular venture, and the amount of risk of the company's investment in it.

At any level, coordinating responsibility for new products in three out of four companies is lodged within a major functional department— usually, marketing. If regular product managers do not have this assignment along with their other duties, it is often held by a full-time manager or unit within the marketing function.

In about one company in five, some or all new-product projects are coordinated outside regular functional departments by separate, specialized units reporting directly to general management.

Most companies have one or more new-product committees. While the role of such committees varies, they are seldom concerned with the day-to-day coordination of projects, but serve more often as communications and review boards, with emphasis on insuring that the new-product program stays on schedule and that cross-functional tangles are avoided.

Apart from these organizational adjustments, managements count most on more thorough-going marketing research to ensure that market needs and prospects are carefully appraised before going ahead with new projects.

Of critical importance, in the opinion of several marketers, is the application of sound research and judgment at the very outset, when the possibility of developing the new product or service is first being considered.

Just because a proposed product gets past this initial hurdle seldom means that it's automatically bound for market. Increasingly, projects routinely move through a series of formal phases—concept testing, feasibility analysis, technical development, field testing, and test marketing—before their full commercialization. And, at the completion of each of these phases, the projects are subject to systematic review and "go, no-go" decisions by management.

Thus the process of developing and marketing new products and services is becoming more formalized and systematized, with more stringent controls and built-in decision points along the way. The minority of firms for whom this is not true are generally the least committed to the new-products race.

CONDITIONS FOR SUCCESS IN MARKETING NEW PRODUCTS

Study of the basic characteristics present in the experience of successful practitioners permits the recognition of some conditions attendant upon success. These "conditions for success" in this important but hazardous undertaking should never be misconstrued as guarantees of success. They are not. Failure to meet them increases the odds of failure. Meeting them *guarantees* nothing.

The first, and most significant, is managerial capacity, including technological capacity, in top management readily available for product planning. Closely allied to this is a favorable attitude toward new-product development. More than lip service is required. The successful marketing of new products creates new demands, perhaps in the face of a relaxed easy life, a high standard of living, and complacency. These new problems, increased financial risk, possible dividend reduction, increased responsibilities—all impact on the way of life of top management. They should *not* be played down. Individuals in this position may agree with the *idea* of the desirability for new products, but actually not be very receptive to new ideas—or to creative individuals. Unless top management actually does possess the favorable attitudes needed in the face of these realizations, the development of new products is bound to run into trouble.

Next is the existence of a real market need. This should be thoroughly identified, refined, and forecast to a reasonable degree of accuracy.

The firm should be aware of its present sales potential and competitive position. In the early stages of the corporate life cycle, the firm's finances are apt to be strained, there is little spare managerial capacity, the plant and equipment may be inadequate to growing needs, and new products merely compound such difficulties. Once corporate maturity has been achieved, the potential satisfied to a reasonable degree, and the share of market established, the finances are apt to be sound, with even excess capital or unused borrowing power and with management not really as busy as it may seem. These are conditions favorable to the additional responsibilities in new-product development.

One further point, almost a prerequisite, is that this entire effort needs to be completely integrated throughout the firm. It is not merely someone's "baby," to be delegated to a committee or department. It is true that an organizational entity is needed for implementation, for providing guidance and control. But this is not enough. Interest in new-product development, willingness to actively cooperate and assume responsibilities, and complete acceptance of the new-product development as a corporate goal are essential.

PRODUCT-LINE DECISIONS

New-product planning should result in new products successfully marketed. However, it should not stand alone. Such a program of growth through innovation should be ruthless in the elimination of *present* products which dilute effort, sap energies, or otherwise impede activities. The hard facts of competition will remove some. What we are referring to here are those others which hang on but contribute little if anything to corporate welfare. Of course, they need identification. One reason for their continued existence is aggregative accounting procedures which fail to isolate these losses. This would seem to be capable of correction, once the need for such screening is recognized—and failure to do so can prolong unidentified losers indefinitely.

Product-Line Simplification versus Standardization

Simplification results from elimination of unnecessary products. A competent analysis of product lines may reveal that, of the total, a few contribute heavily to profit, but at the other extreme, many may be contributing little or nothing, or actually losing money. Elimination can simplify many things, from production, through inventory, to sales and delivery.

Standardization introduces the question of adoption of an industry standard as to specifications. Standardized items invite product substitution. Nonstandard items tend to prevent it but may impede the original sale for that very reason. The competitive position of the firm, seeking market penetration versus product-line protection from competition, is a key factor in this decision.

Planned Obsolescence

Planned obsolescence has been the subject of attack, particularly in the consumer area, by many who mistakenly feel that the interest of the seller is opposed to that of his customer. Others have objected on the basis of too short a planned life. The latter may be a valid criticism in some cases. However, it tends to overlook the satisfactions actually being derived from purchase of the new. Competitive action can be a powerful force to cause the planned life of the product to match the customer preference.

Properly used, planned obsolescence should be a highly desirable policy. It seeks to achieve the "one-horse shay"—a perfect vehicle, with which nothing would ever go wrong or break down until everything did. It starts with a determination of the desired life, in time or operational characteristics, and then seeks to match the life of all components to this target. By this means, the cost of an excessive life of some are saved. Others by the lengthening avoid premature breakdowns and replacement. Ideally, if achieved, customer satisfaction is enhanced at the lowest cost. Obviously, even where most applicable, it is rarely attainable. Yet, practically, it can point the way toward product improvement and increased customer satisfaction.

THE BIRTH OF A NEW PRODUCT

Processing Product Ideas

Product ideas are the oysters from which the successful new products, the pearls, are obtained. The "obtaining" is far from as simple as opening a shell. One perspective of the overall process is offered in **Figure 16.8**. As is indicated in this diagram, product ideas come from many sources. They are submitted in detail to the product-planning and programming entity for initial review and appraisal. This appraisal is typically informal, yet critical and competent. If the idea passes this initial test, it is then processed through the development of all relevant data pertinent to its possible implementation in the "processor."

The results are assembled into a formal product proposal, which is then reviewed by the product-planning committee. This committee is typically composed of representatives from top management of all the major functional divisions of the corporation, including the executive committee. Here the scrutiny is intensified. This committee has the authority and responsibility to reject the proposal, refer it back through the product-planning office for additional data as may be needed, or approve the product as an addition to the corporate line. If approved, it is then programmed, and action implemented.

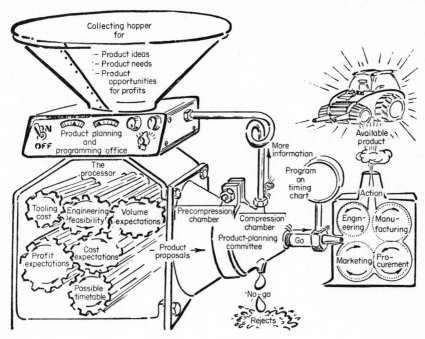

Fig. 16.8 Product planning and programming pelleter. (*Source: Lawrence H. Hodges, Director of Research and Technical Services, J. I. Case Company, Racine, Wisconsin.*)

Implementation involves the determination of a date for product availability, and includes the considerations of further testing, engineering, availability of plant and equipment, production scheduling, advertising and promotion, and product availability (not only in finished-goods inventory, but physical distribution to the appropriate outlets) in order to realize the maximum impact on the market possible by such coordinated efforts. This is recognition of the need for the complete integration and coordination of the efforts of the entire firm in the successful marketing of new products. Such recognition, followed by effective implementation, argues strongly for success in this vital but hazardous undertaking.

Procedure: An Example

No two companies face identical circumstances. No single procedure, even though ideal for one company, is that ideal for others. However, an example of a successful approach is provided by A. Patrick Moran, Manager, New Products, of the Electrical Components Division of Bendix. The recognition of the involvement, the integration of the key factors, and the timing control of the essentials are readily discernible and applicable to most new-product developmental programs.

Moran describes it this way:[5]

> Implicit in any definition of management is "Plan" and "Fact." The plan defines the objective and alternatives of how to reach it. The fact supports, or weakens, or alters the plan. Because "Facts" change with time, "Plans" must be flexible. The planner must have sufficient knowledge of new-product management, and provide sufficient alternatives so that his plan can be adjusted to unsuspected realities as they arise. Wishing won't make harsh facts go away. Flexible management, though, will usually handle them.
>
> Some planners unintentionally "plan-in" failure. They resist some programs because (a) it wasn't their idea, (b) it wasn't their direct responsibility, (c) it wasn't fully understood, or fully explained for engineering, manufacturing, or marketing, or, worst of all, (d) it wasn't given adequate attention. Planners know that anything worth doing is worth doing well the first time. The market and competition doesn't often give one a fair second chance.
>
> Top management has a strong hand in making a product successful. It is top management's responsibility to determine, establish, or approve:
>
> A. That new products are needed and wanted. That new-product possibilities of growth in profits will not disperse the company's energies from the main line.
>
> B. The minimum criteria which any product must meet, then firmly apply and follow them. Although varying from company to company, the following should be established: objectives, market desires, rate of return on investment, profit volume, position, gross margin, budgets, and policies. These are the basic elements for a company and product strategy.
>
> C. Procedures and organization to guide the program and develop information for future management decisions.
>
> D. Checkpoints at critical stages of development. By this method, judgments, based on facts, can and should be *ruthlessly* applied to protect continuing investment of time, energy, and funds in the project. Alternatives should be studied, but judgments should *not* be allowed to fall on project people.
>
> With management supplying the basic incentive, we can now outline a positive approach to planning, organizing, and managing a new-product program.
>
> 1. Define the idea and/or need.
> 2. Reach basic agreement on what is to be done.
> 3. Formulate business plan. Incorporate:
>   a. Objectives.
>   b. Policies.

[5] Used with permission of A. Patrick Moran, Manager, New Products, Electrical Components Division, The Bendix Corporation, Sidney, N.Y.

    c. Technical plan.

    d. Financial plan.

    e. Manufacturing plan.

    f. Marketing plan.

    g. Extract, divide, develop a method to integrate and implement the plans with the objectives.   Provide alternatives.

4. Get management blessing.

5. Establish schedules and assign direct responsibilities.

6. Monitor and control the project—understand it.

7. Check threats and opportunities regularly.

8. Be ready to prepare alternative plans as technology or market conditions demand.   Don't lose the objective.

9. Minimize risk by introducing on a limited scale.

10. Make sure you have the consumers covered—check marketing and distribution results against forecasts.

11. Start another project, because the product life cycle doesn't wait.

Although each of these points will be covered in greater detail, use Figure 16.9 for a checklist.   This is a form to integrate the key points. Flow and overlap can be noted.   This particular figure is for a military marketer, although for nonmilitary marketers, the only significant change is to introduce a test-market phase.   Do notice particularly the parallel, cooperative efforts of engineering and marketing.

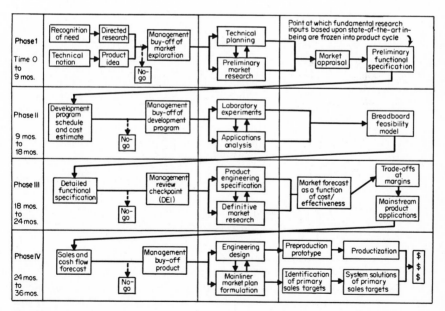

Fig. 16.9 Product development life cycle.   (*Source: Pat Thomas, "Removing the Black Art from Product Planning," "Data on Defense and Civil Systems," Data Publications, December 1963, p. 43.*)

This format can be instituted at any stage of development. To do so though will entail gathering a lot of loose ends together like this:

1. Start off with the idea/need—define it.   In the future, this becomes the problem to be solved, and everyone's understanding of the definition keeps everyone on the same track.   Define it on paper so that it can be referred to, since most people conveniently interpret the results of a meeting to *their* advantage, or all too frequently *forget* exactly what was decided.   Communications are important.   At this point it is necessary to reach basic agreement of all involved on *what is to be done.*   If there is only one idea, a minimal problem scope is involved.   If there are many ideas, a rating system will help choose the best one.

2. After basic agreements on what is to be done are accomplished, the planner must then do first all he can do by himself.   Start off by generating enthusiasm in all who may be involved.   Play politics if he has to.   Save pride, if necessary, but lay groundwork to ease the future path of the program through the personalities and functions of the organization.   Remember people resist change, but it's the planner's job to make "change" a way of life in his company. While the "cajoling" is going on, discuss the idea with people knowledgeable in the field.   It is fine to hold *preliminary* discussions with home-plant people, but before committing any sizable money, the planner must *talk to the outside world for unbiased inputs.*   These discussions are used to formulate objectives and plans in the next step.   Always make sure there is a market for the *specific* product before asking management to push the "go" button.   The planner should do all he can to provide a favorable climate for the product in his own house, but let the *market* decide whether to go into production.   This should help R&D improve its batting average.

3. Now it's time to make a skeleton plan for overall program direction. Let's call this "big picture" the business plan.   It should integrate the objectives and general policies of the company for this product with the plans for engineering, manufacturing, and marketing.

The business plan should tell generally how to reach the objective, and suggest alternatives for consideration.   If the program is big enough, the planner will want to use PERT techniques or critical path methods, or variations of his own to provide checkpoints (especially on financial goals).   These methods emphasize anticipated stumbling blocks or omissions in the plan that might not otherwise be obvious and should work in any organization.   These methods also establish tentative schedules, and oftentimes imply who should be assigned responsibility.   The tentative schedules should' be reviewed to take out any unreasonable delays, thereby being the first step in speeding up the program.   *Any* efforts that reduce program time are well worth taking.   Also valuable are use of a wall planner or tickler file to advise when decision points are near.   This technique is helpful since close-in planning should be in considerable detail, with short times between checkpoints based on ability to measure an *accomplishment.*   As the program stretches out, less frequent checks are scheduled, usually due to their being dependent upon results obtained early in the program.

During this time of skeleton business planning, the planner must get estimates of costs and market size. This sounds easy. It takes time. The technical, manufacturing, and marketing plans usually must be done by different individuals. Many planners work in an area where there is no history available to guide him on estimates. All is "blue sky"—but by breaking the problem down to phases that fit the product and its

ENGINEERING ESTIMATE # ________

Reference ____________________

____

Page ___ of ___ Pages

DETAILED ESTIMATE FOR PHASE # ___

Phase Title ____________________

Work Statement	Work Group (Check one)
	Design ☐ Research ☐ Test ☐ Materials ☐ Adm. Eng. ☐ Exp. Shop ☐ ________ ☐

Estimated Manpower and Material Requirements

Position		Man-hours for Week Weeks from Starting Date of Phase											Total Man-hours	Code Rate	Dollars
Code	Title														
Total Man-hours															
Direct Labor Dollars															
Material Dollars															

Estimate of New Capital Equipment Required

Remarks

Manpower Check List

1. Supervisory Engr
2. Senior Engr
3. Engineer
4. Junior Engineer
5. Senior Tech
6. Shop Skilled
7. Shop Semiskilled
8. Technical Ass't
9. Clerical Ass't
10. Special

Prepared by – Date ____________ Approved by – Date ____________

Fig. 16.10 Sample format for engineering estimates.

requirements, costs and markets are more easily estimated. This same format can be used to establish control, or decision points, or assign budget dollars when the program is approved. Figure 16.10 is an example format for engineering estimates by phases, which are based on a skeleton technical plan. Each work group uses the same format, and occasionally one or more "outside" groups are added. It is usual for each group to conduct more than one phase, since our projects can easily run to 30 individual phases.

The summary sheet of Figure 16.11 is used to collect the totals of

ENGINEERING ESTIMATE # ________

Reference ________________

Page ___ of ___ Pages

Supersedes EE# ______ Dated ________

Project Work Satement

TOTAL ESTIMATED COST
(Summarized from Detailed Phase Estimate Sheets)

Material		$______
Engineering Labor	$______	
Factory Labor	______	
Other Labor	______	
Total Labor		______
Engineering Burden @___%	______	
Factory Burden @___%	______	
Other Burden @___%	______	
Total Burden		______
Total		$______

Note: Engineering labor includes Experimental Shop; Factory labor is "productive" labor only. Other labor includes all "nonproductive" labor (except Engineering) which contribute directly to the Project, for example: the Tool Room.

Estimate of New Capital Equipment Required $________ ; Explain:

Capital equipment only; expense equipment is part of "Total Estimated Cost", above

SCHEDULE
Estimated Completion___Weeks from Starting Date
On chart, below, arrows are drawn from starting to completion dates of each phase
Weeks from Project Starting Date

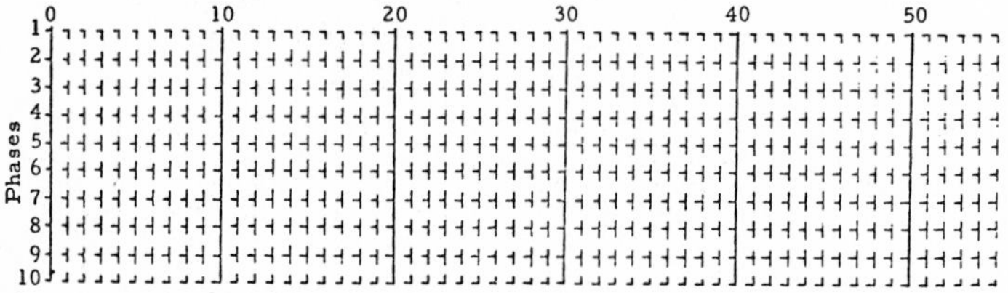

Prepared by - Date

Approved by - Date

Fig. 16.11 Sample summary sheet of engineering estimates.

each work group, then the work group summaries are totaled on the same format, which then becomes the overall engineering budget control of the business plan. This procedure firms up the technical plans, and provides control of funds by phases for easy administration.

Monthly, weekly, or daily spending reports, depending on criticality of function, should be made available from a data processing setup to monitor and chart how close the phase is running to the financial schedule.

While engineering is working on the technical plan, manufacturing should be doing the same for its segment of the program. They will be establishing tentative or firm layouts based on inputs from engineering and marketing. Manufacturing will predict manufacturing costs of the R&D program only, not operating costs.

Manufacturing may base their estimates on either the allocated or incremental cost basis, which should be applied consistently for each project. If this cost estimate appears unfavorable by comparison with existing methods, or if not attractive as compared with the necessary selling price—your program might as well *stop* right then—unless engineering changes or cost reductions can be made.

Materials cost can be the largest item in manufacturing cost. For this reason close attention is given to listing all the materials used, their grade, form, usage per unit or pound of product, and cost per unit.

Labor cost could also be the largest item in manufacturing cost. Techniques are well known to reach an estimate for this factor.

Now look to the marketing plan in more detail. Concurrent with the planning going on in the technical and manufacturing segments, marketing will be establishing their strategy, competition, policies, and the estimated total market, then whittling it down to probable market share. Each firm should establish its own rule-of-thumb ratio of market share to development cost in determining whether to let the development continue.

At the beginning of any program a planner needs really only three key marketing facts to continue with: (1) total market and forecast, (2) selected market and forecast, and (3) market share and forecast. Assess realistically the share of the total market and the selected markets your firm can reasonably expect to penetrate. This will provide your market share and forecast.

4. With the skeleton business plan well in hand, the planner can now extract, divide, integrate, and develop a method to implement the plan in concurrence with his firm's objectives. He will give alternative proposals to allow management to apply *their* techniques of promoting programs, then start on firming up the plan.

But don't spend any time firming up the plans prior to management approval and acceptance of proposed checkpoints.

5. If management *doesn't say* "No" or "Stop," the skeleton plans should be fleshed out by assigning responsibility by name, and scheduled by date, to key individuals. Then, emphasize continually the importance of the individual's function to the whole program. At regular intervals, the planner informs all involved of the status of the program and gives

recognition to *individuals* having outstanding performance. To the responsible planner this project is the most important in his working life today, but to others who have only a small part of the project to accomplish, it's a fleeting problem. But to enhance chance for success, the planner must keep everyone "clued in" on what's happening.

6. Now that the program is rolling, the planner must stay on top of it or it may bury him. Because of this, he must understand what is going on in the whole program every day so that he can monitor and control it. This time is usually when a program-manager post can be most effective. This is the most important time, too, for communications. Some communications must be personal, but much can be done by written reports called for in the business plan. The responsible planner must be sure to promulgate the decisions reached at checkpoints.

7. It should be a matter of course to check threats and opportunities regularly. If communications are good, and the program understood by all, the planner will have a lot of help from program people in this matter. It goes without saying that opportunities should be investigated or grasped immediately, and threats must be evaluated even sooner. If the threats become massive enough to convince the planner the program should be stopped—he must say so! And tell everyone, with fact, reasons, and detail. The planner must remember, others have a lot at stake in the project by now too, and he is going to need the cooperation of these same people in future programs.

8. However, if the program continues to look "go" all the way, feedback on market-needs changes will probably alter the original plan. If the original marketing strategy and testing program were accurate (and if you are lucky) the alternative plans will offer simple "outs" as the market changes. If not, roll with the punches, and change the plans to reflect a new means of reaching the objective. But, if the market change changes your objectives—stop—reevaluate the whole program. Expect that changes in the program will occur. If they are anticipated, they can be schemed around, and perhaps made important pluses in the program. Fit the program to the facts—not facts to the program. Be fair in the appraisal of which facts to use.

9. Don't omit the time for test marketing. This test market or favored customer period will give the planner or marketer time to get customer reaction on all aspects of the product. Take care of design or use problems in this phase, and save lots of dollars that could go into a field service campaign. At this point, make sure the thing works, and can be serviced if that's part of the package.

10. Now the planner and the sales department are ready to count incoming business dollars, determine if supply is going to meet demand, and determine what other markets, not earlier foreseen, are opening. Also check that the customers are getting instant service to keep the products sold. If everything is on schedule and on forecast, give congratulations to all involved. You *and* they were *outstandingly* fortunate.

11. Then the planner can start all over again.

IN ESSENCE

Success in the marketing of new products starts in the earliest stages of development. Careful and thorough attention to the task, *starting in the earliest stages,* and including competent marketability studies, can help eliminate the losers quicker. New-product *ideas* have a very high mortality rate. New products, once commercialized, have a relatively low mortality rate (even though this could be improved). Earlier elimination of the least likely, while concentrating on the most likely, should help. It costs just as much to develop and market a product failure as it does an outstanding success. The essence of success is to produce competent new products for which there is a profitable demand. Skill in the process coupled with improved selectivity are key factors, and they are within the control of the corporation. Here, the highest level of competency obtainable can be the least costly, the most productive, and the most profitable.

RELEVANT READING

Alexander, R. S., "The Death and Burial of Sick Products," *Journal of Marketing,* April 1964, pp. 1–7.

Hopkins, David S., and Earl L. Bailey, "New-product Pressures," The Conference Board *Record,* June 1971, pp. 16–24.

Kotler, Philip, "Phasing Out Weak Products," *Harvard Business Review,* March-April 1965, pp. 108–118.

MacDonald, Morgan B., Jr., "New Product Risk in Industrial Markets," The Conference Board *Record,* November 1967, pp. 26–31.

Management of New Products, Chicago: Booz-Allen & Hamilton, Inc., 1968.

PERT Guide for Management Use, PERT Coordinating Group (Secretary of Defense, Army, Navy, Air Force, Atomic Energy Commission, Bureau of the Budget, Federal Aviation Agency, and National Aeronautics & Space Administration), Washington, D.C.: Superintendent of Documents, June 1963.

Wasson, Chester R., "Common Sense in Sampling," *Harvard Business Review,* January-February 1963, pp. 109–114.

"Why New Products Fail: Survey of Business Opinion and Experience," The Conference Board *Record,* October 1964, pp. 11–18.

CHAPTER SEVENTEEN

Key Services
to Management

TRADE RELATIONS

Reciprocity

Reciprocity favors customers in selecting sources of supply, and it uses the pressure of purchases to aid in obtaining sales.

When two firms are in the position of each needing products made by the other, they might buy from each other, anyway. It *could* happen, without awareness of any reciprocity by either, provided the purchasing and salespeople in each firm did not communicate with each other. Technically, this would be reciprocal buying and selling—but not "reciprocity" as the term is used today.

It should be pointed out that the pressures of reciprocity can exist without top management being aware of them. The pressure can be created by a salesman acting independently and merely reminding his prospect of how much his firm is buying from the prospect's. That may be all that is needed to get the order, and to keep on getting it.

Reciprocity is built on the awareness of the entire situation. It uses this awareness as leverage to create or command preferential treatment. It does not add to the total market; it merely adds to the user's share.

Buying from one's customers is only human and natural. It has been going on for a long time. It undoubtedly will continue in one way or another. So long as all other things are and remain equal, it is hard to criticize this practice. Yet, even under these circumstances, it is discriminatory to favor customers over noncustomers. The proper corporate policy should provide *equal* opportunity for both customers and noncustomers to compete.

A more serious problem arises when other things become less equal. If prices start to go up, or quality and service decline, how far may this go? How much will the buyer pay in such terms to continue to "buy" the sales he is making to such a supplier? This situation harms the buyer. He is not getting the price-quality relationship he could elsewhere. It harms the seller. He is not working as hard to preserve his competitive position by product improvement and efficiency reflected in lower prices as he otherwise might. So both suffer. Competitors are defeated. They cannot compete effectively for that business. Thus competition is restricted and its fundamental advantages destroyed. Under these circumstances it is hard to find anything good in reciprocity—in theory or in practice.

Reciprocity exists over a wide range of intercorporate relationships, all the way from near innocence in buying from a customer to out-and-out connivance in restricting competition in a multifaceted deal.

In the case of small corporations, even with reciprocity, the amount involved in any one relationship may be minuscule. In such cases the reciprocal buying and selling may be completely innocent of a restrictive arrangement to do so. It is obviously both impossible and undesirable to prohibit a firm from buying anything from a customer.

However, as larger corporations become involved and as the volume of reciprocal buying and selling increases, so do the significance and the complications.

In its simplest form, reciprocity simply influences or directs purchasing from the firm's customers. The next step may be to apportion the purchasing from several customers perhaps in proportion to the sales volumes to them. The final step, particularly where larger corporations are involved, is to create a reciprocal arrangement not between two principals alone, but through divisions, subsidiaries, or even favored customers. For example, a manufacturer of electric motors might exert pressure on its wire supplier to buy insulation material from a plastics firm. The plastics firm might be a subsidiary of the motor manufacturer (secondary reciprocity), or it might be a division of a major customer of that manufacturer (tertiary reciprocity).

Such arrangements can become very involved. That simply makes them harder to unravel. It does not, of itself, mean that there is anything wrong. The danger lies in the restriction to competition. If each step continued to exist, with each buying decision reached in the face of open competition, the same situation would be deemed to be beneficial to everyone. It is the curtailment of free choice, the addition of sales considerations as an impediment to the buying considerations, which creates the evil.

The government has long frowned on arrangements which tend to restrict competition. The major difficulties in reciprocity lie in the degree and the proof. A contract or agreement to restrict trade is illegal. This agreement can be inferred from the actions of the parties, if enough trade is involved. Section 7 of the Clayton Act would then be applied. Basically, Section 1 of the Sherman Act prohibits agreements in restraint of trade. Section 5 of the Federal Trade Commission Act and the Robinson-Patman amendment to the Clayton Act might be applicable. Definitely, this is an area for major involvement of the corporate counsel. It is unreasonable to suppose that it will ever cease to exist, even with a growing awareness of the long-run disadvantages of the inherent restrictions of competition. However, steps have been taken by industry to raise the level of intercorporate relationships and to seek to prevent illegal reciprocity arrangements. The creation of the Trade Relations Association, Inc., was a major step in that direction.

Trade Relations and the Trade Relations Association, Inc.

The Trade Relations Association, Inc., was formed in 1962 for the purpose of providing opportunities for association between those individuals whose common interests are the fostering of better and proper business relationships between individuals, firms, or corporations in all walks of industry who may be engaged in commerce with each other.

The association takes a strong professional stand against any kind of unethical procedure that appears to be restrictive or coercive in any way to free and open competition within the business community.

The founding members of the association felt strongly the need for legal guidance and the development of guidelines for trade-relations practice that would fully comply with antitrust law and court cases.

Code of Principles

In 1965, the association adopted a code of principles for trade-relations practice by its members. These principles are:[1]

> 1. To diligently pursue and support the business policies of the company.

[1] Used with permission of Herman Van Fleet, President, Trade Relations Association, Inc.

2. To strive for improved commercial relationships between a company and its customers and suppliers both existing and potential.

3. To understand and support the recognized purchasing principles of best evaluation of price, quality and service.

4. To assist in carrying out the marketing policies of the company and to see that corporate objectives remain in proper priority.

5. To work to further the principle of uniformity between the purchasing and selling policies of his company.

6. To demonstrate in business affairs a code of conduct which effectively contributes to the highest professional stature.

7. To avoid the use of either restrictive or coercive business practice in commercial relationships.

8. To actively support the Trade Relations Association, Inc. in the continued up-grading of professional standards.

9. To be alert to and seek to correct any evidence of malpractice of trade relations activity.

10. To cooperate with all organizations and individuals engaged in activities designed to enhance the development and understanding of trade relations.

Note particularly items 3, 5, 6, 7, and 9. Clearly, if these principles were followed sincerely, reciprocity would be defeated. And yet, the term "trade relations" has been frequently misused by the government, the press, business, and some authors to mean reciprocity. By innuendo this has castigated the Trade Relations Association. Corporations have renamed their trade-relations function to such titles as "corporate relations," "commercial relations," "business development," and "market relations."[2]

Functions of Trade Relations

An examination of the functions involved in trade relations reveals five major categories.[3] First, the information or commercial-intelligence function. This involves the assembly of information on one's own company, on markets, products, distribution, technology, and business developments. The trade-relations executive reviews financial and trade journals, house organs, and annual reports, and learns from day-to-day personal contacts. He acts as a corporate information center or clearinghouse for information.

The second function is to coordinate the activities of corporate divisions and to be sure that maximum use is made of all his information.

[2] Ibid.

[3] Compiled from a talk by Andrew F. Storer, Assistant Vice President, St. Regis Paper Company, "The Role of Trade Relations in Industrial Marketing," given at Clarkson College, April 1970.

Third, the trade-relations man is an ambassador of goodwill, a trouble-shooter, a diplomat at the corporate level. By working with his counter-part in another company, he can quickly identify the real cause of complaints and correct such, as for example, personality clashes at the buying-selling level.

Fourth, he is an auditor of corporate operations. He can obtain and give honest answers quickly. Signs of trouble may be long in surfacing at the divisional or operational level. Another aspect of this function is the development of data on future expansions, new products, and poten-tial developments. Here the goodwill developed between buyer and seller based on a long-term, ethical relationship may be very rewarding in the exchange of such information.

Fifth, the trade-relations man is trained to detect those instances which could lead to legal involvement. He is a watchdog on the firing line. Even though officially prohibited, reciprocity might exist at the buyer-seller level. The perspective of the trade-relations man, coupled with the flow of information regarding corporate operations, puts him in an ideal spot to perform this task. It is inevitable, with hundreds to thou-sands of salesmen in major corporations, that some aggressive salesman, uneducated in antitrust law, may attempt such an approach. His in-ternal request for the necessary information on purchasing, if available to him only through the trade-relations office, can be immediately cor-rected to prevent the reciprocity.

Contribution to Corporate Welfare

Contrary to what some have said, the trade-relations executive is not camouflage for reciprocity. His code and the functions he performs are essential to a diversified, decentralized corporation, if it is to operate at maximum effectiveness.

As corporations continue to acquire and to diversify, the need for commercial intelligence, communications, and an effective preventative of illegal practices will grow, too. This need has been and will continue to be filled by trade relations (under whatever name it may be called) ethically practiced by executives who are rapidly becoming professional in their responsibilities and conduct.

Of paramount importance to their companies are the guidance pro-vided by these executives and the issuance of a well-defined corporate policy on relationships with customers and suppliers covering such things as maintenance and uses of comparative sales-purchase figures, condi-tional purchases, conditional sales, etc. It is this kind of internal educa-tion that is an all-important bulwark against the use of reciprocity in addition to the efforts of the association.

It is unfortunate that trade relations and its professional association have received a setback through adverse publicity, stemming from the very practices they seek to prevent. And yet, good can come from this. Corporate society has now been given notice that it not only must *be* legal and honest in its operations, it must also *appear to be* so. Any new development—and there undoubtedly will be a new development of trade relations—to be successful must be doubly certain of the ethical standards of its participants and of the public's awareness that this is "for real."

It is possible that the trade-relations function, in addition to its insistence upon ethical practices, will gravitate to one under the corporate marketing wing with a basic responsibility of uncovering through interface with many companies future marketing opportunities for a corporation. These two responsibilities are not inconsistent. Rather, their combination into one function can make a most significant contribution to corporate welfare.

THE CORPORATE COUNSEL

The ideal corporate counsel should not even be noticed. If he does his job well, no troubles develop and credit for good performance goes to the line officers, the planners—everyone except him. The primary accolade for such a counsel is his own awareness of the prevention of legal difficulties—not a dramatic courtroom contest, whether won or lost.

The corporate counsel must be intimately acquainted with all aspects of corporate law, and from his background of a thorough knowledge of his own company, he must constantly review and analyze the numerous actions contemplated, ever on the alert for the potential violation.

This means that he must know not only what is going on, but what is being contemplated. He must, to obtain this sort of confidence and information, already have established a high level of rapport with all the corporate planners and administrators. This may not be easy, but it is essential.

Realistically, the corporate counsel cannot depend upon others to volunteer such information, in advance. They may not even be aware of the legal implications involved. He will need to develop his own sources. He will need to be accepted as a confidant. But, unless he is informed, there is little he can do in advance of the fact. The actions taken to remedy a situation after the fact are far less desirable than prevention

Part of the responsibility of the ideal corporate counsel is education. He is the knowledgeable one. But he need not offer dissertations on the law to decision makers or operating personnel. These will be tolerated, not welcomed. Law is restraint on freedom of action. Restraint is frequently resented. But, law is also permissive. Interpretation of what *can* be done may contribute even more to realization of opportunities.

A good start can be to educate people to the pitfalls, to the areas where legal guidance can help, and to the recognition of hazardous situations. Each area has its own special legal problems. Marketing needs to be alert to price discrimination, tying contracts, false advertising, and so on. The industrial relations people need to be fully informed concerning labor law. These matters may seem to be fundamental. They are. It is up to the corporate counsel to keep them in that category, as against a court action.

The corporate counsel must not only know the law, be alert to the trends taken by court decisions, but also be able to interpret both for the guidance of corporate management as to the future. By so doing, he is again fulfilling his primary role, the prevention of difficulties. And this includes not only the current statutes, but those in the making, those which can be anticipated from the trend of current events, from the public attitude, or from the need for remedial action in a given area—a change in tax laws, for example.

This adds up to the need for a knowledgeable man, one who makes friends easily, and one who is willing to really work at his job. It need not mean a "big name." Prestige is not required. Thorough attention to the corporate problems is. Hire the man to do the job—the firm is secondary. If he is interested in politics, so much the better. The grapevine can be a valuable source of advance information. As soon as the job is big enough, bring him into the firm. Your own corporate attorney can be a very wise investment in providing continual attention to your problems on a full-time basis. Even keeping informed on what is going on will require that.

Perhaps one of the greatest requirements of the corporate counsel, as a man, is humility. If he is truly competent and his job is done well, he tends to go unnoticed. He alone may recognize the depth and quality of his contribution to corporate success. Lesser men would demand more recognition. Our man, our ideal corporate counsel, need not do so. He has proved his capabilities to the greatest taskmaster of all—himself. Fortunate, indeed, is the corporation free from legal entanglements, alert to the ever-increasing need to continue eternal vigilance of its own activities, and possessed of such a counsel to help it compete profitably and legally in the complex marketplace of today.

TRADE ASSOCIATIONS IN INDUSTRIAL MARKETING

(*Contributed by Lee Gunlogson, Director of Marketing Services, Carrier Corporation, Syracuse, New York.*)

All large companies and many medium and small companies engaged in industrial marketing belong to one or more trade associations. Since well-managed trade associations can be of considerable value to their members, it is helpful to have an understanding of the range of services they provide.

Definition and Early Development

A "trade association" has been defined as "a non-profit, cooperative, voluntarily-joined organization of business competitors designed to assist its members and its industry in dealing with mutual business problems in such areas as accounting practices, business ethics, market and technical research, standardization, statistics and trade promotion, as well as in relations with the industry's employees, government agencies, and the general public."[4]

The word "trade" is intended to be interpreted broadly to include associations of manufacturers, banks, contractors, transportation companies, and companies providing various services as well as those engaged in retail or wholesale selling. Quite often the word "association" is replaced by some synonym such as "institute," "council," or "federation." For example, the trade association for manufacturers of air conditioning equipment is the Air Conditioning and Refrigeration Institute. Other examples of groups which fit the definition of a trade association but use other designations are the Guild of American Funeral Directors and the Electrification Council.

Associations of businessmen have evolved over many centuries. There were merchant guilds and trade leagues in Europe in the sixteenth century which had many of the characteristics of a trade association. Organizations with the objective or promoting the business interests of particular groups of traders and artisans have long existed in China and Japan.

In America, the oldest organization of businessmen is the New York Chamber of Commerce, formed in 1768.[5] On the national level, the National Association of Cotton Manufacturers (since renamed the Northern Textile Association) was founded in 1854, and the American

---

[4] Jay Judkins, *Directory of National Associations of Businessmen 1961*, U.S. Department of Commerce, 1961, p. 2.

[5] Ibid., p. 5.

Iron and Steel Association (now the American Iron and Steel Institute) was started in 1855.[6]   Several other associations extend back a century or more.

Formation of associations has not proceeded evenly.   During World War I, there was a period of rapid growth.   "In 1900 there were only about one hundred national trade associations; by 1920 there were one thousand."[7]   Another spurt in formations occurred in the 1930s, motivated by the adversities of the Depression.   Many associations were also founded during World War II, when the war effort required coordination of entire industries.   In many cases, trade associations in existence at the start of World War II were able to provide valuable data on the production capabilities and normal material requirements of their respective industries to the mobilization planning agencies.

Number, Size, and Type of Trade Associations

A precise enumeration of trade associations is not available and would be difficult to compile for several reasons.   In the first place, there are several thousand small local associations, many of which are loosely organized without any continuing director or staff.   For example, the merchants of a neighborhood shopping area may form an association to coordinate their promotional activities, or cooperate on street decorations for the Christmas season, and so on.   Since there are no rigid criteria, it is not possible to say just what degree of organizational structure is needed to qualify a business group with common interests as a trade association.

Other definitional problems arise in distinguishing between trade and professional associations.   In general, a trade association is made up of firms and a professional association is composed of individuals.   The objectives of a professional association are oriented more toward advancing knowledge and the sponsorship of journals, but the educational efforts of many trade associations are also extensive and sophisticated. Both trade and professional associations strive to promote the interests of their members by acting as a unified body.   It is perhaps significant that the Columbia Books *Directory* lists national trade and professional associations in a single volume.[8]   The *Encyclopedia of Associations* issued by Gale Research Company[9] does group "trade, business, and

---

[6] Craig Colgate, Jr. (ed.), *1969 Directory of National Trade and Professional Associations of the United States*, Washington, D.C.: Columbia Books, 1972, p. iii.

[7] Ibid., p. iv.

[8] Ibid.

[9] "National Organizations of the United States," *Encyclopedia of Associations*, 6th ed., vol. 1, Detroit: Gale Research Company, 1970.

commercial organization" in one section and other types of organizations in other sections, but this gives rise to some interesting classifications. For example, the National Association of Business Economists is in the section with trade organizations, and the American Economic Association is in the section entitled "Public Affairs."

Despite these enumeration problems, all national trade associations of any significance have been listed in the directories cited in the references. One estimate places the number of national associations at over 3,000 as of 1970. If all local chapters of national associations plus independent local and regional groups are included, the total number is estimated to be about 40,000.[10] There are also over 1,000 professional and learned societies that are national in scope; many of these also have local chapters.

Other evidence on the status of trade-association activity is the fact that association executives have their own trade association. The American Society of Association Executives dates back to 1920, and presently has about 3,500 members, with membership being on an individual basis.

National trade associations vary greatly in size, but "size" has several dimensions. Certainly one measure is number of members. Here we find associations with fewer than 10 members and others with over 100,000 members. The Aircraft Owners and Pilots Association, for example, has approximately 145,000 members. Another dimension of size is the economic importance of the industry represented by the association. The Automobile Manufacturers Association has only about a dozen members, but great influence. Similarly, the Air Transport Association of America with about thirty members represents an industry with a very significant economic impact. Still another measure of the size of an association is the size of its staff or its annual budget. Staff sizes are typically of from two to ten persons, but the Chamber of Commerce of the United States has a staff of over 750. Several other associations have staffs of over 100 people.

Nearly every facet of American industry is represented by a trade association. A quick perusal of a directory of trade associations provides insights into both the scope and the degree of specialization found in modern industry.

Trade-Association Organization and Management

National trade associations typically have a president and other officers and a board of directors who are elected from among personnel of the member firms. They generally serve without compensation and hold

---

[10] Colgate, op. cit., p. iv.

office for a year or two. This group determines the policies, scope of activities, and budget of the association. As a rule, this elected policy-making body is made up of executives who have long experience and have attained a certain stature in their industry.

As full-time employees of their respective firms, these elected officers have only a limited amount of time to devote to association affairs. Therefore, administrative responsibility is placed in the hands of a full-time professional managing director who carries out the policies and service functions of the association with the aid of a staff. The size of the staff is probably more related to the size of the industry represented than to the number of members, per se. Many of the staff members of the larger associations are professionals trained as lawyers, economists, and accountants. Indeed, association management itself has attained a degree of professional status through the designation of certain qualified individuals as a Chartered Association Executive (CAE) by the American Society of Association Executives.[11]

Formerly, almost all associations had staffs of their own, even those with minimal budgets. The great majority still carry their own staffs, but many associations have in the past twenty years chosen to utilize multiple-management firms.

The largest of these multiple association-management firms is Smith, Bucklin & Associates, Inc., with offices in Chicago, Washington, and Geneva, Switzerland. Smith, Bucklin President William W. Carpenter[12] explains the concept this way:

> We note that most trade association executives need not spend full time on their job. Some who are heads of large groups may need to, but the average association executive is only busy because he has to do work that lesser employees or specialists could better be doing. We use specialists and trained workers to back up executives. In this way our executives can effectively manage more than one association. As a result, our clients can afford to retain top-flight executives.

Funds for the operating expenses of an association are derived from membership dues, which may be set at a fixed amount for each member or may be graduated so that larger firms pay more. Judkins states that "the cost of membership in national associations of manufacturers usually is about one-tenth of 1 percent of each firm's annual sales of the products covered by the association."[13] In a typical large association covering a range of products, each major product group or "section"

[11] Ibid., p. iii.
[12] Used with permission of William W. Carpenter, President, Smith, Bucklin & Associates, Inc., Chicago.
[13] Judkins, op. cit., p. 4.

will have its own budget. Thus, a manufacturer who sells products in one section will not have to share in the costs of other sections. Other sources of revenue for trade associations include profits from trade shows, sale of advertising space in association publications, and direct sale of manuals and technical literature.

Expenditures are mainly for salaries, which account for 50 percent or more of the typical association budget. Printing costs are often a major item of expense. Most trade associations are exempt from federal income taxes, although certain criteria must be met.

From the standpoint of a member company, dues represent only part of the cost of belonging to an association. Generally, there are numerous committee meetings which entail travel expense and time away from the job for many individuals. However, these committees serve to work out the details and implementation of broad association policies; consequently they are an essential part of membership.

By location, national trade associations are heavily concentrated in Washington. This reflects the need for frequent interaction between government and industry. New York City and Chicago are also important centers of association activity.

Contribution of the Trade Association to the Member Firm

The range of services provided by different trade associations varies widely. Much of the variation is in the degree to which each service is performed. For example, some associations will have an elaborate public relations program, whereas others will do relatively little in the area of publicity and promotions. Some associations collect primary statistical data, while others merely compile secondary source material or do no statistical work at all. The major functions of trade associations are discussed below under five headings, although any of the classifications could be broken down further. Judkins, for example, lists fifteen major areas of activity and another fifteen secondary areas of service.[14]

Statistics From the viewpoint of the person engaged in industrial marketing, certainly one of the principal functions of trade associations is to collect statistical data from member firms and then summarize these data into industry composites for use by the members. Information is usually collected on sales, which may be measured as factory shipments, or in the case of long-lead-time products, as orders (also referred to as "orders booked"). Often both orders and shipments data are collected on the same product to provide a measure of the relationship between the two. It often happens that the products of an industry

[14] Ibid., p. 5.

are marketed through a channel of distribution that involves manufacturer, wholesaler, and retailer. A trade-association statistical program may attempt to measure sales at the various levels of distribution. If accurate records can be developed on sales at each stage, the manufacturer has a powerful tool for guiding production scheduling and controlling inventory.

Sales data may also be gathered by geographical areas such as states, counties, or trading areas. A "trading area" is usually a group of counties that embrace a major city and its suburbs. Practical problems often arise in compiling geographical data, e.g., some firms which have strong positions in local markets may not report to the trade association, and this tends to distort the market coverage in these areas. However, in a relatively mature industry, such as major appliances, where large firms with national distribution predominate, geographical sales data provide highly useful information for sales management.

In addition to sales data, statistics may be gathered on inventories and various special needs of a particular industry. For example, several associations collect forecasts of industry sales and then summarize these into an average or consensus forecast.

Marketing information is usually of primary concern, but statistics on manpower, financial ratios, and technical characteristics of equipment are also gathered in some cases.

For the most part the statistical data are for the confidential use of members, but many associations release information to the trade press and other interested parties. Usually a trade association will make data available to persons outside the industry who have a legitimate need for it. This may work to a member company's advantage by relief from a certain number of requests from security analysts, students, and others.

Emphasis has been on the collection of primary data which are not available from other sources. However, a trade-association statistical department may also assemble government data pertaining to its industry, and in general, serve as a reference point for secondary data of all types. Among larger associations a close working relationship is maintained with government statistical agencies. This works to the benefit of both.

A limited amount of basic marketing research may be done through surveys of customers, suppliers, and others outside the industry proper. Sometimes the research is initiated by the association and sometimes it is carried out in cooperation with a trade magazine. While it is dangerous to generalize, trade associations are generally less effective in conducting ad hoc surveys than in administering an ongoing statistical program.

Sales Promotion and Advertising   Industrywide promotions are frequently more effective than the sum of the uncoordinated efforts of the individual firms which compose the industry.   During the introductory stage in the life cycle of a new product, it is more important to create public awareness of the product than to promote a particular brand.   Often, no single company can afford the cost of educating the public to try a new or unfamiliar product or service.   However, a cooperative promotion aimed at selling the concept may generate enough demand so that all producers stand to gain.   Later on, after the product has become established, the individual producer generally attempts to hold or gain market share by advertising his particular brand.

No implication is intended that sales promotion should be limited to new products or new uses.   A sustained promotional program on established products may be needed to withstand the inroads from competitive industries.   All forms of advertising media, including magazines, newspapers, television, radio, direct mail, point-of-purchase displays, etc., have been used.   The American Gas Association, for example, has sponsored major television shows.

Trade shows, conventions, and exhibitions under the sponsorship of an association are common.   When properly run, they can be a source of revenue as well as an effective promotion.

Public Relations   "Public relations" refers to those activities aimed at creating a favorable image for the industry among the public at large or among special groups which are important to the industry.   In some cases public relations attempts to enhance the general reputation of an industry.   In other cases, the objective is to refute or counter allegations that will harm an industry if they gain acceptance.

An interesting example of an enlightened public relations program is that of the alcoholic beverage association which advertises against the use of their product by those who plan to drive.   These advertisements are timed to appear just before the start of holidays when travel is unusually heavy.

There are a few industries which have such a persuasive influence on American life that practically any event is newsworthy.   Automobiles are an example.   The introduction of new models is always well publicized, but unfavorable publicity such as factory recalls of defective units is also widely reported.

More commonly, however, the activities of an industry are not of great significance to a general audience.   Occasionally, certain milestones are achieved or some technical breakthrough occurs which can be publicized in the mass media, but usually the public relations activities are limited to supplying news items to trade magazines and other specialized audiences.

Many associations publish a bulletin or magazine on a regular schedule. Copies are sent not only to members but, in some instances, to libraries, state and federal law makers, and others whom the association wishes to keep informed. Circulation is often at a level to attract paid advertisements.

Product Standards and Certification   It is not possible for most potential customers to evaluate . the intrinsic merits of, and advertising claims for, the numerous complex products which they wish to buy. Many trade associations perform a useful public service by drawing up a set of standards for the products of the industry and then certifying those products which conform with the standards. Compliance with trade-association standards is almost invariably on a voluntary basis. A company not wishing to comply may drop out of the association, or in some cases, continue as a participating member in other facets of the association program. However, once an industry standard becomes widely known, it is very difficult for noncertified products to continue to be sold. Specifications are usually written to exclude noncertified products.

Who initiates these standards? It is not the general public, and only rarely are standards directly imposed by law, although in a few cases the adoption of standards may be hastened by the threat of governmental interference. Rather, it is usually a group of firms within the industry which produce high-quality products as a matter of company policy and then find themselves at a disadvantage in competing with firms which produce an inferior product that is difficult for the layman to distinguish from the better product. It is strongly emphasized that there is nothing invidious about offering a lower-quality product; in fact, the consumer deserves to have a range of quality from which to choose. But, potential buyers should have assurance that any product offered meets some minimum standards of performance, reliability, and safety. Also, conscientious producers should not have to compete against misleading claims of less scrupulous competitors. It is this latter condition which frequently gives rise to the adoption of standards.

The development of a standard is a highly technical matter that requires long hours of work and a wide interchange of views by industry experts. Compromises must be worked out between optimal engineering design and economic feasibility. The issue is not so much whether or not a standard is needed, but rather how to develop a fair standard which can be effectively implemented at reasonable cost.

Government Liaison   The influence which government has on business today is hard to overestimate. Taxes are imposed in many forms and at many levels of government. Legislation is constantly being enacted which impinges on business practices and decisions relating to labor, mergers, financing, consumer protection, pollution, foreign trade, and so on. In a broader context, the overall economic policies of the government have a direct effect on every industry.

A trade association has a responsibility to its members to try to influence legislation and government policies which affect the industry it represents, as long as that influence is used with enlightened awareness of the public interest. The word "lobbying" has a disparaging connotation, but the practice which it denotes may be carried on in support of high principles as well as low. It is the responsibility of the trade association to recognize the basic principles of our competitive system and to support that which tends to create increased customer satisfactions, as a prerequisite to the continued welfare of its members.

Evaluation of a Trade Association

The basic reason for the existence of a trade association is to help develop and maintain a healthy economic climate within an industry. The trade association attempts to help its members achieve this goal by acting for them collectively in providing services which the individual members could not obtain acting independently. The key to success in this lies primarily in the quality of the trade-association management, in its leadership, and in its ability to inspire enthusiastic support of all members, most of whom are top executives in their own companies.

Key questions to consider are:[15]

1. Does the association have a dynamic, clear-cut program that all members thoroughly understand and can support? Too many members are only dimly aware, if at all, of what their organization's objectives are and how they are being pursued.

2. Does it provide a program that will deal effectively with industry problems—not just those of the past and present, but also those which are emerging in the future path of a growing industry? Awareness and flexibility are essential ingredients today. Generally, the association that has exactly the same program this year as last year, or five years ago, is a stagnant one.

3. Do the group's programs reach into areas that are generally inaccessible to member companies? It is important that companies complement, not duplicate the efforts of the members.

4. Does it act aggressively to assist in the expansion of the industry's market for its products? It's amazing how many industry problems become minimal when the market for its products is growing rather than decreasing or remaining static!

[15] Used with permission of William W. Carpenter, President, Smith, Bucklin & Associates, Inc., Chicago.

5. Does it provide members with complete and meaningful services in the areas of industry statistics, research, education, standards, conventions and exhibitions, public relations, and government relations?

6. Does it function on revenues derived from an equitable dues structure, one which is acceptable to all member classifications?

7. Is it truly representative of the entire industry, or does it at least show satisfactory progress in its efforts to cut down on the number of "free riders"?

If all these questions can be answered affirmatively, the association has to be doing an outstanding job. If it isn't, or if there are areas of weakness, the member firm should not sit back and wait for others to shape it up. By getting in actively and helping to guide it, the member firm will increase the benefits. If an association did nothing more than acquaint one with his competitors, it would be worthwhile. Trade associations increase in effectiveness in direct proportion to the degree their members want to help themselves by joint effort evidenced by each one's own active participation—or lack of it.

MANAGEMENT CONSULTANTS

Management consultants provide counsel on management decisions to be made and plans and programs for their implementation. There are now an estimated 2,700 firms in the U.S., others overseas, and thousands of individuals offering such counsel. Included in these numbers are many firms and individuals offering consulting on special types of management problems, such as marketing, accounting systems, or executive compensation. Also, many firms and individuals concern themselves with the problems of specific industries, commercial or service types of businesses, hospitals, schools, government agencies, or trade associations.[16]

Management consultants can be grouped into general management consulting firms and specialists. The general management firms offer their services in all areas of management at both the top general management level and in the functional areas, finance, manufacturing, marketing, and so on. "Well-known examples of this type of services firm are McKinsey & Company, A. T. Kearney & Company, Cresap, McCormick and Paget, and some of the larger public accounting firms. These general management consultants to varying degrees offer counseling across all types of management problems and to all types of managements."[17]

[16] *Fact Book, 1970–71*, Chicago: Booz-Allen & Hamilton, Inc., 1971, p. 1.
[17] Ibid.

A few of the general management firms are full-line in scope. They are organized to serve the total needs of their clients, "whether these needs are for counsel and advice, for information and data on which to base decisions or measure results, for actual development or installation of improved operations, products, or processes, or even for actual management of an operation on a contract basis."[18]

> Booz, Allen & Hamilton, Inc. is a multi-national professional services firm and is one of the few organizations in the industry which offers a full line of such services to management. Those which most closely approximate Booz, Allen & Hamilton in size and in scope of services are Arthur D. Little, Inc. and Planning Research Corporation. In addition, there are non-profit institutions offering relatively broad service capabilities, such as the Stanford Research Institute.[19]

The specialists frequently concentrate primarily on one industry. For example, Simat, Helliesen & Eichner, Inc., is one of the largest in the transportation field, particularly aviation. Their clients include airlines, airports, and aircraft manufacturers.

Marketing consultants are specialists who concentrate on marketing. They vary in size from substantial organizations to individuals. Many of these are members of marketing faculties who devote part of their time to consulting. Within marketing, these individuals tend to specialize into functional areas, such as marketing management, advertising, retailing, industrial marketing, market research, and so on.

What Can Be Expected from the Consultant

A major advantage in the use of a management consultant is his perspective, an unbiased approach to the client's problems. This, coupled with the knowledge and experience in his field, competently applied, can be very valuable assistance to the client.

The Conference Board identifies seven major reasons for the use of consultants. They are:[20]

1. Inadequacy of technical knowledge or competence within the organization.
2. Insufficiency of manpower within the organization to carry out a new program or to handle a temporary work overload.
3. Lack of experience in a new business field.
4. Desire for an independent opinion on a decision facing management.
5. Need for stimulation, broadening or specialized training.

[18] Ibid.
[19] Ibid., p. 2.
[20] *Consultants: Selection, Use, and Appraisal,* The Conference Board, Managing the Moderate-sized Company, no. 13, 1970, pp. 1–3.

6. Need for an objective viewpoint on a matter disputed internally.
7. Need for help in selling ideas.

Consultant Usage

One major consideration in connection with the use of a consultant is whether to retain him on a continuing basis, use him as the need arises, or use him only rarely or as a last resort. Reasons favoring the continuing "on-call" type of arrangement are:[21]

> Continuing assistance is obtained on problems that themselves are continuing.
> Continuity of knowledge about the company increases the consultant's effectiveness and saves start-up costs.
> Company executives are more inclined to accept the advice of consultants whom they see regularly.
> Consultants on retainers are more likely to be available when needed.
> Consultants take a greater interest in the company's welfare when they are identified with it over a long period of time.
> Continuing review by a consultant can have the effect of anticipating and preventing problems.

Reasons favoring the use of consultants as the need arises are:[22]

> Unjustified cost.
> Unhealthy dependence on a consultant.
> Loss of objectivity by consultant.
> Possible organizational weakness.

Selection of the Consultant

The nature and scope of the problem(s) go a long way toward indicating the type of consultant to be used. The larger consulting firms frequently have a lower limit to the problems they can afford to accept. The smaller organizations, including the individual, can readily handle these situations. There is overlap, of course.

The nature and degree of complexity of the problem(s) may help determine the appropriateness of the use of a general or specialized firm. Once these basics are somewhat resolved, the next problem is evaluation of qualified consultants to make the final selection. The first step can well be to check with other clients, especially those whose problems were in a similar area. This should be followed by interviews

[21] Ibid., pp. 6–7.
[22] Ibid., p. 8.

between principals of the client and the consulting firm and also between the people who will be working together.

The key points to be explored with the referenced clients of the consultant are:[23]

1. Smoothness of working relationships between consultant and client.
2. Skill demonstrated in dealing with the problem.
3. Practicability of recommendations.
4. Support given during implementation of recommendations.
5. Accomplishment of objectives within cost estimate.
6. Completion of engagement within time estimate.

In the final evaluation, the people to be assigned to the task and their qualifications are more important than the firm. Some companies expect prospective consultants to submit detailed job proposals showing their approach, objectives, time schedule, cost estimate, and so on. This takes considerable time and effort to prepare. It should be remembered that the consultant's stock in trade are his ideas. It is unfair to ask him to outline the solution, and then turn him down. At the same time, the consultant should be able to estimate the time and cost factors reasonably accurately. Confidence in the consultant's ability to perform competently and on schedule is perhaps the key issue. Once this has been demonstrated, there need be no further problem of selection.

Client Responsibilities to the Consultant

The consultant needs cooperative assistance. This can involve considerable time of those who work with him, particularly during periods of training to carry out recommendations. Cooperation will be impeded, unless there is no fear of job security to those who should cooperate. These are important to the effectiveness of the consultant's performance. However, by far the greatest obstacle is the management which hires a consultant to do a job and then fails to do anything about it, once the study is completed.

Along this same line, any consultant who does not insist upon defining just how the recommendations are to be converted into practice is short-changing his job. This practical implementation is an essential step. It will upgrade the quality of the entire task. Unless the firm seeks to benefit from acceptable recommendations, it should not hire the consultant in the first place. But, the considerations of implementation should not be left until the job is done. They should be planned in

[23] Ibid., p. 12.

advance as a part of the total task. One wonders how many thousands of dollars have been paid for research and consultant studies which have been filed away and absolutely nothing done about them!

PROFESSIONAL, RESEARCH, EDUCATIONAL RESOURCES

Professional and trade associations can be valuable to management. The former seeks to keep people informed, motivated, and on top of their fields. The latter, through group action, helps in the tackling of problems common to the group.

Research organizations frequently combine their research skills in the tackling of allied managerial problems with consultation. This is not to be deplored. It is a natural and desirable outgrowth from the providing of the results to the next step—the application and use. Research organizations usually offer both facilities and staff to undertake and complete all aspects of a complete research assignment. This includes everything from defining the problem, planning the research operation, designing the questionnaire, sampling, doing the field interviewing, processing the results by hand or through EDP, through preparation of the report and an effective presentation of it to the client. Consulting services beyond that point are no longer "research," but they may be a desirable addition. Such firms offer the advantage of being able to undertake the research problem of an individual client.

Colleges and universities today frequently are heavily engaged in research of all sorts. A substantial part of the income of many institutions is research grants from many sources and in widely differing amounts. The problems may be highly technical to broad, social studies. Essentially, they utilize the facilities and faculty on current problems. This is to be encouraged. It is beneficial to the sponsor, the academic institution, the faculty, and the students. It is a resource available to business management, if the type of problem can be so researched or studied. It may well be worthy of exploration as a possibility in any such cases.

Not to be overlooked as a source of help are publishers. Many of them provide services in addition to the books and periodicals for which they are well known. Some are engaged recurrently in additional studies within their interest areas. Beyond that, editors as a group are generally informed as to sources of specialized information and major research or studies in process in their areas. Where competitive coverage exists it is well to check with each competitor. An individual engaged in ongoing research tends to become affiliated with one publishing house, particularly if his works are published recurrently. Other publishers then have little or no knowledge of his current activities.

RELEVANT READING

Trade Relations

Adams, Velma, "The Rise of the Trade Relations Director," *Dun's Review and Modern Industry*, December 1964, pp. 35–36ff.

Ammer, Dean S., "Realistic Reciprocity," *Harvard Business Review*, January-February 1962, pp. 116–124.

Finney, F. Robert, "Reciprocity: You Scratch My Back and I'll Scratch Yours," *Sales Management*, Dec. 1, 1969, pp. 33–72. This is an excerpt from a complete report, available from the Marketing Science Institute, 1033 Massachusetts Ave., Cambridge, Mass. 02138.

"Trade Relations Is Not Reciprocity: Storer," *Purchasing*, Dec. 2, 1963, p. 27.

"Trade Relations Serves Dual Aims: Symposium," *Iron Age*, Feb. 11, 1965, p. 100.

The Corporate Counsel

Holloway, Robert J., and Robert S. Hancock, *Marketing in a Changing Environment*, New York: John Wiley & Sons, Inc., 1968, chap. 10.

Kerby, Joe Kent, *Essentials of Marketing Management*, Cincinnati: South-Western Publishing Company, Incorporated, 1970, chap. 24.

Trade Associations

"Are Trade Shows Worth It?" *Dun's Review and Modern Industry*, June 1964, pp. 39–76.

Colgate, Craig, Jr. (ed.), *Directory of National Trade and Professional Associations of the United States*, Washington, D.C.: Columbia Books, $12.50, annual editions.

"Fresh Opportunities for Trade Associations," *Michigan Business Review*, May 1971, pp. 10–22.

Judkins, Jay, *Directory of National Associations of Businessmen, 1961*, U.S. Department of Commerce, 1961.

"National Organizations of the United States," *Encyclopedia of Associations*, 6th ed., vol. I, Detroit: Gale Research Company, 1970.

"What's a Trade Association Worth?" *Dun's Review*, March 1965, pp. 32–60.

Management Consultants

Consultants: Selection, Use, and Appraisal, The Conference Board, Managing the Moderate-sized Company, no. 13, 1970.

Fact Book, 1970–71, Chicago: Booz-Allen & Hamilton, Inc., 1971.

CHAPTER EIGHTEEN

Decision Making

BASIC FALLACIES IN MARKETING THOUGHT

Prior to considering planning and decision making, it is fitting to refresh
our memory of marketing, itself. Marketing is a perspective of business. It is an aid to corporate decision making, provided it is properly
conceived and integrated. Yet it is young, very young. Marketing still
suffers from conceptual fallacies, which need to be recognized and
corrected.

Leo Burnett identifies five fallacies in marketing:[1]

> *The first fallacy is that the people already in the marketing field are*
> *the ones who understand it best and know what the potential customer*
> *wants.*
>
> In this connection, consider how many developments in any field of
> knowledge so often originate *outside* the ken of those specialists sup-
> posedly with the greatest insights.
>
> Of our important railroad devices, not one was invented by a railroad
> man. These were the air-brake, automatic coupling, the refrigerator
> car, and the streamlined train.

[1] Reprinted from *Journal of Marketing*, published by the American Marketing
Association, Leo Burnett, "Marketing Snags and Fallacies," July 1966, vol. 30,
no. 3, pp. 2–6.

The development of tetraethyl lead came from outside the petroleum industry.

And the paperback books—one of the most successful revolutions in selling in our time—were not initiated by the giants of the book publishing business, who entered the field later and only when it was already thriving.

The second fallacy is a limited definition of "competition," under which the chief marketing strategy is to attain the largest possible share of the existing market, rather than create new markets and add to total consumption.

It is true, of course, that many great companies are indeed bringing about innovation; and the overriding marketing strategy is to proliferate and diversify. Obviously, however, there is a tremendous need to *organize for change*—after all, the mere fact of corporate organization tends to conspire against it.

The third fallacy in the marketing world is that competition is a closed system, and that our competitors are those making substantially the same products, or offering the same services, that we are.

It is a mistake to feel that the competition for a Cadillac is either a medium-priced car or another quality car such as a Lincoln or Imperial. The Cadillac is a prestige item. The true competitor of the luxury car is the swimming pool, or the summer place, or the private plane, or the winter vacation, and all the other prestige items dangled before people with large discretionary incomes.[2]

A fourth fallacy is the marketing theory of appealing mainly to present income brackets.

People no longer buy solely what they "need," or even what they "want" for the present. They are anticipating new and future needs; and the industries that have grown most have been the ones catering to this sense of expectation.

All the demographic facts add up to a tremendous new market that is not based on the traditional concepts of "income" and "status" and "education" that have been our bench marks in the past.

In all this we have a dramatic example of *upward mobility*. The more prosperous we become, the higher do our expectations grow, and the more do new people become potential customers for markets that once seemed restricted.

The fifth fallacy is that because we are living in the age of the specialist, only qualified experts with specialized skills will be competent in the future to make basic decisions.

Actually, quite the reverse is happening. Our greatest need today is for the synthesizer, much more than for the specialist. He is not necessarily a computer programer; but he understands how computers work, and what they can do and cannot do.

After all the facts are in from the computers, research, and elsewhere,

[2] Peter F. Drucker, *Managing for Results,* New York: Harper & Row, Publishers, Incorporated, 1964, p. 95.

the "gut" decision finally must be made by a man, or by a very small group of men. And these men cannot afford not to know how their field relates to other fields, and how all of them interlock. The basic decisions in today's economy have much broader and deeper ramifications than ever before.

In the search for a new breed of synthesizer or "generalist," business and industrial leaders are beginning to call for a different kind of graduate from the nation's schools of business; and the schools are responding rapidly.

What we need most in the immediate future are more truly educated men and women, that is, people who know one thing well, but many related things fairly well. And to be educated, in any useful sense of the word, means that you can differentiate between what you know and what you do not know, that you know where to go to find out what you need to know, and that you know how to use the information once you get it.[3]

CORPORATE PLANNING[4]

Everyone plans in one way or another. There is nothing new about that—nor about corporate planning. It has been going on for ages. What is new is the growing recognition of its ramifications and the potential contribution of proper planning to corporate welfare. This has led to the development of organization for planning, and at the same time, the development of full-time corporate planners, specialists in the organization and control of the planning function. These men do not do the actual planning. They do organize, assemble data, coordinate, and present alternatives. They call for the needed contributions of others, integrate and present the results in a unified whole. They make no decisions—but they do help management to do so.

Secretary of Commerce Maurice H. Stans gave real credence to planning when he stated:[5]

> But we cannot build a new and better America by concerning ourselves solely with the day-to-day problems that beset us, as pressing as these are.
>
> We must have the foresight to identify the long-range issues, and the wisdom to plan wisely for their resolution. Otherwise, we shall be compelled to meet every social and economic crisis on an ad hoc basis, employing crash programs and hit-and-run approaches that waste precious resources and are only half effective.

[3] Alfred N. Whitehead, *The Aims of Education,* New York: The Macmillan Company, 1956, pp. 16–17.

[4] To a major extent this section was prepared from contributions made by Morlan J. Grandbois, Corporate Planning Coordinator, St. Regis Paper Company, New York.

[5] © 1971, *Nation's Business*—the Chamber of Commerce of the United States. Reprinted from the February issue, pp. 26–27.

Whereas Mr. Stans was referring to the country as a whole, his comments apply equally forcefully to the corporate entity.

Historically, corporate planning has been largely the prerogative of operational divisions or functions, such as finance, manufacturing, and marketing, usually brought together into a budget, which management amended and finally approved. Overall perspective was provided by top management, but only rarely did this include a detailed appraisal of alternatives beyond those involved in the adjustment of the requests for funds from operating heads to the total economic situation faced by the company, as viewed by top management. This welding of independent and sometimes competitive internal programs and expressing the results in a budget is far short of corporate planning as it ought to be and can be.

Today, many companies are treating corporate planning as an organized process. Plans for the next five, ten, or even more years are common. Such long-range plans force recognition of the many variables affecting corporate welfare. They are frequently accompanied by specific strategies to achieve them. They can be broken down to annual bites. This provides both bench marks for evaluation of progress overall and reference points for individual managers.

All this has been good. It is movement in the right direction. But it still lacks the impact that it could have. Let us go a step further. Let us seek to determine exactly where we are right now, what our potentials for improvement are, and what the alternative procedures for attaining them involve. Let us be specific. Our goal is a corporate strategic plan to provide coordinated direction to the activities of all line and staff groups. It must be operational, practical, and detailed—while providing a bird's-eye perspective.

This is not easy, but it is attainable. Morlan J. Grandbois, Corporate Planning Coordinator for St. Regis, has been working on the development of such a program for his company for several years. The essence of the resultant St. Regis *corporate planning and development program* follows. The basic principles are significant and can readily be adapted with but minor changes in detail to other corporate situations.

Responsibilities of Corporate Planning

Formal planning requires maximum use of the talents and experience of managers (line and staff) and specialists throughout the company. The necessary responsibilities are divided as follows:

Chief Executive and/or Executive Planning Committee: Authorize system; review inputs and analyses; make decisions; allocate resources; authorize action; and review results.

Planning Staff: Design system; train line and staff; make special studies; schedule activities; and assemble plans.

Line and Staff Managers: Before decisions, appraise situations and outlook; prepare special studies; and propose action for approval by top management.

After decisions, program detailed action; assign responsibilities, goals, and controls; and manage the plan.

In essence, there are four phases to St. Regis's corporate planning and development program. The first is an analysis of profit centers. Next is the determination of corporate potential and the planning gap. Third is the planning process which produces the *corporate strategic plan*. Fourth is an annual recycling of the plan.

Profit-Center Analysis

The first step in the implementation of the total program is an audit of the profit performance and trend of each profit center (including plant, division, and operational group) and an evaluation of the relative profit performance of all in terms of assets committed.

The objective is to build background for the planning and development group by means of which management's attention can be directed to improving the areas of strength and correcting or eliminating the areas of weakness.

These data are assembled in a loose-leaf volume, *Corporate Planning Data.* It includes the past five years, together with the current budgeted year. This gives an accurate picture of the relative profit performance of each operation including the return on net assets. The operating income and net cash flow are both converted into equivalent corporate dollars per share. Figure 18.1 shows a sample page.

The Company Potential

As a start, it might be interesting to plot the "go-fishing" line for each major segment of the company and for the company as a whole. This line is the increase in value which would occur if we liquidated the assets of the company and invested the proceeds in securities or bank accounts and went fishing. It is well visualized by the Stanford Research Institute Executive Seminar in Business Planning, as follows:[6]

> One simple measure of the ambitions of a company's top managers is to ask: If you took the present value of your company's assets (or net worth, if you prefer) and simply invested that amount in the best securities you could find, then went on vacation for ten years, what is the minimum growth in value you would expect in that ten years?

[6] Courtesy of Stanford Research Institute.

GROUP _____   PAGE NO. _____

DIVISION _____ PLANT _____

			($000 OMITTED)				
YEAR	ACCOUNTS RECEIVABLE	INVENTORY	PLANT, PROPERTY & EQUIPMENT	EXCESS COST	NET ASSETS	DEPRECIATION	CAPITAL EXPENDITURES
1965							
1966							
1967							
1968							
1969							
1970							
1971							
1972							
1973							
1974							
1975							

YEAR	NET SALES	OPERATING INCOME	NET CASH FLOW BEFORE TAXES	% RETURN ON				EQUIVALENT CORPORATE DOLLARS PER SHARE	
				INCOME		CASH FLOW	CAPACITY		
				OVER SALES	OVER ASSETS	OVER ASSETS	OVER ASSETS	OPERATING INCOME	CASH FLOW
1965									
1966									
1967									
1968									
1969									
1970									
1971									
1972									
1973									
1974									
1975									

NOTES:

Fig. 18.1 Sample page of corporate planning data.

If you relate this question to the compound interest that could be earned from bank deposits, municipal bonds, the average appreciation of common stocks or real estate, you have a first approximation of the minimum growth that good managers should expect from a business over ten years. If the value will not grow any faster than from a simple investment, why work?

Let us next construct realistic potential and momentum lines for this same entity.

The potential line is a projection for a company of the business activity that *could* occur assuming its management exercised *all resources pres-*

ently and potentially available to carry out its explicitly determined ambitions.

To establish a realistic potential line requires critical appraisal by a company's top management of (1) its resources (potentially, as well as those presently available), (2) its awareness of opportunity (those outside of as well as within its present lines of business), and (3) its own commitment to the goals it has set for itself. While all three elements of this critical appraisal are essential to establishing a realistic potential line, the third one—commitment—is key.

A momentum line represents a projection into the future of the level of business activity of the same company *assuming no major change* in today's scope of methods (e.g., it excludes adding of product lines not now handled, acquiring other companies, or going into other businesses unrelated to those already part of the company).

Unless this momentum line is significantly above the "go-fishing" line, why not do just that? Or an improvement in production and/or sales efficiency, a change in products or a divestiture would seem to be in order.

If more than one business is involved in the total company, separate potential and momentum lines can be calculated for each and then a summary made of each total.

Projections should be in those terms most meaningful to top management. It can be one or more of the following: pretax profit as percent of total assets, net profit after taxes, net worth (or equity), return on net worth, or dollar sales.

The Planning Gap

The difference between the potential line and the momentum line is the planning gap. Gap analysis is a process of using the gap as one of the important tools for determining what are desirable and possible actions for the company to undertake.

The usefulness of a gap analysis is entirely dependent on the quality of the information used in making both kinds of projections. Such being the case, it is also true that a good gap analysis is a repetitive process because:

1. It should be updated as new information is made available.
2. Several trials are usually necessary to settle on a realistic potential line.
3. There may be several ways of filling a gap, several trials will have to be tested.
4. It is possible that a projected gap cannot be filled, and may have to be redetermined.

A gap analysis realistically made can be highly useful because it helps a top management mobilize itself and its resources in a way which should make it easier to establish and achieve desirable and feasible goals. Moreover, simply by going through the processes of making a gap analysis, top management will bring together much information it may already know about, but in addition, other information it has not previously assembled in a way to be helpful.

After a few trials of potential-line and momentum-line calculations, the final financial measures can be plotted and a graphic representation of the gap obtained.

A chart or several that represent different sets of assumptions regarding the company's potential and momentum give management a better picture of what can and needs to be done to make the company get where it wants to go.   Figure 18.2 illustrates this.

The individual manager in charge of a profit center should participate in the determination of his potential line, which may be structured under the assumption of use of additional assets. If given these assets, that, plus his personal involvement, will be a most powerful motivation for this manager. With reasonable time to adjust, his planning gap should start to close. If not, either the potential line was wrong (perhaps the

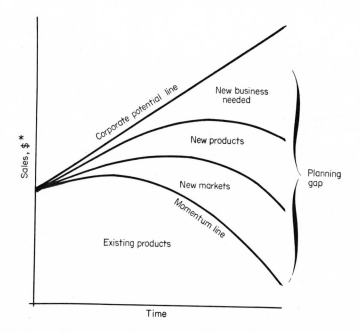

* Or net profit after taxes, net worth (or equity), return on net worth

Fig. 18.2 Gap analysis.

manager overextended himself or was overly optimistic), something happened beyond reasonable expectancy of being foreseen, or the manager just failed to achieve his own goals.   Identification of cause and remedial action are called for.

Corporate Business-Planning System

Individual entrepreneurs have been responsible for building most business operations to the greatness they are now.   These entrepreneurs generally possessed the capabilities required to develop the information to make the adroit decisions necessary for success.

With the increasing size and complexities of business, with the swift advancement of technology and communications, the individual entrepreneur finds it to be a growing problem, in fact virtually impossible, to cope with conditions as his predecessors did when pressures were less complex.   Today it is increasingly difficult to close the planning gap.   Secretary of Commerce Maurice H. Stans confirmed the dilemma of the entrepreneur when he stated:[7] "If there is one thing all Americans can agree on, it is this: We are in a period of change and turmoil such as our nation has rarely experienced—nearly all the problems that mankind has ever faced seem to have converged on us in our time and in this place, and with the force of a hurricane."

The fast movements and complexities of modern business are forcing the individual entrepreneur to give way to organized entrepreneurship. This involves input and decisions by many capable personnel in all phases and stations of a business enterprise.   A business-planning system provides practical direction to identify and link corporate ambitions to the creation of opportunity through orderly management.   It affords a better opportunity for closing the planning gap.   In the last ten to fifteen years, an increasing number of large companies have developed successful organizational procedures using the business-planning system concept.

St. Regis has been involved in planning efforts for many years.   However, these efforts have been uncoordinated and unrelated.   In most cases the effort lacked detailed and valid forecasting of markets and profits.   It tended to extend past activity without adequate analysis to reflect the accelerated rate of change.   The result in most cases has been poor budgeting and vague and unrealistic impressions of expected return on assigned assets.

A formalized business-planning system was recently inaugurated by St. Regis.   It was initiated by the corporate planning and development

[7] © 1971, *Nation's Business*—the Chamber of Commerce of the United States. Reprinted from the February issue, p. 26.

group and approved by a newly appointed executive planning committee. The details of the planning process were completed and introduced in special meetings to selected line and staff executives by the company president and the senior vice president of corporate planning and development.

The objective of the corporate business-planning system is to develop a viable program by which corporate management can encourage and evaluate valid inputs and recommendations by line management and/or find alternative courses of action that are responsive to what needs to be done to meet company current, short-term, and long-range goals. This basically involves:

1. Expanding activity in the more profitable market areas.
2. Improving and broadening the more profitable present product lines.
3. Encouraging new ventures through internal development and/or acquisition to be in tune with environmental change.

This program involves searching, analyzing, appraising, and selecting the more desirable projects and setting priorities. The results are the basis for a *corporate strategic plan.*

A corporate strategic plan, carefully designed, reflects the current, short-term, and long-range objectives of the company. This gives coordinated direction to the activities of all line and staff groups. But it should not be considered a one-time effort. It must be a viable activity that represents the best collective planning effort on the part of all line and staff groups of the company continuously.

All planning effort involved in building a corporate strategic plan must be monitored constantly to assure valid techniques are used (i.e., forecasting, etc.) and that all projects are fully evaluated, selected, and promptly submitted. A close control procedure must be established to constantly compare performance with budget so that prompt corrective action can be taken where necessary.

To cope with the accelerated rate of change in our economy, the corporate strategic plan must be constantly recycled, reviewed, and revised at least once a year to reflect the changes in values and all aspects of the corporate situation. Thus, with the passing of time the vague (six to ten years out) becomes more specific. The specific leads to the actual. The actual is derived from current plans, including the budget.

In building a corporate strategic plan it is of particular importance that the chief executive officer regularly undertake a review of the plan with the operating officers with emphasis on their recommendations and programs for:

1. Further improvement of profitable profit centers
2. Justification of continued operation of those profit centers which fail to meet or contribute to the company goal
3. Development of a long-range program to meet company goals for profit improvement by expansion, acquisition, or divestiture

Mill Economic Analysis

The mill economic analysis can be a most valuable tool in generating a constant flow of valid inputs into the corporate business-planning system. This procedure is not an accounting system, a production plan, or a sales program, per se. It is a composite of all factors that influence profit currently, short term, and long range; it is a total look at an operation; it is a process of "decision analysis" that leads to the better decision at the right time.

The purposes of a mill economic analysis are (1) to fill the need for an accurate overview of each mill, (2) to highlight problem areas and pinpoint profit-improvement opportunities for each operation, and (3) to aid in decision making in the areas of selective selling, operational balance, capital improvement, and expansion.

A mill economic analysis utilizes the systems approach. For example, in the paper industry, it examines the total operation—from raw material, labor, and power requirements through pulping, paper manufacturing, and finishing processes. The study begins with a detailed inventory of all mill facilities and a ten-year projection of supply resources, such as availability of timber by species, water, labor, etc. It proceeds through an analysis of current product mix and machine operations. It then progresses through marketing studies, improved product mix, and improved and expanded machine operations.

A mill economic analysis seeks to:

1. Indicate the optimum earning capability of each mill based on 100 percent standard operation
2. Indicate controllable and uncontrollable variances between actual performance, budgeted levels, and 100 percent standard operation
3. Indicate opportunities for increased profit through an improved selling effort
4. Indicate opportunities for increased profit through capital investment for improved machine performance and a desirable priority of each
5. Indicate opportunities for increased profit through the development and substitution of new products for existing ones

6. Indicate opportunities for increased profit through (a) equipment modifications or substitutions to reduce cost and obtain a more balanced operation, and (b) expansion either internally or by acquisition to keep pace with growing and changing markets

This study is divided into four steps to determine (1) increased profit through selective selling and improved production efficiencies *that require no capital investment,* (2) increased profit from *minor capital improvements* to bring equipment up to rated capability, (3) increased profit through *new-product* development, and (4) increased profit *through expansion* either internally or by acquisition to keep pace with growth opportunities.

Corporate Planning and Development: An Overview

The corporate planning and development program concerns all present and possible new profit centers and the relationship of each to the ever-changing economy when market opportunities are related to production capabilities to produce optimum profit—currently, short term, and longer range.

Phase I in the implementation of the program is the appraisal of the profit performance and trend of each corporate operation (i.e., plant, division, and profit group). This appraisal of profit performance is detailed and summarized in a report entitled *Corporate Planning Data.* It is appropriately the responsibility of the controller's office to continue the appraisal effort and keep the report up to date. The interest of the corporate planning staff is to monitor and coordinate the effort.

In Phase II the "go-fishing," potential, and momentum lines are created. Here the corporate planning staff helps to obtain realism and prevent overenthusiasm. It makes the planning gap analyses and assembles them for top management.

Phase III of this entrepreneurial planning system is designed to assemble the data needed to project courses of action with estimates of consequences before committing resources. It reflects management's decisions in action statements to provide practical direction in identifying and linking corporate ambition to the creation of opportunity through objective management.

Mill and plant economic analyses add specific data on potential results of allocation of resources to improve plant performance and better integrate it with customers' needs. These are rightfully the responsibility of line management. The interest of the corporate planning staff is to help install this tool and to monitor and coordinate this effort.

Phase IV is the annual recycling of these plans to reflect both corporate

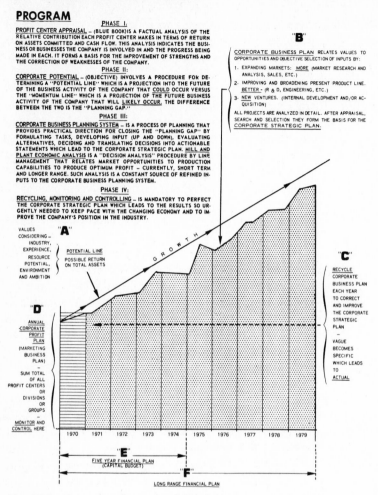

PROGRAM

PHASE I:

PROFIT CENTER APPRAISAL – (BLUE BOOK)IS A FACTUAL ANALYSIS OF THE RELATIVE CONTRIBUTION EACH PROFIT CENTER MAKES IN TERMS OF RETURN ON ASSETS COMMITTED AND CASH FLOW. THIS ANALYSIS INDICATES THE BUSINESS OR BUSINESSES THE COMPANY IS INVOLVED IN AND THE PROGRESS BEING MADE IN EACH. IT FORMS A BASIS FOR THE IMPROVEMENT OF STRENGTHS AND THE CORRECTION OF WEAKNESSES OF THE COMPANY.

PHASE II:

CORPORATE POTENTIAL – (OBJECTIVE) INVOLVES A PROCEDURE FOR DETERMINING A "POTENTIAL LINE" WHICH IS A PROJECTION INTO THE FUTURE OF THE BUSINESS ACTIVITY OF THE COMPANY THAT COULD OCCUR VERSUS THE "MOMENTUM LINE" WHICH IS A PROJECTION OF THE FUTURE BUSINESS ACTIVITY OF THE COMPANY THAT WILL LIKELY OCCUR. THE DIFFERENCE BETWEEN THE TWO IS THE "PLANNING GAP."

PHASE III:

CORPORATE BUSINESS PLANNING SYSTEM – IS A PROCESS OF PLANNING THAT PROVIDES PRACTICAL DIRECTION FOR CLOSING THE "PLANNING GAP" BY FORMULATING TASKS, DEVELOPING INPUT (UP AND DOWN), EVALUATING ALTERNATIVES, DECIDING AND TRANSLATING DECISIONS INTO ACTIONABLE STATEMENTS WHICH LEAD TO THE CORPORATE STRATEGIC PLAN. MILL AND PLANT ECONOMIC ANALYSIS IS A "DECISION ANALYSIS" PROCEDURE BY LINE MANAGEMENT THAT RELATES MARKET OPPORTUNITIES TO PRODUCTION CAPABILITIES TO PRODUCE OPTIMUM PROFIT – CURRENTLY, SHORT TERM AND LONGER RANGE. SUCH ANALYSIS IS A CONSTANT SOURCE OF REFINED INPUTS TO THE CORPORATE BUSINESS PLANNING SYSTEM.

PHASE IV:

RECYCLING, MONITORING AND CONTROLLING – IS MANDATORY TO PERFECT THE CORPORATE STRATEGIC PLAN WHICH LEADS TO THE RESULTS SO URGENTLY NEEDED TO KEEP PACE WITH THE CHANGING ECONOMY AND TO IMPROVE THE COMPANY'S POSITION IN THE INDUSTRY.

"B"

CORPORATE BUSINESS PLAN RELATES VALUES TO OPPORTUNITIES AND OBJECTIVE SELECTION OF INPUTS BY:

1. EXPANDING MARKETS: MORE (MARKET RESEARCH AND ANALYSIS, SALES, ETC.)
2. IMPROVING AND BROADENING PRESENT PRODUCT LINE. BETTER - (R & D, ENGINEERING, ETC.)
3. NEW VENTURES. (INTERNAL DEVELOPMENT AND/OR ACQUISITION)

ALL PROJECTS ARE ANALYZED IN DETAIL. AFTER APPRAISAL, SEARCH AND SELECTION THEY FORM THE BASIS FOR THE CORPORATE STRATEGIC PLAN.

Fig. 18.3   Corporate planning and development summary chart.

and market changes in order to keep the corporate strategic plan viable. Planning, of itself, accomplishes nothing. Planning coupled with appropriate action can be most powerful. The whole planning effort is directed toward improved action. Figure 18.3 provides a concise graphic summary of this program.

THE ACT OF DECISION MAKING

Decision Making versus Problem Solving

Problem solving is the act of providing a satisfactory answer or solution to a question or situation. Decision making is the act of making up one's mind. This provides a judgment. Problem solving can frequently be aided by mathematics and EDP. Decision making can be aided by relevant data, but the deciding is a mental process in the mind of man. And this involves discretion, intangible value judgments.

Problems typically have a correct or one-best answer. In decision making there is rarely a one-best answer. There may not be complete agreement on the criteria to measure it. Even favorable resultant performance is not conclusive that the decision was best. And business rarely has a chance to do it over again under the same circumstances. Decisions produce degrees of results from unfavorable to favorable. The ratio between good and bad decisions, or the extent favorable results are forthcoming, as against the extent of the unfavorable, measures the quality of the decision making—and thereby the capability of the decision maker.

The difference between successful and unsuccessful managers is one of degree in the favorableness of the results obtained from their decision making. Rarely is this a clear-cut matter of good or bad. If the manager can raise his batting average even a little bit, he can become vastly more successful. An exploration of the involvement and act of decision making together with an analysis of the role and types of data may help.

Decisions Defined

"Decisions" are forecasts made in the face of uncertainty. This does not mean forecasts in the usual sense of forecasts of sales or business conditions, but the anticipated results from various kinds of effort. Decisions *would* be simple, if uncertainty and risk were not present. But if they were not present, there would be certainty and absence of risk. There would be no real problem. And, therefore, there would be no need for decision making—or for a decision maker.

Types of Decisions   There is a wide range in scope and involvement in decision making, from the most trivial of matters to multimillion-dollar situations. There are recognizable levels of decision making within this range. First are goals, the short- and long-term objectives, what we would like to achieve. These can be somewhat optimistic and need not be highly accurate or refined. Next, policy decisions refer to the determination of operational guides, criteria to aid in attaining uniformity of effort. Then, strategy, which is the plan, refers to the arrangement and integration of various efforts, to produce the result desired. And tactics are the detailed steps in the implementation of the plan.

Decisions of relatively minor matters and where an immediate judgment is desired or required are most frequently made intuitively, i.e., subjectively. A minimum of forethought is needed. The involvement is low. Promptness is attained. An error does not entail much loss or it may be easily corrected without serious damage. This is a perfectly sound and valid method of decision making when used appropriately.

Intuitive decision making, being subjective, relies heavily upon the evaluation and emotional preference of the individual. There are various other recognizable types of decision making which do this and also add one or more forms of bias. The "seat-of-the-pants" decision maker "feels" that this is what should be done. He may be right. His "feeling," if derived from qualified experience, can be very valuable. The quality of the decision is far more a function of the quality of the man than the method of deciding.

Closely allied to this is the autocrat. He relies on his "better judgment." He is a member of the "unchallengeables." He merely adds his authority or prestige to an essentially subjective reaction. And he resists and resents opposition.

Then there are the habitual decision makers. They base their decisions on history and tradition. "We've been doing it this way for twenty years and it's always worked." Established beliefs need not be wrong, but they are an impediment to creativity.

Some individuals (including managers) decide what they want to do, then look for logical reasons to support it. In this same camp are those who speak or write too soon—then, when challenged, seek to prove that they were right in the first place. Pride of authorship, vanity, can be a serious impediment to reason.

Allied intimately with this is the self-identification with a decision. The decision may have been very soundly reached. But, once reached, it becomes a highly personal matter. Criticize the decision and you criticize the decision maker. Suppose a friend arrives in a new car. If he asks your opinion of it, find out first whether or not he has already purchased it. If he is merely trying it out, he'll welcome your observations—and probably pass them on to the salesman, at least to get a better deal. But, if the car is his, criticize at the risk of endangering a friendship. Self-identification is a very human and very powerful force.

Conflicting Goals: Corporate versus Personal

From a similar point of view, it should be recognized that there are always two goals present in decision making. One is corporate—what is good for the corporation. The other, and most frequently not only the first but the more powerful goal, is personal—what this will do to my job, to me. If the individual's welfare is enhanced, he'll be for the decision. If it is not, he'll come up with as many corporate reasons as he can to oppose it.

Credit versus Blame

In earlier days some of the world's outstanding leaders developed a "foolproof" system of decision making. Julius Caesar, Alexander the Great, and Adolf Hitler relied on a favorite seer before committing their armies. If anything went wrong, it was easy to blame the oracle. If it went well, the leader became successful again.

Unfortunately this practice still exists in some business situations. The inexperienced decision maker would do well to establish clearly both the authority and responsibility inherent in his decision making at the outset. This should be automatic. It is in most cases, but not in all.

Bias versus Objectivity

All human beings are emotional to some degree. In human relations this is all to the good. In business decision making the emotion takes the form of a mental leaning, a partiality, a prejudice. This is a bias and the opposite emotional condition from objectivity. An objective attitude determines its reactions impersonally from the situation being considered, as against the feeling and thoughts—the bias—within the mind of the man.

It is quite difficult to attain and maintain an objective point of view—particularly with subjective personal interests involved—and with seniority, prestige, or authority to permit assertion. To aid in this, the technique of rational decision making can be useful. If the decision maker recognizes his bias, his subjectivity, and yet seeks to be objective, the use of a rational approach can greatly enhance the quality of the decision reached.

Steps in Decision Making

Rational decision making can readily be broken down into a series of steps. It is helpful to visualize the overall decision-making process in this way, to recognize and segregate the steps, and to appreciate the involvement of each. Improvement in the act of decision making should follow from improvement in the performance of each step. Direction is given to thought concerning each. Finally, in the act of decision making, even though one does not necessarily perform all the steps, one by one, a keen awareness of them permits a mental scanning and integration of the factors of the situation, and that will upgrade the quality of the decision reached.

These steps follow:

1. The bird's-eye view
2. The objective(s)—goal(s)

3. The basic issue(s)
4. The immediate issue(s)
5. The data
6. The criteria for evaluation of alternatives
7. The alternatives
8. The evaluation

The bird's-eye view is a perspective of the total situation—but the highlights only, not the minutae of detail. In essence, what is this situation? What is sought here are the *major* elements of the total involvement and their interrelationships. It should be capable of being expressed in far less than a minute. Such perspective is extremely valuable. Many thorough men, "nitpickers" by heart, are all too concerned and readily lost in the important aspects of detail. They really are specialists, competent technicians. They rarely see the problem in its total perspective. They are most competent at administrative detail, but fail completely at the conceptual level of the generalist.

Here, then, is the start. If one aspires to management above the administrative level, the ability to both visualize and conceptualize is most valuable. It is without question a capacity possessed to such an exceptionally high degree by top managers that it becomes almost a prerequisite to successful performance at that level.

Next, the objectives to be attained, including both the corporate and the marketing goals, need to be reapplied to the specific problem at hand. They provide the guiding direction for potential solutions and specific criteria for evaluation of alternative possibilities.

The basic issue(s) is the heart of the problem. There may be one or there may be more than one. The problem at this point is identification. It is very easy to be misled, to accept an immediate issue, a question posed by management, as the basic issue. One test of the fundamental, basic issue is to say, "If I had the answer to this, could I answer everything else automatically?" This is to say that the answer to the basic issue, once obtained, should provide the means to answer logically all the immediate issues. If it does not, there is more than one basic issue—or it is not the correct basic issue in the first place. More analytical thought is called for. The answer to the basic issue should provide that which is needed to answer all lesser, immediate issues, automatically.

The immediate issue(s) are those surface problems to which prompt decision is required. They frequently are pressing in time. They are rarely the basic involvement. Underneath these symptomatic questions lie one or more basic issues, the answer to which provides the means to answer the immediate issues. In practice, the immediate issues are those posed of the manager. They are rarely directed to the heart of the matter. It is up to the manager to recognize the basic problem which, when or if already solved, provides the means to answer the immediate issues.

The data include *all* the quantitative and qualitative information relevant to the basic issue. The key word is "relevant." Any and all information which is relevant is appropriate. Its significance can be subject to weighting. The assembly of these data should never be guided by the anticipation of a potential solution. A fatal but human mistake at this point is to assemble data substantiating a preconceived solution, and to ignore anything opposing it. No potential solution should be considered or discussed—at this point.

The next step is frequently assumed to exist in the minds of the decision makers. Undoubtedly, each one has *some* criteria in mind, but not necessarily the same criteria as the others, nor with the same significance to each. It is well to identify the criteria, discuss them as necessary to reach an agreement on what they are and the relative weight of each one. As a start, corporate goals are involved. Beyond that and depending upon the nature of the problem, other criteria can readily be developed. This provides a uniform base for evaluation of alternatives and can save a lot of needless discussion, if it develops that various managers are actually using different criteria.

Such criteria can form the basis for a rating scale, complete with weights to reflect relative significance of criteria, if the problem is serious enough to warrant that treatment. Sometimes forcing people to express their ideas on paper can help to crystallize thinking and to identify differences. This can be a valuable step in reaching agreement.

Development of the alternatives is far more than listing the obvious possibilities. Of course, there must be at least two reasonably possible alternatives, or there is no choice and therefore no real problem. However, it is a serious mistake to be satisfied to consider merely the obvious ones. Here is a chance for creativity. Here is an opportunity for the imaginative to make a real contribution. The difficult part is to free one's mind of the traditional and to explore the unique. Maybe one alternative is to do nothing and let time take over. Another might be to find out what others have done—and consider the exact opposite. Another approach is to pretend that you are writing a novel on business. How might your hero solve this problem uniquely and advantageously to his company? Businessmen who as decision makers content themselves merely with the exercise of sound judgment are providing good management—but not leadership. They conservatively follow the well-worn paths. They are an impediment to creativity. Let them dream a little—and give them the courage to innovate. All change is not progress, but progress is change. Here, in the development of alternatives, is the businessman's golden opportunity to pioneer, to move in the direction of true leadership.

The evaluation becomes an important but relatively easy task, if the preceding steps have been competently taken. If the basic issue has been correctly identified, if full data, both quantitative and qualitative, are known, if the criteria for evaluation are established, the comparison of the probable results of each of the alternatives to the criteria is simple. It is the unknown which injects the difficulty. Here the human mind must take over. Here the real heart of the decision is a judgment based on the courage, the knowledge of the many intangibles, the foresight of the uncontrollable factors (including competitive reaction), and the degree of risk. The managers who make the decisions recurrently stick their neck out. The risk can be lessened by sound techniques, but never eliminated. Uncertainty creates the need for the decision. This is the ultimate art in industrial marketing and in business. It is learned by the doing. Marketing's greatest contribution is the providing of perspective to the modern decision maker.

Communication: Implementation of the Decision

Once the decision has been reached it must be communicated to others. From the top down this is reasonably easy. Authority and respect pave the way. From the bottom up it is another matter. Here salesmanship is called for. One does not argue a decision. This merely strengthens the opposition to it. One must convince, and in the other man's terms, i.e., by his standards. This includes superiors (who may authorize), subordinates (who act under it), and associates, one's peers (who are impacted by it).

One way to help obtain cooperation is to involve others in the decision-making process. By such involvement they have a chance to be heard, they contribute to the decision, and they learn the basis for the final judgment. Conviction should prevail over compromises. Even assertion by authority is apt to be better than many compromises, which tend to weaken both sides and achieve mediocre results. Try it. If wrong, correct it and try again. Compromises rarely develop the enthusiasm so vital to the wholehearted cooperation needed in effective implementation in today's complex of business.

In the act of communication of decisions, face-to-face confrontations are many times more effective than written. They provide a chance to explore, explain, and discuss ramifications. They are fast. They are human and personal. They show respect for the subordinates. If absolutely necessary to record details of the decision on paper, let it be a follow-up for reference purposes rather than the initial awareness. Goodwill and team spirit grow rapidly if so nurtured.

Errors in Decision Making

It would be a mistake to think that errors in decision making are confined to those who are learning, students and new managers. Experienced businessmen err, too.

It would be a further mistake to assume that businessmen follow through the foregoing steps in decision making in actual practice. That would be quite an assumption. Shortcuts are all too popular. As soon as the decision takes on aspects of major significance, meetings, committees, and ad hoc groups are apt to be involved. This helps spread the blame, but it may or may not contribute to the quality of the decision. Properly conducted, it should increase the scope of considerations. Rarely do such groups initiate. That comes from the mind of a man, a creative individual.

Some of the more common errors in decision making are:

Wrong basic issue. A test as to the correctness of the basic issue is to ask, "If I had the answers to this issue, could all the immediate issues be answered logically therefrom?" If the answer is no, then either it is the wrong basic issue or there is more than one issue involved.

Wrong perspective. Product-oriented in a situation calling for market orientation, for example.

Jumping the gun. Predetermination of the answer, then seeking data to "prove" it is right. Improper, biased consideration with defense of position taken paramount over seeking the most logical conclusion.

Impatience. Failure to give proper consideration to *all* alternatives.

Bias. This takes many forms, in interpretation of data, in determination and weighting of criteria for evaluation, as well as in the final judgment. This is obvious. The real danger here is the more subtle bias in people. Managers may "try to be fair," but little realizing their own prejudices, preferences, or inclinations. Here the outsider, the consultant, or a candid friend who is not afraid to say what he thinks can be invaluable.

Overemphasis on tradition. Inability to overcome habit, tradition, and "what everyone knows" to be true. This is really a failure to recognize and occasionally challenge time-honored assumptions.

Failure to consider the long terms and the fundamental. Short terms may be in conflict with the long term.

Overreliance on data. Failure to recognize that mathematical data can be precise—but inaccurate. Quantitative results are only as good as the validity of the data and the representativeness of the source. At best they are an aid to, not a substitute for, the judgment of the manager.

Failure to give full significance to qualitative data. Intangibility does not mean insignificance. It is dangerous to assume that that which cannot be counted does not count.

The assumption that there is one right or best answer—that all others are wrong. In some cases this can be true. But in many more cases the best answer is really the "best fit" to all the variables and goals to be served. Weighted considerations and ranking of criteria for evaluation may help. Time priorities can be a factor in some cases.

Failure to recognize and honor that which argues for less—or opposes a position taken.

Too heavy a reliance on "better judgment." This is coupled with a failure to develop the full breadth of the considerations—those against as well as those for the decision. Try asking this man to discuss the reasons *opposing* the position taken.

Conservatism. Belief that it is always best to be on the low side in estimating sales results. It makes the manager "look good" to oversell, and he avoids criticism for unsold inventory, if he estimates low. This involves a failure to assess the cost of unfilled orders in terms of goodwill, market position, and additional production runs. It is a failure to plan for success.

Failure to use imagination. This frequently prevents the development of all reasonably possible alternatives. Creativity thrives on knowledge plus imagination. It involves risks and taking chances. But it also offers great rewards. One can be too conservative. At the same time, there is a difference between being courageous and foolhardy.

Fear of risk taking. There is a strong trend toward the "safety" of conservatism in some companies. It sometimes continues until a competitor upsets things drastically in the marketplace.

Failure to generalize. Many businessmen hate to generalize and fight the application of any generalization. They prefer to feel that they are in a unique situation and can cite a myriad of specifics to prove it. This subtly justifies themselves as unique, which pleases the ego, justifies them in their jobs, warrants the salary, and prevents ready replacement—until one wants to change jobs. (Then his experience becomes highly applicable to the new situation.)

Yet, generalization is most valuable as an aid to understanding otherwise complex phenomena. It need not detract from the manager's uniqueness or from the quality of his decision making. Rather, it can improve it. Generalization provides perspective and prevents thinking only within the confines of one corporate situation. Properly understood and applied, generalization can permit critical examination of the truly unique aspects of a situation, a more precise evaluation of them, and thereby an improved guide to overall judgment. Blinders are useful on a race horse to prevent nervous reactions. They do not belong on businessmen.

Fortunately, each of these errors is remedial in nature. About all it takes is recognition, acknowledgment, and a serious desire to improve. It is astounding what conscientious effort can do. The hard part is not the doing, but apparently the making of the effort, initially.

DATA FOR DECISION MAKING

Data versus Decision

As Levitt has pointed out, "Data are not information. Information is not meaning." Data can be processed to yield information. Information can be processed, i.e., applied or related, to produce meaning.[8] Meaning, the significance of the considerations, is the prerequisite to informed decision making.

Decision making is the art of making a judgment. It is forward looking, and when it comes right down to the final valuation, highly qualitative. It is improved by creative and cerebral inputs. The decision is based on data both quantitative and qualitative. However, data availability is but one factor in the decision process.

Today we have almost a plethora of data, with more to come. But this does not mean easier decision making. It may even make it more difficult. Again, as Levitt has observed:[9]

> The enormous prodigality of the computer has so accelerated the process that we often actually know less than we did before. Great masses of data are disgorged in impressively magnificent print-outs. Yet they seldom improve our grasp of the elaborately quantified situations that are depicted.
>
> When we call for more information this must mean a call for more meaning. What is needed is discrimination in the use of data, not its sheer abundance. Abundance is not a liberator. It is a suffocator.
>
> Discrimination cannot be exercised in a vacuum. It has to be relevant to the purpose for which it is exercised. This means that the effective use of information requires a clear understanding of the exact purpose of its use: What is the question it is designed to answer, what is the problem it is designed to illuminate, and what is the issue it is designed to focus?
>
> This suggests that before data can be effectively processed, before information can be effectively arranged and converted to meaning, considerable thought must first be given to their specific uses and purposes.

[8] From *The Marketing Mode* by Theodore Levitt, p. 260. Copyright 1969, McGraw-Hill Book Company. Used with permission of McGraw-Hill Book Company.
[9] Ibid., pp. 260–261.

Otherwise, the recipient will be deafened by an orgiastic outpouring of noise.

The irony is clear: The more data we get, the less time is available for their effective use. Hence the more effective we get at providing data, the greater the requirement that we spend more preparatory time deciding specifically what we want them for—what the issues and relevant questions are. Contrary to the alarmist pronouncements of misinformed pundits on the computerized age, the more data there are, the more, not the less, we shall be obliged to think. The necessity of thinking is intensified, not obviated, by the prodigality of data and information.

The typical executive's pattern of career development lends scant hope that he will be able effectively to deal with the new requirements that the data explosion imposes on him. Most mature, high-level executives reached the top mainly through good management of day-to-day situations. They are men capable of quick decision. They are distinguished by their ability to react to problems, adversity, and opportunity with speed and self-assurance. If they have been lucky, they have won. If they have had a streak of special luck, they have won the top job.

In the new world of abundant data, especially data masquerading as information, they can survive only by first thinking about what the relevant questions are. And that kind of activity is not generally any part of their usual habit or training.

Thus, the first step in the assembly of data is to establish criteria for its selection. This comes from the basic issue, the problem itself. The test is simple. Any and all data *relevant to the problem at hand* should be considered. Other data are simply confusing. But this means what it says, *all relevant* data—both quantitative and qualitative.

The Role of Data

If we had perfect knowledge there would be no uncertainty. Decisions would be simple. Risk would disappear. (And we could fire a lot of expensive decision makers.) Fortunately, this is sheer theory. How dull a life that would be!

In practice, the role of data is to reduce uncertainty. The more we can know about today and tomorrow (at least the whys and probabilities of tomorrow), the better the decision is apt to be. Data for decision making must be relevant to the problem and contribute to reduction of uncertainty. And, to be further practical, the reduction in uncertainty must be worth more than the cost of the data to achieve that reduction.

In many cases it is entirely possible to obtain more data and/or a higher level of accuracy. It simply takes more time and money. This should be done only if the resultant contribution to decision making sufficiently lessens the uncertainty otherwise present to make it worthwhile. This point is easily overlooked. Sometimes rather expensive studies have been undertaken "because it would be a good idea to have more information." This may be true. But, before undertaking such a study, put it to the test of whether or not the results will contribute sufficiently to improved decision making—enough so to warrant the expense involved.

Degree of Accuracy Needed

Obviously, the more accurate the data, the better. That is, it is better assuming the increased accuracy actually increases the quality of the decision or reduces the uncertainty.

There is a strong tendency for people to provide data as accurately as possible. Accuracy is highly associative with quality. People take pride in being accurate. This is all fine—except it frequently is also expensive. Accuracy excessive to the need is a sheer waste of time and money.

The best degree of accuracy is that which is *needed* for decision making. This comes from the nature of the problem and what is needed to solve it. If an approximation will do, why demand precise figures? Proper orientation between manager and data providers, with this point in mind, can save time and money without detracting from decision making.

Degrees of Relevancy

It may be helpful to recognize that relevancy, as with colors, possesses almost innumerable degrees of relevance. It is not merely black or white; many intermediate shades exist. Considerations need to be relevant to a problem to be useful. But how relevant?

As with many things, there is no problem with the extremes. Completely relevant—use it. Irrelevant—forget it. It is in the middle ground that trouble may be encountered. Some may argue for use of a consideration because it is "relevant." Others may oppose, because it is "irrelevant." The probable truth is that it is part of both—in the middle ground. If so, recognition that there are degrees of relevancy can help. It can provide a weight for the factor, based on its degree of relevance. This is a matter of judgment, of course. But it recognizes the problem. It permits the factor to be considered, with an appropriately diminished weighting.

Controllable versus Uncontrollable

One approach to the variable factors involved in decision making is to recognize that there are two major groups. One is composed of "controllables"—those factors over which the manager can exercise a relatively high degree of control. Included here are the product and its production, the package and its pricing, the advertising, distribution, corporate objectives, marketing policies—all matters subject to decision making within the firm.

The "uncontrollables" are those beyond the immediate reach of the firm's influence. In the long run, the firm may be able to affect them, or the industry might by acting in concert. In the short run, and for practical decision-making purposes, they are not subject to the control of the firm. This is not to say they are unaffected. There may be change, but the firm does not control it. Examples are macroeconomic data, governmental rules and regulations, the market generally and its demand, the existing business structure, the cultural, social, and ecological environments, and one of the most significant, the actions and reactions of competitors, individually and collectively, to the decisions of the firm.

The uncontrollables enter heavily into decision making. It is within this total involvement that future changes occur. The decision makers need to know the nature, trends, and predictive probabilities in order that that combination of controllable factors may be made to optimize the future results—in short, to make the most of future market opportunities and best attain the corporate goals.

Quantitative versus Qualitative

Quantitative data measure. They answer the question of how much. Typically they are expressed numerically and explored mathematically to develop interrelationships, significance, and meaning. By the use of a rating scale many qualitative data can be measured, at least relatively, and hence treated quantitatively.

Qualitative data identify. They answer the question of existence and characteristics. A qualitative analysis might seek to determine whether or not a problem exists, its nature, and the factors of its involvement. It can explore the intangibles. It can identify, determine characteristics, impacts, significance, and interrelationships. It is nonetheless meaningful by its nature. Both quantitative and qualitative data are essential to decision making in the broad sense. In practice, their use and significance depend upon the nature of the problem at hand and the relevancy of each class of data to it. Never mistake the volume or the sophistication of mathematical techniques for significance. So long as humans decide on problems relating to human behavior, whether social, political, or economic, the qualitative aspects will continue to be at the heart of the actual decision. Underestimate them at your own risk.

Data Effectiveness

It is meaning we want in decision making. Masses of data may contain volumes of information, but their meaning is obscured by their form.

Busy executives do not have the time to study, absorb, and try to distill meaning from such data, at least in most cases. Hence, such data will be little used.

The effectiveness of data can be greatly enhanced by their treatment. Properly processed information can be developed. This is a big step in the right direction. From information comes meaning and significance. The data provider should seek to contribute information at the very least. If he can go beyond that to the meaning, so much the better. Never let the manager say that this is an impressive set of tables, etc.—but what do they mean? This is a sure sign of incompetency in the presentation. Put the supporting data in an available place, but present the meaning. That's what the decision maker needs and wants. If he is concerned to probe deeper, if he needs more conviction, the provider is ready. His data and his techniques are available for scrutiny. The error is to force the executive to scrutinize in order to, hopefully, arrive at the meaning.

One further point should be made here. In the presentation of data, information, or meaning, it is normally assumed that they are relevant. They probably are, but not necessarily equally so. The hallmark of a quality presentation, and one which will tend to enhance the appreciation of the points being made by a most favorable impression as to technique, is to point out the degrees of relevancy. If the data are relevant, but only to a degree, it is both honest and productive of improved decision making to say so. The danger of this point being overlooked to the detriment of decision making exists.

Scope of Considerations

The technical specialist provides a thorough and in-depth knowledge of his area. By the very nature of this concentration the scope of his considerations is limited. As we move up through middle to top management, the scope increases. The generalist provides a broad scope of considerations. He relies on specialists for depth when needed. This is well known. However, what may be somewhat less appreciated is that the individual at each level tends to feel that his perspective, his scope of considerations, *is* broad—or broad enough, since other matters do not count much anyway.

As authority and responsibility are delegated downward within a corporation, so is decision making. Thus, decisions are made by individuals with ever-narrower scopes of considerations the further this goes. This is not necessarily bad. It depends upon the total involvement in the decisions. As others become involved in the results of decisions, it can be a danger.

Fortunately, there is an effective way to prevent difficulties from arising out of such circumstances. Broaden the scope of considerations of any decision makers whose decisions affect others. The mere appreciation of the real need for this can go a long way. The integration of marketing and marketing considerations throughout the corporation by both marketing and nonmarketing executives is to achieve just this. Let it not stop there. Complete integration of all considerations, financial, production, etc., wherever others are or may be affected, is an excellent goal. It is more than that. It is attainable. And there is no good reason, except for mental insularity of narrow, self-centered individuals, why it cannot be achieved. That exception is not "good" in itself—but it can prevent such achievement.

EDP: The Data Bank

Today, the capability of EDP with its memory and retrieval systems can assemble, store, and when needed, use fantastic amounts of data. The difficulty in using this capability to the fullest does not lie in EDP, the computer, or the programmers. It lies in the newness. Never having had such information, managers are unfamiliar with it. Its introduction means more thought, not less. It means more understanding, but more complications to be handled, not less. It means a better job, but a more difficult one. Fear may exist. It means more responsibility on the decision maker, not less. As more is known about the circumstances, the decision itself becomes a more responsible variable, and with it, the decision maker's performance.

But one should not expect too much. It will be a long time before we market to measurable and predictable automations—devoid of human emotions and infallibly logical in their actions. So long as our end target remains a human being, it will continue to be fallacious to attempt to punch numbers into a computer and determine what will happen in the marketplace.

We are heading toward a major change. Right now quantification and "scientific" management are "in." But the more quantitative data we assemble, the better and more we learn to use it, the more important the remaining variables become. These are the intangibles, the qualitative aspects, stemming from the unpredictable emotional human being we are. It is in this area that we know least, and where the significance is being so rapidly enhanced by the very competency of quantification. The intuitivity of our earlier managers—who never heard of a computer—coupled with their other outstanding qualities of courage, leadership, personality, and ability to motivate others, will again be the deciding factors in business guidance. They may be all the variables that will be left.

Decision making is still the highest art in management. Data for decision making, if competent and relevant, make an invaluable contribution, but it is self-defeating. In the end the decision maker must paint the picture—the artist must practice his art.

As data do not equal a decision, neither does a data processor equal a decision maker. All too many of our young men are becoming enamored of the computer and sophisticated statistical techniques. They look upon this as a ready means of obtaining the answer, as a shortcut to becoming a manager. That they expect too much seems hard for them to realize.

There are a great many situations where the tangibles in business can be quantified with almost fantastic success. Mathematical solutions to these problems are most helpful. Areas within production, purchasing and inventory control, results of market research, transportation, facility location, warehousing, and cost control of numerous operations are excellent examples.

The major point is that the alternatives in such cases are highly capable of quantification with a minimum of qualitative intangibles involved. The major problems of marketing and business are far less quantifiable, far more intangible, require far more creativity, and deal with many unknown and/or uncontrollable considerations which impact in innumerable ways to affect results. To be content with quantification is to fail to appreciate the significance of the crucial factors—to deny the social, political, economic, and human elements comprising the environmental involvement in decision making.

THE DECISION MAKER

Human Relations in Management

Decision making is a most significant segment of management. However, the decisions need implementation, if things are to happen, if the potential is to become reality. Managers must implement their decisions through people. One of the basics involved in this is cooperation.

Cooperation Cooperation is frequently described as a two-way street. To get it, one must earn it by giving it. There is nothing new in this. But perhaps we could explore cooperation a bit more deeply than that.

Cooperation may be received through fear. If cooperation is given through fear, it is compelled, forced from the giver. He does not really want to cooperate. He is most likely, whenever he can get away with it, to be actively uncooperative—and take pleasure in this opposition. He does not like his boss.

It may be received through work pressure under a sense of responsibility of the job. If it is demanded through a sense of duty, ordered—the same thing applies. The man may resent the crack of the whip, the ordering. This man does not really want to cooperate. The individual seeking cooperation in this way is not liked, either.

Robert W. Dugger, vice president of industrial relations, Tenneco, Inc., provides a positive approach as follows:[10]

> If I want you to cooperate with me, some part of it is my inherent desire to have you like me. Here is where the two-way street should be applied. For unless I can like you, sincerely, it is most unlikely that you will, in turn, like me.
>
> If I want to cooperate with you (because I really want you to like me) and if my actions support this, the chances are far greater of causing a favorable reaction on your part and obtaining your cooperation on exactly the same basis—that you want me to like you, too.

This kind of cooperation cannot be bought, ordered, or forced through fear. To get it, it must be given. What we are really talking about here is good human relations, not job performance, as the fundamental issue inherent in the kind of cooperation we seek.

Respect and Like   The manager who socializes seeks to be liked. His goal in this is "like" alone. If this socialization is a cover for lack of ability or inferior performance, respect will not be forthcoming. Such a man will quickly, by failing to earn respect, lose even the "like" he seeks.

The man who ignores or minimizes the "like" can, through his ability and superior performance, earn respect. This can obtain at a very high level. Such a man, although respected, may have very few close friends—may not be liked. To assume that "like" follows respect automatically is a serious mistake. The error is to ignore the significance of good human relations while concentrating on good performance of the job.

It is possible to earn respect but to combine this with fear. An example of this would be a highly competent individual who is autocratic—*the* boss, and no foolin'! This combination of respect and fear prohibits being liked. Such a man will be obeyed—but would never be sought out as a friend for friendship's sake.

The highest degree of attainment is to earn respect for ability and performance—and at the same time to be liked through good human relations. An individual who attains this status is a true leader, a top-quality manager. This combination benefits him and benefits all those

---

[10] Used with permission of Robert W. Dugger, Vice President, Industrial Relations, Tenneco, Inc., Houston, Tex.

with whom he comes into contact. He is most apt to move quickly to a position where he is both respected and not merely liked, but loved by his fellowman. Unfortunately, such men are all too rare—but this rareness makes them all the more valuable.

Leadership   Good managers need to be good leaders. It therefore seems appropriate to examine leadership a bit, too.

Perhaps you have heard someone say, in effect, "You do what you're told—you do it, *I* do the thinking!" Such a leader is identifying himself clearly with one of the two major types of leadership. This man is producing a negative effect upon cooperation. He is asking for the shaft.

Keith Davis aptly describes these two types of leaders as follows:[11]

> This type of leadership is negative and is accomplished through fear.
>
> The negative leader acts domineering and superior with people.
>
> To get work done, he holds over his personnel such penalties as possible loss of job, reprimand in the presence of others, and demotion.
>
> He displays his authority with the false belief that it frightens everyone into productivity.
>
> He allows no exceptions or excuses—except his own.
>
> He is a credit grabber instead of a credit passer.
>
> He is the boss, not the leader.
>
> He seeks to build himself up in the eyes of his subordinates through fear, and feels that people need to be forced to be cooperative and productive because they would not naturally want to be so.
>
> Under negative leadership, the subordinates tend to devote more time to non-productive tasks concerned with pleasing the leader's personal wishes. Much time is spent "covering" oneself for every move. Useless documentation of even trivial decisions, needless memoranda, covering statistics and files (available for post-mortem checks to prove that it was someone else's fault) becomes the way of life. This unnecessary effort is incited simply by fear, instilled in the men under such leadership.
>
> Contrasted with this, we have the other type of leadership—the positive leader. Whereas the negative leader motivates through fear and insecurity by threatening to decrease satisfaction of his employees, the positive leader motivates people by increasing their satisfactions.
>
> The positive leader does not merely issue orders.
>
> He interprets the orders, makes sure his personnel have suitable skills and tools, and delegates the authority to carry out the orders.
>
> He tells his employees why a job must be done—so that their minds and ideas are involved as well as his own.
>
> He recognizes jobs well done as quickly as he does needs for improvement.

[11] From *Human Relations at Work,* 2d ed., by Keith Davis. Copyright 1962, McGraw-Hill Book Company. Used with permission of McGraw-Hill Book Company.

He takes the overall positive viewpoint that people naturally want to do good work if given the opportunity and incentive.

The positive leader exercises power through people—instead of power over people. He leads people, and by so doing, adds their energies to his own to accomplish a high level of productivity. On the other hand, when people are pushed by the boss, they dissipate much of their energies in nervous worries and resistance to him. This lowers productivity and creates troubles.

It is only fair to recognize that both types of leaders get results. The difference is that positive leadership increases satisfactions whereas negative leadership decreases satisfactions and produces dissatisfactions.

Leadership Skills In a broad sense, three types of skills are required of managers: human, technical, and conceptual. Figure 18.4 illustrates their relative distribution by levels of managerial responsibility.

Human skill is the ability to interact effectively with people and to build teamwork. No manager in any type of work or at any business level escapes the requirement for effective human skill. It is a day-to-day part of every manager's job, but he should not depend wholly upon it because conceptual skill is also important. This is the ability to see over-all relationships and to do creative thinking. Conceptual skill enables a manager to deal successfully with abstractions, to set up models, and to devise plans. Conceptual skill deals with *ideas,* while human skill concerns *people,* and technical skill is with *things.*

Conceptual skill becomes increasingly important in higher managerial jobs, because these leaders are dealing more with long-range plans, broad relationships, and other abstractions. This explains why an outstanding department head may make a poor vice-president—different types of functions and different levels of leadership require different mixes of leadership skills.[12]

[12] Ibid., pp. 117–118.

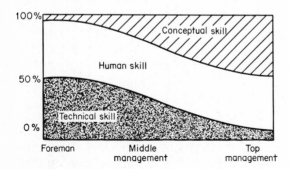

Fig. 18.4 Leadership-skill mix at different management levels. (*Source: "Human Relations at Work," 2d ed., by Keith Davis. Copyright 1962, McGraw-Hill Book Company. Used with permission of McGraw-Hill Book Company.*)

It should be noted that as technical skill is least important, and conceptual skill becomes far more important at the top level, human skill is important to all levels of management—to all decision makers.

What's Needed in the Top Decision Maker?

What makes an ideal decision maker? What qualities should he possess? How can the manager on the way up guide his own development to better qualify for the top job?

Consider this: Suppose competitors have complete data banks on everything quantifiable; that they are equally skilled in its use; that they produce equally satisfactory goods; and that they are equally favorably situated in other respects. What then is left to determine the future welfare of each? The answer should be obvious. It is their management.

Under such circumstances, with full information and equally high-level skills in its use, what qualities are left for the manager to exercise? Now we are getting to the heart of the matter. It is the qualitative—the intuitivity, the ideas, convictions, courage, personality, and leadership of the decision maker. It brings us right back to that same set of characteristics possessed by those pioneering businessmen who made America great in the first place. Pray that these qualities are never lost to us. We've come a long way. Maybe we are approaching a full circle.

Yet, if one out of the blue places great store on intuition, he would be scorned, or worse, ignored, by the quantitatively oriented. Nevertheless, intuitivity, perceptiveness, skill in human relations, integrity, courage, foresight, strength to fight when needed, motivate whenever possible—such things made our earlier leaders great. They may well do so for our future ones, too.

One other distinguishing characteristic of such leadership has been an exceptionally keen desire to lead. This is far more than wanting the top job or the salary. It is a drive, a keen desire to run the show for the sake of running it. It is an eagerness to tackle the job, to face the problems, for the sake of accomplishment. It is an acceptance of the challenge, with the winning more important than the spoils won. Lesser men, too readily satisfied with job security and a complacent way of life, will never know the value of such attainment. It is only because of the difficulties and the risks that the job becomes worthwhile, and success the sweeter.

The man who really wants to lead must not only have the courage to bet his company's money and his own career once in awhile, but also the courage that provides the strength to admit error. He seeks to foster originality in himself and in others. The price of this is mistakes. Being wrong occasionally should not defeat him. It is far easier and much safer to be a follower. There's lots more company in that, too. But whoever heard of a sheep winning a race?

The future executive will need to be broad in his background and perspectives. He should feel as much at home in the world or multinational corporation as his predecessors felt in their essentially national ones. He will need to understand and appreciate the social aspects of decisions. He must be familiar with government and how to work with it. He will need to know how to be selective in obtaining information. He will understand the long-term implications while working with the short terms. He will be dedicated to his job and good at it. He will be very much in demand. Every company in the country is looking for him, right now.

Merritt D. Hill, who after taking early retirement from the Ford Motor Company later became president of J. I. Case, and upon retirement from Case formed his own consulting firm, provides a good overview of the president's spot and why it is so hard to fill. He states:[13]

> Today, there is greater need than ever before for a management team. There are just too many things for any one man to know and understand thoroughly. The president must build a team and depend on men specialized in their particular fields, and then see that they get their respective jobs done properly. Decision making is no longer the sole prerogative of the top man.
>
> A very important factor is total dedication to the job. No chief executive of a company of any size can expect to get the job done working eight hours a day and five days a week. Many young men seem unwilling to give more than forty hours a week to a job. The presidency will not, in my opinion, be offered to men growing up with this time limitation in mind.
>
> Managing has to be done through human beings. This matter of working with and through people to get a job done might be called "human engineering." This is one area where a chief executive should have acquired real skill over a long period of time.
>
> Getting things done is a lot different from planning them. The man at the top must do a lot of pushing and motivating of people in addition to providing guidance to make things happen.
>
> Most top jobs call for a great deal of creative thinking or imagination. This is something frequently lacking in men, even though they are in top jobs. About the only thing they can do under such circumstances is to surround themselves with others who do have this kind of ability.
>
> Credibility is a most important factor. A good reputation and real credibility is one of the most important assets that a man can have. In the top spot it is fatal not to possess it in the highest degree.

[13] Used with permission of Merritt D. Hill, Hill Associates, Incorporated, Bloomfield Hills, Mich.

The top spot will be increasingly filled with a man who offers breadth of knowledge and experience. He must know something of engineering, production, finance, marketing, industrial relations, and people, both customers and people as individuals whatever their position, and be able to understand their problems.

He must know enough about them to be able to measure each one's effectiveness and to help them or determine that they are not qualified and make the necessary changes.

As a result of this he must build an organization as a team, one which works with as little friction as possible, and one which will operate efficiently and smoothly, even without him there to watch it. If the top executive has done a real good job he will have minimized the need for himself. He can and should then concentrate on finding his replacement.

Intelligence and integrity, together with a pleasing personality, empathy, perceptiveness, and culture, are basics. Becoming informed and skilled as a competent decision maker is a good start—but it is not enough. The decision maker as the top manager must also act. He must lead, persuade, sell, fight if need be, stick his neck out, make his ideas work, and bear the risk of failure to obtain the success he seeks. In all of this, he must *like* it.

RELEVANT READING

Ames, B. Charles, "Marketing Planning for Industrial Products," *Harvard Business Review*, September-October 1968, pp. 100–111.

Donnelly, James H., Jr., *Analysis for Marketing Decisions*, Homewood, Ill.: Richard D. Irwin, Inc., 1970, pp. 6–10.

Greene, Mark R., "How to Rationalize Your Marketing Risks," *Harvard Business Review*, May-June 1969, pp. 114–123.

Lesly, Philip, "Effective Management and the Human Factor," *Journal of Marketing*, April 1965, pp. 1–4.

Miller, Edwin L., "Identifying High Potential Managerial Personnel," *Michigan Business Review*, November 1968, pp. 12–17.

"Turning Men into Decision Makers," *Nation's Business*, October 1967, pp. 88–94.

Winer, Leon, "Are You Really Planning Your Marketing?" *Journal of Marketing*, January 1965, pp. 1–8.

Zisch, W. E., "What to Look for in Good Management," *Aerospace Management*, December 1962, p. 36.

Appendix

AIDS TO INTERNATIONAL MARKETING[1]

Trade Centers: The seventh U.S. trade center will open November 17 in Paris. Other permanent centers are in London, Bangkok, Frankfurt, Milan, Stockholm, and Tokyo. The centers are maintained by the Commerce Dept. as showcases for U.S. products. Special shows, which concentrate on single products or product categories, are held at the centers on an average of eight to 10 times each year. The centers also provide conference rooms for sales meetings, seminars, and business consultations. For further information on the trade centers, write: Commercial Exhibits Program, BIC-932, U.S. Dept. of Commerce, Washington, D.C. 20230.

Trade Missions: Organized by industry and supported by the government, trade missions are an effective means of developing and expanding foreign markets. The Bureau of International Commerce assists industry representatives with planning and advance publicity, provides an official to accompany the trade mission's advance agent overseas, and provides detailed information on economic and political conditions and marketing opportunities in countries the mission plans to visit. In addition, U.S. Foreign Service officers help prepare itineraries, arrange meetings, and provide additional information on contracts.

[1] Reprinted by permission from *Sales Management, The Marketing Magazine.* Copyright 1970, Sales Management, Inc., "Tips on a $50 Billion Market," *Sales Management,* February 1, 1970, pp. 39–47.

MOBILE TRADE FAIRS: These are ventures privately organized by industries, states, and communities, aimed at displaying and selling U.S. products through traveling exhibitions.   Contact: Mobile Trade Fairs, BIC-926, Dept. of Commerce.

SAMPLE DISPLAYS: These centers are established and supervised by commercial officers attached to U.S. embassies.   U.S. firms may display their products and sales literature, without charge, for 30-day periods.   These sample display centers are primarily designed for firms that do not have representatives in the host country.   Further information may be obtained from the Dept. of Commerce's BIC-926.

AMERICA WEEKS: America Weeks are held regularly by overseas retailers to promote the sale of U.S. goods.   Announcements of promotions are listed in *International Commerce* (see publications below), with appropriate listings of overseas purchasing offices.   Write: America Weeks, BIC-926, Dept. of Commerce.

JOINT EXPORT ASSOCIATIONS: JEAs are development projects in which private firms and the Commerce Dept. share the costs of overseas market research, advertising, publicity, distribution of technical data and samples, participation in trade exhibits, and sales and service personnel training. Participating contractors represent several firms within their industry. Further information may be obtained by writing directly to BIC.

PUBLICATIONS: In addition to sponsoring major foreign marketing ventures, the Commerce Dept. provides dozens of pertinent reports, pamphlets, brochures, and other publications.   A complete listing of all publications is contained in BIC's *Checklist*.   One of the most essential publications for marketers who hope to extend their overseas sales is *International Commerce*, a weekly news magazine that offers basic, authoritative information on international marketing opportunities.   *International Commerce* is available from the Commerce Dept. at an annual subscription rate of $20.

Although they don't offer financial aid or sponsor trade shows as the Commerce Dept. does, at least 10 other large organizations offer magazines, newsletters, yearbooks, and statistical reports on foreign markets. Here's a checklist:

THE ORGANIZATION FOR ECONOMIC COOPERATION AND DEVELOPMENT (OECD), whose membership consists of the major industrial nations of the world, publishes the monthly newsletter *Activities* containing concise information on publications available and meetings (free).   Write for a subscription from: OECD Publications Office, 2, rue Andre-Pascal, Paris (16°), France.

OECD's *The Engineering Industries in North America, Europe and Japan,* which covers supply, demand, and world trade for various industries, has a reputation for being the best source for comparable statistics in its field   Of special interest are the OECD Economic Surveys published for each member nation, updated annually and made available at 80¢ each or $10 a year.   OECD also offers the *Foreign Trade Statistics,* a periodical issued in three ᴜeries: Series A—over-all trade by countries, $7.50 per year; Series B—trading by commodities in main trading areas, $15; Series C—detailed analysis by commodities and imports and exports, $14.50. These and a catalogue of all publications available may be ordered from OECD Publications Center, Suite 1305, 1750 Pennsylvania Ave. N.W., Washington, D.C. 20006.

THE EUROPEAN FREE TRADE ASSN. publishes the biweekly newsletter *EFTA Reporter* and the annual *EFTA Trade,* which contains statistical information on particular markets. Also available is *Public Procurement in EFTA,* a guide listing public agencies and enterprises responsible for public procurement in its member countries. These and a list of publications available can be ordered from: European Free Trade Assn., Suite 714, 711 Fourteenth St. N.W., Washington, D.C. 20005.

EUROPEAN COMMON MARKET COUNTRIES offer many publications on various markets along with their monthly *Bulletin* (annual subscription: $5). For catalogues and a list of their publications contact the European Community Information Service, 900 17th St. N.W., Washington, D.C. 20006.

GENERAL AGREEMENT ON TARIFFS AND TRADE (GATT) publishes the *Compendium of Sources: Basic Commodity Statistics and Compendium of Sources: International Trade Statistics,* each priced at $5. The latest GATT annual *International Trade 1967,* a review of developments in world trade, is also available. All can be ordered from: National Agency for International Publications, Inc., 317 East 34th St., New York, N.Y. 10016.

THE INTERNATIONAL MONETARY FUND issues a helpful list entitled *International Financial Statistics* for each of more than 100 countries. This and its monthly supplement, *Direction of Trade* (trade-by-country information for almost all the countries in the world, expressed in U.S. dollars), are available at $10 a year from the International Monetary Fund, 19th and H Sts. N.W., Washington, D.C. 20431.

THE INTER-AMERICAN DEVELOPMENT BANK offers the *Eighth Annual Report '67* and *Socioeconomic Progress in Latin America,* the annual report of the Social Progress Trust Fund. Write for these from: Inter-American Development Bank, 808 17th St. N.W., Washington, D.C. 20577.

THE COMMERCE CLEARING HOUSE, INC., which specializes in tax and law reports, issues the biweekly *Common Market Reports,* providing information for Americans doing business in Europe and legal developments in the EEC. A list of their many useful publications can be obtained from: Commerce Clearing House, Inc., 4025 West Peterson Ave., Chicago, Ill. 60645.

THE INTERNATIONAL PUBLICATIONS SERVICE accepts standing orders for various serial publications from the United Nations, the Organization of African Unity, the Center of Planning and Economic Research, and the National Council of Applied Economic Research. For more information about this valuable service and a copy of their source list, write: International Publications Service, 303 Park Ave. S., New York, N.Y. 10010.

Index

Index